# BACKCOUNTRY MEXICO

# BACKCOUNTRY MEXICO
## A Traveler's Guide and Phrase Book

by Bob Burleson and David H. Riskind

University of Texas Press, Austin

Copyright © 1986 by the University of Texas Press
All rights reserved
Printed in the United States of America

First Edition, 1986

Requests for permission to reproduce material from this work
should be sent to Permissions, University of Texas Press, Box 7819,
Austin, Texas 78713.

**Library of Congress Cataloging-in-Publication Data**
Burleson, Bob.
  Backcountry Mexico.

  Bibliography: p.
    1. Mexico—Description and travel—1981–  —Guide-books. 2. Spanish
language—Conversation and phrase books—English.  I. Riskind, David H.
II. Title.  III. Title: Backcountry Mexico.
F1209.B87  1986    917.2'04834    85-22487
ISBN 0-292-70760-6
ISBN 0-292-70755-X (pbk.)

*To the children of Mexico and the United States,*
*with the prayer that they will live forever*
*in peace and harmony, with shared concerns*
*for the well-being of all people, everywhere.*

# Contents

# Preface

**W**e are not linguists, but we have had much experience in backcountry travel in Mexico over a period of many years. David Riskind was born on the Texas side of the border but spoke Spanish before he spoke English. Bob Burleson learned his Spanish by exposure and from necessity. Our combined experience has shown us a need for a phrase book of rural Mexican-style Spanish, an explanation of some of the industries and aspects of rural Mexican culture, and some hints on how to get along. As far as we are aware, there is no such book now available commercially that is oriented toward helping the English-speaking traveler in Mexico's backcountry, where restaurants, hotels, taxis, banks, nightclubs, tours, and so forth, are simply not encountered. What you do find are rural folk who speak simple Spanish and who will gladly communicate with someone from another culture who tries to communicate with them. This book is intended to help the user understand the people and lifeways of rural Mexico. This greater understanding will result in more effective communication.

This book assumes that the user has some basic understanding of Spanish pronunciation and grammar. If you don't have this basic understanding, however, you can get it from the brief guide presented here in Part II or from traveler's guides to Spanish available on record or tape almost anywhere in the United States or from the introduction to a Spanish-English dictionary (see chapter 16 for many valuable references and study aids).

This is a first effort. The grammar may not be the best, but that is true of the rural Mexican's grammar also. If you have suggestions for additions, or comments on how to improve this work, please send them to Bob Burleson, Box 844, Temple, Texas 76503. We hope this book will prove useful to everyone from social workers to scientists to just plain hikers and climbers who hit the Mexican deserts and mountains on foot (*a pie*).

# Acknowledgments

Our thanks to Baudelio Garza, of northern Mexico and San Antonio, Texas, for final grammatical review; to Jane Hunt, Spanish teacher, formerly of Troy, Texas, for early grammatical review; Reuben and Esther Riskind, border merchants and native speakers of Spanish, for border idioms, historical insights, and helpful review; María Araujo, Austin, Texas, and the Reverend Jimmy Smith, Marfa, Texas, for proofing and correcting as well as editorial suggestions. We are particularly grateful to Debbie Ray and Kathy Harrison, both of Temple, Texas, who typed endless revisions of the manuscript, always with good cheer. Any errors, however, are solely ours.

# Tanque la Mula

It is late afternoon in the Chihuahuan Desert of Mexico. In the aftermath of a brief but violent thunderstorm the air is cool, crisp, and unbelievably clear. The sky overhead is a clear blue and the rays of the lowering sun create a jeweled effect as they strike millions of drops of water festooning the low shrubs and cacti that dot the otherwise bare and rocky soil of the ridgetop. Tracks in the fresh mud of the old roadway show where an ever-hungry coyote has just crossed, moving quickly after the storm to search for small rodents driven from flooded burrows. A roadrunner fluffs out every feather, looking twice its normal girth, shakes itself like a wet dog, then hops from its high perch into a wet bush to pick up another load of water drops and complete its bath, perhaps its last for months. Except for muted twitterings from small birds splashing at the edge of puddles, there is complete silence. Only the water-filled ruts of the seemingly abandoned road indicate that humans have ever disturbed this place. In the clear air one can see for twenty miles or more, across low limestone ridges and wide shallow valleys to a chain of saw-toothed peaks marching northward on the western horizon, where the remnants of the recent storm are trapped by mountains reaching up some eight thousand feet above the surrounding desert.

Without warning other than the brief roar of a straining engine and the whine of gears and mudgrip tires, a red 4-wheel-drive pickup lurches and slides up out of the nearby *arroyo*. Covered from top to bottom with a layer of light brown, semiliquid mud, the pickup moves forward, the hand of the driver reaching out from time to time to clear a small spot on his otherwise mud-covered windshield. At the top of the ridge the truck stops, and the occupants dismount to stretch and soak up the beauty of the storm battering itself to death on the peaks in a contest without a winner.

The three men who get out of the truck are obviously not Mexicans, but beyond that little can be seen because of a liberal coating of mud on almost everything from the boots up. Teeth look unnaturally white in their muddy faces as they look back at the last obstacle crossed and ahead at an unknown number of others just as difficult. They have been driving, digging, cutting, and pulling for eight hours straight, and the mountains hardly seem a mile closer. The last sign of human habitation they encountered was a small ranching *ejido* the previous afternoon, where they purchased warm sodas and fresh *tortillas* and gained what information they could about the route and road conditions ahead. The high peaks were their objective and they had no doubt that sooner or later they would get there, but with fatalism born of years of exploration in Mexico they knew it was pointless to worry about the snail's progress they were making. *Pues*, the mountains were moving even more slowly than they were!

"What do you think? Should we camp here and hope the *arroyos* go down and dry up a bit overnight, or push on? We've got a couple of hours of good light still," suggested the driver. There was no immediate response from his companions, but one of them reached into the cab, pulled out a pair of binoculars, and scanned the presumed route ahead of them. After a moment the man with the binoculars spoke up: "All these drainages have been coming from the *sierras*. It's still raining over there, and it may keep it up all night. That's probably the Arroyo de la Zorra ahead of us and the *viejo* said it was the worst to cross. If we can get a good enough view upstream before we drop into it, to make sure there's not a big rise coming down already, I'm for crossing now. It's raining a lot harder over there than it did here, and I really don't care much for spending tomorrow building road." "*De acuerdo*," said the third man, signifying his agreement. On the limestone ridgetop the ruts were shallow, with rock bottoms, and the truck moved easily onward to the edge of the big *arroyo*, where the road plunged down a steep slope into a half-mile-wide expanse of brush and braided streambeds before rising up the opposite bank.

A stop at the top of the bank revealed a full two miles of visibility upstream, without a sign of running water. The path of the road across the *arroyo* was visible for most of its course. "I figure ten to fifteen minutes to cross," said the driver. "What do you all think?" "With the glasses it looks like mostly sand and gravel and pretty well scoured. I see no mud," spoke the man with the binoculars. "Let's check the winch and be sure that last wet crossing didn't short anything out," added the driver, "and David, maybe you had better coil up the snatch strap on the front floorboard, in case you have to jump out and catch a bunch of brush for a quick anchor if we hang up on something." The electric winch worked and the decision was made. It was a calculated risk, but not an extreme one under the favorable circumstances, since they could see enough of the upstream portion of the *arroyo* to know that they had a fair margin of time and safety from a flash flood, even if they did hit a mudhole hidden in the brush that was too deep to cross without the help of the winch.

The crossing safely made, and with no delays, the pickup groaned its way up the opposite bank onto another of the endless succession of limestone ridges. Another hour passed with no serious obstacles and little being said, each man soaking up the beauty and the remoteness of a land little known to most of their countrymen and where fewer still ever venture. "What do you think Mickey would have done back at the big *arroyo* if she had come on this trip?" the third man asked the driver. "She would have jogged across and watched us from the high side," responded the driver, "and probably would have said she didn't come all this way to go boating in a pickup!" "*¡Mire!*" said the third man. "What's that up ahead?"

On the opposite side of a small *arroyo*, on a flat about halfway up the slope and safely above the highest water, stood an outpost of humanity in the form of a one-room *adobe*, formerly whitewashed and with a neat and well-kept roof made of bundled leaves of the *palma*. Nearby was a small dirt stock tank, brimful of fresh water, and a small *corral* made of juniper posts and pickets from the *sotol* plant. There was no horse or burro in the corral and no human in sight, but chickens lining the roof's ridge as they prepared to pass the night out of reach of coyotes and a wisp of smoke coming from a pipe sticking out of the *adobe* wall at a crazy angle indicated that the place was inhabited and that someone, probably the woman, was at home.

Pulling quietly to a stop on the main road, a reasonable distance outside the dooryard of the *adobe*, the men stepped out and called out in Spanish to the presumed occupant of the little house, "*¡Hola, señora! ¿Está en casa!*" A few chickens fluttered at the sound of strange voices and a well-fed cat scuttled from its perch on the sill of a shuttered window to disappear behind the house. The men waited near the truck.

After a few moments a Mexican woman silently cracked the door, took in the scene, and apparently satisfied, stepped out into the bare dirt of the yard. The fact that she rather than her man stepped out and the absence of children peeking from around her skirt or out the doorway indicated that she was alone. The men spoke politely to her, asked permission to visit for a bit, and she graciously welcomed them to Tanque la Mula of the Rancho Las Norias.

Her husband was riding fence and would not be back for at least another day, she said. "What brings you here, are you lost?" "No, *señora*, we are on our way to the *sierras*." She was a slight woman, perhaps five feet tall, and her cotton skirt came within a few inches of her ankles.

A Tarahumar leader sits astride his white horse in the high *sierras* south of Batopillas, Chihuahua. Note the twisted rawhide reins (*riendas torcidas*) in his hands. (Will Thompson photo)

Man and wife of the Tarahumar, walking as usual. The cane staffs and the sandals are traditional, as is the cotton poncho around the man's shoulders. (Will Thompson photo)

A handsome woman of the Tarahumar, wearing traditional clothing. The infant is snug and happy in her shawl. (Will Thompson photo)

Cleotilde Chavez, midwife and spiritual leader of Ejido Melchor Músquiz, Coahuila. (Earl Nottingham photo)

Her face was the color of old saddle leather and crossed with the countless tiny creases that speak of a lifetime of work and exposure to the desert sun and wind, but her brown eyes were clear and intelligent and she was obviously a strong woman of substantial self-confidence, since she was at ease in the presence of three strange *americanos*. Her bare feet were tough and dusty, but her blouse and skirt were clean and in good repair and her wet hair pulled back and tied behind her head was evidence that not long before she had stripped down and taken advantage of the rain shower to wash the desert grime from hair and body. The flour on her hands and on the short apron she wore showed that she was making *tortillas* in anticipation of her husband's return. Her questions and lively conversation were those of a naturally friendly person long accustomed to solitude. Without prying, she clearly wanted to talk and find out what the men were doing, thinking probably of the news of strangers that she could share with her man the next day.

Squatting on their heels in the damp dooryard, munching fresh *tortillas*, the three men explained that they were on a scientific expedition, studying the plants and wildlife of the desert and the mountains of northern Mexico. Under the eaves of her house were numerous and varied plants, hung by the roots to dry in the desert air, along with the dried, skinned remains of a rattlesnake, a common tonic among *vaqueros* when powdered and taken with water. She gladly showed the visitors where she gathered the herbs and gave them the Spanish names and the medicinal uses. She told them they were welcome to camp at the tank for the night, but her visitors thanked her for her hospitality and told her that they wanted to use the last light of the day to make headway toward the mountains. Refusing any payment for the *tortillas*, she asked them what place in the *sierras* they hoped to find.

"We're looking for the road to Rancho El Jardín, where the big spring comes out of the rocks at the base of Pico El Centinela," they said. Standing there, barefooted in the middle of her dooryard, alone and at least thirty miles from the nearest neighbor and at least one hundred miles from a paved road or a town, her last remark was a Mexican classic that the men treasure to this day: "Yes," she said, "I know that place well." "*Pero, Rancho El Jardín está bien retirado*" (But, El Jardín ranch is very remote).

This story, we hope, will introduce you to the real Mexico, a Mexico we love, filled with people more interesting than you can at present imagine, with a million places that are *"bien retirado"* and worth whatever effort and ingenuity it takes to get you there. If with this book we can help you understand and appreciate this independent and varied nation and enjoy the adventure of backcountry travel there, our purpose will have been accomplished.

One final thought. To us it appears that many tourists in Mexico are unhappy, as if they are seeking something they do not find there. The analogy may be objectionable to some, but consider your experience if you visit one of the wildlife parks where exotic animals are displayed in a "natural habitat." Although the animals are beautiful, in a way the experience is not the same as seeing them in their own native habitat, on foot and with an element of risk sharing heightening your sensitivity. The absence of interaction with the animals, the absence of predators, the knowledge that they are "kept" just as much as if they were behind zoo bars, and the certainty that human intervention will save them from flood, drought, and disease all serve to diminish the satisfaction of the experience. By the same token, if you go to Mexico as a typical tourist, stick to the experiences you can buy, stick to the paved roads, the beaten path, the guided tour, commercial food and drinks, fly in and fly out, and insulate yourself from direct contact with all Mexicans except those who know your language and your customs, you will, in time, probably find the experience unsatisfactory. You are, after all, a Mexican, just as you are also an African, Chinese, and Cuban, all of us being of the same species biologically and separated only by humanity's artificial barriers of territory, custom, and language. How often have you wondered what the life of the Mexican working class is really like, what their dreams and goals may be, what their beliefs and fears are, and what their family and village life is really like? With a little work and the right attitude, aided by this book and the other resources we suggest, you can answer these questions and many more and learn firsthand about the unique experience of being a brother or sister to all humankind.

# PART I. CULTURE

# 1. Getting through Town and into the *Campo*

**I**f you cross at one of the typical border towns you will leave the *aduana* (customs) and drive into the bustling streets of a sprawling Mexican town. The streets are narrow, filled with people and too many vehicles, and everyone drives "crazy." There are too many sights, sounds, and smells to take them in all at once, it seems, and since the traffic signs are different and the rules of the road are not the ones you are accustomed to, it is an unnerving experience the first time.

Driving in a busy Mexican city can be a tremendous challenge to the beginner. Unfortunately, you must negotiate it safely before you can hit the open roads to adventure in the backcountry. Here are a few tips to help you pass through cities without too much hassle.

If you are new at this game, do not go with the flow of traffic. The natives are accustomed to driving here and they know the rules and what to anticipate, but you do not. Go slow. Don't let your gaze wander from the traffic and pedestrians ahead (and beside and behind) to look into shop windows or at other interesting sights. Pay extra close attention to your driving and remain ever alert for the unexpected.

Most Mexicans tend to ignore all but two types of traffic signal. One that is always obeyed is the traffic light (*el semáforo*) and the other type is the arrows painted or hung on buildings at intersections. These may be ten or twelve feet above street level, far higher than you would expect, but the arrows denote *tránsito*, *circulación*, or *preferencia* and tell you which way the traffic lawfully flows and who has the right of way. *Preferencia* means that through traffic on that street has the right of way over intersecting traffic.

*Señales* (traffic signs) in Mexico are often in the international design, with symbols rather than words, or symbols combined with words. Although the Mexicans largely ignore them, our advice is to heed stop (*alto*) signs and all other traffic signs and proceed through all intersections with much caution. Likewise be cautious in school zones (*zona escolar*). After the first time you will no doubt remember that the *topes* sign means speed bumps. The impression of your head in the headliner of your vehicle will remind you of the need to reduce speed when you see a *tope*.

To be on the safe side, assume in all instances that you do not have the right of way. If a uniformed traffic policeman is directing traffic, pay close attention to the direction he is facing and his hand movements. If he is facing you or has his back to you, stop. When he turns either side to you, go. No matter that you have the right of way, always watch out for cross traffic, kids, animals, old people, carts, bicycles, stopped vehicles, buses, and anything else unexpected. The buildings extend almost to the street lines, so most corners are blind in the older parts of town.

In the downtown sections of every town are police officials of different types. Most have a uniform of sorts, a pistol, and a whistle. Most are afoot, and they have no radio contact with other officers. This brings us to one of our "How to Avoid Hassles" pointers. Many potentially enjoyable trips have been marred by a tourist-policeman confrontation. Our advice is simple. If at all possible, do not allow yourself to be stopped. Warn your passengers in advance to ignore all whistles, shouts, and arm waving. Everyone should look the other way, intently, at some distant object. Keep driving, even if he is blowing his head off. Unless you are tied up in traffic within a block or so he will be unable to catch you on foot and will give up for easier pickings. Most *tránsitos* (traffic police) are a bit on the heavy side from easy living and will not run after you. Even if the traffic should tie you up and allow him to catch you, just react with a "Who, me?" look and a smile when he comes puffing up. If nobody has looked at him he cannot be sure you actually saw him. If you do get safely away, however, do not forget and pass his way again that day!

After the novice Mexican traveler gets pinched for a minor infraction, such as exceeding the famous 15-kilometer-per-hour speed limit in a school zone, he will appreciate our "keep going" advice. When pinched, however, just play dumb. Stonewall. Listen to the officer carefully. If you understand what he says it is all the better, as he might be telling you something important, such as you're going against the traffic on a one-way street. He may say *preferencia* and point in the appropriate direction, or he may just want to warn you to slow down (*más despacio*). Stay cool, smile, nod your head, say *gracias*, and try to drive off slowly. Do not be antagonistic under any circumstances, but do not be cowed either. Point an imaginary pistol at your head and say, "*Loco gringo*" if you realize you have violated a traffic sign or rule; grin and say, "*Gracias, señor*" and "*Adiós*" as you pull forward. Say little else. Sometimes it is best to speak only English, forcing him to tell you what the problem is and making him find the communication route.

Do not flash a wad of money, and do not instantly whip out cash and offer to pay him off. The art of bribery must be practiced with skill and dignity. If all else fails, then *la mordida* (the bite) is paid, but not until everything else has been tried. Wait for the *tránsito* to initiate the action. If he intimates that you will have to go to the station to clear things up or something like that, then say that you are very short of time and would prefer to settle the matter on the spot. You now have an opening for *la mordida*. You should have in your pocket, easily in reach, a supply of pesos. As of late 1985, 500 pesos were about equal to one U.S. dollar. Two 500-peso notes (about $2.00 U.S.) folded and discreetly handed to the *tránsito* may solve your problem. Hand over the notes, nod your head, say "*Adiós,*" and try to proceed deliberately but cautiously. Several more 100-peso notes should be held in reserve, in case the first 500 do not do the trick. Also, keep in mind that U.S. dollars are preferred. Try two dollar bills at first (no silver) and avoid trying to get by with one dollar, as this may be considered an insult.

We discuss in a later section the problems of traffic accidents (*choques*) in Mexico, where the one who stays is the one who is detained.

Do not get the impression that you are running the gauntlet when you pass through a Mexican city. U.S. speed traps are just as insidious and probably affect more people. Remember, you have little recourse, so keep the old thinking cap on your cool head. It is only on rare occasions that the alert driver will be successfully stopped, or if stopped, will fail to bluff his or her way through a confrontation with a Mexican traffic policeman. *¡Que le vaya bien y buena suerte!*

## LA MORDIDA

It is relatively rare in our experience that Mexican officials solicit bribes or try to force you to pay one. However, it does happen now and then, particularly when there exists some irregularity in your actions or documentation, or when you are asking a special favor.

The more affluent and touristlike you appear, the more unfamiliar you appear with Mexican customs and procedures, the more your dress and attitude show contempt or dismay at conditions, and the more you flash your bank roll, the more likely you are to be bothered. Don't overdress, *or* go scroungy; be modest, polite, quiet, and cool. Don't worry about minor hassles; just play it cool and keep talking and trying every alternative before yielding to *la mordida* (the bite). Try playing dumb. Try asking to see the *jefe* (chief) or ask another official. Sometimes one will overrule the other and you may go on your way without difficulty. Be sure that your car title, driver's license, birth certificate, and voter registration card all have the same name and initials, and that your car title or voter registration card and driver's license have the same address. Any discrepancy can be a technicality that will create an opportunity for a negative head shake or some delay. Just stay cool, play dumb on the suggestions, be slow on the uptake, and you will probably make it through o.k.

*Never* attempt to take guns or ammunition into Mexico. They would be of no use to you under most circumstances, and the penalties for illegal importation are harsh.

In many, many border crossings, only a relatively small number of Mexican officials have attempted to hassle us without reason, so you should approach the crossing with optimism, yet be alert to prepare in advance for the occasional problem. Minor police officials in cities and towns may be the worst problem, but they can be avoided by sticking to the rural areas. Usually the Mexican customs people (*aduana*) are very nice. In fact, we have met with more rudeness and arbitrariness at the hands of U.S. Customs on our return than we ever have encountered entering Mexico.

For short excursions into Mexico, not exceeding 18 kilometers along the border or 23 kilometers into Mexico, no tourist permits or automobile papers are needed. There are checkpoints on the main highways past the 23-kilometer point.

Expect fairness and honesty, but be prepared for *la mordida*. Before an encounter with Mexican officials (usually at border crossings or checkpoints, but sometimes when encountering police officials) put a few dollars, say ten, in one dollar bills in your pocket, where you can pull them out a few at a time if needed. If the circumstances require it, the *mordida* is paid at once, right out in the open, and the transaction is usually quickly over. When it is clear that this is the *only* route, and that persistence or playing dumb will not get you out of the jam or through the border, then resort to *la mordida*. Here are some useful phrases for the border crossing and checkpoints.

| | |
|---|---|
| Is there no other way of solving this problem? | *¿No habrá modo de resolver el problema de otra manera?* |
| Can't anything be done? | *¿No se puede hacer nada?* |
| What remedy is there for the problem? | *¿Qué remedio hay?* |
| Is there no other remedy? | *¿No hay otro remedio?* |
| Is there any way to resolve this problem here and now? | *¿Hay modo de resolver este problema ahorita?* |
| It is worth something to me to resolve this problem now and be on my way. | *Me importa resolver este problema pronto para que me puedo ir.* |

| | |
|---|---|
| Sorry, it can't be helped. | *Lo siento pero no se puede remediar.* |
| There is no remedy. | *No hay remedio.* |
| Will there be an extra charge? | *¿Hay cobro extra?* |
| How much must I pay? | *¿Cuánto tengo que pagar?* |
| Two hundred pesos is too much, but I can afford one hundred pesos. | *Doscientos pesos son demasiado pero cien pesos me acomoda.* |
| Would ten dollars U.S. allow me (us) to pass on? | *¿Me deja (Nos deja) pasar con diez dólares?* |
| That is all I have. | *Es todo lo que tengo.* |
| That is the most I can pay. | *Eso es lo máximo (más) que puedo pagar.* |
| You ask too much of me. | *Me pide demasiado.* |
| Whom do I pay? | *¿A quién le pago?* |
| The money is for you (him). | *El dinero es para usted (él).* |
| Where is the boss? | *¿Dónde está el jefe?* |
| Who is acting as head? | *¿Quién es el jefe?* |
| To whom do I apply? | *¿A quién tengo que dirigirme?* |
| I would like to have a word with him. | *Quiero algunas palabras con él. (Quiero hablar con él.)* |
| May I speak with him? | *¿Puedo hablar con él?* |
| How long must I wait? | *¿Cuánto tiempo debo esperar?* |
| Then I will wait. | *Entonces, esperaré.* |
| Are you alone? | *¿Está usted solo(a)?* |
| How many are you? | *¿Cuántos son ustedes?* |
| Are you together? | *¿Están ustedes juntos?* |
| May I go through? | *¿Puedo pasar?* |
| I wish to cross (enter) here and spend a few days looking around within the border zone. | *Quiero cruzar (entrar) aquí y pasar unos pocos días dentro (de) la zona fronteriza. or (dar la vuelta dentro . . .)* |
| If I stay within the frontier zone, will I need any auto or tourist papers? | *¿Si me quedo dentro de la zona fronteriza, necesito papeles?* |
| In years past I have crossed here several times without problems. | *En años pasados he cruzado por aquí varias veces sin problema.* |
| Why can't I cross (enter) here now? | *¿Por qué no puedo cruzar (entrar) ahora?* |
| I've never had papers before, but the officers didn't give me any trouble. | *Siempre voy sin papeles y nunca me han molestado.* |

I am only going into the frontier zone, and no papers are required.

*Nomás voy a la zona de la frontera y por lo tanto no necesito papeles.*

With your permission I want to cross here and return to the United States.

*Con su permiso quiero cruzar aquí y regresar al otro lado (a los Estados Unidos).*

Where do you wish to go?

*¿Adónde quiere ir?*

We would like to ride around (take a little ride).

*Con permiso, vamos a dar la vuelta.*

I am (We are) going to ———.

*Voy (Vamos) a ———.*

All that we carry is camping and mountain-climbing equipment.

*Nomás llevamos equipo para acampar y de alpinismo.*

We do not carry guns, ammo, or contraband.

*No llevamos carabina, pistola, munición, o contrabando.*

We are alpinists (scientists) studying the mountains of Mexico.

*Somos alpinistas (biólogos; científicos) estudiando las sierras de México.*

We are going to the village of El Veinte to help work on the school.

*Vamos hasta el pueblito El Veinte a ayudar a la gente a trabajar en la escuela.*

We are carrying some supplies for the school to the teacher at La Borrada.

*Llevamos aprovisionamiento para la maestra (el maestro) de la escuela en La Borrada.*

We are going to help the people at El Veinte with sanitation and their water supply.

*Vamos a ayudar a la gente en El Veinte con medidas sanitarias y con el sistema de agua potable.*

We have with us doctors and dentists for a health clinic at El Veinte and La Borrada for one week.

*Vienen con nosotros médicos y dentistas que van a llevar a cabo una clínica higiénica que dura una semana en El Veinte y La Borrada.*

Everything's been arranged.

*Todo está arreglado.*

May we pass?

*¿Podemos pasar?*

Shall I open everything?

*¿Debo abrir todo?*

There is nothing here but ———.

*No hay más que ——— aquí.*

Is that all?

*¿Eso es todo?*

That is all I have.

*Es todo lo que tengo.*

Have you finished?

*¿Ha terminado usted?*

He has no objection to your leaving.

*El no tiene objeción a que salgan.*

Is everything in order?

*¿Todo está bien?*

Will the customs officials let us go through?

*¿Nos dejarán pasar los empleados de la aduana?*

# 2. Culture and Lifeways in Northern Mexico

**M**any, in fact, probably over half, of the rural people in northern Mexico (*la frontera*) came originally from deeper in the interior. There has been a constant movement to the frontier for a number of years, because of overpopulation and lack of work in the interior and because of government resettlement through agrarian programs. Additionally, the lure of work in the United States ensures a regular replacement of frontier *gente* as others cross into Texas (*al otro lado*) and other states.

Thus, although there are still *vaqueros* and their families, who are the result of a long tradition in the northern Mexico cattle industry, most people you meet, including most present-day ranch workers, will be relatively recent migrants into the area. Almost all of the big landholdings formerly held by Anglos have been broken up under Mexico's land reform programs, and a substantial number of the large landholdings (*latifundios*) of Mexican *ricos* (*latifundistas*) have gone the same way.

These once vast holdings, for the most part run as productive cattle ranches, have given way to *ejidos*, or communal ranches established and supported by the government. The result has been a readily observable decline in the quality and productivity of Mexican grazing lands, and essentially a total elimination of most wildlife on *ejido* lands. From our viewpoint, the idea of land reform has merit, but the unmitigated overuse and abuse of once-productive land under the *ejido* system raises serious questions about whether the cure is worse than the disease.

The states of Mexico are divided into local governmental units called *municipios*. The chief (*jefe*) of a *municipio* is the *presidente municipal*. *Ejidos* exist within *municipios*, but are not a subdivision of state government. Each *ejido* has its own more or less democratic form of organization, with a council (*junta*) and *presidente* to manage its affairs. Members of an *ejido* are called *ejidatarios*.

The arid lands of northern Mexico are a tough environment in which to live. There is not much of a resource base for the people, and the idea of conservation is generally not salable to people who are barely keeping body and soul together. Although some of these people are aware of the environment's decline and realize that productivity declines with it, there is little evidence that they are the majority, or that they could do much to stop the slide if they were—the pressures created by Mexico's high birth rate and economic problems are just too great. Increases in brush coverage can be expected, at the expense of the grasslands, and stripping of the mountains for lumber, firewood, posts, and mine timbers is likewise going to continue. Water quality in the streams will drop as the grass cover is stripped and the mountains are degraded, since the mountains "catch" the rains and allow recharge of strata that supply wells and springs in the flatlands around them.

Wherever an *ejido* is established, game animals, such as deer, bear, mountain lion, wild turkey, and quail, soon virtually cease to exist. Incessant unlawful hunting and trapping for furs and food either deprive the area of breeding stock or drive it out. Overgrazing eliminates habitats essential for the survival of game. Some *ejido* lands are biological deserts.

Employment opportunities are very limited in rural areas of northern Mexico. Working cattle, herding goats, cutting posts, mining, or truck driving are the main job opportunities. In certain areas a few families gain some income from timber harvest, from collecting *ixtle* fiber and processing it into rope, or from collecting and processing the *candelilla* plant, a source of quality vegetable wax. With the exception of trucking, none of these jobs do more than furnish the most Spartan living one can imagine. Just to survive to adulthood in northern Mexico's rural areas is a pretty good indication that one is tough as a boot.

With employment opportunities being so limited, it is not surprising that some rural *gente* have started growing marijuana (*mota, hierba*) and smuggling it, and opium poppies are grown in some areas of the western *sierras*. Avoid all contact with drugs and dealers and save yourself a lot of trouble. If you blunder into drug growing or transporting operations, we suggest that you get yourself out of the area at once. These folks can get serious, and so can Mexican army units and drug officials.

The typical rural Mexican family is strongly male-dominated. The husband and father is the head of the house in more than name only and makes most important decisions. Furthermore, his culture tells him that he must show his dominance and must resist all outside forces that try to undermine or destroy it. This creates some potential for problems that the non-Mexican traveler in rural areas needs to avoid.

A *músico* of the Tarahumar. The violin is handmade from local woods of the ash family and is strung with strings made of sheep or goat gut or horsehair, if steel strings are not available from the *mestizos*. (Will Thompson photo)

When you approach a small *rancho, jacal,* or *casita,* either by road or by foot, there are some things you can do that will help you avoid cultural conflict. Consider the following.

If the man of the house is not home, the woman may not even respond to your call or knock. In fact, she may, on rare occasions, run out the back door and into the brush. Off the major roads, it is not uncommon for the women and children to be very shy of *gringos.* Even if you know that someone is within the house, if they do not promptly respond to your call, that means that they do not wish to speak to you. Respect their privacy and go on.

When you approach a house, make a reasonable amount of noise and let them know you are coming from some distance away. Don't just barge up to the house (many of them can be seen into through the cracks or because there are no doors), but stop fifty to seventy-five feet away and call out, *"¡Hola, amigos! Buenos días."* Give them a chance to respond without invading their privacy.

If the woman *(ranchera)* comes, ask her, "Is your husband in the house?" *(¿Está en casa su esposo?),* and she will say he is or *"no está (en casa)."* If the negative, then ask, "Where is your husband?" *(¿Dónde está su esposo?)* and she will say "In town" or "In the pastures" *(Al pueblo,* or *En el monte).* She may also say "He's not going to be home today" *(El no estará hoy en casa).* If further conversation indicates that he will not return soon, you can ask directions or other general information from her, but as a general rule do not enter the house. A strange man has no business in a rural Mexican home with the wife present but the husband absent.

If the husband is there or returning shortly, then say, "I would like to have a word with him" *(Quiero hablar con él* or *Quiero algunas palabras con él),* or you can say, "May I speak with him?" *(¿Puedo hablar con él?)* and conduct your business with him; stay removed from the immediate area of the house until he returns, however.

Never curse at or talk down to a rural Mexican male, or engage in any kidding that insults his manhood. He is bound to defend his masculinity and honor. Unless you know him well, it is best not to get into drinking contests with him or even drink alcohol with him, as U.S.-style social drinking is not the same as rural Mexican social drinking. He may feel compelled to drink you under the table, and neither of you is at your best under the influence of too much alcohol.

Mexicans are rightfully sensitive to *gringos* (a term applied to all Anglo-looking foreigners), and first impressions are very important. They see a lot of rude, arrogant foreigners, and many who only tolerate Mexicans. If you appear arrogant, condescending, or amused at their dress, homes, workmanship, or circumstances, you are off on the

An isolated *rancho* in the Chihuahua highlands. Stone walls keep cattle and pigs out of the cornfields. (Will Thompson photo)

wrong foot. Approach with a smile and handshake, friendly greetings, and waves, and *watch what you say in English to your companions* and you will get along well.

Should you be invited into the home, particularly for a meal, you are expected to eat whatever is served and really get with it. Grab a *tortilla* for a scoop and have at the beans, rice, chile sauce, and show your appreciation. As far as water is concerned, all dug wells are probably polluted, and many streams and springs are. Ask them if the water is safe for you, and if not, drink your own.

Mexicans customarily speak politely to each other when they meet on the trail or street, and handshakes (not bonecrushers) are the minimum way of showing good manners at meeting. A common handshake in northern Mexico is palm to palm with the back of your thumb toward you, as if you were going to arm wrestle; however, the standard U.S. variety is accepted, if not too firmly given.

Mexicans are proud of their race (*la raza*), their language, and their country (*la patria*). Despite what we consider a low standard of living, they are generally a happy people and maintain an intricate social system of which they feel intimately a part. Do not assault their dignity by giving them money or goods except for services rendered, and do not give (or throw) money or candy to their children. Approach them and act toward them as friends and full equals (which they most assuredly are) and do not insult them with materialistic displays. The mere fact that they often live in poverty that may at first shock you and later make you question the values of your own culture is no excuse for condescension on your part.

Occasionally, particularly near the border towns or in or near cities, you may be laughed at or even cursed at in Spanish. This is a rare event. The best way to handle it is to ignore the insult, hold your tongue, and don't get into staring or cursing contests. When you fall into the company of crude or impolite Mexicans, separate from them as soon as you can. Avoid at all times individuals and groups who are drinking heavily.

Foreign women will do well to travel with male company and to "belong" to someone in the group. Women will avoid hassles by avoiding flashy or revealing clothing and "bold" mannerisms. Act shy and discreet until you have formed secure friendships or gained acceptance, and even then you will do well to emulate the Mexican girls and women. Women walking alone should avert their gaze and ignore comments or whistles from males in doorways or on street corners in the cities and even in villages. Try to avoid getting involved in things the Mexicans consider men's business.

Remember, these are generally fine, honest people, friendly to strangers who are friendly to them. Your own behavior will largely determine how the Mexicans treat you. Your risk of getting taken advantage of or ripped off by rural people is less than back home on the Interstate.

# 3. Speaking Spanish

**Y**ou do not have to speak good, correct Spanish to communicate. The goal of this manual is to help you communicate, not necessarily in proper Spanish. If you are thirsty, the expression "want water" conveys as much as a longer, formal sentence. Don't hesitate to simply use a word (we hope the correct one) for an object, a need, a desire.

Learn to supplement your Spanish words and phrases with gestures, facial expressions, and by pointing and showing. If your fan belt breaks, and you (by gross oversight) don't have a spare, open your hood, point at the missing belt, say *banda*, and any Mexican trucker will know what you need or what your problem is.

Pool your Spanish and help each other. If one of you freezes up, which will be common in your earlier attempts, everyone else should pitch in and help. Use imagination and ingenuity to solve communication problems. Listen to what is said in reply. Many Mexicans will help you by slowing down and keeping their conversation simple. Once you recognize words and phrases, plug them into your own vocabulary and use them. Your ability will grow rapidly. After a while, your ear starts getting attuned to Spanish, just as your ear gets attuned to a guitar after practice.

Mainly, just keep plugging away, using this manual and other aids, and you will soon be getting your idea across and understanding the replies. Supplement this manual with a good English-Spanish pocket dictionary and you should easily find the proper noun, verb, or adjective to make a rough sentence.

While in Mexico you should try to speak Spanish all the time, no matter how little you know. That is the only way to learn it.

What is your name?    *¿Cómo se llama usted?*
           *(¿Cuál es su nombre?)*
My name is Bob.      *Me llamo Roberto.*

| | |
|---|---|
| I would like to start a conversation with you to practice Spanish. | *Quisiera comenzar una conversación con usted para practicar el español.* |
| Do you speak Spanish? | *¿Habla usted español?* |
| A little. | *Un poco. (Un poquito.)* |
| I can understand a little but do not speak it well. | *Lo entiendo un poco, pero no lo hablo bien.* |
| Do you understand me? | *¿Me comprende usted?* |
| Do you understand? | *¿Entiende usted?* |
| I understand you very well. | *Lo entiendo muy bien.* |
| I do not understand. | *No entiendo.* |
| Please repeat. | *Repita, por favor. (¿Perdón?) (¿Mande?) (¿Cómo dice?)* |
| What did you say? | *¿Qué dijo usted? (¿Perdón?)* |
| I would like to practice Spanish with you. | *Quisiera practicar el español con usted.* |
| She (He) wants to practice Spanish. | *Ella (El) quiere practicar el español.* |
| What is your friend's name? | *¿Cómo se llama su amigo?* |
| His name is George. | *Se llama Jorge.* |
| We know how to speak a little. | *Nosotros sabemos hablar un poquito.* |
| He speaks broken Spanish. | *Chapurrea el español.* |
| I am learning Spanish. | *Estoy aprendiendo español.* |
| Will you teach me Spanish? | *¿Me quiere usted enseñar el español? (¿Me enseña español?)* |
| Let's talk for a while. | *Vamos a charlar (platicar) un rato.* |
| I have difficulty expressing myself in Spanish. | *Es difícil expresarme en español.* |
| Speak more slowly, please. | *Hable más despacio, por favor.* |
| How do you say ———— in Spanish? | *¿Cómo se dice ———— en español?* |
| What is that? | *¿Qué es eso?* |
| What is the name of that? | *¿Cómo se llama eso?* |
| What is the name of this in Spanish? | *¿Cómo se llama esto en español?* |
| What is the meaning of the word ————? | *¿Qué quiere decir la palabra ————?* |
| What do you mean? | *¿Qué quiere decir usted?* |
| What do you wish? | *¿Qué desea usted?* |
| What is a wrench? | *¿Qué es una "llave"?* |
| What is that thing for? | *¿Para qué sirve? (¿Para qué es eso?) (¿Para qué se usa?)* |
| My wife (husband) | *Mi esposa (esposo)* |

| My daughter (son) | *Mi hija (hijo)* |
| My friend | *Mi amiga (amigo)* |
| What place are you from? | *¿De qué lugar es usted?* |
| | *(¿De donde es usted?)* |
| From Ocampo. | *De Ocampo.* |
| What's your answer? | *¿Cuál es su respuesta?* |
| Where can I find the answer? | *¿Dónde encontraré la solución?* |
| What's he talking about? | *¿De qué está hablando?* |
| What are you laughing about? | *¿De qué se están riendo ustedes?* |
| Do you catch on? | *¿Se da usted cuenta?* |
| It isn't anything about you. | *No es nada concerniente a usted.* |
| May I ask a question? | *¿Puedo hacer una pregunta?* |
| Did you ask him his name? | *¿Le preguntó usted su nombre?* |
| Ask him in. | *Invítelo a entrar (pasar).* |

## GREETINGS, GOOD MANNERS, AND POLITE EXPRESSIONS

Mexicans are more formal and more polite than we are. They speak when they meet and they seek permission before moving into another's territory. By learning and using polite expressions, you will make a better impression and get a much friendlier response. You are not usually actively disliked merely because you are a *gringo*, but rudeness or violation of the customs of the country will cost you the respect and friendship of many people, will close many doors, and will cost you opportunities for friendly interaction.

### Greetings and Polite Openings

| Hi! | *¡Hola!* |
| Hi, friend! | *¡Hola, amigo (amiga)!* |
| How goes it? | *¿Cómo le va?* |
| What's new? | *¿Qué hay de nuevo?* |
| Nothing. | *Yo sin novedad. (Nada, nada.)* |
| Anything new? | *¿Hay novedades?* |
| Nothing new. | *Yo sin novedad. (No, nada.)* |
| How are you? | *¿Cómo está usted? (¿Qué tal?)* |
| Very well, thank you. | *Muy bien, gracias.* |
| So-so. | *Así así.* |
| How do you feel today? | *¿Cómo se siente hoy?* |
| I feel bad (good) (better) (worse). | *Me siento mal (bien) (mejor) (peor).* |
| | |
| What's the matter with you? | *¿Qué le pasa?* |
| I'm weak. | *Estoy débil.* |
| I hope you get better! | *¡Que se mejore!* |

| | |
|---|---|
| Good afternoon. | *Buenas tardes.* |
| Good night. | *Buenas noches.* |
| Good morning. | *Buenos días.* |
| Hello or goodbye. | *¡Adiós!* (This word is used to say goodbye, but also as a greeting, usually with uplifted hand in a casual wave or salute as you meet someone on the trail or street whom you will pass without stopping to visit.) |
| How great to see you here! | *¡Qué milagro verte aquí!* |
| How is your family? | *¿Cómo está su familia?* |
| They are all fine. | *Están todos bien.* |
| Tell your family hello. | *Saludos a la familia.* |
| Thanks. Same to yours. | *Gracias. Igualmente.* |
| Please have a seat. | *Haga el favor de sentarse. (Siéntese.)* |
| Please sit down. | *Siéntese, por favor.* |
| This is Mr. Jones. | *Este es el señor Jones.* |

## Other Polite Phrases

| | |
|---|---|
| Yes. | *Sí.* |
| No, thanks. | *No, gracias.* |
| Please. | *Por favor.* |
| Thanks. | *Gracias.* |
| It has been a pleasure to talk to you. | *Ha sido un placer platicar (hablar) con usted.* |
| Thanks again. | *Gracias nuevamente.* |
| Thanks for the information. | *Muchas gracias por su información.* |
| What a pity! | *¡Qué lástima!* |
| You have been very kind. | *Usted ha sido muy amable.* |
| You are very nice. | *Usted es muy simpático(a).* |
| You're welcome. | *Gracias a usted. (De nada.)* |
| Good, very well, etc. | *Está bien. (Bien.) (Bueno.)* |
| Very well. | *Muy bien.* (Also can be used in shopping to accept the item offered by the vendor.) |
| Excuse me. | *Dispénsame. (Disculpeme.)* |
| Pardon me. | *Perdón. (Perdóneme.)* |
| With your permission. | *Con permiso.* |
| Sure! | *¡Cómo no! (¡Seguro!)* |
| Go on. | *Ándele. (Vaya.)* |

| | |
|---|---|
| After you. | *Pos te.* |
| I'm very sorry. | *Lo siento mucho.* |
| No matter. | *No importa.* |
| It doesn't matter. | *No le hace.* |
| To the contrary. | *Al contrario.* |
| Have a good night. | *Que pase bien la noche.* |
| What can I do for you? | *¿En qué puedo servirle?* |
| Clearly (especially if you agree). | *Claro. (Claro que sí.)* |
| That's right. | *Es verdad.* |
| Thanks for the trouble. | *Gracias por tomarse la molestia.* |
| Do you mind? | *¿Le molesta a usted?* |
| Not at all. | *No, en lo absoluto.* |
| With your permission, or by your leave. | *¿Con su permiso?* |
| You have it. | *Usted lo tiene.* |
| Welcome to my house! | *¡Bienvenido a mi casa!* |
| I'm sorry to bother you. | *Siento mucho molestarle.* |

### Standing Aside (gesture with your hand)

| | |
|---|---|
| Come in. | *Pase adelante. (Pásale.)* |
| Go ahead. | *Pase usted.* |

### Introductions

| | |
|---|---|
| I wish to introduce you to my wife, Mickey. | *Quiero presentarlo a mi esposa, Mickey.* |
| Pleased to meet you. | *Tengo mucho gusto en conocerla, señora.* |
| Equally, I'm sure. | *Igualmente, señor.* |

### Polite Refusal of a Drink

| | |
|---|---|
| Have a drink? | *¿Quiere beber (tomar) algo?* |
| No, thanks, I don't drink. | *No, gracias, no tomo.* |
| As a rule, I don't drink, thank you. | *Generalmente no tomo, gracias.* |
| No thanks, it's not good for me. | *No, gracias. Me hace daño.* |

### Polite Dismissal of an Employee or Servant

| | |
|---|---|
| You can go now, if you wish. | *Usted puede retirarse si le gusta.* |
| You may be excused now. | *Usted puede salir ahora. (Ya se puede retirar.)* |
| Thank you, that's all. | *Gracias, es todo.* |

## Goodbyes

| | |
|---|---|
| Good luck (literally, I hope you go well). | *Que le vaya bien* (very widely used). |
| Have fun. | *Qué lo pasen bien.* |
| I hope to see you again. | *Espero volver a verle.* |
| See you soon. | *Hasta luego. (Hasta pronto.)* |
| See you tomorrow. | *Hasta mañana.* |
| See you later. | *Hasta la vista.* |
| May God be with you. | *Que vaya usted con Dios.* |
| Take care of yourself. | *¡Cuídese usted!* |
| Good luck. | *Buena suerte. (Felicidades.)* |
| Be seeing you! | *¡Nos vemos!* |
| See you there. | *Ahí nos vemos.* |
| Have a successful trip. | *Le deseo muy buen viaje.* |
| It has been a pleasure. | *Ha sido un placer.* |

## Leaving the Table or Arriving When Others Are Eating

Mexicans are very polite when joining another group or taking their leave from the table. Before joining a group one should ask, "*Con permiso*" (By your leave). The response is usually "*Ándele*" (Go ahead) or "*Lo tiene*," meaning "You have it." To excuse oneself from the table, say, "*Buen provecho*" (Good appetite), and they will respond with "*Gracias*."

| | |
|---|---|
| Bon appétit. | *Buen provecho.* |

## Leaving the Room

| | |
|---|---|
| With your permission. | *Con su permiso.* |

## In the Morning

| | |
|---|---|
| How did you sleep? | *¿Cómo pasó la noche?* |
| Did you rest well? | *¿Durmió usted bien?* |
| I slept very well, thanks. | *Dormí muy bien, gracias.* |

## Business

| | |
|---|---|
| How's business? | *¿Cómo van los negocios?* |
| My business is going very well, thank you. | *Mi negocio marcha muy bien, gracias.* |

## To Guests

| | |
|---|---|
| You are in your house (consider this your home). | *Está en su casa.* |

**Toast or Special Occasion**

| | |
|---|---|
| To your health! | *¡Salud!* |
| Happy Birthday! | *¡Feliz cumpleaños!* |
| Merry Christmas! | *¡Feliz Navidad!* |
| Easter or Christmas greeting | *¡Felices Pascuas!* |

**When Given Something**

| | |
|---|---|
| What do I owe you? | *¿Cuánto le debo?* |
| Gift? | *¿Regalo?* |
| Something extra? | *¿Pilón?* (The term *pilón* has an interesting history. In the small neighborhood stores [*tienditas*] the shopkeeper would often give the children of shoppers a small pinch of *piloncillo* [brown sugar] to sweeten the deal.) |

**Try Again, Please**

| | |
|---|---|
| What did you say? | *¿Mande?* (polite) (*¿Qué?*) (*¿Cómo dice?* [informal]) |
| Repeat it, please. | *Repita, por favor.* |
| I didn't catch his name. | *No entendí su nombre.* |

## GETTING TO KNOW EACH OTHER AND THE TERRITORY

Perhaps the toughest step in a difficult journey is the first one, when you launch yourself into a new adventure. The adventure of communication in a foreign language, spoken in a foreign land, in the midst of a very different culture, requires a strong first step. *You* must take that step, or wander silently and uncomprehendingly through Mexico and also be doomed to miss much of the grandeur of the country and its remarkable people. That first step is to initiate conversation at every opportunity in Spanish, no matter how fractured it may be, no matter how gross your errors, no matter if you forget all the carefully memorized vocabulary and all the phrases and sentences given in this book, and no matter if all you get at first are blank expressions, spread hands, and *"No comprendo, señor."*

Take the first step with a smile and friendly greeting, grin at your own mistakes, laugh with the Mexicans at yourself, but keep on trying and you will soon be communicating and find yourself understanding the people you meet. At first you will mentally translate from English to Spanish and back again, but soon you will find you can think in Spanish, and you are then on your way.

Most Mexicans are very cooperative and will give you the correct word, with the correct pronunciation, if you make a mistake. If you have to communicate by a combination of individual words, facial expressions, pointing, and gestures, don't worry. Mexicans are expressive people, and gestures and communication by "body language" are natural to their culture. Just carry that old pocket dictionary and get with it!

One of the best ways to get folks to talk to you is to ask them about themselves, their family, their work, and then tell them the same about yourself. This can be expanded to questions about their farm, ranch, or village, places where they feel at home, and about the surrounding country. There may be many better ways to get acquainted with strangers, but the following dialog will help you get started.

F = foreigner; R = ranchero; W = wife

| | |
|---|---|
| (F) Good day. | *Buenos días.* |
| (R) Good day. | *Buenos días.* |
| (F) How are you doing? | *¿Cómo está usted?* |
| (R) Very well, thank you. And how are you? | *Muy bien, gracias. ¿Y usted?* |
| (F) Very well, thanks. May I have a word with you? | *Regular, gracias. ¿Puedo hablar con usted?* |
| (R) Yes, why not? | *Sí. ¿Cómo no?* |
| (F) What is your name? | *¿Cómo se llama usted?* |
| (R) My name is Jaime Diego. | *Me llamo Jaime Diego.* |
| (F) My name is Bob Burleson. I am glad to know you. | *Me llamo Roberto Burleson. Tengo mucho gusto en conocerle.* |
| May I present to you my wife, Mickey. | *Jaime, le presento a mi esposa, Micaela.* |
| (R) It is a pleasure to know you, Madam. | *Tanto gusto en conocerla, señora.* |
| (W) It is equally my pleasure, Sir. | *Igualmente, señor.* |
| (R) Do you speak Spanish, Roberto? | *¿Habla usted español, Roberto?* |
| (F) Yes, a little. I need practice. Jaime, please speak a bit more slowly. | *Sí, un poco. Me falta práctica. Jaime, hable más despacio, por favor.* |
| (R) Do you understand me now? | *¿Me entiende ahora?* |
| (F) Yes, now I understand. This ranch is very interesting. With your permission, may we visit your *rancho?* | *Sí, ahora entiendo. Su rancho es muy interesante. Con su permiso, ¿podemos visitar su rancho? (¿Nos permite visitar?)* |

(R) Why not? Go ahead!  
Where do you come from, Roberto?  
*¿Cómo no? ¡Adelante!*  
*¿De dónde viene (es), Roberto?*

(F) I'm a Texan.  
*Soy tejano. (Vengo del Norte.)*

(R) Where do you go from here?  
*¿Adónde va de aquí?*  
*(¿Para dónde va?)*

(F) We're just riding around.  
*Vamos a dar la vuelta.*

(F) Jaime, does this ranch have both goats and cattle?  
*Jaime, ¿hay vacas y cabras en este rancho?*

(R) No, we have only goats.  
*No, tenemos puros chivos.*

(F) Are you a goatherd?  
*¿Es usted pastor?*

(R) No, I am the foreman. The goatherds are in the pastures.  
*No. Soy el caporal. Los pastores están en el monte (pasto) (campo).*

(F) Where do you live, Jaime?  
*¿Dónde vive usted, Jaime?*

(R) I live in that stone house.  
*Yo vivo en esa casa de piedra.*

(F) Is this *rancho* an *ejido*?  
*¿Es este terreno parte de un ejido?*

(R) No, this is all private property.  
*No, es propiedad privada.*

(F) Do you have a family, Jaime?  
*¿Jaime, tiene usted familia?*

(R) Yes, I have a wife and two sons, but they live in Músquiz.  
*Sí, tengo esposa y dos hijos, pero ellos viven en Músquiz.*

(F) Who owns this ranch?  
*¿De quién es este rancho?*

(R) The owner is Mr. Raúl García.  
*El dueño es el Señor (Don) Raúl García.*

(F) Where does the owner live?  
*¿Dónde vive el dueño?*

(R) He also lives in Músquiz.  
*El vive en Músquiz también.*

(F) Do you have pure water here?  
*¿Hay agua potable aquí?*

(R) Yes, there is a good spring in the canyon.  
*Sí, hay un buen ojo de agua en el cañón.*

(F) There come two horsemen.  
Who is the older man?  
*Allá vienen dos jinetes.*  
*¿Quién es el viejo?*

(R) He is my uncle Jacinto.  
*Es mi tío Jacinto.*

(F) Who is the other man?  
*¿Quién es el otro hombre?*

(R) He is Joe, a gatherer of plant fibers.  
*Es José, un ixtlero.*

(F) How is the weather?  
*¿Cómo está el tiempo?*

(R) It is fine.  
*Hace buen tiempo.*

(F) Did it rain much yesterday?  
*¿Llovió mucho ayer?*

(R) I'll say it did!  
*¡Ya lo creo!*

(F) Has traffic been getting through on this road?  
*¿Ha pasado tráfico por este camino?*

(R) Yes. There is no problem.  
*Sí. No hay problema.*

(F) Are there caves on this ranch?  
*¿Hay cuevas en este rancho?*

(R) Yes, there are many in the mountains.  
*Sí, hay muchas cuevas en las sierras.*

| | |
|---|---|
| (F) Are there good waterholes in the mountains? | *¡Hay tinajas buenas en las sierras?* |
| (R) Yes, there are three large ones. | *Sí, hay tres tinajas grandes allá.* |
| (F) Is there a trail to the caves and waterholes? | *¡Hay una vereda (un rastro) a las cuevas y a las tinajas?* |
| (R) Yes, there is a trail from here. | *Sí, hay una vereda (un rastro) de aquí.* |
| (F) Where does the trail start? | *¡Dónde comienza la vereda?* |
| (R) It starts just beyond that little hill over there. | *La vereda comienza del otro lado de esa lomita.* |
| (F) With your permission, I would like to take a walk along the trail. | *Con permiso, quiero caminar por esa vereda.* |
| We plan to return in a few hours. | *Pensamos regresar en tres o cuatro horas.* |
| (R) Go ahead. Good luck. (May you go well.) | *Adelante. Que le vaya bien.* |
| (F) Thanks. With your permission I will leave. | *Gracias, Jaime. Con su permiso, yo me voy.* |
| (R) O.K. | *Bueno.* |
| (F) Goodbye, friend. | *Adiós, amigo.* |

The above dialog is an example of a typical conversation with a *ranchero*. If you stop and visit and show courtesy and interest, you will usually be allowed entry and can explore many points of interest. Each time you visit, you pick up some conversational points and become more confident in your ability. Just hang in there and keep trying!

# 4. In Your Vehicle

## WHERE AM I?

What (city) (town) is this?

¿En qué (ciudad) (pueblo) estamos? (¿Qué pueblo es este?)

Where is the center of the town?

¿Dónde está el centro de la ciudad?

Where is the (street) (square) (hotel)?

¿Dónde está (la calle) (la plaza) (el hotel)?

Where can I find road maps?

¿Dónde se pueden conseguir mapas con carreteras y caminos?

Won't you please draw me a map of the route?

¿Quiere hacerme el favor de dibujarme un mapa del camino?

Draw me a map, please.

Dibújeme un plano (un mapa), por favor.

Put a cross on the map to show where we are.

Ponga usted una cruz en el mapa para señalar dónde estamos.

Certainly, I'll do it for you.

Se lo haré, con mucho gusto.

Can you give (sell) us a map?

¿Nos puede dar (vender) un mapa?

Can you show me the town on the map?

¿Puede usted mostrarme el pueblo en el mapa?

Is there a gasoline station near here?

¿Hay una gasolinera cerca de aquí?

Where is the next gasoline station?

¿Dónde está la próxima gasolinera?

How far away is it?

¿A qué distancia? (¿Qué tan lejos?)

Is there a gasoline station on this road?

¿Hay una gasolinera por este camino?

May I use your phone?

¿Puedo usar su teléfono?

I wish to telephone.

Quiero telefonear.

Is this the road to ———?

¿Este camino llega a ———?

Which is the road to ———?

¿Cuál es el camino a ———?

Take me there, please.
Is this the public road?
How many kilometers to ———?
How do I get to ———?
Am I going the right way?
I'm lost.
I got lost because I took the wrong road.
How do I get back to ——— from here?
Can you direct me to ———?
Please point!

Which way is north?
Where is it?
Is it far?
How far?
Is it close?
Can you find your way all right?

The roads fan out from the town in all directions.
A fence runs along the road.

Does either of these roads lead to Músquiz?
Either one is satisfactory.

Both roads will take you all to Músquiz.
Where do I turn east?
Go due north until you come to the river, then turn east.

Follow the old riverbed for 5 kilometers.

*Lléveme allá, por favor.*
*¿Es este el camino real?*
*¿Cuántos kilómetros a ———?*
*¿Cómo llego a ———?*
*¿Voy bien?*
*Estoy perdido(a).*
*Me perdí porque me equivoqué de camino.*
*¿Cómo vuelvo a ——— de aquí?*

*¿Me puede dirigir a ———?*
*¡Sírvase apuntar! (Sírvase señalar.) (Por favor, señale.)*
*¿Dónde está el norte?*
*¿Dónde está? (¿Dónde queda?)*
*¿Está lejos?*
*¿Qué tan lejos?*
*¿Está cerca?*
*¿Podrá usted encontrar el camino sin dificultad?*
*Los caminos salen del pueblo en todas las direcciones.*
*Hay una cerca a lo largo del camino.*
*¿Va hacia (Pasa por) Músquiz alguno de estos dos caminos?*
*Cualquiera de los dos es satisfactorio.*
*Los dos caminos le llevan a Músquiz.*
*¿Dónde volteo hacia el este?*
*Vaya usted derecho hacia el norte hasta que llegue al río, entonces voltee al este.*
*Siga el viejo cauce del río cinco kilómetros.*

## Compass Points

| North | *Norte* (m.) |
| East | *Este* (m.); *Oriente* (m.) |
| South | *Sur* (m.) |
| West | *Oeste* (m.); *Poniente* (m.) |

Informal roadside sign pointing the way to Mexico's highest waterfall, Cascada de Basaseachic, Chihuahua. The name has several spellings. (Will Thompson photo)

## FINDING YOUR WAY

| | |
|---|---|
| Please show me the road to ———. | *Por favor, enséñeme el camino a* ———. |
| How far away is ———? | *¿Qué tan lejos está ———?* |
| I'm lost. | *Estoy perdido(a).* |
| I need some information. | *Necesito cierta información.* |
| Am I going the right way? | *¿Voy bien?* |
| How do I get back to ——— from here? | *¿Cómo vuelvo a ——— de aquí?* |
| How can I get to ———? | *¿Cómo puedo llegar a ———?* |
| Please point. | *Sírvase apuntar. (Sírvase señalar.) (Sírvase indicar.)* |

| | |
|---|---|
| Please point it out to me. | *Sírvase señalármelo.* |
| Where does this road go? | *¿A dónde va este camino?* |
| Where will that road take us? | *¿A dónde nos lleva ese camino?* |
| Please tell me where the ford (river crossing) is? | *¿Hágame el favor de indicarme dónde está el vado?* |
| Show me the way to the ford, please. | *Enséñeme el camino al vado, por favor.* |
| How do I go to ———? | *¿Por dónde voy a ———?* |
| (At a junction) Which road must I take? (Note: a y in a road is called *igriega*.) | *¿Qué camino debo tomar en la confluencia?* |
| Which way should I go? | *¿De qué lado debo ir?* |
| Where do I turn? | *¿Dónde me doy la vuelta?* |
| What is the shortest way to ———? | *¿Cuál es el rumbo más corto para ———?* |
| Is this the way to ———? | *¿Se va por este camino a ———?* |
| On the road to ——— | *Por el camino de ———* |
| Where can I see ———? | *¿Dónde puedo ver ———?* |
| Where can I find a village? | *¿Dónde puedo encontrar un pueblo?* |
| Go back by way of ———. | *Regrese por ———.* |
| At what place or point? | *¿En que punto?* |
| How does one go? | *¿Por donde se va?* |
| Is this the (direct) way to ———? | *¿Este es el camino (directo) a ———?* |
| How long will it take to go? | *¿En cuánto tiempo se llega? (¿Cuánto tiempo se hace?)* |
| When will we arrive at ———? | *¿Cuándo llegaremos a ———?* |
| Can I get something to eat on the way? | *¿Se encuentra en dónde comer?* |
| We're going to blaze a new trail! | *¡Vamos a abrir un nuevo sendero!* |
| Where have you come from? | *¿De dónde viene usted?* |
| Have you all come through the Puerta de la Boquilla? | *¿Pasaron por la Puerta de la Boquilla?* |
| Did you all pass near the Rancho El Jardín? | *¿Pasaron cerca del Rancho El Jardín?* |
| Is the road passable from here through the Puerta de la Boquilla? | *¿Podemos pasar por este camino desde la Puerta de la Boquilla? (¿Se puede pasar por el camino desde aquí hasta la Puerta de la Boquilla?)* |
| Can you drive to Rancho El Jardín on this road? | *¿Se puede llegar al Rancho El Jardín por este camino?* |

What route did you take from El Jardín to here?

*¿Qué ruta llevó desde El Jardín a aquí? (¿Qué ruta tomó del Jardín aquí?)*

Is there a better way to get to ———?

*¿Hay un mejor modo de llegar a ———?*

Do you know the road from Tanque la Mula to El Jardín?

*¿Conoce usted el camino del Tanque la Mula al Jardín?*

Can the road be traveled in an ordinary pickup?

*¿Se puede pasar en una camioneta?*

Is there any road into the lower (upper) end of El Diablo Canyon?

*¿Hay algún camino a la parte baja (alta) del Cañón el Diablo?*

How can I get there from here?

*¿Cómo puedo llegar allá?*

Can I go by way of ———?

*¿Puedo ir vía ———?*

Go by way of ———.

*Váyase por ———.*

What is this (next) town?

*¿Cómo se llama este (el próximo) pueblo?*

Do you go near ———?

*¿Pasa usted cerca de ———?*

Do I keep to the left or the right?

*¿Debo seguir a la izquierda o a la derecha?*

Turn left (right) when you get to the fork in the road.

*Doble hacia la izquierda (la derecha) cuando llegue usted al cruce del camino.*

Where do the roads join?

*¿Dónde se juntan los caminos?*

How far is it to the river?

*¿Qué distancia hay al río?*

When I get to the Paso de las Cabras, should I go around to the east side of the sierras or go through it?

*¿Cuándo llegue al Paso de las Cabras, cómo voy: al lado este de la sierra o atravieso el paso mismo?*

Is there any way to pass by truck from Rancho El Jardín down the canyon to the west, so as to meet the highway to Boquillas?

*¿Hay paso por camioneta del Rancho El Jardín por el cañón hacia el oeste para tomar el camino a Boquillas?*

Is there a road over which I can drive my truck to the top of the cliff and look off to the west?

*¿Hay algún camino que vaya hasta la orilla de la sierra? Quiero ver el panorama hacia el oeste.*

Where can I find (get on) that road?

*¿En dónde queda (puedo tomar) este camino?*

Which is the best road to the top of the mountain?

*¿Cuál es el mejor camino que sube la sierra?*

You can't get through the mountain pass at this season.

*No puede usted franquear el paso de las sierras en esta estación (temporada).*

| | |
|---|---|
| How long will it take us to pass through the canyon? | *¿Cuánto tiempo nos tardaremos en atravesar el cañón?* |
| The road runs parallel to the river. | *El camino va paralelo al río.* |
| The river lies to your right. | *El río queda a su derecha.* |
| On this side of; before you get to ————. | *Más acá de; de este lado de ————.* |
| On the other side of; beyond. | *Más allá de; al otro lado.* |
| Just beyond ————. | *Un poco más allá de (pasado de) ————.* |
| This way. | *Por aquí; por acá.* |
| That way. | *Por allá; por allí.* |
| A little more (farther). | *Más allá; un poco más.* |
| Going in the right direction. | *Ir al rumbo; ir bien.* |
| To the left. | *A la izquierda.* |
| To the right. | *A la derecha.* |
| Straight ahead. | *Siempre derecho; adelante; derecho.* |

(Note: *derecha* [right] and *derecho* [straight ahead] can cause confusion. Watch where your informant points.)

## ROAD CONDITIONS

In rural Mexico you may encounter very difficult roads. It is best to travel with a heavy-duty pickup or 4-wheel-drive vehicle, with good clearance and substantial 6-ply or 8-ply tires, preferably mudgrips. Also, follow the custom of the Mexicans and carry a set of tire chains, as nothing else will get you across slick clay flats in the rainy season. Most roads get only infrequent grading, and you should be prepared to do some minor roadwork, such as building up a washout where the road crosses an *arroyo* (creek). Drive slowly and watch carefully for large rocks (small boulders) that Mexican truckers use to hold up their trucks while changing tires, or as chockstones on slopes, as they habitually drive off and leave them in the road. However, don't forget that large stones are also used to mark (warn of) dangers on the road.

### Descriptive Road Terms

| | |
|---|---|
| Bad | *Malo(a); muy feo(a); muy malo(a)* |
| Better | *Mejor; mucho mejor* |
| Bridge | *Puente* (m. or f.) |
| Built-up road with deep bar ditches on both sides | *Bordo* (m.) |
| Cattle guard | *Cuida vaca* (f.) |

| | |
|---|---|
| Detour | *Desviación* (f.) |
| Dip | *Bajada* (f.) |
| Dry | *Seco*(*a*) |
| Dry lake holding water after rains | *Playa* (f.); *laguna* (f.) |
| Dunes | *Dunas de arena* (f.); *médanos* (m.) |
| Dusty | *Polvoriento*(*a*); *polvoroso*(*a*) |
| Fence | *Cerca* (f.); *alambre* (m.) |
| Flat or level | *Plano*(*a*) |
| Ford (river crossing) | *Vado* (m.) |
| Gate | *Puerta* (f.) |
| Good | *Bueno*(*a*) (*lo mejor* = the best) |
| Gravel | *Grava* (f.) |
| Gully | *Arroyo* (m.) |
| Jungle mudhole | *Fanga*(*o*) |
| Landslide or rockfall | *Derrumbe* (m.) |
| Loose | *Suelto*(*a*); *flojo*(*a*) |
| Muddy | *Lodoso*(*a*); *zoquetoso*(*a*) |
| Mudhole | *Charco* (m.); *aguada* (f.); *atascadero* (m.) |
| Narrow | *Angosto*(*a*) |
| Passable | *Pasable* |
| Pavement | *Pavimento* (m.) |
| Remote; beyond nowhere | *Retirado*(*a*); *lejano*(*a*) |
| Rocky | *Rocoso*(*a*); *roqueño*(*a*) |
| Rough | *Borrascoso*(*a*); *áspero*(*a*) |
| Route | *Ruta* (f.) |
| Rut | *Rodada* (f.) |
| Sand | *Arena* (f.) |
| Shortcut | *Atajo* (m.) |
| Shoulder (of road) | *Borde* (m.); *saliente* (m.) |
| Slippery | *Resbaloso*(*a*) |
| Small lake or big puddle | *Aguada* (f.); *laguna* (f.) |
| Steep | *Precipitoso*(*a*); *muy alto*(*a*) |
| Stuck | *Atascado*(*a*) |
| Washout | *Derrubio* (m.); *fracaso* (m.) |
| Wide | *Ancho*(*a*) |
| Wire gap | *Falcete* (m.) |

Typical Mexican roads in unfenced rural areas soon separate into a veritable maze of routes, most of them eventually leading to the same destination, so that they are the same (*lo mismo*) to the Mexicans. In other words, if one route (*ruta*) gets too bad (*malo*), they just take off across the brush (*monte*) and make a new path around the washout

A mountain road on the east side of the Sierra Maderas del Carmen in Coahuila. If you're *muy macho*, you put the truck in low gear and forge ahead without looking. We looked, parked the truck, grabbed our packs, and took off walking! (David H. Riskind photo)

Mexican road construction methods in the *barranca* country of Chihuahua. In-stead of moving the heavy boulder, they just put some props under it. (Will Thompson photo)

(*derrubio*) or mudhole (*charco*) that is creating the problem. Thus, you will be confronted with many choices. Usually, you should stay with the road showing the greatest degree of travel and the most recent signs of travel, even if the other choice may at first glance look like the better road. Mexicans, like wildlife, take the path of least resistance, and they are very good at avoiding the worst spots on their roads. Just as a game trail will get you up the mountain or canyon with the least expenditure of effort, following the road the Mexicans themselves follow will usually (but not always) get you there with the least effort and risk.

Do not, however, drive as fast as the Mexicans do on these rural roads; they know every bump and washout intimately, can move faster than you dare, and they do not seem to mind long waits for repairs or a ride.

Tarahumar men employed as a road construction crew. Much road work in the Sierra Madre is done by hand. (Will Thompson photo)

In the rainy season (*tiempo de las aguas*) there are real problems to be found in valleys with clay or silt soils that were formerly tobosa grass flats, now reduced by years of overgrazing to flat clay pans cut by *arroyos*. Some low, unvegetated areas are called *lagunas*. The roads usually follow the valleys, to avoid the rocky hills, but this also makes them very subject to washing and huge mudholes. One particular series of mudholes is called Charcos de Risa (Mudholes of Laughter), as so many vehicles get stuck in them. It has taken us as long as twelve hours to go 20 or 30 miles under these conditions, even with 4-wheel drive and winches. Be prepared with highlift jacks and strong boards, shovels, cables, and the like, to self-rescue from a *charco*.

Most Mexicans do not have 4-wheel drive vehicles. They get by with mudgrip tires, liberal use of tire chains, and by making long running starts into mudholes, driving as though there is no tomorrow. Four-wheel drive is called *doble tracción* (double traction). If you have it, they may well think you can go anywhere, so be sure you question them well about the road conditions. Mexicans have a tendency to understate the degree of difficulty ahead, particularly if they have just come through it themselves. Also, being agreeable people, they may well tell you what you want to hear, whether it is accurate or not. We once asked a Mexican coming out of a miles-long *charco* if the road was passable, and he said *bueno*. As we were stuck a few hundred yards ahead and looking for some tree big enough to tie a winch line on, we found where he had camped in the mudhole for several nights. True, the *charco* was "passable" as both he and we got through it; the only problem was that he failed to tell us how much time and labor would be required!

There are many abandoned roads, totally impassable and even dangerous, in mountains and deep canyons. Use good judgment. Scout ahead. Stop while you can still turn back, and if you just *have* to go up that road, walk it out first. In really remote areas, serious damage to your vehicle can strand you for a long time. It is also possible to fall off a mountain in your vehicle and end up as a long-term resident of a Mexican *campo santo* (graveyard).

In Mexico many streams are crossed by fords (*vados*) rather than bridges. This calls for some thought and skill on your part. Always be extra careful if the stream is muddy, as it may be in flood. If there is rain or stormy weather nearby, be careful that there is no headrise coming down to catch you broadside in the middle of the river. Put a stick at the water's edge and wait to see if it is going up or down. Then, if you cannot see the bottom and the route clearly, someone should wade the stream and test the bottom and depth. Next, check the opposite bank for good winch anchors, such as trees or large boulders. If the water is high, you may wish to remove your fan belt, as this will eliminate a common source of water splashed into the ignition system. Drive slowly so as not to create a "bow wave" ahead of you, as this has a tendency eventually to roll back and flood you. Remember that fording streams may get water or sand in your wheel hubs, axles, and transmission, and you should repack bearings frequently if you are having to do a lot of fording. Check for water in the crankcase, axles, transfer case, and so on.

For getting out of mudholes, a strong nylon "snatch strap" about 30 feet long is better than tow chains, as it allows a lighter vehicle to get a running start and pull a heavier one (the extra length lets the pulling vehicle stay on better ground). These straps have give built into them, so don't be shy about a running start. To avoid having to unload your vehicle in a mudhole to get at emergency gear, build a subfloor or platform of 2 × 6's topped with plywood and store shovels, axes, snatch straps, and chains under the floor so you can easily pull them out anytime.

There are usually high roads and low roads to the same place. The low road is best except in wet weather. To build "roads," use the trunks of giant dagger (*palma*; preferably dead ones), brush, rocks, or anything handy. You need a good high-lift jack, some heavy boards or a metal plate to support the jack in mud, and lots of WD-40 to keep it working. The quickest way out of a bad mudhole (if you have no winch) is to jack up *all four* wheels one at a time and put rocks, boards, *palma* trunks, or cut brush under and in front of them. Then all but the driver push and give a big yell (*grito*) and make a run out of the hole. *Never* carry a spare tire *under* a vehicle (as it comes from the factory), or you will have trouble getting to it under muddy conditions. Mount your *two* spares on top, on the front, or inside near the rear.

*Never* take down a fence across a road, and do not enter a locked gate without permission. On *ejido* lands, see the *presidente*, if possible. In some very remote communities you will be expected to look up the local *jefe* to get "official" permission to explore, camp, or visit. Just take your time and feel your way along until you understand the local customs. In places where few foreigners go, you may be suspected of being a drug buyer, hunter, or scout for a mining or timber company. Since such people do cause problems for the rural folk, do not be offended if they ask what your business is. A little delay for friendly conversation will ease their minds and facilitate your passage.

## Road Condition Phrases

(Note: As a general rule, try *not* to provide an answer in the question: "What is the road condition?" not "Is the road good?")

| | |
|---|---|
| What is the condition of the road? | *¿Cuál es la condición del camino?* (*¿En qué condición está el camino?*) |
| This is a narrow road. | *Este es un camino angosto.* |
| Is the road passable? | *¿Es el camino pasable?* |
| This time of year the roads are impassable. | *En esta época (estación) del año los caminos están intransitables.* |
| Is it hard surface or dirt? | *¿Está pavimentado o es de tierra?* |
| Is the road good or bad? | *¿Está bueno o malo el camino?* |

This road is full of ruts.

*Este camino está lleno de surcos (rodadas).*

Are the creeks (rivers) running too high to cross?

*¿Podemos cruzar los arroyos (ríos)? (¿Los torrentes no están muy altos?)*

It cannot be passed.

*No hay paso.*

Go ahead.

*Pase adelante.*

Which is the public road?

*¿Cuál es el camino real?*

Are there detours on this road?

*¿Hay desviaciones?*

Yes, there is a detour six kilometers from here.

*Sí. Hay una desviación a seis kilómetros de aquí.*

Did it rain yesterday?

*¿Llovió mucho ayer?*

How much?

*¿Qué tanto? (¿Cuánto?)*

I should say it did! Two inches!

*¡Ya lo creo! ¡Dos pulgadas!*

Are there mudholes in the road?

*¿Hay charcos en el camino?*

Is the road very muddy?

*¿Está el camino muy lodoso?*

Is there another route?

*¿Hay otra ruta?*

Are these roads the same?

*¿Son los caminos iguales?*

Is the road washed out?

*¿Está desviado (derrubiado) el camino?*

There is a steep grade on the other side of the hill.

*Al otro lado del cerro hay una pendiente muy pronunciada.*

There is a great gorge two kilometers from here.

*A dos kilómetros de aquí hay una gran cañada (barranca).*

You must use caution in crossing the river.

*Tiene que tener cuidado al cruzar este río.*

It's dangerous to cross the bridge unless the river falls.

*Es peligroso cruzar el puente si el río no baja.*

The road goes through the cut in the mountains.

*El camino pasa por el puerto.*

Have they cleared the road yet?

*¿Han despejado ya el camino?*

The roadbed is in bad condition.

*El firme del camino está en malas condiciones.*

There's an obstruction across the road.

*Hay un obstáculo atravesado en el camino.*

Are there many turns ahead?

*¿Hay muchas vueltas más adelante?*

Who's ahead?

*¿Quién va adelante?*

Where does that road go?

*¿Adónde va aquel camino?*

Which road goes to Rancho el Jardín?

*¿Cuál camino llega al Rancho Jardín?*

Can you get there by pickup?

*¿Se puede ir allá en camioneta?*

Is the road passable in my pickup?

*¿Puedo pasar con mi troca (camioneta)?*

Is the road open?
The road is such that it can be traveled only on foot.

*¿Está abierto el camino?*
*El camino está en tales condiciones que sólo se puede recorrer a pie.*

Have there been any big rains recently?
Has other traffic been getting through?
Can this pickup cross the arroyo safely?
Where can we cross the stream?

*¿Ha llovido mucho recientemente?*

*¿Ha pasado tráfico?*

*¿Puede cruzar esta troca el arroyo con seguridad?*
*¿Por dónde podemos cruzar la corriente?*

The river's rising fast!

*¡El río está creciendo rápidamente!*

How deep is the water? Show me, please.
Will you wade ahead and show me the crossing?
Certainly, I'll do it for you.
Supposing it rains, can we use that road?
No, you cannot pass in the rainy season.
Is there a better road to ———?
The next stretch of road is not bad.

*¿Qué tan hondo está el agua? Enséñeme (Muéstreme), por favor.*
*¿Puede chapotear (vadear) el vado y enseñármelo (mostrarme)?*
*Lo haré, con mucho gusto.*
*¿Suponiendo que llueva, podremos utilizar ese camino?*
*No hay paso en el tiempo de las aguas.*
*¿Hay un camino mejor a ———?*
*El próximo trecho del camino no está mal.*

Is this the principal road to ———?
Are there any locked gates across the road?
Do the gates have locks?

*¿Este es el camino (directo a) principal a ———?*
*¿Hay puertas bajo llave (con candado) a través del camino?*
*¿Las puertas están bajo llave (con candados)?*

May I go through?
Where can we get permission to pass through?
May I go in?
Where is the key hidden?
Where can I find the key?

*¿Puedo pasar?*
*¿En dónde (A quién) podemos pedir permiso para pasar?*
*¿Puedo entrar?*
*¿En dónde está la llave escondida?*
*¿En dónde puedo encontrar la llave?*

Who has the key?
Where does he live?
Is there another truck coming down the mountain after you?

*¿Quién tiene la llave?*
*¿Dónde vive él?*
*¿Viene otra troca (otro camión) en seguida?*

How many more do we have coming?

¿Cuántos más tenemos (vienen)?

Are there any loaded trucks coming down?

¿Vienen otras trocas cargadas?

Did you meet anyone on the road?

¿Se encontró con alguien en el camino?

Watch out! There comes another truck.

¡Cuidado! ¡Allí viene otra troca (otro camión)!

Can two trucks meet and pass on this road?

¿Pueden pasar dos trocas en este camino?

What cargo are you hauling?

¿Qué carga lleva?

The first good rainstorm will wash it away.

La primera lluvia fuerte que caiga se lo llevará.

Last night's storm washed out the road.

El aguacero de anoche ha cortado el camino.

There is a ditch on each side of the road.

Hay una zanja a cada lado del camino.

A fallen tree (rock) barred our way.

Un árbol (Una piedra) caído(a) obstruía el paso.

The road is in bad condition.

El camino está en mal estado.

The road is muddy.

El camino está lodoso.

How well can this truck take rough ground?

¿Marcha bien esta camioneta por un terreno quebrado?

The road is getting steadily worse!

¡El camino está cada vez peor!

One more heave and we'll have the pickup out of the mud!

¡Un empujón más y sacaremos la camioneta del lodo (zoquete)!

Let's stop and get our bearings before we go any farther.

Vamos a orientarnos antes de continuar.

Can I drive over to that mountain (canyon) on a road?

¿Puedo llegar a esa sierra (ese cañón) por camino?

Where does the road start?

¿Dónde comienza el camino?

What route does it follow to the mountain (canyon)?

¿Qué rumbo (ruta) sigue a la sierra (al cañón)?

Are they cutting timber in those mountains?

¿Están cortando madera en la sierra?

Are the mines being worked at this time?

¿Hay minas en operación ahora?

Are there ore trucks (logging trucks) ahead?

¿Hay camiones cargados con minerales (troncos) adelante?

Is there a better road around this mudhole (creek)?

¿Hay una ruta mejor alrededor de este charco (arroyo)?

Is there a road up the canyon to the top?

¿Hay un camino más arriba que sube a la cumbre?

| | |
|---|---|
| Is there a road alongside the river? | ¿Hay algún camino a lo largo del río? |
| Where can I find a road to the river? | ¿Dónde puedo encontrar el camino al río? |
| Is the bridge safe? | ¿Es seguro el puente? |
| That bridge is not strong enough to support such weight. | Ese puente no está bastante fuerte para aguantar tanto peso. |
| Traffic on this road is always light. | El tráfico por este camino es siempre poco. |
| Let's take another try at getting up this hill! | ¡Haremos un nuevo intento para subir la loma! |
| Give the wheel a turn! | ¡Déle una vuelta a la rueda! |
| The road got worse as we went along. | A medida que avanzábamos el camino empeoraba. |
| We'll come back by the mountain road. | Volveremos por el camino de la sierra. |
| In a way, we're lucky to be here! | ¡En cierta forma es una suerte estar aquí! |
| As long as we've come this far we might as well go on! | ¡Puesto que hemos llegado hasta aquí, deberíamos seguir adelante! |
| Loaded | Cargado(a); con carga |
| Fully loaded | Con carga completa |

## DRIVING AT NIGHT

Most tourist guides advise strongly against driving at night in Mexico. This is generally good advice, particularly if you attempt to drive in the same manner as you would back home. However, since occasions will arise when you will want or may be forced to drive after dark, we shall discuss some of the hazards and how to avoid them and give you some tips.

You may find it hard to believe, but the main highways are more dangerous at night than are the rural roads we usually travel on. The primary difference is your speed. On a paved highway you will tend to drive much faster, even at night, than you will on a rough and tortuous dirt road. On most country roads you will do well to average 15 to 20 mph and over long stretches you will be driving in lower gears at even slower speeds. The slower your speed, the more time you have to spot a problem and react to it, and the shorter your stopping distance. Therefore, the first rule of night driving in Mexico is slow down! Even on paved roads—particularly on paved roads—we rarely exceed 35 or 40 mph at night and 30 mph is *mucho mejor* for a number of reasons.

The best of Mexican roads are inadequately marked to warn of *current* conditions and *recent* hazards. *Gringos* are in the habit of expecting the Highway Department to take care of drunks and fools as well as the careful driver. Not so in Mexico, where inspections and repairs are infrequent, and a "warning" for a serious washout may have been that large white rock you found in your lane about 100 yards back.

You will get lost. Only the most important road junctures are marked with any form of directional or informational sign. Signs that may have existed are often run over by trucks, cut down for firewood, or pulled up for posts. In fact, one of the most common road signs is the one begging people to refrain from destroying the signs!

Horses, burros, cattle, and other large animals migrate to the roadside at night, as traffic falls off and they can often find better grazing alongside the pavement due to the extra moisture that strip gets from rain runoff. Hit a cow or horse at 20 mph and you have a chance of a bent fender and a slight inconvenience. Hit one at 45 or 50 mph and both your trip and you may end there.

From dusk on, you must watch like a hawk (owl?) for unlighted vehicles. Mexican vehicles often have no lights of any kind, yet are operated for as long as drivers believe they can see. After all, they know the road very well (a road is merely an improved trail) and, to their way of thinking, anyone else traveling at night must know it equally as well. Even if the Mexican vehicle has lights that operate, there is a tendency to "save" them until absolutely necessary, much as your grandmother probably refused to turn on her new electric lamp until full dark. In the United States we are encouraged to turn on our headlights in full daylight, rather than risk being unseen. In Mexico headlights are rarely switched on until "needed," and this need varies not so much with the presence or absence of light as with the individual viewpoint of the driver.

Mexican trucks often have no sign of taillights, brake lights, directional signals, warning flashers, or even reflectors. If they have them, they may be covered entirely with mud or dust. Thus, you may suddenly happen on a heavily laden truck, perhaps barely moving or even stopped, without a sign of a light to the rear.

When a truck breaks down, there is no point in getting it off the road; that just complicates the repair. It just sits there in the traffic lane until the driver gets it rolling again. Some few drivers, when their vehicle has broken down, will go back up the road 30 or 40 yards and put a couple of warning rocks in the road (they are invariably left there after the truck moves on), but that is the exception rather than the rule. Thus you may happen upon disabled trucks in your lane at any time or place, without any sort of warning.

Bridges or roads may wash out in heavy rains, or mud and rocks may fall from above, making a road highly dangerous, but warnings of such recently created hazards are rarely found. Again, when warnings are given, they may be a tree branch cut and laid across the road, or a boulder or two rolled out onto it.

Chugholes or potholes are never marked. You drive where the road is best, irrespective of the lane of travel.

On main roads, particularly mountain roads, you may encounter the Mexican high-speed bus. Bus drivers, to our way of thinking, are among the best, and also the most dangerous, drivers in Mexico. They generally go at top speed, night and day, and are very good. But they are also *muy machos* (they don't give an inch, and they never slow down, as that is a sign of fear or weakness), and tend to take their half out of the middle. They can literally run you off the road, and they take a frightening toll of livestock and pedestrians.

You must remember that you may also encounter *la gente* (the people) at any place, at any hour of day or night, on foot, on a bicycle, in a burro-drawn wagon, in an ox cart, or mounted on a horse, using the roads as if they were village paths. They neither have nor carry lights or reflectors, and you can kill someone easily if you drive at normal U.S. speeds at night.

How can you safely survive all these perils? Try the following suggestions:

Slow down!

Use your headlights early, even if the Mexicans do not.

Everyone in the vehicle should be helping the driver keep watch.

Reduce speed even more at the first sighting of anything questionable or different.

Consider all objects in the road to be warnings of danger ahead; this includes rocks, sticks, leafy branches, or a white rag tied on a roadside bush.

If heavy rains have fallen recently, slow down to a crawl in all low spots. Do not try to drive across flooding streams.

Do not drive in rainstorms, but be careful where you stop. Find a place where you can pull far off the road. Mexicans keep driving in rainstorms.

If you have a light bar with auxiliary lights, this is a great asset. Use your extra lights.

Do not be misled by a smooth stretch of road, as a rough spot is surely coming up.

At the very hint of roadside *gente* or livestock, slow down and creep past them. Movements of people and animals can be totally unpredictable at night, and also can be very rapid.

Respond to any flicker of light, as the only warning you receive may be the reflection from an animal's eye.

Unless you know the road well, stop if conditions get really bad, and before it becomes impassable or dangerous.

In mountain areas, be wary of blind corners or blind hilltops and creep around or over them. Rockfalls, stalled vehicles, or washouts may lurk beyond them.

Stay in your lane in all areas where visibility is limited.

Give the right of way to all Mexican drivers. Their rules of the road are not the same as yours, so just stay out of their way.

Consider all bridges to be narrow (*puente angosto*) and avoid meeting another vehicle on a bridge.

Avoid cities and towns at night if you can, as there is much more chance of people, wagons, and unlighted vehicles being on the road in and near population centers. Reduce speed to a crawl in populated areas.

Driving at night in Mexico is much like IFR conditions in a light aircraft. It takes all your alertness and navigating skill just to stay level and alive!

## IF YOU HAVE AN ACCIDENT

In the United States you are taught to stay at the scene of an automobile accident and render all possible aid, cooperate with the investigation, and stop even if you are merely a witness. In Mexico, although the law says you should remain, this may not be the thing to do.

Under Mexican law, any party to an accident, even a witness, can be held in custody until the investigation is complete. This process may take some time. As a result, most Mexicans immediately leave the scene of an accident if there is any way they can do so. Witnesses do not stop or identify themselves. Neither do most drivers stop and render aid. If a cow, chicken, or burro is struck and killed, nobody stops to locate the owner and pay for it.

What you do will depend on your conscience and your humanitarian instincts. If a human life hangs in the balance, most of us will probably stop. On the other hand, you cannot ignore the consequences of stopping when you could have gone safely on your way. Since the Mexicans presumably know their country and its legal system far better than we do, the fact that they almost universally flee the scene of accidents is highly persuasive.

Merely having insurance on your vehicle from a U.S. carrier, even "Mexico Coverage, Limited," does not satisfy Mexican financial responsibility laws. You should secure Mexican liability insurance coverage from a reliable Mexican insurance company if you plan to drive far in Mexico, particularly on the main highways. Liability coverage is cheap and you can buy it by the day or week, so that you pay only for the period when you need coverage. However, even having Mexican liability insurance will not prevent your being detained until all matters regarding the accident are settled.

Fortunately, in *el monte*, where we suggest that you spend your time, accidents are few and police officials are fewer. Most problems occur in the cities and in towns through which tourists pass on the main highways.

Mexico is not a land of horror stories, but it has a very different culture, a different legal system, a different political system, and different customs from those you are used to. It will pay you to learn all you can about the nation if you plan to travel there; we hope that the frank discussions in this book will assist you.

## VEHICLE TROUBLE PHRASES

| | |
|---|---|
| I want to ask you a favor. | *Quiero pedirle un favor.* |
| I need help. | *Necesito ayuda.* |
| Let me help you. | *Déjeme ayudarle.* |
| My (car) (pickup) has broken down. | *Se me descompuso (el carro) (la camioneta).* |
| Can you please help me? | *¿Por favor, puede usted ayudarme?* |
| I have run out of gasoline. | *Se me acabó la gasolina.* |
| Could you give me some gas? | *¿Puede darme usted un poco de gasolina?* |
| The old tire blew out. | *La llanta vieja se reventó.* |
| The tire is flat. | *La llanta está desinflada.* (On the border, *desinflada* may be replaced by *ponchada* or *rota*.) |
| Help me fix the tire, please. | *Ayúdeme a reparar la llanta, por favor.* |
| Put on the spare. | *Ponga la extra, por favor.* |
| Where is the car repair shop? | *¿Dónde hay un taller de (reparación) (mecánico)?* |
| Where is the tire repair shop? | *¿Dónde hay un vulcanizador?* |
| Do you have a jack? | *¿Tiene usted un gato para la llanta?* |
| Can you help me jack it up? | *¿Puede usted ayudarme a alzar el carro con el gato?* |
| Is there gasoline near? | *¿Hay una gasolinera cerca?* |

Gassing up from a rural source, west of Parral, Chihuahua. In the backcountry most gasoline is found in steel drums and is of questionable quality. (Will Thompson photo)

| | |
|---|---|
| How much is gasoline per liter? | *¿Cuánto vale el litro de gasolina?* (You may be getting it out of a drum!) |
| Fill up the (gasoline tank) (radiator) (battery). | *Llene (el tanque de gasolina) (el radiador) (la pila).* |
| Please check the (oil) (water). | *Por favor, revise (el aceite) (el agua).* (Frankly, you should do your own checking.) |
| Did you check the oil? | *¿Revisó usted el aceite?* |
| Is there any charge for this service? | *¿Hay que pagar algo por este servicio?* |
| What do you charge? | *¿Cuánto me cobra?* |
| You're charging too much! | *¡Usted me pide demasiado!* |
| How much do I owe you? | *¿Cuánto le debo?* |
| Do you fix flats? | *¿Repara usted tubos ponchados (llantas ponchadas)?* |

Change the tire, please. / Cambie la llanta, por favor.

This tire needs pumping up. / Hay que inflar esta llanta.

Put some air in the tires, please. / Por favor, ponga aire en las llantas. (Note: carry your own air gauge, as theirs will be metric.)

Do you sell tires? / ¿Vende usted llantas?

Is there a mechanic there? / ¿Hay un mecánico allí?

Can you fix it? / ¿Puede usted componerlo?

We cannot fix it today. / No podemos arreglarlo hoy.

We don't have the parts. / No tenemos las refacciones correspondientes.

We must send for them. / Tenemos que mandar a buscarlas.

It will take four days. / Tomará cuatro días.

We can fix it temporarily. / Podemos arreglarlos temporalmente.

That's enough. / Basta. (Bastante.) (Está bueno.)

Can you tow the pickup into town? / ¿Puede usted (remolcar) (jalar) (llevar) mi camioneta al pueblo?

It does not work! / ¡No sirve! (Slang: ¡No quiere! ¡No jala!)

I can't move. / No me puedo mover.

It's in the ditch! / Está en la zanja.

It broke! / ¡Se quebró!

It is broken. / Está quebrado(a).

Can you send a mechanic (wrecker) right away? / ¿Puede usted mandar un mecánico (una grúa) lo más pronto posible?

I need a wrench. / Necesito una llave.

Where is an auto parts store? / ¿Dónde está (queda) una refaccionaria? (¿Dónde hay una tienda de partes automotriz?)

A little farther. / Un poquito más allá. (Más adelante.)

Will you go after the parts? / ¿Quiere usted ir por las piezas?

A little more, please. / Un poco más, por favor.

Give me 20 liters of gasoline. / Déme veinte litros de gasolina.

I need a push (a tow), please. / Necesito un empujón (remolque), por favor.

Give the pickup a push. / Déle un empujón a la camioneta.

Stop the engine and let it cool off. / Pare usted el motor y deje que se enfríe.

Try once again. / Pruebe otra vez.

It does not run well. / No anda bien.

| It runs well. | Anda bien. (Corre bien.) |
| Will you take me to a garage? | ¿Quiere usted llevarme a un garaje? |
| Can you tow (push) me? | ¿Puede usted remolcarme (empujarme)? |
| How long will it take to fix? | ¿Cuánto tiempo tomará para arreglarlo? |
| How long will it take? | ¿Cuánto tardará? |

## BASIC AUTO PARTS

| Alternator | Alternador (m.) |
| Auto parts | Refacciones (f.) |
| Axle | Eje (m.) |
|   front |   eje delantero |
|   rear |   eje trasero |
| Ball joint | Rótula (f.) |
| Battery | Acumulador (m.); batería (f.); pila (f.) |
| Battery cable | Cable de acumulador (m.); cable de pila (m.) |
| Bearings, ball | Baleros (m.) |
| Bearings, front wheel | Baleros de las ruedas delanteras (m.) |
| Brakes | Frenos (m.) |
|   master cylinder |   cilindro maestro de frenos (m.) |
| Brake fluid | Líquido de frenos (m.) |
| Carburetor | Carburador (m.) |
|   float |   flotador (m.) |
|   jet |   esprea (f.) |
|   choke |   ahogador (m.); aire (m.) |
| Clutch | Embrague (m.) |
|   disc |   disco de embrague (m.) |
| Coil | Bobina (f.) |
| Coil springs | Resortes (m.) |
| Condenser | Condensador (m.) |
| Cylinder | Cilindro (m.) |
| Differential | Diferencial (m.); maza (f.) |
| Dipstick (oil or transmission) | Bayoneta (f.) |
| Distributor | Distribuidor (m.) |
|   cap |   tapa de distribuidor (f.) |
| Drive shaft | Flecha cardán (f.) |
| Electrical system | Sistema eléctrico (m.) |

| | |
|---|---|
| Exhaust pipe | *Tubo de escape* (m.); *mofle* (m.) |
| Fan | *Ventilador* (m.); *abanico* (m.) |
| belt | *banda de ventilador* (f.) |
| Frame | *Bastidor* (m.) |
| Fuel line | *Tubo* (m.); *manguera de gasolina* (f.) |
| Fuel pump | *Bomba de gasolina* (f.) |
| filter | *filtro de gasolina* (m.) |
| Fuse | *Fusible* (m.) |
| Gas cap | *Tapón de gasolina* (m.) |
| Gas tank | *Tanque de gasolina* (m.) |
| Gasket | *Empaque* (m.); *junta* (f.) |
| head | *empaque de cabeza* (m.) |
| Gauge | *Calibrador* (m.); *manómetro* (m.) |
| Gear | *Engranaje* (m.); *rueda dentada* (f.) |
| Generator | *Generador* (m.) |
| Grease | *Grasa* (f.) |
| Ground | *Tierra* (f.); *conductor a tierra* (m.) |
| Headlights | *Focos* (m.); *faro* (m.) |
| Horn | *Klaxon* (m.); *bocina* (f.) |
| Hose | *Manguera* (f.) |
| Hose clamp | *Abrazadera* (f.) |
| Ignition key | *Llave de switch* (f.) |
| Ignition switch | *Switch de ignición* (m.) |
| Leaf springs | *Muelles* (m.) |
| Leak | *Gotera* (f.) |
| Manifold | *Múltiple* (m.) |
| Master cylinder | *Cilindro maestro de frenos* (m.) |
| Motor | *Motor* (m.); *máquina* (f.) |
| Muffler | *Mofle* (m.); *silenciador* (m.) |
| Oil | *Aceite* (m.) |
| filter | *filtro de aceite* |
| pump | *bomba de aceite* |
| Parts | *Piezas* (f.) (of machine) |
| spare part | *pieza de repuesto* (f.); *pieza de recambio* |
| Patch | *Parche* (m.); *remiendo* (m.) |
| Points | *Platinos* (m.) |
| Pressure plate | *Plato de presión* (m.) |
| Radiator | *Radiador* (m.) |
| cap | *tapón del radiador* (m.) |
| hose | *manguera del radiador* (f.) |
| Relay | *Relé* (m.) |

| | |
|---|---|
| Rings | *Anillos* (m.) |
| Rotor | *Rotor* (m.) |
| Seal | *Retén* (m.) |
| Shaft | *Flecha* (f.) |
| Shock absorber | *Amortiguador* (m.) |
| Solenoid | *Solenoide* (m.) |
| Spare wheel | *Rueda de repuesto* (f.); *extra* (m.) |
| Spark plug | *Bujía* (f.) |
| wire | *cable de bujía* (m.) |
| Starter | *Marcha* (f.); *arranque* (m.) |
| Steering gear | *Caja de dirección* (f.) |
| Steering wheel | *Volante* (m.) |
| Stop or taillight | *Farito trasero* (m.); *calavera* (f.); *trasera* (f.) |
| Stud | *Birlo* (m.); *perno prisionero* (m.) |
| Switch | *Switch* (m.) |
| Taillight | *Foco trasero* (m.) |
| Tail pipe | *Tubo de escape* (m.); *mofle* (m.) |
| Thermostat | *Toma de agua* (f.); *termostato* (m.) |
| Throw out bearing | *Cojarín* (m.) |
| Tie rod | *Varilla de dirección* (f.) |
| Tie rod end | *Terminal de varilla de dirección* (m.) |
| Tighten | *Apretar* |
| Timing gear | *Engranaje de árbol de levas* (m.) |
| Transmission | *Transmisión* (f.); *caja* (f.) |
| Tune | *Afinar* |
| Tune up | *Afinación* (f.) |
| Turn signals | *Direccionales* (f.) |
| Turn signal flasher | *Destellador* (m.) |
| Universal joint | *Cruceta y yugo* (f.); *cardán* (f.) |
| Vacuum advance | *Avance* (m.) |
| Valves | *Válvulas* (f.) |
| Voltage regulator | *Regulado de voltaje* (m.) |
| Water pump | *Bomba de agua* (f.) |
| Weld | *Soldar* |
| Wheel | *Rueda* (f.) |
| Wheel cylinder | *Cilindro de frenos* (m.) |
| Window | *Ventana* (f.); *vidrio* (m.) |
| Windshield | *Parabrisas* (m.) |
| Windshield wiper | *Limpia parabrisas* (m.); *limpiadores* (m.) |
| Windshield wiper blade | *Pluma* (f.) |

| | |
|---|---|
| Wire | *Alambre* (m.) |

## Vehicles

| | |
|---|---|
| Station wagon | *Vagoneta* (f.) |
| Pickup | *Camioneta* (f.) |
| Truck | *Camión* (m.); *troca* (f.) |
| Big truck | *Tortón* (m.) |
| 4-wheel drive | *Doble tracción* (f.) |

## HITCHING A RIDE

| | |
|---|---|
| Lift | *Aventón; llevarme* |
| Where are you going, friend? | *¿A dónde va, amigo?* |
| Where to? | *¿Adónde?* |
| I'm going to Ocampo. | *Voy a Ocampo.* |
| I'm traveling by thumb. | *Viajo por aventón.* |
| I have no means of transportation. | *No tengo medios de transporte.* |
| I've got real problems! | *¡Tengo problemas!* |
| I'm in a tight spot! | *¡Estoy en un aprieto!* |
| I need help. | *Necesito ayuda.* |
| I need a ride. | *Necesito un aventón.* |
| Can you help me, please? | *¿Por favor, puede ayudarme?* |
| Will you give me a ride to Ocampo? | *¿Me da un aventón a Ocampo?* |
| Take me to Ocampo, please. | *Lléveme a Ocampo, por favor.* |
| I want a lift, please. | *Quiero un aventón, por favor.* |
| Take me to the nearest town, please. | *Por favor, lléveme al pueblo más cercano (próximo).* |
| Can you give me a lift in your truck to the next town? | *¿Puede usted llevarme en su troca al próximo pueblo?* |
| Can I bring a friend with me? | *¿Puedo traer a un amigo conmigo?* |
| We like to bum around! | *¡Nos gusta vagabundear!* |
| Take me there. | *Lléveme allá.* |
| What time do you leave? | *¿A qué hora sale usted?* |
| I will pay. | *Yo pago.* |
| What will you charge to take me to Ocampo? | *¿Cuánto me cobra por llevarme a Ocampo?* |
| What do I owe you? | *¿Cuánto le debo?* |
| Please leave me at the square. | *Favor de dejarme en la plaza.* |
| Let me off at the next corner. | *Déjeme bajar en la próxima esquina.* |
| Jump on! | *¡Salte usted!* |
| Get in. | *Súbase.* |

| | |
|---|---|
| Get in the pickup. | *Súbase a la camioneta.* |
| Would you like to ride in my truck? | *¿Quiere usted venir en mi troca?* |
| Would you like a ride? | *¿Quiere usted un aventón?* |
| I'll give you a ride if you will show me the way to Ocampo. | *Lo llevo si me enseña la ruta a Ocampo.* |
| I'm going to get (off) at ———. | *Me voy a bajar en ———.* |
| Can I ride (in the back) (on top) (inside)? | *¿Puedo subirme (atrás) (arriba) (adentro)?* |
| Where do I get off? | *¿Dónde me bajo?* |
| Please tell me where to get off. | *Por favor, dígame donde debo bajarme. (Haga favor de decirme donde me bajo.)* |
| Get off here. | *Bájese aquí.* |
| At what time does the next truck leave for Músquiz? | *¿A qué hora sale la próxima (siguiente) troca para Músquiz?* |
| Where can I get a truck going to Músquiz? | *¿Dónde puedo tomar una troca a Músquiz?* |
| I will take you over there. | *Yo le llevo allá.* |
| Where can I take the bus? | *¿Dónde puedo tomar el autobús?* |

If riding in the back of a bus or a truck and you want to get off, just bang on the cab top or shout, "*¡Baja! ¡Baja! Por favor*" (Down, please) or "*¡Aquí, por favor!*" (Here, please).

*Aventón* can also mean the same as *empujón* (push or shove) but is most commonly used to mean "a free ride" (*una llevada gratuita*).

# 5. Travel by Foot, Mule, Horse, Burro, or with a Guide

**T**his section offers some handy phrases that will be useful in several areas of Mexico, primarily the major mountain ranges, where most travel is still by foot or *bestia* (horses, mules, or burros). In many of these areas it is wise to have a guide to handle and pack the stock and keep you on the route.

The burro is the jeep of Mexico. A good *arriero* (mule or burro driver) can take you across deserts or into the most rugged *sierras*. Burros can get by on almost no water, except that from plants they eat, for several days. They can thrive on cactus and other plants that most animals would starve on.

## BURRO OR MULE COMMANDS

| | |
|---|---|
| Forward | Click with tongue (*tsk, tsk, tsk*) |
| Forward | *¡Hiya! (ee-ya)* or *¡Arre!* |
| Forward | Whack with stick |
| Stop or "steady" | Hiss (*ssssss*) |
| "Line 'em out!" | *¡Hi-Lo! (ee-lo)* |

In general, burros are also a pain in the neck to travel with. You must be patient to a point, and almost cruel on occasion. It seems that you beat burros up the mountain and chase them down. Going out, they seem listless and near death, but homeward bound they can muster a trot! To get a burro train up a really tough mountain trail, you arm yourself with a stout stick about 2.5 feet long (a *vara* or *garrote*), get behind the rear burro or any laggard, shout *hiya*, and whack the burro on the rump. Between whacks and various maledictions in Spanish you get it to the top. To stop it, you hiss between your teeth like a snake (*sssssssssss*). Any offense, such as biting its neighbor, trying to pass on a narrow trail, or trying to rub off its packsaddle (*aparejo* or *fuste*) is punished by a sharp whack with the *vara*. The load (*carga*) is

In much of mountainous Mexico the remote villages and ranches are supplied by pack trains such as this one in the State of Durango. (Will Thompson photo)

tied on with a locally made rope of *ixtle* fibers from small agave (century plant) type plants, most commonly *lechuguilla*. The rope is called *mecate*. A carved wooden *honda* helps form a friction-free running loop in one end of the *mecate*, and the *arriero* is very adept at balancing the load and tying the proper hitches.

When camp is made, a pair of hobbles (*las trabas; maneas*) is placed on the forefeet of the burros, so that they cannot run or walk off. They move by raising both front feet together and lunging forward. If a burro is very wild (*muy liviano*) it may be belled and tied neck and neck to a stronger and more docile burro. They are tied with a rope yoke (*mancornador*). Hobbled, they rarely get more than a half-mile away overnight, and the *arriero* is very skilled in "thinking like a burro" and seems instinctively to go in the right direction to find them when needed (actually, he tracks them or bells them).

In desert conditions, or dry camps, *sotol*, a desert plant with a succulent and nutritious heart protected by leaves with hooked spines, is chopped with a *machete* to feed the burros and give them some plant moisture.

Other burro gear items are saddlebags (*alforjas*); saddle blanket or packsaddle pad (*corona*); *ixtle* fiber bag hung from the packsaddle or neck of the burro (*morral*); *ixtle* fiber bag for holding large loads (*costal*). Burros are sometimes fitted with a riding saddle (*una silla de montar*) and ridden, but generally you walk along behind them while they carry the load. A burro can easily carry over one hundred pounds up a mountain.

## BASIC COMMUNICATION WITH YOUR GUIDE

Where can I find a good guide?
*¿Dónde puedo encontrar un buen guía?*

Do you know these sierras, the trails, the water sources, and the camps well?
*¿Conoce bien estas sierras (montañas), las veredas, los ojos de agua, y los campos?*

Do you have pack animals and know how to handle them and pack them?
*¿Tiene burros (bestias) y sabe como cargarlos(las) y arriarlos(las) cargados(as)?*

Have you ever traveled into the Barranca del Cobre before?
*¿Ya ha viajado a la Barranca del Cobre?*

I wish to take a trip through the mountains.
*Quiero hacer un viaje por la sierra.*

What salary do you want?
*¿Qué sueldo quiere? (¿Cuánto me cobra?)*

How much money per day?
*¿Cuánto (dinero) por día?*

I wish to rent a horse (mule) (donkey).
*Quiero rentar un caballo (una mula; una acémila) (un burro).*

I need two pack mules and one to ride, with pack saddles and riding saddle.
*Necesito dos mulas acémilas y una para montar (dos mulas con aparejos [fustes] y una con silla de montar).*

Is this one for sale?
*¿Quiere vender éste? (¿Se vende éste?)*

What is the price?
*¿Cuál es el precio? (¿Cuánto cuesta?)*

I will pay you —— pesos per day.
*Le pagaré —— pesos por día.*

How much do I owe you?
*¿Cuánto le debo?*

| We need many provisions for the trip. | Necesitamos muchas provisiones para el viaje. |
| Where can we spend the night? | ¿Dónde podemos pasar la noche? |
| I would like to hire a reliable guide who knows these mountains (canyons) well. | Quiero emplear un guía seguro que conozca bien estas sierras (estos cañones). |
| None of us has been there. | Jamás hemos estado allí. |
| What will be the cost per day for the guide? | ¿Cuánto cuesta el guía por día (a diario)? |
| I will furnish the guide food and a sleeping bag. | Yo le doy al guía la comida y el paquete de cama. |
| What will be the cost per day for the animals and their gear? | ¿Cuánto cuestan por día (diariamente) los animales (las bestias) con equipaje? |
| I will pay one-half the money for the guide and the animals in advance. The rest I will pay when we return. | Pago por adelantado la mitad por el guía y los animales. Le pago lo demás cuando regresemos. |
| Do you need money for the house while we are gone (absent)? | ¿Necesita dinero (socorro) para la casa durante nuestra ausencia? |
| How much do you need? | ¿Cuánto necesita? |

(Note: In many areas it is customary to leave some money [advance pay = socorro] with the guide's wife for the family expenses while the husband is gone.)

| When could you start working? | ¿Cuándo podría usted comenzar a trabajar? |
| Are the trails suitable for horses, or only for burros or mules? | ¿Las veredas sirven para caballos o nada más para mulas? |

(Note: Mules and burros are superior to horses on steep trails and are calmer. Mules are called *mulas*, *machos*, and *acémilas* in different places.)

| I am planning to walk through the canyons. | Pienso caminar a pie por los cañones. |
| I plan to go by foot. | Pienso ir a pie. |
| Let's take a hike through the gap. | Hagamos una caminata por la quebrada (barranca). |
| There's a big gap between the mountains. | Hay una gran abertura (puerta) entre las sierras. |
| Let's stop and get our bearings before we go farther. | Vamos a orientarnos antes de continuar. |
| We're going to blaze a new trail! | ¡Vamos a abrir un nuevo sendero! |

| | |
|---|---|
| I would like to have a reliable man or boy to go with me and show me the trails. | *Me gustaría conseguir un hombre o muchacho de confianza para que me enseñe las veredas.* |
| I wish to travel along the canyon trails from —— to ——. | *Quiero caminar por las veredas del cañón desde —— a ——.* |
| What experience do you have? | *¿Qué experiencia tiene usted?* |
| Have you been along that route before? | *¿Conoce la ruta?* |
| Do you know how to swim? | *¿Sabe usted nadar?* |
| Are there many places where the trail crosses the stream? | *¿Hay lugares en donde la vereda cruza corrientes?* |
| Where can we cross the stream? | *Por dónde podemos cruzar la corriente?* |
| We'll have to swim the river. | *Tendremos que cruzar el río nadando.* |
| How many days of walking will this trip require? | *¿Cuántos días hay que caminar a pie en este viaje?* |
| How long will the trip take? | *¿Cuánto durará el viaje?* |
| Is there good drinking water along the way? | *¿Hay agua potable (un ojo bueno) por el camino?* |
| Is this water safe for me to drink? | *¿Puedo tomar esta agua con seguridad? (¿Es agua potable?) (¿Es agua pura?)* |
| Is the water pure enough to drink? | *¿Está buena el agua para beber?* |
| Is there an empty house or shed in the village (rancho) that we can sleep in? | *¿Hay un jacal (una casita) o cobertizo desocupado(a) donde podemos dormir?* |
| Where does the trail start? | *¿Dónde comienza (empieza) la vereda (el sendero)?* |
| Will you point it out to me, please? | *Enséñemelo, por favor.* |
| Go at a walk. | *Vaya usted al paso (despacito).* |
| Go faster. | *Vaya usted más aprisa.* |
| Go at full speed. | *Vaya usted a todo correr.* |
| Don't hurry. | *No se apure usted.* |
| Where are we now? | *¿En dónde estamos ahora?* |
| We are within 10 kilometers of our destination. | *Estamos a diez kilómetros de nuestro destino.* |
| Let's take a walk. | *Vamos a pasearnos.* |
| Do you think we can walk it in an hour? | *¿Cree usted que podremos llegar a pie en una hora?* |
| It's a long walk from here to the canyon. | *Es una caminata larga de aquí al cañón.* |
| Can we go on foot? | *¿Podemos ir a pie?* |

| | |
|---|---|
| Take the path that runs along the river. | *Tome el sendero (rastro) que va a lo largo del río.* |
| Let's stop here and catch our breath. | *Detengámonos aquí para tomar aliento.* |
| When do we get a breather? | *¿Cuándo tenemos un respiro (descanso)?* |
| Stop here. | *Párese usted aquí.* |
| We are there already! | *¡Ya estamos! (¡Ya llegamos!)* |
| Let's go and see! | *¡Vamos a ver!* |
| Let's go! | *¡Vámonos!* |
| What do you need? | *¿Qué le hace falta? (¿Qué necesita?)* |
| What are you looking for? | *¿Qué busca usted?* |
| I am hungry. | *Tengo hambre.* |
| I am hot. | *Tengo calor.* |
| I am thirsty. | *Tengo sed.* |
| I am tired already. | *Estoy cansado(a) ya. (Estoy un poco cansado(a).) (¡Ya me cansé!)* |
| This trail is burning hot! | *¡La vereda está que quema!* |
| Let's go back. | *Regresemos, por favor.* |
| Let's stop here a while. | *Paremos (Parémonos) aquí un rato.* |
| Let's go home. | *Regresemos a casa.* |
| Let's go on foot. | *Vayamos a pie.* |
| Will you go with me? | *¿Quiere usted acompañarme?* |
| I'm afraid I will lose my way. | *Temo extraviarme. (Tengo miedo de perderme.)* |
| I can ride well. I want a good horse (mule) (burro). | *Puedo montar bien. Quiero un buen caballo (una buena mula o buen burro).* |
| I don't ride well. | *No puedo montar bien.* |
| Is this horse gentle or wild? | *¿Es manso o bronco este caballo?* |
| Is it difficult to reach that village? | *¿Es difícil llegar a ese pueblo?* |
| Where shall we pitch the tent? | *¿Dónde armaremos la tienda de campaña?* |
| Do you have an axe? | *¿Tiene una hacha?* |
| Air the bedding first. | *Primero, ponga la ropa de cama al aire libre.* |
| Brace the tent, a storm is coming up! | *¡Asegure la tienda de campaña, se acerca una tormenta!* |
| The wind will blow the tent away! | *¡El viento se va a llevar la tienda de campaña!* |

| | |
|---|---|
| They drove in stakes to hold the tent down. | *Fijaron estacas para asegurar la tienda de campaña.* |

(Note: In tropical Mexico you will find only two seasons, wet and dry. The dry season runs from about November to April or May. The wet season covers about June through September, depending on latitude. June and September are the wettest months in most years. The coolest months are usually January and February and are good hiking months. March, April, and May can get very hot, with much haze and smoke in the air from the burning of jungle slash, left to dry when cornfields are hacked out of the jungle.)

| | |
|---|---|
| I'm going to light a fire. | *Voy a encender una lumbre.* |
| We're going to break camp tonight. | *Vamos a levantar el campo a la noche.* |
| He travels by night. | *Viaja de noche.* |
| I'm tired, let's hit the sack. | *Estoy cansado(a), vamos a dormir.* |
| We shall return in five days. | *Regresaremos (Volveremos) en cinco días.* |
| I'm going to return tomorrow. | *Voy a regresar mañana.* |
| I want you to leave us here, and return to this same spot on the morning (evening) of the third day to pick us up. We will spend two nights here, and on the third day we will expect to see you and the pack animals (truck). | *Déjenos aquí y venga a recogernos a este mismo sitio en la mañana (la tarde) del tercer día. Nos quedaremos aquí dos noches y esperamos verlo el tercer día con las bestias (la troca).* |
| I wish to hire a driver and a good truck, to carry us to the mountains (canyon) (mine) (ranch) and drop us off. Then, after three nights and three days, return for us on the morning of the fourth day. | *Quiero emplear un cochero (chofer) con una troca buena para que nos vaya a dejar a la sierra (el cañón) (la mina) (el rancho). Y para que nos recoja después de tres noches y tres días en la mañana del cuarto día.* |
| Do you understand well? | *¿Entiende bien?* |
| Will you be here to meet us on the morning of the fourth day? | *Bueno, ¿está bien entendido que nos encontramos en la mañana del cuarto día?* |
| Here is half of your pay now. I will pay you the other half when you meet us and return us to this village. | *Le voy a pagar la mitad ahora. Lo demás se lo doy cuando vuelva y nos lleve de regreso al pueblo.* |
| What's the cause of the delay? | *¿Cuál es la causa de la tardanza (el retraso)?* |

The date you are to return for us is Monday, April 20, 1983.

El día que volverá es lunes, veinte de abril de mil novecientos ochenta y tres.

Why didn't you come yesterday?

¿Por qué no vino usted ayer?

Is it a deal?

¿Hecho? (¿De acuerdo?)

It's a deal!

¡Trato hecho!

Lead off, I will follow you.

¡Ándele! Yo lo sigo.

Go on ahead and I'll catch up with you.

Siga usted adelante y yo le alcanzaré.

Stop at the next level place for pictures.

Por favor, párese en el nivel próximo para una foto.

## HIKER'S TERMS

| | |
|---|---|
| Backpack | Mochila (f.); saco (m.) |
| Backpacker | Mochilero(a) |
| Mountaineer | Alpinista (m. or f.) |
| I am a backpacker (mountaineer). | Soy mochilero(a) (alpinista). |
| Tent | Carpa (m.); tienda de campaña (f.); casita de campamento (f.); pabellón (m.) (large tent or mosquito net) |
| Bedroll | Tendido (m.); mochila (f.); liacho (m.) |
| Sleeping bag | Paquete cama (m.); bolsa de dormir (f.) |
| A long walk or hike | Caminata (f.); andada (f.) |
| On foot | A pie |
| To walk | Caminar; andar |
| Trail | Vereda (f.); sendero (m.); rastro (m.) |
| To walk up | Subir |
| To take a walk | Recorrer a pie; andar a pie |
| Mosquito net | Mosquitero (m.); pabellón (m.) |
| Mosquitoes | Zancudos (m.); moyotes (m.) |
| Are there many mosquitoes here? | ¿Hay muchos zancudos aquí? |
| There are many mosquitoes here because of the swamp. | Aquí hay muchos zancudos (moyotes) a causa del pantano (de la ciénaga). |
| The mosquitoes kept buzzing all night. | Los zancudos continuaron zumbando toda la noche. |
| Panting and out of breath | Jadeante |
| I'm out of breath! | ¡Estoy jadeante! |

| | |
|---|---|
| To break camp | *Levantar el campo* |
| It's getting late. | *Se hace tarde.* |
| Let's go home. | *Vámonos a casa (campo).* |
| Are they dry? | *¿Están secos(as)?* |
| Are you tired? | *¿Está cansado(a)?* |
| Rest a while. | *Descanse un poco.* |
| League | *Legua* (f.) (Technically a league is 5,572.7 meters, or 3.5 miles, but *legua* is sometimes used to mean "an hour's walk," which varies from 1.5 to 3.0 miles, according to topography.) |
| Canteen | *Cantimplora* (f.) |
| Walking stick | *Bastón* (m.) |
| A day's walk | *Jornada* (f.) |
| Jungle mudhole | *Fanga* (f.); *fangar* (m.) |
| Spiny palm (a hazard along jungle trails) | *Palma espinosa* (f.) |
| Small jungle village | *Colonia* (f.) |
| Jungle | *Selva* (f.) |
| Opening in jungle | *Abra* (f.) |
| There are only two seasons in the tropics. | *En los trópicos hay solamente dos estaciones.* |

## ARCHAEOLOGICAL TERMS

| | |
|---|---|
| Ancient ones | *Antiguos* (m.) |
| Archaeologist | *Arqueólogo* (m.) |
| Archaeology | *Arqueología* (f.) |
| Arrow | *Flecha* (f.); *saeta* (f.) |
| Arrowhead | *Punta de flecha* (m.); *punta de saeta* (f.) |
| Artifact | *Artefacto* (m.) |
| Dart | *Dardo* (m.) |
| Dart point | *Punta de dardo* (f.) |
| Hollow reed | *Cañuto* (m.) |
| Indian camp | *Campo de los indios antiguos* (m.) |
| Indian cave | *Cueva de los indios antiguos* (f.) |
| Rock art | *Dibujos de los indios* (m.); *pinturas de los indios* (f.) |

(Note: Sometimes Indian art on rock walls is called *los altares* [altars].)

| | |
|---|---|
| Roofless walls | *Tapias* (m.); *ruinas* (f.) |
| Ruins | *Ruinas* (f.) |
| Spear or dart thrower | *Atlatl* (m.) |
| Flints (arrow points) | *Pedernales* (m.) |

## TRAILS, ROUTES, SPRINGS, AND WATER HOLES

| | |
|---|---|
| Is there a good trail up the mountain? | *¿Hay una vereda (un sendero) buena(o) subiendo la sierra?* |
| Is there a good trail down into this canyon? | *¿Hay una vereda (un sendero) buena(o) bajando este cañón?* |
| Show me the trail, please. | *Por favor, enséñeme la vereda (el sendero).* |
| Where does the trail start? | *¿Dónde comienza (empieza) la vereda (el sendero)?* |
| Can you take me to where the trail starts up? | *¿Puede llevarme a donde comienza la vereda?* |
| Please point out the route of the trail. | *Enséñeme la ruta de la vereda. (Indíqueme dónde sale la vereda.)* |
| Are there any good springs along the trail? | *¿Hay buenos ojos de agua al lado de la vereda?* |
| Where are the springs to be found? | *¿Dónde están los ojos de agua?* |
| Will the springs have water at this season? | *¿Hay agua en los ojos en este tiempo?* |
| Are there any good water holes in the canyons? | *¿Hay algunas tinajas buenas (algunos charcos buenos) en los cañones?* |
| Will the water holes have water at this season? | *¿Hay agua en las tinajas en este tiempo?* |
| Where are the water holes to be found? | *¿En dónde se encuentran las tinajas?* |
| Is the trail passable with horses or only mules and burros? | *¿Sirve la vereda para caballos o nada más para mulas y burros?* |
| Where does the trail take you? | *¿Dónde sale la vereda? (¿Adónde va la vereda?)* |
| Are there any people living along the trail? | *¿Vive gente al lado de la vereda?* |
| Is the trail manmade or is it a game trail? | *¿La vereda es hecha por gente o natural?* |
| Is there any place where the trail forks or becomes hard to find? | *¿Hay lugares en dónde se pierde la vereda?* |

| | |
|---|---|
| Where would that be? | *¿En dónde? (¿Adónde?)* |
| Should I go right or left? | *¿Voy al lado derecho o izquierdo? (¿Tomo la derecha o la izquierda?)* |
| Are there any Indian caves or Indian camps in the mountains (canyon)? | *¿Hay cuevas o campos de los indios en la sierra (en el cañón)?* |
| Where are the Indian camps or caves located? | *¿Dónde están los campos o las cuevas de los indios?* |
| Can you take me there and show me? | *¿Puede llevarme y enseñarme?* |
| You will find the climb steep and difficult. | *Encontrará usted la subida empinada y difícil.* |
| We climbed to the top of the bluff. | *Escalamos hasta la punta del risco.* |
| I'm going to return tomorrow. | *Voy a regresar mañana.* |
| Ups and downs | *Subidas y bajadas (f.)* |
| On the way down | *De bajada* |
| Downward slope or path | *Bajada (f.)* |

## GUIDES AND DIRECTIONS

| | |
|---|---|
| Let's get a drink of cool spring water. | *Vamos a tomar un poco de agua fresca del ojo de agua.* |
| How far are we from the spring? | *¿A qué distancia estamos del ojo de agua?* |
| You can't miss the spring if you follow this trail. | *Usted no puede errar el ojo de agua si sigue por esta vereda.* |
| The spring is not far from our house. | *El ojo de agua no está lejos de nuestra casa.* |
| Show me the exact spot you mean. | *Enséñeme el lugar exacto a que se refiere usted.* |
| Point out the place you told me about. | *Indíqueme el lugar de que me habló.* |
| I'll wait for you. Don't let me down. | *Yo esperaré, pero no me deje plantado(a).* |
| Straight ahead. You can't miss. | *Vaya derecho. Usted no puede errar.* |
| Which one of those mountains is the farthest away? | *¿Cuál de esas sierras queda más lejos?* |
| How much farther do we have to go? | *¿Cuánto más tenemos que andar?* |

Burros and hikers switchbacking up a steep trail in the Sierra del Carmen, Coahuila. By the use of burros one can carry enough water into arid mountains in the dry season to stay several days. (Will Thompson photo)

How far are the mountains from here? — ¿A qué distancia de aquí están las sierras?

Be there without fail! — ¡Esté allí sin falta!

What is your excuse for being late? — ¿Qué razón tiene para llegar tarde?

I would have been here sooner but I had to walk. — Hubiera llegado antes si no tuviera que venir andando.

It is a straight road. — Es un camino recto (derecho).

How far is it to the top of the mountain? — ¿A qué distancia está la cima de la sierra?

The road winds through the mountains. — El camino tuerce por las sierras.

Are we within walking distance of the canyon? — ¿Estamos bastante cerca del cañón para ir a pie?

It's too far to walk. — Está demasiado lejos para ir a pie.

I'm down here. — Estoy aquí abajo.

There it is. — Allá está.

How many times have you made the trip by canoe? — ¿Cuántas veces ha hecho usted el viaje en canoa?

There is a very good view from that hill. — Desde ese cerro hay una vista muy buena.

Where does this road (trail) lead? — ¿Adónde va (¿Adónde nos lleva) este camino (esta vereda)?

This road goes as far as Mina el Popo. — Este camino llega hasta Mina el Popo.

You can rely on him. — Usted puede confiar en él.

I'm counting on your help. — Cuento con su ayuda.

When will you come? — ¿Cuándo vendrá usted?

Which way are you going? — ¿En qué dirección va usted?

Will you come tomorrow? — ¿Vendrá usted mañana?

Without a doubt. — Sin duda.

Have you ever gone through the Barranca del Cobre? — ¿Ha pasado usted por la Barranca del Cobre?

Lend me the binoculars so I can see it better. — Présteme los gemelos (miralejos) para verlo mejor.

There is a forest (jungle) along the river. — Hay un bosque (una selva) a lo largo del río.

Is it very far from here? — ¿Está muy lejos de aquí?

They are very far away. — Están muy lejos.

What place is this? — ¿Qué localidad (lugar) es ésta?

First, we have to find out where they live. — Primero, tenemos que localizar en donde viven.

We'll meet on Thursday morning. — Nos veremos el jueves por la mañana.

| | |
|---|---|
| We can meet in the middle of the afternoon. | *Podemos vernos a media tarde.* |
| We are halfway there. | *Ya estamos a medio camino.* |
| The river has its source in the mountains. | *El río nace en las sierras.* |
| That part of the country is heavily wooded. | *Esa parte del país está llena del bosque (de la selva).* |
| I know this place like the palm of my hand. | *Conozco este lugar como la palma de mi mano.* |
| I have to ask him for permission. | *Tengo que pedirle permiso.* |
| What are your references? | *¿Cuáles son sus referencias?* |
| Do you know how to get to that place? | *¿Sabe usted cómo llegar a ese lugar?* |
| He has gone so many times that he knows the place very well. | *Ha ido tantas veces que conoce muy bien el lugar.* |
| It is a long time since I've been there. | *Hace tiempo que estuve allí.* |
| There is a bad stretch of road. | *Hay un trecho malo en el camino.* |
| Are there many ups and downs along the trail? | *¿Hay muchas subidas y bajadas por el rastro (la vereda)?* |
| Yes, there are many ups and downs along the trail. | *Sí, hay muchas subidas y bajadas por el sendero (la vereda).* |
| It will be important to arrive on time. | *Será importante llegar a tiempo.* |
| I will not arrive late. | *No tardaré en llegar.* |
| I am looking for a guide who knows how to cook. | *Busco un guía que sepa cocinar.* |
| I will give five pesos to the boy who shows me his house! | *¡Le daré (Le doy) cinco pesos al muchacho que me enseñe su casa!* |
| Does he live here? | *¿Vive él aquí?* |
| Have you seen him anywhere? | *¿Lo ha visto usted en alguna parte?* |
| They live beyond (on the other side of) the river. | *Viven más allá (al otro lado) del río.* |
| They live in a thatched house. | *Viven en una casa de paja (un jacal).* |
| All around; all about | *A la redonda* |
| Look here. | *Mire aquí.* |
| Look around you. | *Mire alrededor.* |
| Let's ask if he's in. | *Vamos a preguntar si está en casa.* |
| The "one who really knows." | *Él es el "mero, mero." (El es el que sabe.)* |

| | |
|---|---|
| Are there any soldiers around here? | *¿Hay por aquí algunos soldados?* |
| How far is it? | *¿Qué tan lejos está?* |
| How far is it from La Linda to Ocampo? | *¿Qué tan lejos es de La Linda a Ocampo?* |
| We want to go to Boquillas. | *Nosotros queremos ir a Boquillas.* |
| Where do you suggest we go? | *¿Dónde sugiere que vayamos?* |
| He will go with me to Boquillas. | *Él irá conmigo a Boquillas.* |
| If it rains we won't go. | *No iremos si llueve.* |
| She is out. | *Ella ha salido.* |
| He will be back at four. | *Él volverá a las cuatro.* |
| To whom do you wish to speak? | *¿Con quién quiere hablar?* |
| There is nobody by that name living here. | *Nadie con ese nombre vive aquí.* |
| He is away in the country. | *Él ha salido para el monte.* |
| He went that way. | *Él se fue por allí.* |
| Is this the end of the road? | *¿Es este el final del camino?* |
| Where is the entrance? | *¿Dónde queda la entrada?* |
| Is there an entrance fee? | *¿Hay que pagar entrada?* |
| What is beyond the hill (mountain)? | *¿Qué hay más allá de la colina (sierra)?* |

# 6. Entering Private Land

**M**any of the most beautiful and best-preserved natural areas of Mexico are behind the fences and gates of large private holdings. Because of the pressures of agrarian reform, some landowners are very hesitant to allow strangers to enter. Most *vaqueros* (cowboys) you will see will not have the authority to permit you to enter. Arrangements should be made in advance, if possible, to locate the owner and secure permission; try to get a letter of consent to show the local foreman (*caporal*).

Mexican ranch owners are usually well educated and successful, many have been educated in the United States, and most speak some English. You may encounter them on your journey, and the following may help you gain permission.

The Mexican landowners (private) are very concerned about their wildlife (game animals), since wildlife is a scarce and valuable commodity. It is important to let them know that you do not hunt and have no guns (*armas*).

Never enter private lands without permission. Never cut chains or wire or destroy locks or gates. Sometimes you will run into fences recently built right across a road. This is *usually* a sign of a dispute between agrarians (*agrarianistas*) and a private landowner, so be on the alert and avoid trouble with either side.

| | |
|---|---|
| What is the name of this ranch (*ejido*)? | *¿Cómo se llama este rancho (ejido)?* |
| May we enter this ranch? | *¿Nos permite entrar a este rancho?* |
| We would like to explore in those mountains and canyons. | *Queremos explorar la sierra y los cañones.* |
| Are you allowed to camp here? | *¿Se puede acampar aquí?* |
| May we camp here? | *¿Podemos acampar aquí?* |
| We are interested in the plants and wildlife of Mexico (your ranch) (this ranch). | *Tenemos interés en la vegetación y fauna silvestre de México (su rancho) (este terreno).* |

| | |
|---|---|
| We will not hunt or harm anything. | No vamos a cazar o molestar ninguna cosa. |
| We would like to camp near the mountain (canyon) for a night or two. | Nos permite acampar cerca de la sierra (el cañón) por una noche o dos. |
| Is there a spring or good water to camp near? | ¿Hay un ojo de agua o agua potable para acampar cerca de allí? |
| Where is it located? | ¿Dónde queda? |
| What sort of wildlife is found on the ranch? | ¿Cuáles tipos de fauna (vida) silvestre se encuentran en su rancho? |
| Is there any big game near here? | ¿Hay caza mayor cerca de aquí? |
| We will leave a clean camp and will close all gates. | Dejaremos el campamento bien limpio y cerraremos todas las puertas. |
| Who owns this ranch? (Who are the owners?) | ¿De quién es este rancho? (¿Quiénes son los dueños?) |
| Where does the owner live? | ¿Dónde vive el dueño? |
| Does he live here? | ¿Vive él aquí? |
| What's the area of the ranch? | ¿Cuál es el área del rancho? |
| This property extends for many kilometers on all sides. | Esta propiedad se extiende por muchos kilómetros a la redonda. |
| The owner owns a vast extent of land in this area. | El patrón es propietario de una vasta extensión de tierra en esta zona. |
| Who owns (controls) that mountain (canyon) over there? | ¿De quién es esa sierra (ese cañón)? |
| Is this ejido land? What ejido is it? | ¿Este terreno es propiedad de un ejido? ¿Cuál es el nombre de este ejido? |

(Note: *Ejidatarios* are sensitive about "ownership," as their lands are communal.)

| | |
|---|---|
| Where can I go to get permission to go see that mountain (canyon)? | ¿En dónde puedo sacar permiso para ir a esa sierra (ese cañón)? |
| Can I drive nearer to the mountain (canyon) in my truck? | ¿Puedo arrimarme más cerca a esa sierra (ese cañón) en mi troca? |
| We plan to stay two nights and leave on the third morning. | Planeamos quedarnos dos noches y salimos (e irnos) en la próxima mañana. |

|  |  |
|---|---|
| Is there any big timber on (the) high peaks? | ¿Hay un bosque con árboles grandes en los cerros más altos? |
| Are there permanent streams in any of the canyons? | ¿Hay corrientes en algunos cañones? |
| Where is the best spring in the mountains? | ¿Dónde está el mejor ojo de agua en toda la sierra? |
| Are there any locked (padlocked) gates? | ¿Hay puertas con llave (con candado) (bajo llave)? |
| Have you got a key to fit this lock? | ¿Tiene usted una llave para abrir esta cerradura? |
| Where can we get a key? | ¿En dónde podemos conseguir la llave? |
| Is the key hidden near the gate? | ¿Está la llave escondida en un lugar cerca de la puerta? |
| Where is the key hidden? | ¿Dónde está la llave escondida? |
| The key is on the nail on the tenth post to the right of the gate. | La llave está en el clavo en el décimo poste a la derecha de la puerta. |
| Where shall I leave the key? | ¿Dónde dejo la llave? |
| Who is the foreman or person in charge with whom we should check? | ¿Quién es el caporal conque debemos hablar? (¿Quién es la persona encargada de este rancho [terreno]?) |
| Are all of the roads passable in a pickup? | ¿Podemos pasar todos los caminos en esta camioneta? |
| Is livestock grazed in the high mountains? | ¿Hay ganado en los potreros más altos de la sierra? |
| We do not hunt and have no guns. | No vamos a cazar y no tenemos armas (escopetas; carabinas). |
| We do not bother any wild game. | Nosotros no molestamos la caza. |
| We are alpinists, and wish to climb those mountains. | Somos alpinistas y deseamos escalar esos cerros. |
| In years past, we have climbed these mountains from the other side. | En años pasados hemos subido estos cerros por el otro lado. |
| Mr. Diego has allowed us to camp and climb the mountains on Rancho El Bonito in years past. | En años pasados, el señor Diego nos ha dejado acampar y subir a las sierras aquí en Rancho El Bonito. |
| I have been to (climbed in) these mountains in years past. | He subido a estas sierras en años pasados. |

## LEAVING YOUR VEHICLE

| | |
|---|---|
| May I please park my pickup here? | *¿Por favor, puedo estacionar mi camioneta aquí?* |
| I will return in three days. | *Regreso en tres días.* |
| Can I leave my pickup there (here)? | *¿Puedo dejar mi camioneta allá (aquí)?* |
| I want to leave my pickup here overnight, please. | *Quiero dejar mi camioneta aquí durante la noche, por favor.* |
| Where should I leave my pickup? | *¿Dónde debo dejar mi camioneta?* |
| Where can I park my pickup? | *¿Dónde puedo estacionar mi camioneta? (¿Dónde puedo dejar mi camioneta?)* |
| You can put your pickup here. | *Puede usted poner su camioneta aquí.* |
| Move your pickup back a little bit. | *Mueva su camioneta hacia atrás un poco.* |
| The pickup is parked behind the house. | *La camioneta está estacionada detrás de la casa.* |
| Keep an eye on my pickup, please. | *Vigile usted mi camioneta, por favor.* |
| Is the pickup safe here? | *¿Está segura la camioneta aquí?* |
| Will you keep an eye on my pickup and equipment? | *¿Puede cuidar mi camioneta y mi equipaje?* |
| I would like to have my pickup watched tonight. | *Quiero que me guarden mi camioneta por la noche. (Quiero encargar mi camioneta por la noche.)* |
| I will be glad to pay you for your trouble (time). | *Con gusto pago por su molestia (tiempo).* |
| What do I owe you? | *¿Cuánto le debo?* |
| I will pay you the balance when I return. | *Le pago el saldo cuando regrese.* |
| Are you allowed to camp (there) here? | *¿Se puede acampar (allá) aquí?* |
| I am planning a trip on foot through the mountains. | *Pienso caminar a pie por las sierras.* |
| I'm going alone. | *Pienso ir solo(a).* |
| I will return. | *Ya vuelvo.* |

## AVOIDING RIPOFFS

In the most rural areas of Mexico you are safer from the threat of violent crime or theft than you would be along the Interstate. In many
years of travel in the backcountry of Mexico, including numerous
times when we have left a vehicle unguarded for a week or more while
we backpacked into a mountain range, we have never suffered a break-
in or ripoff. However, such events can occur, and the risk is increased
directly as you move nearer to population centers.

We do know of several instances of thefts from backpackers who
have carelessly left packs along main roads or trails while making a
side excursion, and of several from parked vehicles. There are also professional thieves in the markets and public places of Mexico, just as in
the United States.

To avoid theft from your vehicle or the theft of the vehicle itself,
there are several things that you can do to greatly reduce this risk.

Devise a secure and substantial lock for your hood to protect against
theft of the battery and vital parts.

Use locking gas filler caps. An expanded metal guard underneath
will prevent draining of gas by removal of gas lines under the chassis.

Make a habit of rolling up windows and locking doors any time you
leave the vehicle, even for a short while.

Devise locks for any externally attached spare tires, extra gas cans,
or cargo racks on the top.

Camper windows can be backed up by expanded metal guards that
will prevent reaching into the interior of the camper by merely breaking a glass or plastic window. The usual camper latch can be supplemented with a good security hasp and a stout padlock.

Keep your gear and valuables out of sight in the vehicle. Use a tarp to
cover the gear and keep it on the floorboards, in the truck, in the
camper, etc.

Install a second ignition lock or antitheft cutoff between coil and
distributor or at some other place. There are time-switch devices available. Use a cable or rod lock from brake pedal to steering wheel.

Leave your vehicle at a *rancho* or business where someone agrees to
watch out for it.

Ripoffs from the person or the camp most often happen when your
attention is focused on something else, such as a side trip from a base
camp, swimming while leaving the camp unguarded, while you are
traveling on train or bus, or while moving through a crowd at a market
or *fiesta*. The following steps will make your property more secure and
will minimize the adverse consequences of such crimes.

Keep your money, tourist and vehicle papers, and your identification on your person at all times. These items can be carried in a money belt under your clothing, in a leg wallet (a cloth bag with zipper or Velcro closure affixed to an elastic band that goes around your calf under your pants leg), or in a bag slung on a band around your neck. Wallets that look like the shoulder holster of a detective's pistol are available from many places. Pack pockets are not safe, since they can be slashed open from the bottom in a crowd.

When swimming, bathing, or exploring, try to leave someone to watch the camp.

If you must make a stash of the camp gear, to enable you to make a side hike, make your stash after dark or just before dawn. Leave no tracks and look around carefully, since you are often observed without knowing it.

If you must leave your camp, use cable locks to secure your pack pockets and secure the pack to a tree. Close the tent and get all gear out of sight.

Never flash a roll of money. Keep small amounts of money in various pockets and deal out of them.

Women should never carry a handbag or purse. They are easily snatched or cut away from you in crowded markets.

You can sew pockets into the inside of shirt or pants, with secure fasteners, to hold vital money and documents.

Never leave your gear and turn your attention to anything else in markets or crowds.

If you must carry a shoulder bag, get one with a very stout strap and secure closures and keep it with you at all times.

Keep a low profile, avoid camping near habitations or around cities or villages, and keep on the move.

Consider carrying a duplicate set of personal identification and citizenship documents, or of switching so that each person carries the spare set of his or her partner.

Consider paying a small fee to leave your locked pack at a hotel before going to the market.

Generally, stay as far in the *monte* as possible, as most troubles come in population centers, along main roads, or on trains or buses.

# 7. Camping in Mexico

**T**his is not a camping guide. Only the more important differences between camping in Mexico and in the United States will be covered, and a few tips given.

In general, you will not find handy campgrounds; nor will you find many state or national parks or other places where campsites are prepared. Even parks shown on maps may not exist, as it is the custom in Mexico to put planned improvements on maps, so that the map will not be out of date when and if the improvement is built.

| | |
|---|---|
| Is the park open to the public? | *¿Está el parque abierto al público?* |
| Is camping permitted there? | *¿Se puede acampar allá?* |

We assume that you will be on paved or main roads only long enough to get to the *monte* and that most of your camping will be in really rural areas. We do not suggest camping near major urban areas, as problems of theft and other crimes increase the nearer you get to the cities, the same as in the United States.

"Camping," as used here, really means camping out of your vehicle. Backpackers have more freedom of choice and can avoid most problems by simply camping late and leaving early while staying in the most remote areas.

If you follow these suggestions, you should be able to camp with confidence.

Stay as far off the main road as possible. Roadside camping is not recommended in many areas, not so much from the standpoint of crime as from the risk of being hit by a truck or disturbed by noise.

Remain as inconspicuous as possible. Don't try to draw a crowd and don't pick a spot where you know many people will pass or be inclined to stop.

If possible, pick your site before dark. On the other hand, it is sometimes better to arrive and camp after dark and break camp at dawn.

Turning down side roads, even roads that appear to go nowhere, will often get you away from the noise of traffic and into a place of privacy and solitude. Do not, however, open gates to get there.

If there is a nearby house, get permission to camp.

High spots with a good breeze will have fewer mosquitoes (*zancudos*) than a spot down low or near water. Also, cold, damp air tends to settle in low spots such as canyons or river bottoms. Don't camp in streambeds or where a sudden flood may catch you.

| | |
|---|---|
| Are there many mosquitoes here? | *¿Hay muchos zancudos aquí?* |
| There are many mosquitoes here because of the swamp. | *Aquí hay muchos zancudos a causa del pantano.* |

Don't be surprised if you draw a crowd. You may find ten or fifteen people, adults and children alike, squatting in a circle around your camp and silently watching. After all, you're the "only show in town"! If things get too bad, you might ask, "Can't we have any privacy around here?" (*¿No podemos estar solos por aquí?*). But don't expect any mass exodus! If you want to be rude, you can say, "Go away!" (*¡Váyase!*), but this will result in hurt feelings and you will miss out on lots of chances to visit and learn.

Avoid ostentatious displays of material goods. Keep your gear under cover.

Don't litter. Even though you may come to believe that no Mexican ever puts anything in a trash can, there is a distinct difference between their littering their country and your doing the same.

Avoid passing around booze, candy, and cigarettes, as this will just draw a bigger crowd and give you less privacy. If you wish to share, a big pot of coffee is always appreciated, and a batch of popcorn makes an economical treat that goes a long way.

You can practice your Spanish and learn a lot by visiting with the *gente* who come near your camp. Since they will come with or without an invitation, you might as well make the best of it and get to know them. It can be very enjoyable. Break out the guitars and sing a while.

When you wish to go to sleep, just politely rise, say, "*Estamos muy cansados. Con permiso, buenas noches,*" put out the fire, douse the lights, and hit the sack. Don't expect anyone to leave as long as anything interesting is going on!

For privacy, camp as far from all signs of habitation as possible.

The most inviting streams can be found. But wear a bathing suit to take your bath; many Mexicans are offended at public displays of nudity.

Rig a privacy tarp if anyone in your party has problems with people wandering up or by at delicate moments.

In jungle areas, watch out for a plant called *mala mujer* (bad woman). It looks like a cross between a castor bean tree and a Texas bull nettle. It is covered with stinging hairs, and to contact one with a tender part of your anatomy is like the touch of a red-hot poker. Since they grow fifteen feet tall or more, any part of your body is at risk; therefore, learn to identify them and be alert for them on roadsides and stream-sides in the tropics.

Along jungle trails also watch out for the spiny palm (*palma espinosa*), with sharp, stabbing spines hidden among the fronds. You cannot "brush by" a spiny palm!

## SOME PRODUCTS OF INTEREST

While backpacking, safe water is always a problem. Your intestinal flora are not the same as the intestinal flora of rural Mexicans, and there are bacteria and other invisible varmints in most springs and in all water holes and rivers that can make you sick. Until recently, iodine tablets and boiling were the only sure solutions, and the taste thereby imparted to the water was horrible. Now, there are available from most backpacking supply houses ceramic filters with pumps that will allow you to use even polluted water sources with safety. These should be ideal for travelers in rural Mexico, particularly the ones with both filters and purifiers of silver nitrate and activated carbon.

In years past, jungle tents had to be made at home, as none of the backpacking supply houses carried these handy tents with sewn in floors and walls and roof totally of nylon mosquito netting. Now you can purchase tents that are cool and comfortable, with special nylon netting to keep out sandflies as well as mosquitoes and larger pests. In case of rain, there is a waterproof fly that goes over the tent. These are not cheap, but they are very effective and the best shelter for hiking or camping in tropical Mexico. Jungle hammocks, used by us when available after WWII, soon turned to cheap copies from the Orient and just did not hold up. The tents can be used anywhere, and at no greater weight penalty than the lightest hammock.

Insect repellants have improved greatly in recent years. The best locally available to all of us is Johnson's Deep Woods Off in lotion form, a white cream. Best of all is Muskol, which you generally must order from a backpacking supply house. We have tested both of them as far south as Central America and they do work. For those who really wish the ultimate, there are now available cotton mesh jackets impregnated with repellant, which even have a hood. You store them in a plastic container that "recharges" them for the next use.

For footgear, the Vietnam War has had some beneficial side effects. The Vietnam jungle boots, now mostly made in Korea but still of pretty good quality, are ideal for both hiking and canoeing in all of Mexico. They are equally good in desert or jungle and keep the feet healthy by allowing them to dry out quickly. In desert hiking, this cools the feet, and in jungle hiking this helps keep them from becoming waterlogged. On canoe trips, they furnish good footing on wet banks and in shallow wading and also serve well for side hikes without having to change shoes. We often carry one pair for wet wear and a spare dry pair for use after the day's boating is finished.

The new fabrics that are waterproof and yet still "breathe" are super rainsuits and ponchos for hikers and campers. One of the problems with rain protection for active people has been getting rid of the moisture your body normally puts out. Thus, much of the old-style raingear would keep the rain out, but if you were climbing or bushwhacking through jungle, you got just as wet inside the gear as outside, because of the trapping of body moisture. The new fabrics avoid that and keep you dry from the rain while still allowing for active exercise without the "greenhouse effect."

## A WARNING

While hiking or driving in the Sierra Madre of western Mexico, and in other remote places, don't forget to steer clear of drug operations, fields of marijuana (*mota*) or opium poppies (*amapola de opio*), and processing areas. It is natural to be curious, but curiosity killed the cat. Tourists have no business near drugs of any sort, and the drug operations are among the few real human dangers you may encounter in rural Mexico. Don't tarry!

You may from time to time encounter, or even be stopped or searched by, Mexican federal narcotics agents or army units in the Sierra Madre. If this happens, don't make any jokes or threaten to call your congressman, as it is serious business. Stay clean, keep cool, and you'll not likely have any trouble. Smart off or get found with drugs in your possession and you can become one of the several hundred *gringos* in Mexican jails, where the rules of civil rights are not enforced.

In some villages you may be asked if you want to buy some pot. Always turn down all such offers at once. Don't think you are making friends by buying or using dope. Most of the Mexicans don't smoke it. They just sell it to stupid *americanos*!

A *leñero* passes by after selling most of his load of wood to housewives in Santa Elena, Chihuahua. (Will Thompson photo)

## FIREWOOD AND FIRES

Firewood is *leña*. Those who cut firewood and sell it are called *leñeros*. Because of heavy use of wood for many purposes, from fence building to home building, and because of its extensive use for cooking and warming homes and camps, the deserts of Mexico are often nearly devoid of decent firewood. *Leñeros* dig up old stumps, collect driftwood along *arroyos* and rivers, and with axe (*hacha*) or *machete* cut bundles of wood, often green, and load their burros with high loads. Small boys often go for miles to gather or cut firewood, and elderly women and men can be seen trudging up mountain trails with a load on their back or on the head. Mexico, in the desert areas, is a place where you "dig for wood," meaning you often get more wood from the unearthed roots of dead desert plants such as mesquite than from the dead top.

The people of Mexico usually build small fires, use them wisely, and sit up close. *Gringos* build bonfires and stand back, wasting wood.

In the winter, or in the high *sierras*, the morning sun is the poor man's fire. Mexican men and boys will line the east wall of a house or building, soaking up the first warmth of the sun's rays. When they get warmed up enough, they go to work.

Much wood is made into charcoal, or *carbón*, which is used both in cooking and by local blacksmiths in the forges. *Carboneros*, as the men are called who make charcoal, sack up their wares in huge sacks, to be trucked to the cities for use in home cooking fires. The smell of burning wood is the typical early morning smell of all of Mexico.

Firewood is sold by the piece (*por pedazo*), by the handful (*por mano*), or by the load (*carga*). If you cannot tell the difference between green wood and dry wood, better carry a gasoline stove and forget the *leña*!

| | |
|---|---|
| I'm going to start a fire. | *Voy a encender (hacer) una lumbre.* |
| Please gather some small wood. | *Haga el favor de recoger leña menuda.* |
| Chop it up small. | *Píquelo (Córtelo) muy chico.* |
| Will you light the fire? | *¿Quiere prender el fuego?* |
| Stir up the fire! | *¡Atice el fuego!* |
| Strike a match. | *Encienda un fósforo (cerillo).* |
| May I trouble you for a match? | *¿Lo puedo molestar por un fósforo?* |
| Wet firewood does not burn well. | *La leña mojada no arde bien.* |
| The cinders were still smoking. | *Las cenizas (brasas) todavía humeaban.* |
| Be careful, it is very flammable. | *Tenga usted cuidado porque se inflama muy fácilmente.* |
| Let's cut some wood for the fire. | *Cortemos un poco de leña para el fuego.* |
| Isn't that fire giving off a good blaze! | *¡No da ese fuego buena llama!* |
| The fire is blazing nicely now. | *El fuego está ardiendo ahora muy bien.* |
| I like to see a bright fire. | *Me gusta ver un fuego llameante.* |
| Please build a fire in the fireplace. | *Haga el favor de hacer el fuego en la chimenea.* |
| The wood is so dry that it will easily catch fire. | *La leña está tan seca que prenderá fácilmente.* |
| He blew on the embers until they flamed up. | *Sopló el rescoldo (las ascuas) hasta que se hizo llama.* |
| What do you use for fuel? | *¿Qué usa usted como combustible?* |

The fire spread rapidly.

What started the fire?

The chimney caught on fire and the house burned down.

Their home burned down.

The house burned to the ground.

The fire destroyed three houses.

Lightning struck the house and set it afire.

*El incendio se extendió rápidamente.*

*¿Qué fue lo que causó el incendio?*

*Se incendió la chimenea y se quemó toda la casa.*

*Su casa se quemó por completo.*

*La casa se abrasó.*

*El incendio destruyó tres casas.*

*Cayó un rayo e incendió la casa.*

# 8. Canoeing the Río Grande, Río Conchos, and Other Mexican Streams

**C**anoeing is a great way to pass through wilderness country. Big Bend National Park and the Río Grande below it have some fine canyons to canoe, with Mexico on the right-hand side. The Río Conchos, flowing from the highlands of Chihuahua into the Río Grande (Río Bravo del Norte) at Ojinaga-Presidio, has some nice canyons and remote villages along its lower stretch, including Peguis Canyon with its major rockfall obstacle hidden in the depths. There are many fine whitewater streams deeper in Mexico worth searching out, although dams and hydroelectric projects have taken their toll.

Remember that some of the interior rivers of Mexico originate in rain forest and high mountains, with steep gradients, high discharge volumes, and difficult access. They all bear scouting, the bigger ones from the air in a chartered plane before launching blindly downstream into a canyon. Some are hairy beyond belief.

Older Mexican maps are not always reliable, but the new ones are better. We have seen topographic maps from the same government office, one ten years older than the other, showing the same river on opposite sides of the same substantial mountain range. Be sure to scout the rivers, as there are some places, such as Puente de Dios near Valles, where the river drops into a cavern and goes underground for some distance. In other places narrow canyons hide waterfalls without a safe way out or around.

Since few Mexicans boat these rivers, they are usually not reliable informants about the obstacles to boating found within them. They may consider a rapid "impossible" that we rate as an easy Class III. On the other hand, they may also tell you a canyon is passable when in fact it is impassable or highly dangerous to pass through.

Certain warnings that are given related to "bad" rivers are included below. Consider them carefully, whether you heed them or not.

| | |
|---|---|
| Bank (river) | *Orilla* (f.); *banca* (f.); *ribera* (f.) |
| Beach | *Playa* (f.) |

Rugged dissected limestone terrain of the Big Bend–Sierra del Carmen country of Texas and Coahuila, Mexico. This aerial view shows a part of Boquillas Canyon and the Sierra del Carmen with Schott Tower, or Pico del Cerdo, in the background. (David H. Riskind photo)

| | |
|---|---|
| Boulder | *Peña* (f.); *roca* (f.) |
| Bow (of canoe or raft) | *Proa* (f.) |
| Canoe | *Canoa* (f.); *lancha* (f.); *chalupa* (f.); *barca* (f.); *piragua* (f.) |
| Channel | *Canal* (m.); *cauce* (m.) |
| Current | *Corriente* (m.) |
| Danger (risk) | *Riesgo* (m.); *peligro* (m.) |
| Dugout canoe | *Cayuco* (m.) |
| Eddys, waves, and whirls | *Remolinos* (m.); *olas* (f.) |
| Flood | *Crecida* (f.); *creciente* (f.); *inundación* (f.) |
| Kayak | *Lancha* (f.); *kajak* (m.) |
| Life jacket | *Salvavidas* (m.) |
| Logjams or obstructions to the flow of the river | *Estancamientos* (m.) |
| Mud | *Lodo* (m.); *zoquete* (m.) |
| Narrow passage | *Estrecho* (m.) |
| Oar | *Remo* (m.) |
| Paddle | *Pala* (f.); *remo de canoa* (m.) |
| Patch | *Remiendo* (m.) |
| Raft | *Balsa* (f.) |
| Rapids | *Chorros* (m.); *rápidos* (m.) |
| River basin | *Hoya* (f.) |
| Row | *Remar* |
| Shipwreck | *Naufragio* (m.) |
| Shoal | *Bajo* (m.); *bajío* (m.); *banco de arena* (m.) |
| Shore | *Orilla* (f.); *playa* (f.) |
| Splice | *Ayuste* (m.) |
| Stern (of canoe or raft) | *Popa* (f.) |
| Torrent | *Torrente* (m.) |
| Valley | *Valle* (m.) |
| Waterfall | *Salto* (m.); *salto del agua* (m.); *caída* (f.); *catarata* (f.); *cascada* (f.) |
| Without danger | *Sin riesgo; sin peligro* |

This is not a canoeing guide, nor a guide to river travel in Mexico, but we throw in some phrases that may be useful to the traveler by canoe or raft in Mexican inland waters.

| | |
|---|---|
| Is this the ——— River? | *¿Este es el Río ———?* |
| What is the name of this river? | *¿Cómo se llama este río?* |

(Note: In Mexico, many local people call a river by the name of the nearest town. Thus, the Río Valles, near Valles, may be the Río Salto when it is near El Salto del Agua, or the Río Naranjo when it is near the village of El Naranjo.)

| | |
|---|---|
| How far is it to the source (head) of the river? | *¿A qué distancia queda el nacimiento del río?* |
| Can we safely pass down this river to ——— in a canoe? | *¿Podemos navegar en canoa y pasar este río sin riesgo (peligro) hasta ———?* |
| Have others passed down this part of the river in canoes? | *¿Han pasado otros esta sección del río en canoas?* |
| What problems or obstructions do you know about between ——— and ———? | *¿Conoce usted problemas o obstrucciones entre ——— y ———?* |
| How far is it to the mouth of the river? | *¿A qué distancia queda la desembocadura del río?* |
| This river empties into a big lake. | *Este río desemboca en un lago (una presa) grande.* |
| Are there canyons downstream (upstream)? | *¿Hay cañones río abajo (río arriba)?* |
| Are there big rapids (waterfalls) downstream (upstream) from here? | *Hay chorros (cascadas) grandes río abajo (río arriba)?* |
| Are there logjams across the river downstream (upstream)? | *¿Hay estancamientos río abajo (río arriba)?* |
| Is there a trail around the waterfall that I can carry my canoe around on? | *¿Hay vereda alrededor de la cascada en donde puedo cargar mi canoa?* |
| Where does the trail start? | *¿Dónde comienza la vereda?* |
| On which side does the trail start? | *¿De qué lado comienza la vereda?* |
| Are there any villages alongside the river downstream (upstream)? | *¿Hay pueblos río abajo (río arriba) a la orilla del río?* |
| You'll find a settlement about 10 kilometers downstream (upstream). | *Encontrará usted una colonia (aldea) a unos diez kilómetros al río abajo (río arriba).* |
| How far is it to the other shore? | *¿A qué distancia queda la otra orilla?* |
| The two rivers meet below the town. | *Los dos ríos confluyen más allá del pueblo.* |
| This is only a branch of the river. | *Este es sólo un brazo del río.* |
| Can we cross the river in this canoe? | *¿Podemos cruzar el río en esta canoa?* |

The trip by canoe will take five days.

*El viaje en canoa durará cinco días.*

Can I land at ———?

*¿Puedo desembarcar en ———?*

Let's dive in!

*¡Vamos a zambullirnos (echarnos de cabeza) (tirar un salto)!*

He swam to the nearest bank of the river.

*Nadó hasta la orilla más cercana.*

The water's so clear we can see the bottom.

*El agua está tan clara que se ve el fondo.*

What are the names of the villages I will pass?

*¿Cómo se llaman las aldeas por donde voy a pasar?*

Is there a road crossing downstream (upstream) from here?

*¿Hay un cruce con el camino río abajo (río arriba)?*

How far from here?

*¿Qué tan lejos? (¿A qué distancia de aquí?)*

Is there a bridge crossing the river downstream (upstream) from here?

*¿Hay algún puente río abajo (río arriba)?*

Do the downstream villages have access by bus (truck)?

*¿Hay autobús (troca) (camión) en los poblados río abajo?*

Would you like a ride across the river?

*¿Le gustaría cruzar el río en canoa?*

Take me across the river, please.

*Lléveme al otro lado del río, por favor.*

Get in my canoe, I'll take you over.

*Súbase a mi canoa y le llevo al otro lado.*

Sit in the stern (bow) while I row.

*Siéntese en la popa (proa) mientras yo remo.*

Sit down on the bottom and keep steady.

*Siéntese en el fondo de la canoa y estése quieto.*

Don't rock the canoe, it's liable to tip over.

*No mueva usted la canoa porque se puede volcar.*

Be careful not to swamp the canoe.

*Tenga cuidado de no hundir la canoa.*

Now, get out, keeping your balance.

*Bájese y mantenga su equilibrio.*

Watch out! We nearly turned over that time!

*¡Cuidado! ¡Esta vez casi nos volcamos!*

Is this water safe to swim in?

*¿Podemos nadar aquí sin riesgo?*

I want to go swimming.

*Quiero ir a nadar.*

I'm going out for a swim.

*Voy a nadar un rato.*

Show me how you use your dugout canoe, please.

*Por favor, enséñeme cómo usar su piragua (canoa).*

| | |
|---|---|
| May I try it? | *¿Puedo probarlo?* |

(Note: Except in the far south and in the coastal sections of the largest rivers, most dugouts are paddled by one person standing in the stern and using a long paddle. They are mainly used for ferrying across the river, and not for downstream or upstream travel.)

| | |
|---|---|
| Be careful not to hit that stump (rock)! | *¡Tenga usted cuidado de no tropezar con ese tronco (piedra)!* |
| The raft struck a rock! | *¡La balsa chocó con una roca!* |
| We shoved the raft into the water. | *Empujamos la balsa adentro del agua.* |
| Let's pull the raft farther up on shore. | *Arrastremos la balsa más arriba en la orilla.* |
| The raft pushed off from shore. | *La balsa se alejó de la orilla.* |
| We beached the canoe. | *Encallamos la canoa en la playa (orilla).* |
| The waves tipped our canoe over! | *¡Las olas voltearon nuestra canoa!* |
| You'll have to row too. | *Usted tiene que remar también.* |
| The only way you can fix that is to patch it. | *La única forma (manera) de arreglar esto es remendándolo.* |
| A fallen tree blocked our way. | *Un árbol caído obstruía nuestro paso.* |
| What is the name of this village? | *¿Cómo se llama este pueblo?* |
| Is there a grocery store in the village? | *¿Hay un mercado (tendajo) (una tienda de abarrotes) en el pueblo?* |
| Will you help me carry my canoe and equipment around this waterfall (rapids)? | *Me ayuda por favor a cargar mi canoa y equipaje para rodear esta caída (este chorro)?* |
| I need a porter. | *Necesito un cargador.* |
| I'll be glad to pay you for your trouble. | *Le pago por la molestia.* |
| What do I owe you? | *¿Qué le debo? (¿Cuánto le debo?)* |
| Can I (we) camp here? | *¿Puedo (Podemos) acampar aquí?* |
| Is there safe drinking water nearby? | *¿Hay agua potable cerca?* |
| Where is the nearest spring with good water? | *¿Dónde queda el ojo de agua más cercano?* |
| May I visit your camp (ranch) (farm) (village) (*ejido*)? | *¿Puedo visitar su campo (rancho) (granja, pueblo) (ejido)?* |
| Is there anyone here who has a truck that I can hire to drive me and my canoe back to ———. | *¿Hay alguien con camión de alquiler que puede llevarme a mí y a mi canoa a ———?* |

| | |
|---|---|
| What will it cost me to hire this truck and driver? | ¿Cuánto me cuesta por emplear este camión y su chofer? |
| Wind at your back! | ¡Viento en popa! |
| Load up and let's go! | ¡Cargue y vámonos! |

Some of the following warnings may be given you about rivers the natives believe are inherently dangerous.

| | |
|---|---|
| This is a bad river, with many waterfalls! | ¡Es un río muy feo, y hay caídas de agua muy altas! |
| It is all canyon! | ¡Es puro cañón! |
| Steep-walled canyon, water from wall to wall! | ¡Hay puro cañón, con río de lado a lado! |
| The river is badly swollen after the summer rains. | El río está muy crecido después de las lluvias de verano. |
| The river's rising rapidly. | El río está creciendo rápidamente. |
| This river is very deep. | Este río es muy hondo. |
| The water is pretty rough here! | ¡El agua aquí está muy agitada! |
| Be careful of the waves and swirls when you swim! | ¡Tenga cuidado con las olas y los remolinos cuando vaya a nadar! |
| The current zigzags back and forth! | ¡La corriente zigzaguea de un lado a otro! |
| There are many great waves and swirling eddies! | ¡Hay bastantes ondas y remolinos muy grandes! |
| The rapids are stronger this year than last. | Los rápidos del río son mas fuertes este año que el pasado. |
| Have your life jackets ready! | ¡Tengan listos los salvavidas! |
| Man overboard! | ¡Hombre al agua! |
| We had a narrow escape! | ¡Escapamos por un pelo! |
| You're taking a big chance, and I'd think better of it if I were you! | ¡Usted va a correr un gran riesgo; yo, en su lugar, lo pensaría mejor! |
| I'd think twice about that if I were you. | ¡Si yo fuera usted, lo pensaría dos veces! |
| There are many waterfalls on this river. | Hay muchas cascadas en este río. |
| The river has a strong current. | El río tiene una corriente muy fuerte. |
| Let's approach carefully! | ¡Acerquémonos con cuidado! |
| We had better take that coil of rope along in the raft. | Sería mejor llevar ese rollo de cuerda en la balsa. |
| He almost drowned. | Por poco se ahoga. |
| The water is very cold. | El agua está muy fría. |
| He was dragged along by the current. | Lo arrastró la corriente. |

| | |
|---|---|
| The water's very inviting. | *El agua está muy tentadora.* |
| The canoe (raft) has a leak. | *La canoa (balsa) tiene un agujero.* |
| How many times have you made this trip by canoe? | *¿Cuántas veces ha hecho usted el viaje en canoa?* |
| This is a very dangerous waterfall. | *Este salto de agua es muy peligroso.* |
| They went up the river. | *Remontaron el curso del río.* |
| The water became muddy because of the rains. | *El agua se enturbió con la lluvia.* |
| We followed the course of the river. | *Seguimos el curso del río.* |
| The river carries a huge volume of water. | *El río lleva un gran caudal.* |

(Note: Over many small canyons and narrow rivers in tropical Mexico, we have seen the natives cross on wires or cables, using a hook that they carry with them, with a short rope attached for a harness. They hook on and hand-over-hand across. The crossing is done with ropes and cable or rope bridges across the smaller streams. To see a native going hand-over-hand along a wire across a canyon over a raging torrent is interesting and a challenge to you to try it the same way.)

## SCOUTING RIVERS AND MOUNTAINS BY AIR

Light aircraft are generally available in Mexico, and under the right conditions it is safe to hire a plane and pilot to scout rivers and mountain ranges (or canyons) from the air. From the air, with good binoculars, you can estimate the frequency and severity of rapids, determine whether or not there are waterfalls, assure yourself of a chance to portage the unrunnable obstacles, get an idea of the lay of the land for hiking, find roads that will furnish easier access around or to certain spots, and check the validity of information from local informants. Keep in mind, however, that flying in Mexico is substantially more risky than in the United States due to less-reliable maintenance on the aircraft, unnecessarily bold pilots, very rough country, and lower-quality aviation fuel.

The following suggestions may help you avert a crash or forced landing.

Select your aircraft and pilot carefully and get all the information you can about both before chartering. Don't just take whatever is available. Professional charter services that regularly fly into remote mines, ranches, and villages are probably the best bet under most circumstances.

Don't overload. One pilot and two observers is the maximum. Don't carry anyone who is not an experienced observer and who cannot read a topographical map and a chart.

High elevations, heat, and humidity are ingredients of a dangerous flight, since these conditions require more runway and reduce the rate of climb of the aircraft.

Avoid flying on days with high winds or thunderstorms in the area.

Be sure the pilot maintains at least 2,000 feet of clearance over all ridges and mountains. Don't let him just skim over the tops. Use binoculars for a better view below.

Cross ridges and mountain tops at a 45-degree angle, and then straighten out after you have passed through any downdraft that may be found on either side. If you hit downdrafts, the 2,000 feet of clearance will give you time and room and the 45-degree angle will allow the aircraft to turn toward lower terrain in an emergency.

Arrange your flight for morning hours, when weather is usually best and air currents more stable. In the afternoon weather starts developing rapidly in mountain regions. Avoid routes flying directly into the sun.

While flying a canyon (to scout a river), fly the side of the canyon, not the middle. Fly the updraft side (if the wind is coming from your left, the downdraft side is to your left, so the updraft side would be to your right).

Fly canyons from top to bottom (downstream) not from bottom to top (upstream). It is all too easy for the pilot to run out of altitude at the upper end, and find that he has neither power to climb out nor room to turn around. Canyon walls (or surrounding mountains) can hem the aircraft in. Flying one side or the other may not feel as safe as flying the middle, because you feel like you have more room in the middle, but by flying the middle you are cutting your available turning space in half. If you do wish to fly a canyon at a low altitude, for closer inspection of the river, rapids, waterfalls, trails, villages, roads, you should always fly from the higher end to the lower.

Stay out of very narrow canyons. Flying up a narrow canyon with a charter pilot is just not smart. You cannot assume that his instincts for self-preservation are strong enough to keep him flying a relatively safe route. If you don't like what he is doing, tell him "no" and make it stick.

Winds generally blow upcanyon in the mornings and downcanyon in the evenings, another good reason to fly canyons from top to bottom and in the morning.

Never fly in weather when visibility is bad because of clouds, fog, or rain. You probably could not see much on the ground anyway under those circumstances, and you need full visibility when flying around mountains or canyons.

Topographic elevations shown on Mexican maps and even on U.S. air navigation charts may be erroneous. There are many high peaks in Mexico that have never been accurately measured or charted. Allow for elevations to be higher than those charted.

The effects of density altitude must be considered when a takeoff with a loaded aircraft is attempted at higher elevations. For example, an aircraft that requires 1,000 feet of runway for takeoff at sea level may require 2,000 feet of runway at a strip having an elevation of 5,000 feet. Because the performance of the aircraft is adversely affected by altitude, heat, and humidity, the rate of climb is reduced in many circumstances encountered in mountain flying. This factor requires increased distance clearances from obstacles to enable the aircraft to climb safely over. It is also possible to land on a strip at high altitude from which a safe takeoff with an equal load cannot be made. All of these factors change constantly and must be kept in mind by the person in charge of the charter. Do not put blind trust in a strange pilot and aircraft.

If the weather forecast is for winds aloft to exceed 35 mph, you should consider postponing the flight, as winds near mountains and canyons typically exceed the velocities reported a few miles away. Downdrafts are to be expected on the lee side of all peaks, cliffs, and mountain passes, and these may commonly reach velocities of 1,500 to 2,000 feet per minute. It is for this reason that substantial clearance margins are advised.

On the lee or downwind side of all peaks, ridges, cliffs, or steep canyon walls, you can expect to encounter the "mountain wave" effect. There is usually a fairly smooth updraft on the upwind side, followed by turbulent air and strong downdrafts on the immediate lee side. The rate of downdraft can exceed the climb capability of the aircraft, causing a crash not far over the ridge or cliff on the lee slope. In most of the mountain areas of Mexico prevailing winds are from the west, but local conditions can create opposite effects, so the only safe approach is that of additional clearance gained before encountering the downdraft conditions.

# 9. Rural Mexican Village Life

This section does not purport to be a sociological study, or even a guide to the Mexican village. It is merely an outline of some of the activities, trades, and institutions found in many rural Mexican villages. The variety of lifeways across Mexico is extremely wide, from the deserts of the north to the cool central highlands and the rain forests in the tropics. Rainfall, temperature, elevation, topography, house styles, and Indian-*mestizo* racial mixtures all vary widely across Mexico, so that only limited generalizations can be made about village life. All these differences make Mexico a most interesting nation for the patient, friendly, and curious traveler.

When we speak of villages, we are talking of rural villages, sometimes only scatterings of *jacales* (small houses) or *rancherías* (clusters of farmsteads) or *pueblos* (small towns, with no more than a few hundred inhabitants). We are also speaking mainly of the type of village one might encounter along a rutted country road in north Mexico or perhaps in the Sierra Madre of the west.

## SOME VILLAGE TERMS

*El horno:* clay or stone beehive ovens used for baking. These are usually separate from the house.

*Ixtle:* a fiber made from plants of the *agave* family, such as the *maguey* or century plant, or the yucca (*palma*). Rope made of *ixtle* is called *mecate*.

*Los músicos:* groups of local musicians, who play locally made guitars and violins, as well as other instruments, such as the Mexican harp or *arpa* in some areas.

*La ollera:* someone, usually a woman, who makes clay pottery in the old way.

*Las escobas:* brooms locally made from stiff, springy branches of certain trees or woody plants tied in bundles.

Chihuahuan desert village, west of Manuel Benavides, Chihuahua. The buildings and yards are typical of desert Mexico. (Will Thompson photo)

*El canastero:* someone who weaves baskets from split palm or other woody fibers.

*La cobijera:* the weaver, usually a woman, who weaves on a simple but effective loom made locally. Blankets are a common woven product.

*El maíz:* corn, in all its varieties. In many rural areas the soil in the small fields (*milpas*) is tilled with a wooden plow pulled by a mule (*mula*) or ox (*buey*) and planted by hand, the planter dropping grains into holes punched with a sharpened stick. Planting is done in a traditional manner called *sembrando en cruz* (planting in a cross), in holes two steps apart in rows one step apart. Plants in alternate rows are staggered, so there is a "cross" pattern. This allows the corn plants to get plenty of wind, believed essential for good *maíz*.

*El maíz chapolote; el esquite; las palomitas* (preferred): popcorn. Most Mexicans enjoy popcorn as a treat.

*Las elotes:* fresh corn on the cob. These are good eaten on sticks after roasting. Vendors sell them on the streets.

*Las mazorcas:* dried ears of corn. Corn is often stored dry and on the cob, in sacks, or in elevated storage structures.

*El carozo; el zuro; el zuro de la mazorca de maíz:* corn cobs; used often as fuel and for scrubbing.

*La saca; el costal:* large palm-leaf or *ixtle* fiber sack in which rural people carry ears of corn or store dried ears.

*La panocha:* raw sugar; made from the boiled juice of sugarcane in tropical areas. Much *panocha* is made from sugarcane juice squeezed between iron rollers in a mill turned by a burro walking in a circle. After the juice (*miel de caña*) is slowly cooked until it forms sugar, it may be formed into small cones of hard brown sugar. These are called *piloncillo.* Sugar is also called *azúcar.*

*La tejedora:* a weaver of hats made of split palm leaves.

*El carbón* (*carbonero* = maker of charcoal): charcoal, fuel for cooking and blacksmith's forges.

*La olla:* water jug of fired clay, usually hung in *mecate* slings so that evaporation will cool the water inside. Also used by women to carry water home from streams or wells.

*El herrero:* the village blacksmith. With a charcoal forge, and only a few of the traditional smith's tools, he can fix almost anything.

*El carpintero:* the village carpenter, who uses very simple tools and ingenious hand-powered lathes and other interesting devices to make items of wood.

*Los adobes:* bricks made of sun-dried mud, with tempering agents of sand or straw.

*El ladrillero:* the local brick maker, who fires clay bricks in a kiln made of the bricks themselves, stacked in ranks.

*La ramada:* a shady shelter with thatched roof and no walls, usually made of four corner posts set in the ground and holding up the superstructure. Such items as dried corn are stored atop the *ramada*, to keep them away from the pigs that keep the yard clean. A notched log or a ladder goes to the top.

## WATER SOURCES

Mexican villages exist only where there is water. It can come from springs (*ojos*) or wells (*norias*) or seeps (*ciénagas*) or rivers (*ríos*) or just from erosional ditches (*arroyos*). In some few places rainwater is collected from roofs. In other areas, nearby ponds (*aguadas*) furnish the drinking water supply. In the limestone areas of southeastern Mexico, deep natural wells, actually sinkholes (*cenotes*), furnish water. Some remote desert villagers must haul water from long distances in dry seasons.

The village water supply in the Chihuahuan Desert country of Coahuila. Most village wells like this are polluted. (Will Thompson photo)

Family water supply: the well of Victorio Hernández, in Santa Elena, Chihuahua. The windlass is made of a cottonwood log. (Will Thompson photo)

It is always interesting to inquire about the local water source. Since only a few villages have potable water supplies, it is not usually safe for foreigners to drink the water without treatment or boiling. You will need to carry your own water purification equipment and iodine tablets or drink only from springs high above all habitation.

## LOCAL INDUSTRIES

It is also interesting to see what is made locally, or what the local industries are, whether agricultural, mining, timbering, or manufacturing. A stop for a few minutes can turn into hours of interesting watching. Sawmills in tropical regions are interesting for the great variety of color and texture of the different logs, all of them strange to us. In the arid regions you can observe the making of mud bricks and the making of rope from the fibers of desert plants. In the mountains of the tropics the weaving of hats, baskets, and other products from split palm leaves is of great interest. (See chapter 11 for more information.)

## MARKETS

In many villages, particularly in Indian areas, there are central open-air markets with vendors having their wares spread about in neat and inviting stacks, sometimes on fiber mats (*petates*) also used for sleeping pads in many rural homes. The sight of a *gringo camioneta con doble tracción* (4-wheel drive truck) with its big tires and all its special gear will draw a crowd in a market. Park at a distance and walk to the market and you will see it in a more natural state.

## SLASH-AND-BURN AGRICULTURE

Much agriculture in Mexico is carried on under difficult conditions. There is almost no level arable land left unused in the nation, and in heavily populated areas people farm slopes that you can hardly stand on. The result is ruinous erosion and muddy rivers.

In tropical areas, one technique still in use is to cut all the jungle flat, allow it to dry, burn the slash, and plant a corn crop into the ashy soil. Squash is planted as a low crop between the corn plants, and beans are likewise planted among the corn rows. After a couple of crops the nutrients are depleted and the farmers abandon the field (*milpa; labor*) to the jungle and go cut and burn a new one. This is wasteful and contributes to soil erosion, but it has been an enduring form of subsistence agriculture in the tropics for perhaps a thousand years and shows little sign of dying out. A cleared area where jungle or brush is cut away is called a *desmonte* after the fields are abandoned.

## VILLAGES REACHED ONLY BY TRAILS

The tropical lowlands and mountainous regions are full of villages that are so remote that not even a jeep trail reaches them. Where these trails run, centuries of foot travel and erosional cutting have made trails several feet deep. The only roadside indication of the location of many of these villages is the small groups of people, some with sacks of corn on their backs, with a tumpline to the forehead, or with sacks of produce, bundles of live chickens tied together, or *morrales* (fiber sacks) holding their possessions, standing beside the highway waiting for a truck or bus. In the tropics many of these trails lead off for miles through swampy ground to small clusters of huts and fields cut out of the jungle.

## BUILDING TECHNIQUES

Once we were lucky enough to come upon a group of farmers cutting jungle for a cornfield. They showed us how they peeled the red bark from long straight poles for use in houses, how they saved the bark for tying the house together, and how they split the twenty-foot leaves of the *cohune* palm (*coquito de colima*) to make their water-shedding thatch roofs. We watched the construction of such a home from the ground up, and not a single nail or piece of wire went into a serviceable house for a family of four, complete with sleeping loft, walls, open windows, and the usual dirt floor. It took two men, equipped with one old axe and a machete, about twenty-four hours to build it. It sure as heck beats slaving all your life to pay for a $90,000 all-electric marvel that you cannot survive in when the power goes off! A close inspection of the Mexican village cannot help but leave one wondering a bit about the validity of many of our ideas of the "necessities of life." Such a house will last several years with no repairs, and for a lifetime with reasonable maintenance.

## RURAL HOUSING

We are not architects and do not pretend to know the proper names of all the various styles of Mexican houses. This brief section is only intended to make you aware of some of the construction materials, techniques, and styles of the owner-built homes of rural Mexicans. Most of these houses are made with locally available materials, whether ani-

Desert home of Ramundo and María Chávez, Ejido Melchor Músquiz, Coahuila. Summer sleeping platform, made of sotol *quiotes*, is at left. Water, hauled by burro, is stored in the drums. (Mickey Burleson photo)

mal, vegetable, or mineral. They usually cost nothing except time and labor. Generally speaking, they are best suited for hot to moderate temperatures, since really cold weather is not that common in Mexico except at high altitudes. Therefore, when a blue norther blows across Texas and it freezes in the Rio Grande Valley, you can bet your boots that there are some cold *gente* huddled under whatever cover they have available to them.

Although these houses may appear at first to be nothing more than hovels, and totally unsuitable for human habitation, they are often happy homes and a source of genuine pride to the inhabitants. Look carefully and you often find that the woman of the house has managed to maintain a small garden, or pots of flowers or herbs used for seasoning. Generally, except under the worst conditions, the dooryard is swept clean daily with a homemade broom, and bedding is aired in the sun. Most semipermanent homes have a small kitchen garden (if water is available) in which are grown beans, chile peppers, cilantro, and other food and seasoning plants. Herbs are gathered in *el monte* and can be seen drying under the roof edge or in the rafters. Where conditions permit you will find caged birds and lard cans used as pots for flowering plants. All are carefully tended by the *ranchera*.

Most of the houses are rather dark inside, since electricity is uncommon and windows of the sort we have are generally not available. Instead, there are either no windows, or the unscreened openings are shuttered. In fair weather, much cooking is done outside, perhaps under a *ramada* (arbor). In foul weather, the house is closed tight and any of a number of forms of heating, all dangerous, are used. A 55-gallon drum (*tanque*) may be cut in half, the bottom filled with sand, and used as an open hearth. Or a 55-gallon drum may have a door cut in the side, a pipe attached, and serve as a stove. Some homes have commercially made kerosene heaters, or wood-burning stoves. A few of the older ones made of rock have a fireplace and chimney, but this is a real rarity except on old ranches. Now and then a propane hotplate or space heater is seen. Propane bottles must be carried many miles to be refilled.

General styles of houses range from the desert adobe, to the house near the river made of polished, flood-worn boulders from the mountains. On formerly large ranches, many houses of ledgestone remain, the stones usually having been laid with only mud for mortar. Some of these have fireplaces. We have not seen much new construction of rock houses, indicating that less permanent types of housing have come to the fore. In the mountains, particularly near sawmills, houses are made of slabs of fresh-sawed lumber, often roofed with the exterior slabs of bark. In other areas where tall evergreen timber is found, traditional log cabins are raised. If caves are handy, they are often walled up and used for homes. Dugouts are made if a cutbank is handy.

A friend decided to climb up to one of the caves in Indian country to see if it had been recently occupied. He called out loudly and got no reply, then, thinking the cave unoccupied, he started up the steps hewn into the rock wall of the canyon. About halfway up, a fist-sized rock came arcing out the door of the cave, barely missing him. He decided that someone was surely claiming that cave and did not insist on his visit!

In several areas we have visited, where large piles of weathered granitic boulders are found, homes have been constructed under huge boulders, the builder simply walling up sides and front and having a solid rock rear wall and roof. A more snug dwelling can hardly be imagined. They last a long time as well, as one of the best examples, at Rancho San José de las Piedras, Coahuila, has been known to be in ex-

istence and occupied since at least 1856, when it was sketched by a
U.S. military engineer. It was still the home of a *pastor* when we were
last there only a short time ago. Pictographs on the boulders prove that
the Indians used the shelters even before the Mexicans adopted them.

Timber is scarce in the northern deserts of Mexico. Most of the
streamside trees (particularly species of cottonwood [*álamo*] and ash
[*fresno*]) have long ago been cut to provide posts and beams for houses.
In some areas where permanent streams support the growth of cottonwoods, the people preserve the main trunks of the cottonwoods and
simply cut off the larger limbs from time to time, as if harvesting a
crop. This is called in English "pollarding," obviously not a Mexican
term. The term comes from the word "poll" for "head," and literally
means to "dehorn" the tree, as you might dehorn a cow. Check the
cottonwoods and other fast-growing trees near a Mexican village and
you will see evidence of this harvest. The limbs go to make structural
parts of houses, or for furniture, cottonwood being easily worked.
Along the more populated stretches of the Río Grande, the cottonwood has nearly been eliminated because of overharvest.

Roofing materials also vary widely. Grass and *palma* (yucca) leaf
thatching is still used. In mining and lumber camps the primary roofing material is a corrugated black asphalt-felt seen all over Mexico. In
some areas, locally made reddish roof tiles are used, either half-round
or flat. Again, sheet iron roofs are found where money is more plen-
tiful, and occasionally one sees roll roofing of the sort available in the
United States for cheap roof covering. In government housing, corrugated asbestos cement roofing is common, but this is not seen except
in the newest *ejido* communities of concrete block houses with case-
ment windows. Among the most common rural roofs is the old standby,
wet earth mixed with ashes. In the tropics split palm fronds prevail.

To make an earthen roof, the Mexicans first frame it out with poles
then overlay a solid deck of whatever material is available, small
branches, river cane or reeds, bloomstalks of *sotol*, *lechuguilla*, or
other desert plants. Over this is put tar paper, if they have it, cardboard
if they don't. Sometimes a layer of grass or woven matting, or anything
handy, to keep earth from sifting down through the cracks is used.
Over all are piled several inches of puddled (wet) *adobe* soil mixed
with ashes.

Walls of houses not made of brick, rock, or adobe usually start with
four poles at the corners, and sometimes a central pole to help support
the ridgepole and roof. In between will be placed staves, and more
slender branches will be woven between the staves. River cane, if available, will be used for walls, supported by and tied to the staves. We
have seen walls made of anything and everything. Sometimes *adobe*

San José de las Piedras, Chihuahua. This house has been occupied and abandoned off and on since the early 1800s. It was completely refurbished and occupied when we last visited in 1984. Note the substantial stone roof, the painted *portales*, the *metate* and *horno* (oven), and the living compound perimeter fence (*cerca*), and brooms (*escobas*) to sweep the compacted dirt floor and the yard. (Jim Belamy photo)

Typical rock and *adobe* walls for gardens and livestock pens, near San Francisco del Oro, Chihuahua. (Will Thompson photo)

A *mestizo* family in their hillside house near La Bufa, Chihuahua. Note the log and green slab lumber construction. (Will Thompson photo)

Details of stone house construction, near La Mula, Chihuahua. The kitchen (*cocina*) is tacked on at the right, and water is hauled by burro from the river. (Will Thompson photo)

is plastered over the basic wall to seal it against the weather, sometimes not.

The cheapest houses are obviously those of the poorest people. We have seen *jacales* with walls of stacked or upright yucca plants, and roofs of split dagger trunks (making a half cylinder) with one turned up and the two on either side turned down, for a "corrugated" roof.

Nails, bolts, metal hinges, and the like are very rare, and to the Mexican not necessary (earlier in this chapter we described a house made by two men in about twenty-four hours without a nail or even a piece of wire going into its construction). Hinges can be made of wood, and often are. Just as often a few strips of old truck tires will be nailed by one end to the doorpost, and the other end to the door, making neat, nonsqueaking hinges that last forever. We ran over one of these hinges one time, with the nails sticking up, and it gave us a quick flat tire.

The luxury of glass windows has hardly reached rural Mexico. These are usually found only in the cities and in the country homes of *ricos* (people of wealth). More likely, windows are closed by a wooden shutter, or by a blanket, piece of an old tarp, or a goatskin. However, even

This hut in remote Coahuila is thatched with *palma* (*Yucca carnerosona*) over sotol *latillas*. The door is of scrap lumber with tire-tread hinges. The *palma* is attached with either scrap wire or *lechuguilla* fibers. The ridge pole is a *quiote* of a large agave. (David H. Riskind photo)

the most humble *jacal* may have an iron wire strung up as an antenna; battery-powered radios are a source of pride and pleasure.

Floors are almost always unadulterated dirt, the native earth. In some *adobe* dwellings, a floor of puddled *adobe*, or even of *adobe* bricks is used, but the order of the day in rural housing is the earthen floor. In areas where timber and sawmills are found, the floors are rough planks, as are the ceilings and interior walls. Flagstones are rarely used.

The idea of double walls or insulated walls is unheard of. The conventional stud wall, slab-on-grade house that we slave all our lives to pay for is never seen in rural areas, except in the more recent *ejidos* or mining areas.

Take the time to look at the housing, at the materials, techniques, and lack of manufactured items that go into them. Consider that each house was built by a family for itself, generally with only the help of neighbors and whatever grew or could be found nearby. There are many valid alternatives to the wasteful and materialistic lives we lead in the United States, and this is one of them.

## Housing Questions

| | |
|---|---|
| May I go in? | ¿Puedo entrar? (¿Me permite entrar?) |
| How old is this? | ¿Cuántos años tiene esto? |
| When was it built? | ¿Cuándo fue construido? |
| Who built it? | ¿Quién lo construyó? |
| Is the house wired for electricity? | ¿Tiene instalación eléctrica esta casa? |
| The roof is covered with sheet metal. | El tejado está cubierto de chapas metálicas (de lámina). |
| It's a makeshift house. | Es una casa improvisada. |
| Adobe bricks | Adobes (m.) |
| Beam | Polín (m.); viga (f.) |
| Board | Tabla (f.) |
| Corner | Rincón (m.; inside); esquina (f.; outside) |
| Door made of roughsawn planks | Puerta de tablones (m.) |
| Doorway (or opening) | Entrada (f.); puerta (f.); vano (m.) |
| Earth or stone beehive-shaped oven | Horno (m.) |
| Fired bricks | Ladrillos (m.) |
| Floor | Piso (m.); suelo (m.) |
| Forked corner or center post | Horqueta (f.) |
| Foundation (occasionally of concrete, usually of stone, and only under walls of brick or adobe) | Fundación (f.) |
| Giant yucca (dagger) plants | Palma (f.); yucca (f.) |
| Horizontal latticework between upright posts, usually made of sotol or agave flower stalks | Quiotes (m.); piquetes (m.) |
| Hut | Choza (f.); jacal (m.); hogar (m.) |
| Joist | Viga (f.) |
| Kitchen | Cocina (f.) |
| Lime concrete (pea gravel aggregate) used to top off a dirt roof in old but well-built buildings | Chipichil (m.); tipichil (m.) |

Holes for muskets or rifles to fire through, found in very old stone buildings — *Troneras* (f.)

Mold for brick making (also concrete form) — *Molde de madera* (m.)

Mortar — *Mezcla* (f.); *mortero* (m.); *cemento* (m.)

Nail — *Clavo* (m.)

Outhouse or latrine — *Excusado* (m.); *común* (m.); *sanitario* (m.); *baño* (m.); *alcantarillado* (m.); *letrina* (f.); *retrete* (m.)

Outspout, to keep water from roof away from the base of an *adobe* wall — *Canal* (m.)

Palm leaf hut — *Palapa choza* (f.)

Plank — *Tablón* (m.)

Reinforced concrete — *Concreto armado* (m.)

River cane used for roof decking — *Carrizo* (m.); *caña* (f.)

Roof — *Techo* (m.); *tejado* (m.)

Roof beam or rafter — *Morillo* (m.); *viga* (f.)

Roof cross-decking — *Latillas* (f.); *savinos* (m.); *latas* (f.); *tablas* (f.)

Roof (flat) — *Azotea* (f.)

Screen (windows and doors) — *Tela metálica* (f.)

Steps — *Escalones* (m.)

Tiles — *Tejas* (f.) (usually hooked over or nailed to *tablas*)

Tin house — *Casa de estaño* (*lata*) (*lámina*) (f.)

Unwalled arbor for shade — *Ramada* (f.)

Upright pickets used in house walls — *Palitos* (m.); *estacas* (f.)

Upright pickets made of *agave* or *sotol* flower stalks — *Quiotes* (m.); *piquetes* (m.); *palisadas* (f.)

Wall — *Muro* (m.); *pared* (f.)

Wall (*adobe*) — *Tapia* (f.)

Wall of upright posts, pickets, or *quiotes* — *Palizada* (f.); *empalizada* (f.)

Well — *Noria* (f.); *pozo* (m.)

Window — *Ventana* (f.)

Wire — *Alambre* (m.)

Wood frame house — *Casa con armazón de madera* (f.)

The house walls are sometimes covered with adobe or mud plaster, to chink the cracks. The *adobe* is a mixture of clay (*barro*), straw (*paja*), and ashes (*ceniza*). Walls and fences or compound walls are also made of *ocotillo* stalks. Sometimes a wattle-and-daub construction is used, with slender *quiotes*, pieces of cane, or *ocotillo* stalks interwoven and plastered with *adobe* mud.

Where sawmills are nearby, the people use the outside sawn slabs (with bark on) as parts of house walls and roofs. These slabs with the bark on are called *cáscaras de madera* or *costeros de madera*.

Near the main roads entire houses may be roofed and walled with discarded 55-gallon drums. The Mexicans cut the ends out with a cold chisel, cut down the side seam the same way, and flatten the cylinder out into a rectangular sheet. Large tin cans can be used in the same way.

Near industrial or mining areas you will see corrugated sheet iron (*lámina*) or scraps of plywood (*triplex*) in use. In short, no possible building material is rejected. A piece of rusted metal on a laboring Mexican's *jacal* may have an unwritten history of having been a part of a dozen buildings, in as many locations, over half a century!

## HOUSEHOLD CUSTOMS, FOODS, AND TERMS

Because the home (*la casa*) is so important to family life, you will need to know some basics of household conversation. In a rural setting, particularly in the very remote regions, the Mexican people do not have a lot of variety in their diet. Lack of refrigeration, electricity, and modern stoves, plus the long distances over which supplies often must travel, all operate to limit the choices of foodstuffs and force selection of foods that can be stored for long periods without refrigeration.

Staples of the rural Mexican diet are dried beef (*carne seca*), onions (*cebollas*), rice (*arroz*), potatoes (*papas*), peppers (*chiles*), canned tomatoes (*tomates*), tomato sauce or paste (*salsa de tomate*), canned sardines (*sardinas*), cheese (*queso*), salt pork (*tocino*), spaghetti (*fideo*), *tortillas* of corn (*masa*) or wheat flour (*harina*), beans (*frijoles*), squash (*calabaza*), together with whatever fresh meat, vegetables, herbs, or supplements are available. Coffee (*café*) is a beverage used when it can be obtained or afforded, and in the tropics *chocolate* is prepared in many ways. For children most milk is powdered whole milk (*leche de vaca entera en polvo*), usually the brand named Nido in a pale yellow can (*bote*). Cooking oil (*aceite comestible*) is purchased in large plastic jugs, but hog lard (*manteca*), usually purchased in metal buckets, is the best for frying and for making tortillas. If fowl are kept, as they usually are at most small *ranchos*, the diet will be supplemented by

Blanched, salted strips of meat and *tripa* (washed intestines) dry in the mountain air in the State of Durango. There is no ice or refrigeration in the rural areas, so drying is the only way of preserving meat. (Will Thompson photo)

eggs (*blanquillos; yemas*) or by chicken (*pollo*) or turkey (*cócono*). Pigs (*marranos*) and kid goats (*cabritos*) round out the diet as available.

Parts of the animal or fowl that we do not normally eat are eaten with gusto by the Mexicans. Food prejudices should not be allowed to spoil your enjoyment of the country or its people, as most people around the world cannot afford to have the food prejudices we have. Try it all; you may well enjoy blood tacos! The most delicious *tamales* are made from the meat found on the head of a hog, and the head of a cow, wrapped in burlap and buried in the earth with live coals turns out to be mouth-watering *barbacoa*. Fried pork or beef tallow and skin (cracklings) are hung in a cloth bag from a rafter. These *chicharrones* are eaten in cornbread, with eggs, or alone. In hard times the diet may be *"puro tortillas,"* meaning that all the family can get or afford is corn *tortillas*.

Remember when talking about peppers (*chiles*), eggs (*huevos; blanquillos; yemas*), and milk (*leche*) that there are some dangers in using the verb *tener* (to have) when asking for these food items, since there are some secondary meanings that can cause you to be the butt of a joke. For example, *chile* is also slang for penis, and *huevos* is slang for testicles. If you ask a man *"¿Tiene usted chiles?"* he may grin and reply that he has "a big one," or if you ask "*¿Tiene usted huevos?*" he may again grin and reply that he indeed has "two big ones." To ask a young woman, "*¿Tiene usted leche?*" may be understood as "Do you have a flow of milk?" Therefore, with respect to peppers, eggs, and milk, use the verb *haber* instead of *tener*, and say "*¿Hay chiles?*" "*¿Hay huevos?*" and "*¿Hay leche?*" These questions will not cause any laughter and will avoid your getting embarrassed.

Most Mexican housewives in rural areas cook either over open fires, using a tripod (*trípode*) to support the pot or pan or a flat sheet of steel as a griddle (*comal*), or they cook over stoves made from 55-gallon steel drums, standing on end, with a firebox inside and using the top of the drum for a cooking surface. The bottom of the drum is filled with earth to give a platform for the fire to be built on, a hole is cut in the side to put wood or charcoal fuel in, and a hole is cut in the top of the drum for a piece of pipe to serve as a flue. Closer to the main routes one will find propane hotplates or kerosene stoves, but when this fuel runs short the *ranchera* resorts to wood. The pungent odor of wood smoke is typical in the morning all across Mexico. Utensils are few and very basic.

Cleotilde Chávez in her open-air kitchen at Ejido Melchor Músquiz, Coahuila. The oil drum stove and the *comal* sitting in another oil drum stove are typical of many rural Mexican kitchens. (Mickey Burleson photo)

Reyna Mota and daughter visit with María Chávez. María is patting out *tortillas* to be cooked on the *comal*. Notice the laying hen (*gallina ponedora*), the mobile garbage disposal unit of the Mexican kitchen. (Earl Nottingham photo)

## Around the House

| | |
|---|---|
| Bed | *Cama* (f.) |
| Bench | *Banca* (f.) |
| Blanket | *Cobija* (f.); *frazada* (f.); *manta* (f.) |
| Boiler | *Caldera* (f.) |
| Box | *Caja* (f.) |
| Broom | *Escoba* (f.) (small whiskbroom for cleaning the *comal* is an *escobetilla* [f.]) |
| Bucket | *Balde* (m.); *bote* (m.) |
| Cabinet | *Gabinete* (m.) |
| Candle | *Candela* (f.); *vela* (f.) |
| Chair | *Silla* (f.) |

| | |
|---|---|
| Chest of drawers | *Cómoda* (f.) |
| Closet (almost never seen) | *Ropero* (m.) |
| Crumbs | *Migas* (f.) (slang = "supper") |
| Detergent | *Detergente* (m.) |
| Dresser | *Tocador* (m.) |
| Dust | *Polvo* (m.) |
| Dustpan | *Pala de recoger la basura* (*el polvo*) (f.); *recogedor* (m.) |
| Fan | *Abanico* (m.); *ventilador* (m.) |
| Fire | *Lumbre* (f.); *fuego* (m.) |
| Furniture | *Muebles* (m.) |
| Groceries | *Abarrotes* (m.); *comestibles* (m.) |
| Lady of the house | *Ama de la casa* (f.) |
| Lamp | *Lámpara* (f.) |
| Light | *Luz* (f.) |
| Mat | *Petate* (m.) |
| Match | *Cerillo* (m.); *fósforo* (m.) |
| Mattress | *Colchón* (m.) |
| Mirror | *Espejo* (m.) |
| Mop | *Trapeador* (m.) |
| Pictures | *Cuadros* (m.); *fotos* (f.); *retratos* (m.) |
| Pillow | *Almohada* (f.) |
| Quilt | *Colcha* (f.); *cobija* (f.) |
| Radio | *Radio* (f.) |
| Refrigerator | *Refrigerador* (m.) (very rare) |
| Sack | *Saco* (m.); *costal* (m.) |
| Sewing machine | *Máquina de coser* (f.) (usually a treadle type) |
| Sheet (bed) | *Sábana* (f.) |
| Shelf | *Estante* (m.); *anaquel* (m.) |
| Sink (kitchen) | *Fregadero* (m.) |
| Soap | *Jabón* (m.) |
| Stool | *Taburete* (m.) |
| Sweep | *Barrer* |
| Table | *Mesa* (f.) |
| Towel | *Toalla* (f.) |
| Trash | *Basura* (f.) |
| Trunk | *Baúl* (m.) |
| Tub | *Bañera* (f.); *batea* (f.) |
| Washbasin | *Lavabo* (m.) |
| Water barrel | *Barril de agua* (m.); *tanque* (m.) |
| Wick | *Mecha* (f.) |

## In the Kitchen (*la Cocina*)

| | |
|---|---|
| Bottle | *Botella* (f.) |
| Bowl | *Batea* (of wood) (f.); *cuenco* (m.); *tazón* (m.) |
| Butter | *Mantequilla* (f.) |
| Can | *Lata* (f.); *bote* (m.) |
| Coffeepot | *Jarra de café* (f.); *cafetera* (f.) |
| Cook | *Cocinera(o)* (f. or m.) |
| Cup | *Taza* (f.) |
| Dishes | *Vajillas* (f.); *trastes* (m.) |
| Food | *Comida* (f.); *alimento* (m.) |
| Fork | *Tenedor* (m.) |
| Frying pan | *Sartén* (f.) |
| Glass | *Vaso* (m.) |
| Griddle | *Comal* (m.); *plancha* (f.); *tartera* (f.) |
| Grill | *Parrilla* (f.) |
| Grinding handstone | *Mano* (f.) |
| Grinding slab | *Metate* (m.); *molcajete* (m.) |
| Groceries | *Comestibles* (m.); *abarrotes* (m.) |
| Ice | *Hielo* (m.) |
| Icebox | *Hielera* (f.) |
| Knife | *Navaja* (f.); *cuchillo* (m.) |
| Ladle | *Cucharón* (m.); *cazo* (m.) |
| Mixing bowl | *Batea* (f.); *bandeja* (f.) |
| Napkins | *Servilletas* (f.) |
| Pan | *Cazuela* (f.) |
| Pepper | *Pimienta* (f.) |
| Plate | *Plato* (m.) |
| Platter (large) | *Fuente* (f.); *trinchero* (m.) |
| Pot | *Olla* (f.) |
| Refreshments | *Refrescos* (m.) |
| Salt | *Sal* (f.) |
| Saltshaker | *Salero* (m.) |
| Saucepan | *Cacerola* (f.) |
| Skewer | *Broqueta* (f.); *alambre* (m.); *palito* (m.) |
| Spatula | *Espátula* (f.) |
| Spoon | *Cuchara* (f.) |
| Stove | *Estufa* (f.) |
| Sugar | *Azúcar* (m.); *panocha* (f.); *piloncillo* (brown) (m.) |

| Sugar bowl | *Azucarera* (f.) |
|---|---|
| Teapot | *Tetera* (f.) |
| Tortilla press | *Prensa* (f.) |
| Water | *Agua* (f.) |
| Water jug | *Jarra* (f.); *garrafón* (m.); *jarrón* (m.); *olla* (f.); *olla de barro* (glazed clay pot holding one liter of water)(m.) |

## HOUSEHOLD, JUNGLE, AND VILLAGE PESTS AND OTHER VARMINTS

Mexico does not have any corner on the pest market; millions of dollars are spent annually in the United States to try to control or eradicate pests. However, due to the more open and primitive living conditions in Mexico, and the lack of refrigeration, trash collection systems, or sewage systems, in most small rural villages, the presence of such pests may be more obvious than at home, although it is debatable whether there are really more of them in Mexico or whether they are merely more visible. Mexicans do not like them any more than you do, but necessity often requires higher tolerance levels. Mexicans do not prefer to live in unsanitary conditions, and if they must, it is usually due to financial necessity, the remoteness of the area, the lack of the general government services we take for granted, or lack of good public health education and assistance. Where circumstances permit, Mexican homes are as spotless and neat as any you will find the world over, but in remote, rural villages and *ejidos* you cannot expect to find pristine conditions and must raise your personal tolerance level if you intend to visit these people. We find it to be no problem and don't think that you should let a few pests keep you from doing effective work or enjoying the experience.

In jungle hiking, ticks and chiggers can be a worse problem than mosquitoes. Neko brand soap helps take them off. When picking off ticks, pluck them gently and stick them to a strip of duct tape or freezer tape, then wad up and throw into the fire. Conduct regular checks of head and body, particularly the nooks and crannies. Check each other over, after the fashion of the monkey (*el mono*).

MOSQUITOES (*zancudos; moyotes*): not common in large numbers except in swampy areas or in the tropics. Good repellant works on them. Sleep under netting.

FLIES (*moscas*): common in most villages due to the presence of small livestock and fowl about the houses.

FLYSWATTER (*matamosca*): from *matar*, "to kill."

FLEAS (*pulgas*): common around most *jacales*, usually the common dog flea. They may bite, but don't live on you. Repellant is the answer.

TICKS (*garrapatas*): not usually a problem, except in jungles, although you may run into occasional infestations in woodlands or brush. Repellant and regular visual checks are the answer.

LICE (*piojos*): can be present and a problem, but in twenty years of Mexico travel we have held many children and patted many a head without coming home any more lousy than we were at the start. *Piojoso* in Spanish means the same as our slang word "lousy."

BEDBUGS (*chinches*): hide in the cracks and under Mexican bedsteads, so the *ranchera* often puts the bedstead out in the sun to kill them or pours boiling water into the cracks. Since you will bring your own bedroll (*mochila; tendido*) and will sleep apart from the village in most instances, these should not present a problem.

CHIGGERS (*niguas; chigoes*): the worst jungle pest in tall grass areas. Use repellant.

GNATS (*jejenes; moscos*): found in tropical and mountain areas, particularly in the rainy season. The black ones have the most potent bite; the pale ones bite without pain but leave a circular, itchy spot. Good repellant and a headnet help.

ANTS (*hormigas*): common, but only in the low coastal areas or the tropics are they much of a pest or hazard. Even a *gringo* should have enough sense to avoid sitting or camping on an ant bed.

MOTHS (*polillas*): eat Mexican blankets and other woolens (when in the larval stage) just as they eat ours. Wool is *lana*.

WEEVILS (*gorgojos*): very common pests in stored corn or meal or flour of any kind. The mealworm is also found, being the larval stage of another flying varmint. Just sift them out and the meal or flour is fine, or just ignore them and they cook up nicely. People on short rations cannot afford the luxury of throwing out food just because of a few harmless varmints.

WORMS (*gusanos*): wear shoes in Mexican villages to avoid the hookworm. Wash your hands before preparing food or eating and eat under sanitary conditions to avoid the other kind. All meats and fish should be fully cooked to avoid tapeworm and flukes, just as in the United States, and the same cooking of pork and bear meat kills the cysts of the trichina.

RATS (*ratas*): present mainly in the cities and larger towns, or in abandoned mining or timbering camps. Most rats you see in the *monte* (rural areas) will be wood rats or pack rats, neither of which pose any serious health threat, although they may carry away keys, earrings, or small objects, so these should not be left out at night.

MICE (*ratones*): the house mouse, has followed humankind all over the world and is recognized as a commensal. Mexico has mice, but they present no health hazard to you. If you don't like them, carry a mousetrap (*ratonera*) with you.

CONENOSED BUG (KISSING BUG) (*bicho*): generic for "bug"; we do not know the specific Spanish name for this blood-sucking insect, but it can transmit Chagas' disease. It has a long, piercing mouthpart, folded back under a head that seems too small and thin for the rest of the body, and the length of the body is usually less than one inch. The bug appears flattened when viewed from above, with flat wings on the upper body surface. The edge of the abdomen shows outside the wings when viewed from above, and has a checkered edge design of alternating orange and black rectangles. This insect is reclusive during the day, coming out at night to feed. Avoid it by not sleeping in old huts or sheds and by making your bed away from rodent dens or the immediate area of camp lanterns, since it is attracted to lights at night.

SCORPIONS (*alacranes*): found all over Mexico just as in the United States, and the sting, although painful, is usually not harmful. There are two species on the Arizona border that have a neurotoxic venom and are considered dangerous. The species *Centruroides durangensis* is found in northern Mexico, and can also be potentially dangerous to humans. Scorpions can be avoided by the following steps. When going to bed, don't leave clothing or boots on the ground and make camp in as barren an area as you can find. When arising, shake out your clothing and boots before putting them on; this should become standard practice in all camp situations. When collecting rocks or firewood, you may find scorpions under rocks, under the bark of dead wood, or inside rotted wood. Whack the wood on the ground before gathering it to your body. Wear leather gloves for turning rocks or gathering firewood.

TARANTULAS (*tarántulas*): large, hairy, black or brown spiders occasionally seen in the desert. They are generally harmless, and they bite only when provoked and handled. The bite is painful, but not poisonous to humans. If handled gently, they can be allowed to crawl up your arm or leg. The hairs of the tarantula are easily shed and are very irritating to the eyes, mouth, etc., so it is best to avoid kissing them.

SPIDERS (*arañas*; *sartenes*) (spider web = *telaraña*): the Spanish names of the brown recluse and the black widow (other than *viuda negra* for the latter) are unknown to us, but they are found in Mexico just as in the United States. Avoid old buildings with dark corners, old privies, and don't reach into spots where you cannot see. Shake out clothing before putting it on. Since you will not usually sleep inside a Mexican hut, you have little risk of exposure to these spiders.

COCKROACH (*cucaracha*): found in any village or town, but much less commonly in the very rural areas. They do no harm if you keep prepared food properly covered.

SNAKES (*culebras*): scarce and seldom seen in the deserts, but they are there. They are mostly nocturnal, preferring to remain hidden during the day. In cold weather they are torpid, but in warm weather they are active at night. The rattlesnake exists in several species, and is generally called *cascabel* or *víbora*. The coral snake (*coralillo*) and copperhead are found, but very rarely. Generally, use a flashlight when walking at night, avoid stepping or reaching into spots where you cannot see clearly, and make plenty of noise while walking to give them time to retreat. In tropical Mexico, the *barba amarilla* (yellow beard) is found in jungle and canebreak and is aggressive and dangerous, as is the *fer de lance*, or lancehead viper. All are related to the rattlesnake (pit vipers). Just exercise caution and avoid walking at night in jungle or carelessly walking through thick undergrowth without keeping a very sharp eye out for them.

BATS (*murciélagos*): common and mostly harmless. You will sometimes find them flitting overhead near your camp lantern, or swooping low across ponds or stock tanks, feeding on insects. In caves you should avoid areas of heavy bat infestation, as rabies can on rare occasions be caught from the airborne virus. Avoid stirring up the dust of bat guano (bat manure), as some diseases can be contracted from organisms in it. Wear a dust filter mask or use a doubled bandana across mouth and nose when exploring such caves and old mines. In the deep tropics, where the vampire bat (*vampiro*) is found, sleep under netting.

SKUNKS (*zorrillos*): common enough that you will occasionally encounter one after dark. It is rare but possible that you might encounter a skunk with rabies, just as you might in the United States. If a skunk wanders into your camp, such behavior is probably not natural, and the animal may be rabid; therefore, avoid contact. A quick whack with a machete will behead without stink, if you are good with the instrument! If courage fails, just herd the animal out of camp by making lots of noise. Most people who are bitten by skunks are bitten at night while sleeping on the ground. Sleep on a cot or in a tent and you avoid this remote risk.

CATTLE (*vacas*): may be wild enough to make a run at a person on foot. Usually, they just run from the odd odor of the *gringo*. Watch out for range bulls with horns, and avoid getting between young calves and their mothers. If no safe spot is available, shout, wave your arms, and "charge" the oncoming cow, and she will usually yield to your bluff and retreat.

VILLAGE DOGS (*perros*): common in Mexico and usually thin, underfed curs of shorthaired breeds and of medium or smaller size. They are sneaky and will slip up behind you. Since the *gringo* odor is strange to them, they often react with alarm or occasionally with hostility. Approach them with a friendly word, as you would a strange dog back home, and stop to let the dog sniff you. We sometimes extend the back of a hand to the dog to sniff, but do not attempt to pet or play with them. Once they are aware that you are not a threat, you normally have no trouble with them. If bitten in Mexico, seek rabies treatment with DEV in the United States. Do not allow your children to tease or play with them, as they are not usually handled as kindly as family pets are here and may be snappish. In a real tough situation, quickly stoop and act as if you are picking up a rock to throw, and they will usually retreat. (Better still, pick up a rock and clobber the cur!)

VINEGAROON (*vinagrón* or *alacrán gigante*): harmless but dangerous-looking member of the whip scorpion family. It looks like an overgrown scorpion with a whiplike tail (no stinger) and much heavier pincers. The name comes from the vinegarlike odor that the insect releases when disturbed. They will come to lights at night, scuttling across the desert floor in search of insect prey. They grow to a length of six inches in the Mexican deserts, but are harmless curiosities and should not be killed.

From this list of pests and varmints, you can see that Mexico has about the same problems as we have, and none of them are anything approaching a real hazard that would keep you from enjoying your trip in Mexico. Just use good judgment and restraint, and no serious problem should be encountered from any of them; but if all else fails:

| | |
|---|---|
| Beware of the dog! | ¡Cuídese del perro! |
| Will this dog bite? | ¿Muerde este perro? |
| He won't do a thing! | ¡No pica! |
| His bark's worse than his bite! | ¡No es tan fiero como parece! |
| Chase him out of here. | Échelo de aquí. |
| Chase that dog away! | ¡Ahuyente ese perro! |
| Throw the damn cat out! | ¡Eche afuera al maldito gato! |
| He's not worth a damn! | ¡Maldito sea! (¡No vale un comino!) |
| That dog is very gentle. | Ese perro es muy dócil (manso). |

## FOOD PREJUDICES TO OVERCOME

The roadrunner (*el paisano; el corre camino*), a large ground-dwelling bird of the cuckoo family, is sometimes eaten for food and is also used by *curanderos* (healers) as an ingredient in a curative stew. The flesh is tough and a bit gamey by our standards, but not nearly as tough as boiled whole vulture (*zopilote*), a folk remedy for venereal disease! When eaten as food, the roadrunner is usually stewed to tenderize it.

In many of the northern desert areas you can commonly see the kangaroo rat (*rata canguro*) out foraging at night. A long tail helps balance these powerful runners and jumpers (broadjumps of fifteen feet or more are not uncommon when the rodent is pressed) and the hindquarters are very well developed, looking much like frog legs when skinned. The Mexicans use vehicle headlights or flashlights to blind the kangaroo rats and club them with a stick, or they trap them. They become the desert equivalent of frog legs at parties and beer busts. They taste much better than frog legs, so don't hesitate to eat them.

The wood rat or pack rat, found in both desert and mountain habitats in Mexico, is better eating than any squirrel. You can easily trap a mess of them overnight in any mining or lumbering camp with snap traps (*ratoneras*) baited with a mixture of peanut butter and rolled oats. Fry them and ¡Qué sabroso!

In the Indian areas of the western Sierra Madres the small boys are constantly hunting for any form of small game: wood rats, chipmunks, rock squirrels, tree squirrels, any form of bird life, large lizards, and snakes, all go into the pot. The mountain streams are full of small, circular rock fish traps, and it is not uncommon to encounter a small boy with a green branch strung full of fish we would consider too small for bait, all headed for the pot.

The iguana is a large lizard of the western tropical regions (which can be found to extend into the bottoms of the deep *barrancas* of the western *sierras*) growing to a length of several feet. It looks horrible, but has white meat better than chicken. It goes into the pot!

If a fat puppy is here one day and gone the next, say, "*Buen provecho*" in its memory!

The rattlesnake (*cascabel*) is more of a folk medicine (possessing powerful curative effects because of its known venom in life) than a dietary supplement, but you will find skinned rattlesnakes dried and hanging under the *ramada* of many Mexican homes, and lots of tough old *vaqueros* eat a little *molida de cascabel* nearly every day to ward off illness.

The burro is not only a pet but good eating! A fat young burro is favored fare of the mountain lion, and generations of lions can't be wrong! Much burro meat is made into *carne seca* and used in *machacado*, which can be either a dried meat stew or a scramble of dried meat, peppers, and eggs. Alone, burro meat is sold as *machaca* or *carne seca*.

*Menudo* is a soup or stew made of *nixtamal* (hominy) and the feet or lower legs of a steer, plus *tripa de leche* (washed beef intestines). It can be one of the best meals you ever ate! If it smells good, don't hesitate to dive right in!

Generations of tough, healthy, and happy *campesinos* cannot be wrong, so gut up and try these strange foods when they are available to you. Will Rogers once said that there are two things you do not want to see made: legislation and sausage. Most of you eat sausage all the time, and we can promise you that most of the above food items, properly prepared, are not only cleaner but lots better than most sausage!

## EJIDOS

The following list of questions will not get all the information you may want about *ejidos* but it will cover some of the areas that we are interested in. Although there are certainly successful and prosperous *ejidos*, there are also a great many that linger on the edge of survival. Most of them seem to lose rather than gain in population, particularly in the more marginal lands of the arid north. It is a tough life in the arid-land *ejidos*, and most of the people are there only because it was worse where they came from, or because they like the freedom and independence that a struggle for existence in a harsh environment provides.

We have noted a high death rate among children. Most of the graves you see in new *ejidos* are those of children. The small mounds, fenced with *quiotes* of the *sotol* plant, often fill us with sadness and make us thankful for the readily available medical care and the adequate diet that our children benefit from.

Before launching off into this type of informal sociological study, make friends with your informant. Some of these questions are apt to be considered personal, so wait until you are at ease with the informant and feel that the time is right.

| | |
|---|---|
| Where do you get your drinking water? | ¿Dónde obtienen su agua potable? |
| How is the water transported to the *ejido*? | ¿Cómo traen el agua al ejido? |
| Does the water supply ever dry up? | ¿A veces el manantial de agua se seca totalmente? |
| Does the water come from a river, spring, or well? | ¿De dónde viene el agua? ¿Del río? ¿De un ojo o de una noria? |
| Is the water treated in any way to make it potable? | ¿Tratan el agua con químicos u otro modo para hacerlo potable? |

Does the government provide any direct assistance to members of the *ejido*, such as money, food, or equipment?

¿El gobierno da asistencia directamente a los ejidatarios, como moneda, comestibles, o equipaje?

What direct assistance is furnished?

¿Qué clase de asistencia está proveída?

How many children have died in the *ejido* in the past five years?

¿Cuántos niños han muerto en este ejido en los cinco años pasados?

What is the most common cause of death?

¿Cuál es la causa de mortalidad más común?

Is there any medical care available?

¿Hay asistencia médica disponible?

Where is the nearest doctor or clinic?

¿Dónde está el médico o la clínica más cerca (próxima)?

Do any public health doctors or nurses ever come?

¿Vienen médicos al ejido?

How often?

¿Con qué frecuencia?

Are the *ejido* lands fenced?

¿(Todo) El terreno del ejido está bajo alambre (cerca)? (¿(Todo) El terreno del ejido está separado con cerca?)

How many hectares are in the *ejido* lands? (1 hectare = 2.5 acres)

¿Cuántas hectáreas hay en el terreno del ejido?

Where are the corners or property markers located? How are they marked? Are there markers on the boundaries?

¿Dónde se encuentran los límites del ejido? ¿Cómo están marcados? ¿Hay jalones o monumentos en las esquinas?

What is the full name of the *ejido*?

¿Cuál es el nombre completo del ejido?

How many people are in the *ejido*?

¿Cuántos habitantes tiene el ejido?

Is the *ejido* growing or getting smaller?

¿El ejido está en crecimiento, o va reduciendo?

What is the reason for people leaving?

¿Qué es la razón por qué la gente va dejando? (¿Cuál es la razón por qué la gente se va yendo?)

What do you think the future holds for the *ejido*?

¿Qué hay para el futuro (el porvenir) del ejido?

Are any of the men holding jobs outside the *ejido*?

¿Algunos de los ejidatarios tienen trabajo afuera del ejido?

What kind of work are they doing? And where?

¿En qué trabajan y dónde?

Is there a school for the children? | ¿Hay una escuela para los niños?
Is there a teacher for the school? Full time? | ¿Hay maestro (maestra) para la escuela? ¿Constante?
How long have you been living in the *ejido*? | ¿Desde cuándo vive usted (viven ustedes) en el ejido?
Does the *ejido* have any trouble with its neighbors (miners) (timber cutters)? | ¿Hay problemas con vecinos (con mineros) (con leñadores)?
What sort of troubles do they have? | ¿Qué clase de problemas tienen?
Do the people ever suffer from lack of food? | ¿La gente sufre de alimentación deficiente? (¿Los habitantes sufren de alimentación deficiente?)
When food is scarce, what do the people eat? | ¿Cuando el alimento está escaso, qué come la gente?
Does the government provide any emergency food? | ¿El gobierno les da substancia alimenticia en emergencias?
Are any foods grown in the *ejido*? What kinds? | ¿Crecen algunos alimentos en el ejido? ¿Cuáles tipos?
What kind of *ejido* is this? | ¿Qué tipo de ejido es?
We are trying to better living conditions here. | Estamos tratando de mejorar aquí las condiciones de vida.
We will be better off if we move. | Estaremos mejor si nos mudamos.
What is your name? | ¿Cómo se llama usted? (¿Cuál es su nombre?) (Dígame su nombre.)
My name is Michael Vargas. | Me llamo Miguel Vargas.
How old are you? | ¿Cuántos años tiene usted? (¿Qué edad tiene?)
I am thirty. | Tengo treinta años.
When were you born? | ¿Cuál es la fecha de su nacimiento?
I was born January 1, 1953. | Yo nací el primero de enero de mil novecientos cincuenta y tres.
Where were you born? | ¿Dónde nació usted?
I was born in Durango, Mexico. | Yo nací en Durango, México.
Where do you live? | ¿Dónde vive usted? (¿Dónde está su domicilio?)
I live on Las Norias ranch. | Vivo en Rancho las Norias.
What education do you have? | ¿Qué educación ha tenido usted?
I have no education. | No tengo educación. (Nada.)
I do not read or write. | Yo no sé leer ni escribir.

| | |
|---|---|
| Are you married? | ¿Es usted casado(a)? |
| No, I'm single. | No, soy soltero(a). |
| Yes, I'm married. | Sí, soy casado(a). |
| What is the name of your wife? | ¿Cuál es el nombre de su esposa? |
| My wife is María Vargas. | Mi esposa es María Vargas. |
| Do you own your house? | ¿Es usted propietario de su casa? |
| Yes, I own it. | Sí, mi casa es mi propiedad. |
| Do you get money from the government? | ¿Recibe dinero del gobierno? |
| No, I do not receive money from the government. | No, no recibo dinero del gobierno. |
| What work do you do? | ¿Qué clase de trabajo tiene usted? |
| I am a cowboy. | Soy vaquero. |
| Always a cowboy. | Siempre vaquero. |
| Do you like your work? | ¿Está contento con su trabajo? |
| Yes, sir. | Sí, señor. Estoy muy contento. |
| Are you happy here? | ¿Está usted contento aquí? |
| Yes, I'm happy. | Sí, estoy alegre (contento). |
| Do you really feel abused? | ¿De veras siente usted que le tratan mal? |
| | |
| Where do your parents live? | ¿Dónde viven sus padres? |
| My father is dead. My mother lives in Músquiz. | Mi padre está muerto. Mi madre vive en Músquiz. |
| Do you have brothers or sisters? | ¿Tiene usted hermanos? |
| Yes, three of them. | Sí, tengo tres hermanos. |
| Where are they? | ¿Dónde están sus hermanos? |
| They also live in Músquiz. | Viven en Músquiz también. |
| How is your family? | ¿Cómo está su familia? |
| They are all well. | Todos están bien. |
| May I accompany you home? | ¿Me permite acompañarle a su casa? |
| | |
| Yes, but we can only accommodate three more people. | Sí, pues, podemos acomodar solamente a tres personas más. |
| I wish to introduce you to my mother, Jane. | Quiero presentarlo a mi madre, Juana. |
| Mother, this is my friend Roberto. | Mamá, este es mi amigo Roberto. |
| I'm very pleased to meet you, Madam. | Tengo mucho gusto en conocerla, Señora. |
| Equally, Sir. | Igualmente, Señor. |
| Are you four acquainted? | ¿Se conocen ustedes cuatro? |
| We met them by accident. | Los encontramos por casualidad. |

## PERSONAL AND COMMUNITY HISTORY

(Note: The following is not intended as a conversation.)

Who were the original inhabitants? — *¿Quiénes fueron los primeros habitantes?*

I was born and reared on a farm (ranch). — *Nací y me crié en una granja (un rancho).*

My parents are still living. — *Mis padres viven aún.*

We live in central Chihuahua. — *Vivimos en el centro de Chihuahua.*

Do you live here? — *¿Vive usted aquí?*

Where are you staying? — *¿Dónde se aloja usted?*

I live here. — *Vivo aquí.*

I'm staying with friends. — *Vivo con unos amigos.*

What subjects did you study in school last year? — *¿Qué asignaturas materias estudió usted en la escuela el año pasado?*

What happened next? — *¿Qué pasó luego?*

What made you come here? — *¿Qué móvil tuvo usted para venir aquí? (¿Por qué vino usted aquí?)*

We have lived here many years. — *Tenemos muchos años de vivir aquí.*

How long did you stay there? — *¿Qué tanto (Cuánto) tiempo se quedó (pasó) usted allí?*

When did you leave El Veinte and how did you travel from there to here? — *¿Cuándo salió de El Veinte y cómo viajó de allá a aquí?*

How did you come from La Linda to Las Norias? — *¿Cómo vino usted de La Linda a Las Norias?*

Are you married? — *¿Es casado(a)?*

Are you single? — *¿Es soltero(a)?*

Yes, I'm married. — *Sí, soy casado(a).*

Tell me, please. — *Dígame, por favor.*

Tell me, what is your name? — *¿Dígame, cómo se llama usted?*

Where were you born? — *¿En dónde nació?*

In Mexico. — *En México.*

In what state and town? — *¿En qué estado y pueblo?*

I was born in Músquiz, Coahuila. — *Nací en Músquiz, Coahuila.*

How long have you been here? — *¿Qué tanto tiempo tiene usted aquí?*

Of what country are you a citizen or a national? — *¿De qué país es usted ciudadano o nacional? (¿Cuál es su ciudadanía o nacionalidad?)*

Where are you from? — *¿De dónde viene usted?*

From Durango. — *De Durango.*

Tell me the name of the ranch, the town, the state, and the country. — *Dígame el nombre del rancho, del pueblo, del estado, y del país.*

What country were you born in? — *¿En qué país nació usted?*

Where do you live now? — *¿Dónde vive usted ahora?*

In El Veinte, near La Linda. — *Yo vivo en El Veinte, cerca de La Linda.*

What is your permanent address? — *¿Cuál es su dirección permanente?*

Did you leave your family in El Veinte? — *¿Dejó su familia en El Veinte?*

On what day, month, and year were you born? — *¿En qué día, mes, y año nació usted?*

What is your birthdate? — *¿Cuál es la fecha de su nacimiento?*

I was born April 2, 1938. — *Yo nací el dos de abril de mil novecientos treinta y ocho.*

What education do you have? — *¿Qué educación tiene usted?*

None. I cannot read or write. — *Nada. Yo no sé leer ni escribir.*

How long have you had ———? — *¿Desde cuando tiene usted ———?*

Do you live alone? — *¿Vive usted solo(a)?*

Have you been away? — *¿Ha estado usted fuera?*

How long? — *¿Cuánto tiempo? (¿Qué tanto tiempo?)*

What part of the country do you hail from? — *¿De qué parte del país viene usted?*

Does Santiago live here? — *¿Vive Santiago aquí?*

Do they live here? — *¿Viven ellos aquí?*

## PHOTOGRAPHS

When you encounter someone in rural Mexico, it is best to use care and courtesy and show respect for the privacy that all Mexicans value highly. Before wandering up to someone and taking his or her photograph or taking one of home or yard, pass some pleasantries and ask for permission. In Indian areas some of the more rural folk do not wish to be photographed for various reasons, all good enough for them and therefore good enough for us.

Is picture taking permitted? — *¿Se puede (permite) tomar fotos?*

May I please take your photo? — *¿Por favor, puedo tomarle una fotografía?*

Can I take your picture? — *¿Puedo (Permite) tomarle una foto?*

A *ranchero* of Chihuahua, with pistol on his hip, writes his address for use in sending him a print of his picture. There seem to be more firearms carried in the western *sierras* than in most other parts of Mexico. (Will Thompson photo)

| | |
|---|---|
| Photograph | *Retrato* (m.); *fotografía* (f.); *foto* (f.) |
| Please stand over there. | *Por favor, párese allá.* |
| Your (house) (yard) is very interesting (pretty). | *Su (casa) (jardín) es muy interesante (bonita).* |
| May I take a photo of it? | *¿Puedo (Permite) tomar una foto de su (casa) (jardín)?* |
| Do you mind if I watch your work? | *¿Le molesto si veo (observo) su trabajo?* |
| May I take a photo of the type of work you are doing? | *¿Puedo tomar una foto de su trabajo (de usted trabajando)?* |
| I am interested in the many different styles of houses. | *Me interesan los diferentes estilos de casas.* |
| Your house is in a different style. | *Su casa es de un estilo diferente.* |

(Note: See the section on rural housing for more information and vocabulary.)

| | |
|---|---|
| Do you come from a distant state? | *¡Viene de algún estado lejano!* *(¡Viene de otro lugar!)* |
| May I photograph your house? | *¡Por favor, puedo fotografiar su casa!* |
| May I see the inside of the house? | *¡Me permite ver el interior de la casa!* |
| Yes. Let's go inside. | *Sí, entremos.* |
| They are building a new house. | *Están construyendo una casa nueva.* |
| Do you mind if we come along? | *¡Le molesta a usted si le acompañamos!* |
| How is your work coming along? | *¡Cómo va su trabajo!* |
| Your children are beautiful. | *Sus niños son muy hermosos.* |
| May I take their photograph? | *¡Los puedo (Permite) fotografiar!* |
| I will give (send) you a copy. | *Le doy (mando) una copia.* |
| Could you send this to me? | *¡Podría usted mandarme esto!* |
| Do you have mail service out here? | *¡Hay servicio de correo aquí!* |
| What is your name and your mailing address? | *¡Cuál es su nombre y su dirección particular de correos!* |
| Here is my address. | *Aquí están mis señas. (Aquí está mi dirección.)* |
| Please write your name and mailing address. | *Escriba su nombre y su dirección de correos.* |

The Polaroid and Kodak instant cameras so readily available in the United States can, if properly used, be helpful in establishing friendly relations in rural areas. Don't just hop out of your truck and start shooting; take the time to visit and demonstrate courtesy and genuine interest. Then, if there are children about the *rancho*, particularly *niños* in arms or toddlers, a tasteful snapshot, taken with permission and given to the mother as a gift (*regalo*), is almost always appreciated.

Certain Indian groups have a near-phobia of having their photographs taken. You should respect their wishes. Among other Indian groups the portrait is a very serious event, and you can hardly coax a smile, so forget "cheese" and adapt to their customs.

Once you break the ice, be sure you have enough film packs for everyone nearby, as a flood of children may threaten to engulf you! Always be fair and develop a feel for the relative status of your subject or family. In other words, do not leave out the child or grandchild of the *jefe*!

## RESPECT FOR THE DEAD

The backcountry traveler may encounter family and community activities related to terminal illness, death, and burial of members of the group. It is important to have some basic understanding of the rural Mexican's attitude toward death and dying and some of the customs and traditions that accompany death and burial. Because of the very diverse racial, ethnic, and religious background of rural groups from different geographical areas, it is not within the scope of this work to give complete treatment. Some of our generalizations may not apply everywhere, for example, in traditional Indian areas where customs and practices may vary even from village to village. However, if you understand the typical attitude toward death and dying, and if you are sensitive to the feelings of people around you, you should be able to avoid actions that might be considered rude or thoughtless.

Because of the relatively high death rate among children, the relatively low standard of living, and the lack of adequate health care delivery systems in most remote areas, most rural Mexicans have a fatalistic attitude toward death. It is often regarded as an entity, a distinct "being," rather than the result of natural or accidental processes of termination of life. Some believe that a person is foreordained for a particular manner and time of dying. Others believe strongly that "fate," "destiny," or "luck" (*suerte*) is the determining factor and that humanity is essentially helpless to change its destiny or its luck. Men, in particular, perhaps in part because of their more *macho* image, are more inclined to fatalism and to strict self-control of the outward appearances of emotion around the dead and dying. On the other hand, in certain locations and among certain people you will see outpourings of grief as demonstrative as any you have ever witnessed at home. If you see the men sitting around at a wake, drinking alcoholic beverages and playing at cards, you may wonder whether they are callous or unfeeling, but please do not prejudge them. Remember that this is not your culture, and that your understanding (like ours) is imperfect.

If you encounter a situation related to terminal illness, death, burial, or a wake, we have several suggestions that should help you avoid mistakes. If you drive into a village where a funeral is in process, pull over and stop at once and get out of the way. The procession is usually on foot. Cut off your engine, turn off any radio or tape deck, and don't just pile out of the vehicle and scatter. Remove hats and stand by quietly and with respect (*respeto*) until all have passed. You may bow your head in prayer or give the sign of the cross as the mourners pass. Avoid taking photographs or otherwise acting as if the procession or other burial activity is a form of entertainment. You will be best served and make a better impression by appearing to understand and join in their grief and by appearing to understand the serious nature of the event. Remember that emotions may be on edge and near the surface, and that your reception as a stranger may be affected adversely by any intrusive or unthinking attitude on your part. If, contrary to our advice, you are looking for the *cantina*, you will do well to go on to some other spot. Even if the men gather at the *cantina* after the funeral, they may not be in a good mood, and the chance of some form of confrontation is increased. Respect and reverence are expected perhaps more of you than of the Mexicans, since they know very well what is acceptable and what is not, whereas you are forced to guess. Guess on the side of good manners and human sympathy and you will rarely go wrong.

When a family member dies, many Mexicans go through a period of formal mourning. *Estar de luto* and *tener de luto* convey the idea of both public or formal mourning and private mourning. The form and degree of public mourning is expressed most often in the clothing worn. The wearing of only black clothing means one is *en luto completo* (in complete mourning), whereas one *en medio luto* may wear white, gray, or purple. The more conservative and traditional the family and the community, the more strictly the dress code is followed, and women seem to follow it more closely than men in all areas. Some widows remain *de luto* for the rest of their lives, whereas others follow the dress code for a definite period of from one to as long as twenty years. In less traditional communities and families, *luto* is not observed beyond the funeral.

The graves of loved ones are regularly visited, and one can often find evidence of recent family visits, usually in the form of a tin can filled with fresh or recently wilted flowers, in even the most remote cemeteries.

Along the roads and highways you will encounter numerous crosses and occasionally even small concrete or stone altars. These usually signify the location of the accidental death of a family member. Where a bus or truck loaded with people has been involved in a fatal wreck (*choque*), you may find a dozen or more crosses or altars, one for each person killed. Even though these places do not represent the burial site, you will find that many of these small markers are visited and maintained over a period of many years and fresh flowers and/or candles may be placed nearby from time to time.

Actual mortuary customs vary widely, depending on the geographical area, the degree of religious influence in the area, the particular religious practices of the family, the degree to which the family and community is traditional and conservative, and whether the racial and

Roadside crosses and small altars are regularly placed by the families of accident or murder victims, located as near as possible to the scene of the tragic event. Here, the death obviously occurred in the canyon far below this roadside cross. Relatives frequently maintain these crosses year after year. (Will Thompson photo)

ethnic composition of the community is predominantly Indian or *mestizo*. Generally, the more complex and elaborate public observances and funerals are found in areas where the people are mostly Catholic and of Indian extraction.

Although we have insufficient experience to give detailed accounts of the funeral process, we can give some generalizations that may help you understand what is going on. In most remote areas there are no churches nearby and the activities take place mainly at the home of the deceased or a relative. There is usually a wake, where the family serves refreshments, cigarettes, sometimes alcohol, coffee, and the like. The wake usually lasts from death until the funeral. The women gather and chat quietly, sometimes praying for the soul of the deceased and for the family; the men also gather and may play cards or drink. Often a cross of lime and sand is poured onto a piece of paper on the floor or a table near the head of the bed (*cabecera*) and this cross is "raised" in a later ceremony. There is often a second short wake about nine days after death, at the time of the "raising of the cross." A third and usually final overnight wake may be held one year after death.

There is usually a formal funeral procession on foot to the burial site, and a cross on which is carved or painted the name of the deceased and the date of death is placed on the grave. An old practice that is still used on occasion is the noting of three letters on the grave marker: E.P.D. (*En Paz Descanse*), the equivalent of our RIP. In rural areas the fresh grave is usually covered with heavy stones to ward off coyotes, or a small fence of thornbush is built around it for the same purpose.

Funerals for adults are occasions for demonstration of grief and are usually solemn, but the funeral for a child may be considerably different in tone. Many (but certainly not all) rural Mexicans hold to the Catholic belief that the soul of a child goes directly to Heaven; thus the funeral of a child may have more of the appearance of a celebration. In areas with this tradition, the child is dressed as a little angel (*angelito*), often in sandals covered with gold paper and in robes or gowns befitting the innocent new angel. A garland of flowers may be placed about the head, and ribbons often adorn the body. The music or singing at a child's funeral under such circumstances is often light and gay, befitting a happy occasion. Despite the outward appearances, it has been our observation that among the immediate family members the personal grief over the loss of a child is usually every bit as deep as that experienced in our own culture.

In essentially pure Indian communities their own tribal traditions are observed, often with little admixture of Catholic beliefs and practices. We cannot be much more specific than this, because we cannot communicate with the Indians in their own languages and cannot be sure that we understand the meaning to them of the things we have observed. However, the rules of polite conduct suggested above should serve you well in any area of Mexico.

In many areas of Mexico we have encountered one particular flower that older women often grow in the dooryard because it has long-lasting blooms for use in funerals and at wakes. This is *cresta de gallo*, an amaranth native to tropical Mexico and widely planted both there and in this country, where we know it also by the name cockscomb. We speculate that it may have a very long history of domestication and mortuary use in Mexico.

Some of the following words or expressions may be of use to you when you encounter death, burial, and mourning.

| | |
|---|---|
| Cemetery | *Panteón* (m.); *camposanto* (m.); *cementerio* (m.) |
| Grave | *Sepultura* (f.); *tumba* (f.) |
| Hole (in ground) | *Hoyo* (m.) |
| Coffin | *Ataúd* (m.); *caja* (f.) |
| Gravestone | *Lápida* (f.); *monumento* (m.) |
| Burial | *Entierro* (m.); *sepultura* (f.) |
| Bury | *Enterrar*; *inhumar*; *sepultar* |
| Funeral | *Funeral* (m.); *exequias* (f.) |
| In mourning | *De luto* |
| Wake | *Velorio* (m.); *velatorio* (m.) |
| Hold a wake | *Velar* |
| Mourn | *Lamentar* |
| All Saints' Day, November 1 | *Día de Todos los Santos* |
| All Souls' Day, November 2 | *Día de los Difuntos* |

# 10. Work, Building, and Processes in Northern Mexico

**I**t is most interesting to stop and watch the people of Mexico at work. Many of their methods are primitive by our standards but efficient. In general, Mexico is a labor-intensive nation, and the "primitive" technology of its rural *gente* is an appropriate technology under the circumstances. Oftentimes they make do with very little, in the materialistic view that colors our observations. Many of their methods and processes are age-old, handed down through the generations and refined by the hands and minds of their ancestors.

Rather than just intrude into their privacy, it is best to seek permission politely before stopping to watch or take pictures. Permission is generally freely granted.

| | |
|---|---|
| What are you doing? | *¿Qué hace usted?* |
| This is interesting work. May I watch you? | *Su trabajo es interesante. ¿Me permite verlo?* |
| Do you mind if I watch your work for a while? | *¿Si no le molesta, puedo (permítame) observar su trabajo?* |
| How do you do that? | *¿Cómo le hace?* |
| Will you show me how you make that (do that)? | *¿Por favor, enséñeme cómo hacerlo?* |
| There's an art to it. | *Hay una técnica para ello.* |
| Will you sell this work? | *¿Vende su trabajo?* |
| It is very interesting and I would like to buy it and take it home to show my family. | *Es interesante y me gustaría comprarla(lo) para llevársela(lo) a mi familia.* |
| I will trade you this ——— for that ———. | *Quiero canjear esto por ———.* (*Quiero cambiar esto por ———.*) (*Le cambio esto por ———.*) |
| ——— pesos is all I can afford to pay. | *——— pesos es todo lo que puedo pagar.* |
| May I photograph your work? | *¿Puedo tomar una foto de su trabajo?* |

| | |
|---|---|
| What cargo are you hauling? | *¿Qué carga lleva?* |
| Are you always busy? | *¿Está usted siempre ocupado(a)?* |
| I have nothing to do. | *No tengo nada que hacer.* |
| What's that strange-looking object? | *¿Qué es ese objeto tan raro?* |
| Do you mind if we come along? | *¿Le molesta a usted que le acompañemos?* |
| How is your work coming along? | *¿Cómo va su trabajo?* |
| May we watch the work? | *¿Podemos ver el trabajo?* |
| May I take pictures? | *¿Puedo (Permítame) tomar fotos?* |
| Is there a kiln or drying yard for the timber (boards)? | *¿Hay secador para la madera (los tablones)?* |
| What types of trees are you cutting? | *¿Qué clase de árboles están cortando?* |
| What is the name of this tree (pointing)? | *¿Cómo se llama este árbol?* |
| What is the name of the tree this log came from? | *¿Cómo se llama el árbol de esta madera? (¿De qué árbol sacan esta madera?)* |
| This is very beautiful. | *Esto es muy hermoso.* |
| The house is well built. | *La casa está bien construida.* |
| How old is this? | *¿Cuántos años tiene esto?* |
| When was it built? | *¿Cuándo fue construido?* |
| The house was built in 1945. | *La casa fue construida en mil novecientos cuarenta y cinco.* |
| Who built it? | *¿Quien la construyó?* |
| May I see the inside of the ———? | *¿Puedo ver el interior de ———?* |
| May I go in? | *¿Puedo (Permítame) entrar?* |
| It's closed. | *Está cerrado(a).* |
| No admission. | *Se prohibe la entrada.* |
| Let's go inside. | *Entremos.* |
| What is that used for? | *¿Para qué sirve eso? (¿Para qué es eso?)* |
| That is used for ———. | *Eso sirve para ———. (Es para ———.)* |
| Where is the boss? | *¿Dónde está el jefe (patrón)?* |
| What area is he working in? | *¿En qué zona trabaja él?* |
| The work has become harder. | *El trabajo se ha hecho más difícil.* |
| They have cut down most of the trees for firewood (posts). | *Han cortado la mayor parte de los árboles para leña (postes).* |

## TWO NORTHERN MEXICO COTTAGE INDUSTRIES

### Rope Making

In much of the Chihuahuan Desert region, which comprises most of north central Mexico, there grows a family of very useful plants known as *agaves* to the scientist and to the Mexican as *maguey* (century plant) or *lechuguilla* or *mezcal*, depending on their size. *Magueyes* usually occur on the mountain slopes and are generally more or less isolated plants, but may grow in large colonies. *Lechuguilla* is a much smaller *agave* found in dense stands on limestone flats, ridges, and slopes, sometimes becoming so dense as to require *"lechuguilla* stomping" with sturdy boots to walk through it. The leaves of both plants are armed at the tips with strong spines, and they also have hooked spines along the lateral leaf margins. The leaves of the giant dagger (*yucca; palma*) also furnish fibers and are used in much the same way.

These plants have abundant, long fibers (*ixtle*) within the fleshy leaves. Because the leaves sprout from a heart in the base of the plant and grow outward and upward from the common base, they often have a center section of newer leaves closely pressed together in the form of a spine-tipped conical bunch, the *quiote* (*jiote*). The *ixtlero* (gatherer of *ixtle*) walks through the *lechuguilla* with a sack (*morral*) slung over his shoulder and a special tool with a sharpened iron ring and a short wooden handle in his hand. He fits the iron ring down over the *quiote* and quickly snaps or cuts it off, leaving the long, round, tapered *quiote* free to grasp and stuff into his sack. The *ixtlero* is also called a *quiotero*, or "one who gathers *quiotes*." The *campo* of the *ixtlero* may be just a tarp or sheet thrown over the *matorral* or *chaparro* (brush) for shade. A local rope-making enterprise is a *fabrica*.

These leaves (*pencas*) are then taken to camp or home, separated, and over a wooden, slanted form known as a *burro*, or over a fence rail, a barrel, or other handy support, the individual leaves of the *agaves* are cut free of spines and scraped (with a *sacador*) to remove the flesh of the leaf and expose the *ixtle* fibers. Some *ixtleros* use a flat rock to pound the pulpy flesh away from the fibers. The pulp soon sours, so the odor of an *ixtlero* camp is pretty rank, about nine on a scale of ten! The fibers are then hung over a fence or wire and dried in the sun for a few hours, turning from wet yellow to white in the process. Then fibers are carded and placed randomly in a pile or in a shallow pan (*batea*). From there, they are plucked and twisted by one of several different methods, including use of the fingers (twisting two strands of fiber clockwise while also bringing one strand around the other counter-clockwise); rolling them on the maker's hip; using a small

These *lechuguilla quiotes* bundles, top photo, are ready for transport by the *ixtlero* to a place where the fibers will be extracted. Below: a sophisticated extraction plant for *lechuguilla* fibers near Torreón, Coahuila. Note the stockpile of fibers behind the *trabajador* (worker) that will be made into fiber bags, *costales*, or rope, *mecate*. (Jim Henrickson photos)

handmade twisting and twirling device called a *tarabilla* (a two-person job); or using a small home rope-making machine such as is described in some Boy Scout or outdoor manuals, the device having a crank on it to accomplish the twisting. Sometimes an old truck steering wheel (*volante*) is mounted on a post and used to rapidly twist the rope. The resulting two-ply cord can be doubled and again twisted, twisting the individual plies one direction while bringing them about each other in the opposite direction. The end result is *mecate*, or *ixtle* fiber rope. The opposite twists of adjoining plies serve to exert counterforce, which prevents unraveling. The ends are tied off in a knot to keep them together. This rope is very harsh on *gringo* hands, but it is the primary rope of rural Mexico and does a good job. When carefully made it is of uniform diameter and strength. As each fiber ends, new ones are twisted in, and friction holds them together as a single fiber.

## Wax Processing

The *candelilla* plant grows in a large section of central northern Mexico, extending very slightly into Texas in the Big Bend region. It seems to prefer shallow, rocky soil, mainly on limestone rock. As a defense against aridity, the plant secretes a high-quality vegetable wax (*cera*) that is much used as a waterproofing agent and in polishes, chewing gum, and candles. In Mexican folk medicine, practitioners (*curanderos*) often prescribe the plant, with its milky sap, as a cure for syphilis.

The plant grows in compact bunches of gray-green, leafless stems about the diameter of a pencil and up to three feet tall. It grows in dense stands, tiny flowers appear at the top when conditions are favorable, and it is a soil builder and holder.

The wax is exuded by the plant as a defense against desert dryness and obviously is produced in greater quantity under the most extreme conditions of dryness. The outside of the round, pencil-thin stems is covered with flakes of wax (*cera*). It takes a number of years (four to seven) for the plant to mature and become wax-laden, thus an area that has been overharvested can rapidly suffer a drop in production. The hottest, driest summers and the coldest winters seem to promote the greatest production of wax.

Commercial growing of the plant in rows has never worked, as it fails to produce sufficient wax under the more favorable conditions of agriculture. It even sprouts leaves and turns a much brighter green when placed in fertile soil and given more water than it naturally gets in the desert, causing it to look like a totally different plant. Such plants produce little usable wax.

The Bank of Mexico has, by government decree, control of the harvest and sale of *candelilla* wax in all of its range in Mexico. It is unlawful in Mexico to harvest the plant or sell the wax except within the quota system of the Banco de México or to sell or export the wax for sale without compliance with Mexican law. It is not, however, illegal to import the wax into the United States as long as it is declared to Customs, and there is no duty on its importation. The Banco usually pays a price slightly higher than market price to entice producers to sell to it, but since there are long delays in payment after delivery, and since there is a ready market for the wax if smuggled to the Texas side in the Big Bend region, much wax crosses by burro train and in other ways into Texas, where it is sold for quick cash. Some of these burro trains travel hundreds of miles from interior Mexico to the dealers on the Texas border, particularly if prices are good.

Into the hills goes the wax gatherer (*cerero,* also called *arrancandor,* "one who pulls up") with his burro. He pulls the plant up by its roots, using his hands, which become as tough as sole leather. He ties the plants in small bundles with *mecate* cords, and windrows the plants (*yerba*) until he has enough to suit him. Then he expertly packs them onto his burro using the packsaddle (*fuste; aparejo*) and a long *mecate* with a wooden loop (*honda*) at one end. It is tied off with a special packer's knot.

Back at the wax camp, the *cerero* dumps his load of green weed (*yerba*) and fills a large vat (*paila; caldera*) with water from a nearby *tinaja,* river, or spring. A firepit under the *paila* (which is usually located on the edge of a cutbank) is cleaned of ash and some dry weed (*yerba seca*) from previous processing is placed in it and fired off, producing a hot fire that brings the water to a boil. Fuel is scarce, and dried *yerba* is the major fuel, so processing takes place only when a sufficient amount of dry weed has accumulated.

When the fire is going and the water heating, the vat is charged with green weed from the nearby pile and sulfuric acid (*ácido oscuro*) is added to the water. A heavy steel grate (*parrilla*) holds all the weed below the water level and leaves a few inches of water above the submerged grate. When the water boils, the wax starts to come off and rise as a tan foam. It is scooped up with a perforated tin skimmer (*espumador*), which collects the hot waxy foam but lets water run back into the vat. As the water continues to boil, and more waxy foam rises, the wax maker continues to scoop the foam off and places it into a mold to cool and harden. Anything can be used as a mold, from a simple dirt dam to the cut off head of a 55-gallon drum. After a period of boiling and skimming, another charge of acid is added, to get the last of the wax off the plants. Then the *cerero* drops a handful of ashes into one corner of the vat, and the resulting reaction between the acid water and the basic ashes drives the last of the wax across the surface

*Candelilla* wax workers (*cereros*) near San Carlos, Chihuahua. This view looks directly into the firebox as the *cerero* is sweeping up an *espumador* (perforated scoop) of melted wax from the top of the boiling water. It is then poured into the steel drum to cool. (Bob Burleson photo)

of the vat to another corner, where it is skimmed off.

The wet weed is forked out of the vat, the vat is recharged, and the cycle commences again. Wet weed can be carried away by two men by putting a pile of it on two poles, which are then carried away as one would carry a stretcher.

The wax dries and cools and becomes a hard, brownish substance with impurities in it (*cerote*). It is broken up with a hammer or a handy stone and placed in *costales* (burlap bags). These can be hauled away by burro or truck, and either legally sold to the Banco or smuggled into Texas for sale.

In Texas the wax is refined further by heating it alone, without water but with a bit of acid, in a larger vat, then cooking off the water that was caught up in the wax at the camp and letting impurities either float to the top or settle to the bottom of the vat. The wax is allowed to run onto a concrete cooling floor with shallow walls around it; it then is about 98 percent pure.

The *candelilla* camp from another view. The green, unprocessed plants are stacked in the background, after being carried to the camp on burros. The lever of wood holds down steel grates, which in turn push the green weed beneath the surface of the boiling acid-water mixture. The wax floats to the top, to be skimmed off. (Bob Burleson photo)

In line with the Mexican custom of using all resources to the maximum, even the dried, dewaxed weed is used for many purposes. Not only is it a major fuel source but it makes thatch for the shelter of the *cereros*; a bundle makes their beds; it is a common tempering agent in *adobe* bricks; and it is fed to goats and burros. The green weed is toxic to animals and is never eaten, but both goats and burros relish the acid-flavored dry weed after processing.

Wax gathering and processing is a tough life and demands many hard hours in the *monte*. It takes about one hundred pounds of green weed to produce one pound of wax—pretty hard work for little pay! The camps are for men only, and wives and family are left at home. It is a most interesting operation to watch, and you should do so, after getting the *cereros'* consent, whenever you run into a camp along the Río Grande or back in some canyon deeper in Mexico.

## FARM WORK AND LIFE

| | |
|---|---|
| Where is your husband? | ¿Dónde está su esposo? |
| He is in the field. | Está en la labor. |
| What will grow in this soil? | ¿Qué se puede cultivar en esta tierra? |
| This is very rich wheat land. | Esta labor es muy buena para el trigo. |
| The land here is poor for farming. | La tierra aquí es mala para el cultivo. |
| This ground is not very fertile. | Esta tierra no es muy fértil. |
| They are plowing the land. | Están arando la tierra. |
| They dug a ditch to irrigate the land. | Cavaron una zanja para regar la tierra. |
| They planted corn in some fields and wheat in others. | Sembraron maíz en algunas milpas y trigo en otras. |
| The corn's doing well this year. | El maíz está bien este año. |
| There will be a big crop of corn this year. | Este año habrá una cosecha grande de maíz. |
| The crops failed last year. | Le cosecha se malogró el año pasado. |
| The dry weather has done a lot of harm to the crops. | Le sequía ha dañado mucho a la cosecha. |
| The well is fifty feet deep. | El pozo tiene cincuenta pies de profundidad (hondura). |
| Let's cut across this field. | Atravesemos esta milpa. |
| Is the fruit ripe enough to pick? | ¿Está suficientemente madura la fruta para cogerla? |
| Is the soil ready? | ¿La tierra está lista? |
| We sow broadcast. | Sembramos mantiado. |
| We plant by hand. | Sembramos a mano. |
| We plant corn in a cross pattern. | Sembramos el maíz en cruz. |
| We will plant in June. | Vamos a sembrar en junio. |
| One man makes the hole with a pointed stick. | Un hombre hace el pozo con un palo puntiagudo. |
| Make the hole with a stick. | Haga el pozo con un palito (palo). |
| They are ready to pull. | Están listas(os) para estirar. |
| You can pull them by hand. | Puede estirarlos (arrancarlos) a mano. |
| We gather corn by hand. | Cosechamos el maíz a mano. |
| Harvest has ended. | La cosecha está terminada. |
| Is the soil dry? | ¿Está seca la tierra? |
| The soil is a little hard. | La tierra está un poco dura. |

| | |
|---|---|
| The grain is ready for harvest. | El grano está listo para la cosecha. |
| The harvest season is drawing near. | Se acerca la temporada de la siega (cosecha). |
| It's an off year for crops. | No es un buen año para la cosecha. |
| It's been a lean year for farmers. | Ha sido un año malo para los labradores (rancheros). |
| They pulled up the plants by the roots. | Arrancaron las plantas con todo y raíz. |
| Pull them by hand. | Estirarlos (Arrancarlos) con la mano. |
| Do you know how to milk cows? | ¿Sabe ordeñar vacas? |
| Be careful that cow doesn't switch her tail in your face! | ¡Tenga cuidado que la vaca no le dé con la cola en la cara! |
| I hope this cow doesn't kick! | ¡Espero que esta vaca no dé coces (patadas)! |
| Is it sharp? | ¿Tiene buen filo? |
| I get up soon after I hear the rooster crow. | Me levanto poco después de oír cantar el gallo. |
| Dig this hole a little deeper. | Excave usted ese hoyo un poco más. |

## RANCH WORK AND LIFE

| | |
|---|---|
| He keeps all classes of stock on his ranch. | Tiene toda clase de ganado en su rancho. |
| How many goats do you have? | ¿Cuántas cabras tiene usted? |
| I have fifty-five goats. | Tengo cincuenta y cinco cabras. |
| How many cows do you have? | ¿Cuántas vacas tiene usted? |
| I have twenty cows. | Tengo veinte vacas. |
| This land is good for grazing cattle. | Esta tierra (Este campo) es buena(o) para el ganado (las vacas). |
| The ranch is enclosed (fenced). | Este rancho (La propiedad) está cercado(a). |
| The cold was so severe that the animals froze! | ¡El frío fue tan intenso que se helaron los animales (los ganados). |
| The grass is parched this summer. | Este verano se ha abrasado el zacate. |
| The grass did not come up this spring. | El zacate no salió esta primavera. |
| The calf was born this morning. | El ternero nació esta mañana. |

| | |
|---|---|
| Is that lariat made of rawhide? | ¿Es de cuero crudo esa reata? |
| Is that bag made of calfskin? | ¿Es de piel de ternera esa bolsa (ese morral)? |
| This afternoon we are going to butcher two steers. | Esta tarde vamos a matar dos novillos. |
| We are going to brand cattle this afternoon. | Esta tarde vamos a marcar con hierro los novillos. |
| Whose brand is on that cow? | ¿De quién es el hierro de esa vaca? |
| Does it have a brand? | ¿Hay alguna marca que lo distinga? |
| It has none. | No hay marca de hierro. |
| Catch hold of the rope. | Agarre usted la cuerda (el mecate; la reata). |
| Can you tie a loop? | ¿Puede usted hacer un lazo? |
| Hold the rope tight! | ¡Mantenga firme la reata! |
| Be careful; that's a mean animal! | ¡Tenga usted cuidado; ese animal tiene muy mal genio! |
| Tie the rope tight to the tree. | Amarre bien la reata (el mecate) al árbol. |
| Loosen the rope a little. | Afloje usted un poco el mecate (la reata). |
| Try to hold on a little longer. | Trate de aguantar un poco más. |
| Hold the rope tight. | Agarre usted bien el mecate. |
| Get a good grip on the rope! | ¡Agarre la reata firmemente! |
| This knot is very tight. | Este nudo ha quedado muy apretado. |
| Be careful, it is a mean bull! | ¡Cuidado! ¡Es un toro muy bravo! |
| Watch out or the bull will charge you! | ¡Cuidado con el toro; puede embestir! |
| Be careful, the bull has sharp horns! | ¡Tenga cuidado, el toro tiene las astas (los cuernos) puntiagudas(os)! |
| He hasn't got any fight left in him! | ¡No le queda ni el ánimo de reñir! |
| He dodged the bull! | ¡Hurtó el cuerpo al toro! |
| There was a roundup last week. | Hubo rodeo (un recogido) la semana pasada. |
| They are going to turn the steers loose now. | Ya van a largar los novillos. |
| They drove the steers out to the pastures. | Sacaron los novillos a los pastos. |
| Hitch the mule to the wagon. | Enganche usted la mula a la carreta. |
| Help me hook this. | Ayúdeme a enganchar esto. |

| | |
|---|---|
| He forgot to bar the pasture gate. | Olvidó trancar la portilla (la puerta) del pasto. |
| The fence needs new posts. | La cerca necesita unos postes nuevos. |
| The posts are spaced three paces apart. | Los postes están separados tres pasos de distancia entre sí (a cada tres pasos). |
| I'm going to cut a switch to use on my burro (mule) (horse). | Voy a cortar una varita para darle a mi burro (mula) (caballo). |
| Who is going to shoe the horse? | ¿Quién va a herrar el caballo? |
| I hope this horse doesn't kick! | ¡Espero que este caballo no dé coces! |
| They are going to turn the goats loose now. | Ya van a largar las cabras. |
| The dog watched over the goats all night. | El perro guardó (cuidó) las cabras toda la noche. |
| We will have to separate the kids from the goats. | Tendremos que separar los cabritos de las cabras. |
| We will feed the kids first. | Les daremos de comer a los cabritos (pequeños) primero. |
| Do the goats come and go at will? | ¿Van y vienen las cabras a su antojo? |
| You can get there faster (easier) on horseback. | Usted puede llegar allí más pronto (fácil) a caballo. |
| Where can I get a horse? | ¿Dónde puedo conseguir un caballo? |
| Do you have horses to rent? | ¿Renta usted caballos? (¿Tiene usted caballos de renta [alquiler]?) |
| This bridle does not have a bit! | ¡Esta brida no tiene el bocado! |
| He couldn't (can't) control the horse. | No podía (puede) contener el caballo. |
| He got very mad! | ¡Se puso muy bravo! |
| Don't ride that horse. He'll throw you! | ¡No monte usted ese caballo porque le tirará (desarzonará)! |
| Be careful your horse does not throw you! | ¡Tenga usted cuidado de que su caballo no lo tire (desarzone)! |
| He has ridden horses all his life. | Ha montado a caballo toda su vida. |
| How far have you ridden? | ¿Qué distancia ha usted recorrido? |
| How long does this ride last? | ¿Cuánto dura este trayecto (recorrido)? |
| We rode to the canyon on horseback. | Fuimos a caballo al cañón. |

*Vaqueros* in the process of hauling out three cows that broke from the herd and fell into a dry well about twenty-five feet deep. They were stacked one on top of the other. All survived, a tribute to the toughness of Mexican livestock. (Earl Nottingham photo)

Cow number three comes out "hooking." The *vaqueros* are pulling her up but are ready to scatter. Antonio Chávez, *at left*, is breaking for her tail, to "tail" her and keep her from getting a horn into one of the men in front of her. (Earl Nottingham photo)

Antonio Chávez, a *vaquero* all his fifty-odd years, has caught a cow *a media cabeza* (by the half-head) and flicks his *lazzo* to release her. (Earl Nottingham photo)

| | |
|---|---|
| They mounted their horses and left. | *Se montaron a caballo y se fueron.* |
| Attach the trailer to the pickup. | *Enganche el carro de remolque a la camioneta.* |
| Don't forget to water the horses. | *No se le olvide dar agua a los caballos.* |
| He knotted the rope securely. | *Amarró la cuerda (el mecate) fuertemente.* |
| Help me undo this rope. | *Ayúdeme a desatar esta cuerda (este mecate).* |
| Help me untie this knot. | *Ayúdeme a desatar este nudo.* |
| I cannot untie this knot. | *No puedo deshacer (sacar) este nudo.* |
| That knot is loose. | *Ese nudo está flojo.* |
| Don't let go of the rope until I tell you to. | *No suelte la cuerda (reata) hasta que yo le diga.* |
| Pass the rope through here and tie it securely. | *Pase la reata por aquí y amárrela fuertemente.* |
| Pull the rope tight. | *Estire el mecate (la reata) tirante.* |
| Wind up the rope. | *Enrolle la reata (el mecate).* |

| | |
|---|---|
| The rope got snarled. | *Se enredó el mecate.* |
| Hold on to the reins. | *Agarra usted bien las riendas.* |
| Many cows are sold on (from) this ranch. | *Se venden muchas vacas en (de) este rancho.* |
| I am going to the other side of the canyon. | *Voy al otro lado del cañón.* |
| Santiago is going to the pasture. | *Santiago va al pasto.* |
| The steers are coming in from the pasture. | *Los novillos vienen del pasto.* |

## RANCH AND FARM TERMS

In northern Mexico the dominant form of land use is ranching, but there are occasional irrigated areas and there are usually small subsistence plots (*milpas*) where corn is grown.

### Ranching

| | |
|---|---|
| Back (of an animal) | *Lomo* (m.) |
| Barbed wire | *Alambre de púas* (m.) |
| Ride bareback | *Montar en pelo* |
| Barn or stable | *Establo* (m.); *bodega* (f.); *troje* (m.); *granero* (m.) |
| Big steer | *Buey* (m.) |
| Blinders (for animal) | *Anteojeras* (f.) |
| Brand | *Fierro* (m.); *marca* (f.) |
| Bridle | *Brida* (f.); *frena de caballo* (f.); *cabestro* (m.) |
| Brush | *Chaparro* (m.) |
| Bull | *Toro* (m.) |
| By the half head | *A media cabeza* (said of a loop that catches the cow only by one horn and the face) |
| Calves | *Becerros* (m.); *terneras* (f.) |
| Cattle | *Vacas* (f.); *ganados* (m.); *res* (m.) |
| Cattle guard | *Cuida vaca* (f.) |
| Chaps (leg protectors) | *Chivarras* (f.); *chaparreras* (f.) |
| Chicken | *Gallina* (hen); *gallo* (rooster); *pollo* (chicken; m.) |
| Cleared area (abandoned field) | *Desmonte* (m.) |
| Colt | *Potro* (m.) |
| Cowbell (also bell for goats, cattle, and ranch animals in general) | *Cencerro* (m.) |
| Cowboy | *Vaquero* (m.) |

| | |
|---|---|
| Cow dung | *Boñiga* (f.) |
| Dog | *Perro* (m.) |
| Dogs (hound) | *Perros juanes* (m.) |
| Dogs (hunting) | *Perros de caza* (m.); *sabuesos* (m.) |
| Dog dung | *Canina* (f.) |
| Duck | *Pato* (m.) |
| Dung (manure) | *Boñiga* (f.); *estiércol* (m.) |
| Fat | *Gordo(a)* |
| Feed (ground) | *Molida* (f.) |
| Feed trough (usually long and of wood) | *Canoa* (f.) |
| Female animal | *Hembra* (f.) |
| Fence | *Cerca* (f.) |
| Fence (boundary) rider | *Pastero* (m.) (it is the custom of the *pastero* to cut a green, leafy branch from time to time and hang it over the fence, to prove how recently he has passed) |
| First rooster to crow in the A.M. | *Primer gallo* (m.) |
| Foot of animal | *Pata* (f.) |
| Forefoot of animal | *Mano* (f.) |
| Foreman | *Caporal* (m.); *jefe* (m.); *rallador* (m.); *mayordomo* (m.) |
| Fowl | *Aves de corral* (f.) |
| Gate | *Puerta* (f.) |
| Give it a turn (rope) | *Dar una vuelta* |
| Goat | *Cabra* (f.); *chivo* (m.) |
| Grass | *Zacate* (m.); *pasto* (m.) |
| Grassland | *Zacatal* (m.) |
| Halter | *Cabestro* (m.) |
| Hay | *Pastura* (f.) (bale = *paca*) |
| Heifers | *Hembras* (f.) |
| Herd or flock | *Rebaño* (m.); *hato* (m.) |
| Hobble | *Maniota* (m.); *traba* (f.); *manija* (f.) |
| Hoof (of horse) | *Casco de caballo* (m.); *mano* (f.) (front foot) |
| Horn | *Cuerno* (m.); *cuerna* (f.) |
| Horse | *Caballo* (m.) |
| Horse breaker | *Jinete* (m.) |
| Horse breaking | *Jineteada* (f.) |
| Horse dung (slang = horseshit) | *Cagajón* (m.) |
| Horse herd | *Caballada* (f.); *remuda* (f.) |
| Horse herd led by a bell mare | *Tropilla* (f.) |

| | |
|---|---|
| Kid goat | *Cabrito* (m.); *chivito* (m.) |
| Knot (hard knot) | *Nudo ciego* (m.) |
| Lamb | *Cordero* (m.) |
| Lasso | *Lazo* (m.); *reata* (f.) |

(Note: The *vaquero* may use a "rope" of rawhide, called a *reata*. These are made of several strands of untanned [raw] steer hide that are either twisted together [*reata torcida*] or braided together [*reata trenzada*]. Usual length is eight *brazadas*, the distance between palms of outstretched arms, or between 45 and 48 feet. The strongest *reatas* will have six strands. *Reatas* are also made of horsehair [*crin; tejido de crin*] from the mane and tail, twisted together like *ixtle* ropes.)

| | |
|---|---|
| Lead mare (bell mare) | *Madrina* (f.); *caponera* (f.) |
| Leather | *Cuero* (m.) |
| Loop of rope | *Lazada* (f.) |
| Male animal | *Macho* (m.) |
| Mare | *Yegua* (f.) |
| Mares under a stallion | *Manada* (f.) |
| Maverick bull (no ear marks) | *Toro orejano* (m.) |
| Mesquite land | *Mesquital* (m.) |
| Mutton goat | *Castrado* (m.); *capado* (m.) |
| Norther, severe winter storm (kills goats) | *Mata cabras* (f.) |
| Owner | *Dueño* (m.); *patrón* (m.) |
| Ox | *Buey* (m.) |
| Pack animals | *Bestias* (f.) |
| Pasture | *Pasto* (m.) |
| Pen | *Corral* (m.) |
| Pig (hog) | *Marrano* (m.); *puerco* (m.); *cerdo* (m.); *cochino* (m.) |
| Plant, bush, or shrub | *Mata* (f.) |
| Post | *Poste* (m.); *palo* (m.) |
| Pump | *Bomba* (f.) |
| Rat dung (slang) | *Cagarruta* (f.) |
| Rawhide | *Cuero crudo* (m.) |
| Reins | *Riendas* (f.) |
| Saddle | *Silla de montar* (f.); *montura* (f.) |
| Saddle blanket | *Corona* (f.) |
| Saddle stirrup | *Estribo* (m.) |
| Saddle toe fender | *Tapadero* (m.) |
| Salt box (for livestock) | *Salera* (f.) |

(Note: To keep cattle from eating too much expensive ground feed or protein meal such as cottonseed meal, the Mexican rancher often mixes salt with the feed [*molida con sal*].)

| | |
|---|---|
| Second-in-command | *Segundo* (m.) |
| Seedling | *Plantula* (f.) |
| Shaded spot where livestock rest during heat of the day | *Sesteadero* (m.) |
| Shearer of sheep or goats | *Trasquilador* (m.) |
| Shed for goats or sheep | *Cobertizo* (m.); *redil* (m.); *tejadillo* (m.); *tinglado* (m.) |
| Sheep | *Borrego* (m.); *oveja carnero* (f.) |
| Sheep boss | *Vaciero* (m.) |
| Shepherd | *Pastor* (m.) |
| Skinny, Mexican longhorn cattle | *Corrientes* (m.) |
| Small holding pasture or meadow | *Potrero* (m.); *trampa* (trap) (f.) |
| Small shelter for kid goats, made by leaning two flat rocks against each other | *Chiquero* (m.); *chivetero* (m.) |
| Spanish goat (for eating) | *Española* (f.); *cabrito* (m.) |
| Spur | *Espuela* (f.) |
| Steers | *Novillos* (m.) |
| Strap | *Correa* (f.) |
| Straw | *Paja* (f.) |
| Sway-backed horse | *Caballo de loma hundida* (m.) |
| Tame | *Manso(a)* |
| Tank (earth stock tank) | *Tanque* (m.) |
| Thicket | *Monte* (m.); *chaparral* (m.); *matorral* (m.) |
| Thin | *Flaco(a)* |
| Trail | *Sendero* (m.); *vereda* (f.); *rastro* (m.) |
| Turkey | *Cócono* (m.); *guajolote* (m.); *pavo* (m.) |
| Water trough (circular) | *Pila* (f.) |
| Wild | *Bronco(a)*; *liviano(a)*; *cimarrón* (m.) |
| Windmill | *Papalote* (m.) |
| Wire | *Alambre* (m.) |
| Wire gap | *Falcete* (m.) |
| Wooden stave fence | *Empalizada* (f.) |
| Yoke | *Mancornador* (m.) |

| Those cows are fat (thin). | Esas vacas son gordas (flacas). |
| I want to sell them. | Quiero venderlas. |
| The grass is tall here. | El zacate es alto aquí. |
| I see the goats. | Veo los chivos. |
| The coyotes are killing the young goats. | Los coyotes matan a los cabritos. |
| Give it (rope) a turn. | Dar una vuelta. |

## Farming

(For animals, see Ranching; other terms may be used in both farm and ranch work.)

| Bale | Paca (f.) |
| Baler (hay) | Empacadora (f.) |
| Bank (of ditch or stream) | Orilla (f.) |
| Bed (soil) | Bordo (m.) |
| Careless weed | Quelite (m.) |
| Chisel plow | Pico (m.) |
| Crop (harvest) | Cosecha (f.) |
| Crop duster (airplane) | Avión fumigador (m.); aeroplano (m.) |
| Crop dusting | Polvear; envenenar |
| Cultivator | Cultivador (m.) |
| Disc plow | Disco (m.) |
| Domestic fowl | Aves de corral (f.) |
| Farm worker | Sembrador (m.); labrador (m.) |
| Farmer | Granjero (m.); ranchero (m.) |
| Field | Milpa (f.); labor (m.); sembrado (m.) |
| Garden | Jardín (m.) |
| Grass | Zacate (m.) |
| Harrow | Rastrillo (m.) |
| Harvester | Cosechador (m.) |
| Hay hook | Gancho (m.) |
| Hoe | Azadón (m.) |
| Irrigate | Regar |
| Irrigation | Riego (m.) |
| Irrigation ditch | Acequia (f.); zanja (f.); ditche (m.) |
| Leaf | Hoja (f.) |
| Level | Plano(a) |
| Machine | Máquina (f.) |
| Mouth; gap; opening | Boquilla (f.) |
| Ox cart | Carreta (f.) |
| Pipe | Pipa (f.); tubo (m.) |

| Pipeline | *Tubería* (f.) |
| Plant | *Sembrar* |
| Planter | *Sembradora* (f.) |
| Plow | *Arado* (m.) |
| Pump | *Bomba* (f.) |
| Roots | *Raíces* (f.) |
| Row | *Surco* (m.); *raya* (f.) |
| Scarecrow | *Espantapájaros* (m.) |
| Scythe | *Guadaña* (f.); *alfanje* (m.) |
| Seed | *Semilla* (f.) |
| Short pipe | *Tubo corto* (m.) |
| Shovel | *Pala* (f.) |
| Sickle | *Hoz* (f.) |
| Stalks | *Matas* (f.) |
| Tractor | *Tractor* (m.) |
| Weed | *Yerba* (f.) |
| Yoke (for oxen) | *Yugo* (m.); *mancornador* (m.) |

## THE GOATHERD

In many areas of Mexico you are likely to encounter the *pastor* (goatherd) and a large flock (*majada*; also used for the goat pen or shed) of varicolored goats (*cabras*; *españolas*; *chivos*) usually moving actively through brushy areas, along creeks or canyons, or in scrub woodlands. Goats being chiefly browsers, rather than grazers of grass, they move along and nip off the leaves of trees, shrubs, and forbs, often climbing low trees or standing on their hind legs to reach low branches.

These Spanish goats are primarily eating goats, the young kids (*chivitos*; *cabritos*) being killed for meat about the time of weaning or shortly thereafter. Little is wasted from the goats; the kidneys, blood, and the other organs are cooked in various ways and consumed in addition to the meat (*carne*). Cooked kid goat is commonly called *cabrito*. If cooked over open coals it is *cabrito al pastor*; if cooked in an oven, it is *cabrito al horno*.

The goats are probably related to the Nubian milk goat of Africa, and some milk is produced from fresh nannies (*hembras*; *cabras*) and used for cheese and for drinking by infants. *Queso asadero* is a white cheese made from goats' milk and is very tasty, although some find it a bit salty. The fermentation process is interesting in that often a piece of the lining of a cow's stomach (*cuajo*) is used as a natural rennet to start the process.

These goats are very destructive of the environment; they consume (just as folklore has it) almost anything. Just as a burro will eat cactus pads with three-inch spines, as calmly as we would munch a tortilla, the goat will eat thornbush, weeds, and even *lechuguilla*, which is supposedly toxic to them. Although they are not immune to poison, and certainly can starve to death like any other animal, we can say with almost no fear of contradiction that the goats will be the last to go!

Some interesting events take place in the management of the kids. Instead of allowing them to run along with the adults, and thereby become subject to predators or become lost or dehydrated, the kids are either kept in a small pen and fed on freshly cut branches of oak (*encino*) or other palatable trees and shrubs, or they are tied by a forefoot (*mano*) with a soft rope (*mecate*) to a stake or stretched wire (*rayo de alambre*) near a small individual kid house (*chiquero*) made of two flat rocks tilted against each other to form an inverted V roof. This allows the kid to get under shelter from wind, rain, and sun. Many kids are thus staked out together each day, in long rows, in what we call a "*goataría*." The nannies are penned overnight, and each kid taken to its mother each night to spend the night with her and nurse. In the morning, the kids are carried to the *goataría* and staked out for the day, and the *pastor* leaves with the nannies. In the evening, the kids are again put with the nannies to nurse. This continues until they become of marketable size, or large enough to run with the herd.

Of considerable interest is the goat dog (*perro cuida cabras*). This animal appears to be an ordinary cur, of almost any shape, size, or color. Any resemblance between a Mexican goatherd's dogs and the border collie or other famous breed is purely coincidental! However, the nondescript appearance can fool you, as these dogs are very good at their work. In fact, they stick with the goats as though they were goats themselves (because they do think of themselves as goats!). A puppy is taken from the bitch shortly after whelping and before its eyes are open and is put to nurse on a fresh nannie goat. The goat is tied to prevent injury to the puppy or puppies, and they nurse right along with the kid. They grow up with goats and as goats and pretty well identify with goats, it seems. They go forth daily with the goats, and it is only by instinct that they act like dogs. When a predator, such as a bobcat (*gato de montes*) or coyote comes around, the dog instinctively barks at it, gives alarm, and protects the goats. The system works pretty well, as some *pastores* rely solely on the dogs for protection and do not actually herd the goats themselves.

With or without dogs, the *pastor* in many places will be found with the goats from dawn until dusk. His day starts early and ends late. It is a lonely existence, with nobody to talk to during most days, and only the goats and dogs for companionship. In fact, you often have to look very carefully around the *matorral* to find them, as they do not always show themselves. Where there are goats, however, there is usually a *pastor* nearby. *Pastores* often become very silent individuals, difficult to talk with, since they spend so much time alone. If they are married, their families usually live in a *jacal* near some *corrales* (pens) made of thornbush limbs, *quiotes*, or *piquetes*. The family lives nearly as lonely a life as the pastor does, and only the poorest people become *pastores*. The *pastor's* children often have young goats as pets (*sanchos*). The boys are constantly playing *vaquero* by roping goats, and they become very adept with the *lazo* or *reata* (roper's rope).

The *pastor* carries his lunch in a fiber bag (*morral*) slung over his shoulder and usually carries a staff (*bastón*), often the *quiote* of a *sotol* plant. If water is near, he usually carries no canteen (*bule*, or gourd jug) but drinks with the goats from river or spring. The *pastor* is habituated to hardship and all sorts of weather and usually carries only a wool *poncho* or merely a blanket in cold weather. His shoes are sandals with old tire treads for soles (*huaraches; guaraches*). He often carries a slingshot (either the old-style classic sling or *honda*, or the modern "shooter" with rubber bands, the *tirador de goma*) and is accurate with it. He throws rocks by hand with great force and accuracy also, killing small game for the pot. His only shade in summer is his *sombrero* or the occasional and temporary shade of desert shrubs.

Because of his constant outdoor life, and the slow progress of his flock across the country, the *pastor* has much time to observe and is very knowledgeable about all forms of wildlife and about such matters as caves, Indian camps, water holes, springs, trails, and the location of plant life, in his particular area. His world is generally small, however, and he rarely knows much more about the country than the area where he has spent his time with the flocks.

The total material assets of a *pastor* and his family could be carried by any foreign adult in a large gunnysack; they live at the extreme edge of subsistence. Time spent with them, visiting and observing their life and their goats, is time well spent, however, and their life, although rough, is not necessarily unhappy.

## THE TRUCKER

If you drive for any distance in Mexico, from the most remote deserts to the mountaintops, you will soon find that Mexico is a nation of trucks. Everything goes by truck. On a Sunday, the trucks that have been working all week, hauling ore, wood, charcoal, livestock, fruits and vegetables, and other products turn out and haul *la gente* into town. It is not unusual to see a truck with twenty or thirty people of every age, size, sex, and shape sprouting from every possible place of purchase or foothold. Long lines of trucks and people converge on the larger towns on weekends, with all the passengers expecting high adventure.

The Mexican trucker (*el troquero*) is *muy macho*, bold, stubborn, proud, virile, romantic, and boastful. His truck (*camión; troca*) is an extension of himself, an expression of his own tradition and personality.

The trucks are generally well cared for. You will find *troqueros* washing their rigs in roadside creeks, puddles, and even at river crossings. Trucks are usually painted in distinctive ways. White wheels, floral designs, stripes, geometric patterns, bold colors are all used to identify and express the *troquero*'s personality.

Trucks are uniformly loud. In fact, nothing is quite as loud as a Mexican truck (especially the DINA trucks made in Mexico) with a load on a long upgrade. Mufflers are a luxury; straight pipes announce to the world the coming of the *troquero* and his steed.

The cab is the throne. Fringed curtains (*cortinas*) are strung across the front windshield, and various crosses, medallions, and other objects of religious art may hang from any handy spot.

*Troqueros* are bold to the point of being reckless. Enough said! Watch out for them on mountain roads, narrow bridges, and detours. If a trucker flashes his lights at you, he is coming through! His lights may not work, so it is safer to assume he is coming through in all instances.

*Troqueros* can haul the most dangerous loads into places angels fear to tread! Once we came upon a big truck stuck in a deep *charco* (mudhole) with a broken driveshaft. The load (*carga*) was covered with tarps. There was hardly room for our truck to pass, and sloppy mud and water made the passage one calculated to cause a sideswipe if anything went wrong. Calmly the *troquero* motioned us to "make a run for it" and we went lurching and sliding by, without a collision. We then gave the *troquero* a lift to the nearest city (one hundred miles distant) and on the way asked him what he was hauling. "*Dinamita*" came the reply! He said it didn't bother him, as he had been hauling dynamite to the mines for seven years, and "if anything goes wrong, you won't feel a thing!" Thunderstorms and lightning were all about as he sat in the *charco* with his load of dynamite. He said the only thing that really bothered him was hail.

*Troqueros* are born mechanics. We have seen them literally take a truck apart on the roadside and fix it with none of the fancy tools our local mechanics seem to need. They can keep a truck running on parts borrowed (cannibalized) from other trucks and wrecks of trucks, long past U.S. trade-in time. How they keep them running is beyond understanding. We have seen logging trucks made of WWII and Korean War

Mexican *troqueros* engaging in a friendly game of chance in the *plaza* of San Carlos, Chihuahua. Avoid such games until you understand the language and the customs fully. (Will Thompson photo)

deuce-and-a-halfs (*doble tracción*) with the army beds removed, loaded with logs, and running laden down mountain grades, with not a sign of a brake other than low gear and engine compression! When you hear one "winding up" as it comes down the one-lane road toward you, you had better hunt for a wide spot, *muy pronto*, or be prepared to outrun it down the mountain in reverse gear. When they stop, the helper jumps off and blocks the wheels with rocks (a good practice for anyone on mountain roads).

The philosophy of the *troquero* is expressed in sayings variously called *dichos*, *bravos*, or *letreros*, painted most often on the front and rear bumpers of the trucks. These can be religious, boastful, sex-oriented, comic, or dead serious. While going through Mexico, take special pains to observe these *dichos* and make a list of them. Here are a few of them, in rough translation, just to give you an idea of what to look for:

| | |
|---|---|
| Don't you believe it! | *¡No Lo Creas!* |
| Speed without direction | *Velocidad sin rumbo* |
| I'm grunting, but I'm getting there. | *Pujando pero llegando.* |
| Fearless one | *El atrevido* |
| Go with God. | *Vaya Con Dios.* |
| I'll swap you my new tire (woman) for your old one (woman). | *Te cambio Mi llanta nueva por tu Vieja.* |
| The spent cartridge | *El cartucho quemado* |
| Faith in God and onward | *Fe en Dios y adelante* |
| Step aside, cockroach, here comes your DDT. | *Hasta un lado, Cucaracha, aquí va tu DDT.* |
| Watch out: the brakes are mush. | *Precaución: Frenos de atole.* |
| My guide . . . is my destiny. | *Mi guía . . . es mi destino.* |
| Life is worth nothing. | *La Vida No Vale Nada.* |
| The pedestrian flattener | *Planchada de peatones* |
| For one bitten by this serpent there is no remedy in the drugstore. | *A quién pica esta víbora No hay remedio en la botica.* |
| We're going where we're not criticized. | *Vamos a dónde no nos critiquen.* |
| I'll take you if you bathe. | *Te llevo si te bañas.* |
| For wine and women, drivers were born. | *Pa' el Vino y las mujeres nacieron los choferes.* |

Make your own list and send it in to us for the future. The variety is endless! Double entendre is common, so meanings cannot always be taken literally.

## Special Trucks

| | |
|---|---|
| A former army 4-wheel drive truck adapted to civilian use. | *Comando* (m.) |
| 4-wheel drive truck with canopy and flat bed, used as a jungle and mountain bus in *el monte*. | *Ruta* (f.) |
| An armored *comando*, such as an old armored car, halftrack, etc., used as a logging truck or log skidder. | *Comando blindado* (m.) |
| Trailer truck (tractor trailer) | *Camión con remolque* (m.) |
| Trailer | *Carro de remolque* (m.) |

## TOOLS AND EQUIPMENT

Sometimes it is worth an awful lot to have the right tool at the right time. If you don't have it, and don't know how to say it in Spanish, you are in trouble. Here are some of the more commonly used tools that you may need on the road or in *el monte*.

| | |
|---|---|
| Allen wrench | *Llave de alan* (f.) |
| Axe | *Hacha* (f.) |
| Blocks (chain) | *Bloques* (m.) |
| Bolt | *Tornillo* (m.); *cerrojo* (m.) |
| Box-end wrench | *Llave astria* (f.) |
| Cable | *Cable* (m.) |
| Chain | *Cadena* (f.) |
| Chain saw | *Motosierra* (f.) |
| Cold chisel | *Cincel* (m.) |
| Cotter key | *Chaveta* (f.) |
| Crank | *Manivela* (f.); *manubrio* (m.) |
| Crescent wrench | *Perico* (m.); *cresciente* (m.) |
| Crowbar | *Barra* (f.) |
| Drill and bits | *Taladro* (m.) *y pizcas* (f.) |
| Equipment | *Equipaje* (m.) |
| File | *Lima* (f.) |
| Funnel | *Embudo* (m.) |
| Gear puller | *Extractor de engranes* (m.) |
| Grease gun | *Inyector de grasa* (m.) |
| Hacksaw | *Cegeta* (f.) |
| Hammer (sledge; maul) | *Maza* (f.); *marro* (m.); *pisón* (m.) |
| Hammer | *Martillo* (m.) |
| Hatchet | *Hacha* (f.) |
| Hoe | *Azadón* (m.) |
| Hook | *Gancho* (m.) |
| Hose | *Manguera* (f.) |
| Jack | *Gato* (m.) |
| Jumper cables | *Cables (para cargador de batería)* (m.) |
| Knife | *Cuchillo* (m.) |
| Level | *Nivel* (m.) |
| Lever or handle | *Palanca* (f.); *maneral* (m.) |
| Lug wrench | *Llave de cruz* (f.) |
| Nail | *Clavo* (m.) |
| Needlenose pliers | *Alicates* (m.) |
| Nut | *Tuerca* (f.) |
| Open-end wrench | *Llave española* (f.) |

| | |
|---|---|
| Phillips screwdriver | *Desarmador de cruz* (m.) |
| Pick | *Pico* (m.) |
| Pin | *Perno* (m.) |
| Pipe wrench | *Llave Stillson* (f.) |
| Pliers | *Pinzas* (f.); *tenazas* (f.) |
| Pocketknife | *Cortapluma* (f.); *navaja* (f.) |
| Pump (generic) | *Bomba* (f.) |
| Punch (or awl) | *Punzón* (m.); *sacabocados* (m.) |
| Sandpaper | *Papel de lija* (m.) |
| Saw | *Sierra* (f.); *segueta* (f.); *serrucho* (m.) |
| Scissors | *Tijeras* (f.) |
| Screw | *Torno* (m.); *chilillo* (m.); *tornillo* (m.) |
| Screwdriver | *Desarmador* (m.) |
| Shaft | *Flecha* (f.) |
| Shovel | *Pala* (f.) |
| Socket wrench | *Llave de dado* (f.) |
| Spark plug wrench | *Llave de bujía* (f.) |
| Spring | *Resorte* (m.) (coil); *muelle* (m.) (leaf) |
| Square (carpenter's) | *Escuadra de carpintero* (f.) |
| Staples | *Grampas* (f.); *grapas* (f.) |
| String; cord | *Mecate* (m.); *cuerda* (f.) |
| Tape | *Cinta plástica* (f.) |
| Tape measure (metric) | *Cinta métrica* (f.) |
| Tool (generic) | *Herramienta* (f.) |
| Tool box | *Caja de herramientas* (f.) |
| Vise | *Tornillo* (m.) |
| Vise grips | *Pinzas de presión* (f.) |
| Washers | *Arandelas* (f.) |
| Water pump pliers | *Pinzas de extensión* (f.) |
| Wedge | *Cuña* (f.) |
| Winch | *Malacate* (m.) |
| Wire | *Alambre* (m.) |
| Wrench (generic) (also means "key") | *Llave* (f.) |
| How do you operate this machine? | *¿Cómo trabaja (funciona) esta máquina?* |
| Is the machinery out of order? | *¿No funciona la maquinaria?* |
| Fixing it will be a simple operation. | *El arreglarlo será un trabajo sencillo.* |
| Could you explain how this machine works? | *¿Puede usted explicar cómo funciona esta máquina?* |

Do you know the term for this part of the machine?

¿Sabe usted cuál es el nombre de esta parte de la máquina?

Could I borrow your tools?

¿Podría usted prestarme sus herramientas?

Where are the tools?

¿Dónde están las herramientas?

The tools are here.

Las herramientas están aquí.

## WORK AND BURDENS

Are you idle at the moment?

¿Está usted desocupado(a) en este momento?

Do you earn enough to keep your family?

¿Gana usted lo suficiente para mantener a su familia?

It is getting hard to make both ends meet!

Se está haciendo difícil vivir con lo que se tiene.

They labor from morning till night.

Trabajan de la mañana a la noche.

It is too heavy to lift.

Es demasiado pesado para levantar.

That is too heavy a load for the burro.

Es una carga demasiado pesada para el burro.

We have to lighten the load.

Tenemos que aligerar la carga.

The burros were carrying (are carrying) heavy packs.

Los burros llevaban (llevan) cargas pesadas.

How many men are there?

¿Cuántos hombres son?

He pulled with all his might.

Tiró con todas sus fuerzas.

He made a great effort.

Hizo un poderoso esfuerzo.

Where will I be out of the way?

¿Dónde me puedo poner para que no le moleste?

The men are working with picks and shovels.

Los hombres trabajan con picas y palas.

Is the ladder steady enough?

¿Es bastante firme la escalera?

Steady the ladder so I won't fall.

Sostenga la escalera para que no me caiga.

This needs a steady hand.

Esto necesita una mano firme.

I go off duty at 5:30.

Estoy libre de servicio (trabajo) a las cinco y media.

I'm on duty all night.

Estoy de trabajo toda la noche.

I'm done in working in all this heat.

Estoy agotado(a) de trabajar en este calor.

Let's stop working and call it a day.

Dejemos de trabajar y demos por terminado el día.

Is that bundle too heavy to carry?

¿Es demasiado pesado ese bulto para cargar?

| | |
|---|---|
| I cannot lift this; it's too heavy. | *No puedo levantar esto; pesa demasiado.* |
| The workers are cutting the brush (shrubs). | *Los trabajadores están cortando los matorrales (arbustos).* |
| Let's put aside our work and go get a drink. | *Dejemos a un lado el trabajo y salgamos a beber algo.* |
| I would like to talk to the foreman. | *Quería hablar con el caporal.* |
| I'll talk with you when you are not busy. | *Hablaré con usted cuándo esté desocupado(a).* |
| They lead such a hard life. | *Llevan una vida tan dura.* |
| How do you find the work? | *¿Cómo encuentra usted el trabajo?* |
| It is a thankless job. | *Es un trabajo muy ingrato.* |
| We need more workers. | *Necesitamos más obreros.* |
| It cannot be moved. | *No se puede quitar (moverlo).* |
| It is stuck fast. | *Está fijo (bien pegado).* |
| Do you have Saturday off? | *¿Tiene usted libre el sábado?* |
| How do you manage to do this? | *¿Cómo se maneja usted para hacer esto?* |
| Do it this way. | *Hágalo usted de esta manera.* |
| What material is this made of? | *¿De qué material está hecho esto? (¿De qué está hecho?)* |
| What material is used to make this? | *¿Con qué material se hace esto?* |
| Watch what they are doing. | *Observe usted lo que hacen.* |
| Do you know how to drive a truck? | *¿Sabe usted manejar un camión?* |
| I know how to do that type work. | *Yo sé hacer esa clase de trabajo.* |
| What work does your husband do? | *¿Qué trabajo hace su esposo?* |
| He is a cowboy (ranch hand). | *Es un vaquero.* |
| What is your occupation? | *¿Cuál es su ocupación?* |
| I am a truck driver. | *Soy troquero.* |
| Where do you work? | *¿Dónde está su lugar de empleo? (¿En dónde trabaja?)* |
| At the Cuatro Palmas Mine. | *En la mina Cuatro Palmas.* |
| Do you have much work? | *¿Tiene usted mucho trabajo?* |
| Yes, I have plenty of work. | *Sí, tengo bastante trabajo.* |
| How much do you earn a week? | *¿Cuánto gana usted por semana?* |
| I make $20 a week. | *Gano veinte dólares (pesos) por semana.* |
| How many workers are employed here? | *¿Cuántos obreros emplean aquí?* |
| Who do you work for? | *¿Para quién trabaja usted?* |
| Who is he working for now? | *¿Para quién trabaja él ahora?* |
| What does he do for a living? | *¿Qué hace para ganarse la vida?* |

| This job has no future. | Este trabajo no tiene porvenir. |
| Is that too heavy for you? | ¿Es eso demasiado pesado para usted? |
| How are you going to haul it? | ¿Cómo lo va a arrastrar? |
| How much do you pay? | ¿Cuánto paga? |
| He's carrying the bag on his back. | Lleva el saco en la espalda. |
| I'm looking for another job. | Estoy buscando otro empleo. |
| What is it used for? | ¿Para qué se usa? |
| He is cutting the trees. | El está cortando los árboles. |
| He is cutting them. | El está cortándolas(los). |
| What is it good for? | ¿Para qué sirve? |
| To be very difficult | Costar mucho trabajo |
| Like this | De este modo |
| He makes use of | Se sirve de |
| Make it. | Hágalo. |
| Put it here. | Póngalo aquí. |
| Let me show you how to do it. | Déjeme enseñarle cómo se hace. |

## MINING

| San José | Patron saint of miners |
| Copper | Cobre (m.) |
| Fluorite | Florita (f.) |
| Gold | Oro (m.) |
| Lead | Plomo (m.) |
| Silver | Plata (f.) |
| Ore | Mineral (m.) |
| Ore mill (hand- or burro-powered) | Tahona (f.); arrastra (f.) |
| Mill (general) | Molino (m.) |
| Mine | Mina (f.) |
| Miner | Minero (m.) |
| Pan (for collecting gold dust) | Batea (f.) (usually a shallow wooden bowl) |
| Pan (for gold) | Batear |
| Prospector | Gambusino (m.) |
| Pocket (of ore) | Bolsa (f.) |
| Shaft | Pozo (m.); tiro (m.) |
| Strike (rich ore) | Bonanza (f.) |
| Tunnel (mine) | Túnel (m.) |
| Value | Ley (f.) |
| Vein (ore) | Veta (f.) |
| Veinlet (ore) | Hilo (threadlike) (m.) |
| Mining is very heavy labor. | El trabajo en las minas es muy pesado. |

A day's work for a miner is a long grind.

Un día de trabajo para un minero es un calvario.

They are working a silver mine.

Están explotando una mina de plata.

Are there many unemployed workers at present?

¿Hay muchos obreros sin trabajo estos días?

Yes. The mine is shut down.

Sí. Está parada la mina.

The majority of those men work in the mine.

La mayoría de aquellos hombres trabajan en la mina.

What work do you do? (What is your job, etc.?)

¿Qué trabajo hace? (¿En qué trabaja usted?) (¿Qué clase de trabajo hace usted?) (¿En qué se ocupa usted?) (¿Cuál es su ocupación?)

I work in a mine.

Trabajo en una mina. (Soy minero.)

The frame of the mine should be finished in a day or two.

La armazón de la mina debería acabarse en uno o dos días.

Is the mine always open?

¿Está abierta la mina siempre?

At what time does the mine open?

¿Y a qué hora se abre la mina?

Are the mines being worked at this time?

¿Se están trabajando esas minas ahora?

Can we visit your (mine) (mill) (camp)?

¿Podemos visitar su (mina) (molino) (campo)?

What sort of ore is this?

¿Qué clase de mineral es este?

May we go into the mine and look around?

¿Podemos entrar a la mina a observar?

Where does the ore (the timber) go from here?

¿A dónde va el mineral (la madera) de aquí?

# 11. Eating and Staying Well on the Road and Trail

**R**estaurants are not to be found in the backcountry. Small outposts (*puestos*) or individual housewives (*rancheras*) along the road may serve *tortillas*, beans, or a few other staples, or may have occasional eggs and peppers or even some meat stew (*guisado*). The custom is to dig in and eat up, using a folded *tortilla* for a scoop if there is no spoon. The price is always very reasonable. The following phrases may get you nowhere in the best restaurants in the cities, but will probably get you fed in the *monte*.

| | |
|---|---|
| It's time to go to dinner. | *Es la hora de (comer) las migas.* (*Las migas*, "the crumbs," is a slang or idiomatic expression to signify dinnertime.) |
| Come to dinner. | *Venga a comer.* |
| Is there lunch (food)? | *¿Hay de comer (comida)?* (*Lonchería* is slang for quick-lunch counter; *lonche* is sandwich or sack lunch.) |
| What is there to eat? | *¿Qué hay de comer?* |
| I want something to eat. | *Quiero algo de comer.* |
| I'm very hungry! | *¡Tengo mucha hambre!* |
| I'm thirsty. | *Tengo sed.* |
| Are there corn *tortillas*? | *¿Hay tortillas de maíz?* |
| Are there flour (wheat) *tortillas*? | *¿Hay tortillas de harina?* |
| Are there beans? | *¿Hay frijoles?* |
| What do you want to eat? | *¿Qué quiere comer?* |
| Anything you have will be o.k. | *Cualquier cosa que usted tenga está bien.* (*Lo que tenga está bien.*) |
| I want to eat ———. | *Quiero comer ———.* |
| I want (beans) (soup) (stew) (scrambled eggs) (*tortillas*). | *Quiero (frijoles) (sopa; caldo) (carne guisada) (huevos revueltos) (tortillas).* |

What do you eat for supper?

¿Qué come usted para la cena?
(¿Qué cena usted?)

Would you like to eat beans and rice?

¿Desea usted comer frijoles y arroz?

I have to prepare the meal.

Tengo que preparar la comida.

May I stay with you in the kitchen?

¿Me permite quedarme en la cocina con usted?

I like sausage and eggs.

Me gusta el chorizo (salchicha) con huevos.

I want a couple of eggs.

Quiero un par de blanquillos.

We want to eat at about 6 o'clock.

Queremos comer como a las seis.

When may I (we) eat?

¿Cuándo puede (podemos) comer?

One (You) may eat now.

Puede comer ahora.

What are you eating?

¿Qué está comiendo?

This pepper burns my tongue!

¡Este chile me quema la lengua!

Is it your custom to eat breakfast so early?

¿Acostumbra usted a desayunar tan temprano?

Is the food good there?

¿Está buena la comida allí?

I want cabrito.

Quiero cabrito, por favor.

There is no other meat but chicken.

No hay otra carne más que pollo.

Bring me beans.

Tráigame frijoles, por favor.

What do I owe you?

¿Cuánto le debo?

I like scrambled eggs (stew) (soup).

Me gustan los huevos revueltos. (Me gusta la carne guisada.) (Me gusta la sopa; el caldo.)

The meal is very good.

La comida está muy sabrosa.

This is a good meal.

Esta es una buena comida.

I want hot sauce.

Quiero salsa de chile roja (red) (verde [green]) (also chile macho; salsa picante; salsa; pico de gallo).

Where can I get a good meal?

¿Dónde se come bien? (¿Dónde puedo conseguir una comida buena?)

You can eat here.

Puede comer aquí.

What do you eat for breakfast?

¿Qué desayuna usted?

Would you like to eat dried beef and eggs?

¿Le gustaría comer machacado con huevos?

What do you suggest?

¿Qué me recomienda usted?

I like ranch-style eggs.

Me gustan los huevos rancheros.

I would like a typical Mexican meal.

Me gustaría una comida típica Mexicana.

| | |
|---|---|
| Do you need anything else? | ¿Desea algo más? |
| You can eat now. | Usted puede comer ahora. |
| May I have another bowl of soup? | ¿Puedo tomar otro tazón de caldo (sopa)? |
| Don't let this soup cool too long. | No deje enfriar mucho el caldo (la sopa). |
| Mess of food or "chow" | Rancho (m.) |

## COOKING

| | |
|---|---|
| What do you want instead? | ¿Qué desea en lugar de eso? |
| This pot leaks. | Esta cazuela se sale (gotea). |
| The pot is leaking. | La cazuela está goteando. |
| This is the kind of food I like. | Esta es la clase de comida que me gusta. |
| How can people live on this food? | ¿Cómo puede vivir la gente con esta alimentación? |
| It's almost time for lunch. | Es casi la hora del almuerzo. |
| Will you lunch with me? | ¿Quiere usted almorzar conmigo? |
| Do you have any meat today? | ¿Tiene usted carne hoy? (¿Hay carne hoy?) |
| Meat is scarce. | La carne está escasa. |
| Would you like half a chicken? | ¿Quiere usted medio pollo? |
| I only want a little. | Solamente quiero un poco. |
| Put a pan of water on the stove (fire). | Ponga usted una cacerola con agua en la estufa (el fuego). |
| In a few minutes the water will boil. | Dentro de poco hervirá el agua. |
| The pot is boiling over. | Se está tirando la cazuela. |
| Have the chickens been plucked? | ¿Han desplumado los pollos? |
| Let's have dinner now. | Vamos a comer. |
| Chop it up small. | Píquelo (Córtelo) muy menudo. |
| I like meat roasted on a spit. | Me gusta la carne al asador. |
| You can get a square meal there for very little money. | Con poco dinero usted puede conseguir una comida abundante en ese lugar. |
| Squeeze some lemons for lemonade. | Exprima unos limones para la limonada. |
| Wait until I finish eating. | Espere hasta que acabe de comer. |
| Who wants a second helping of stew? | ¿Quién quiere repetir del guisado? |
| What is that stuff you are eating? | ¿Qué es eso que come usted? |
| This meat is very tough. | Esta carne está muy dura. |

| | |
|---|---|
| This food is not nourishing enough. | Esta comida no es alimenticia (nutritiva). |
| I'm thirsty. Let's have a soda. | Tengo sed. Vamos a tomar una soda. |
| Is there drinking water? | ¿Hay agua para tomar? |
| What are you going to drink? | ¿Qué va a beber usted? |
| What time is chow? | ¿A qué hora dan la comida? |
| He ate a plate of calf's brains. | Comió un plato de sesos de ternera. |
| Are you still hungry? | ¿Todavía tiene hambre? |
| He likes to try everything. | Le gusta probar todo. |
| Get some water from the well. | Traiga usted un poco de agua del pozo. |
| What a delicious flavor this meat has. | Qué rico sabor tiene esta carne. |
| It is burro meat. | Esta es la carne de burro. |
| What time will the meal be served? | ¿Cuándo se sirve la comida? |
| What drink do you prefer? | ¿Qué bebida prefiere? |
| I prefer ———. | Prefiero ———. |
| Please give me the glass of water. | Me permite el vaso de agua. |
| Do you like chicken? | ¿Le gusta el pollo? |
| What do you eat? | ¿Qué come usted? |
| Have you already eaten? | ¿Ya comió? |
| I have already eaten. | Ya comí. |

## CABRITO

You will often pass a *pastor* (shepherd) with a flock of goats (*cabras*). A tender, milk-fed kid goat (*cabrito*) freshly killed and cooked over open coals is a treat. The best kids for eating are between forty-five and sixty days old. The kids are usually back at the corrals, where they are kept tied by a forefoot near a small shelter made of two slabs of rock that lean together to make a little tent. The nannies are brought to them twice daily to nurse. The *pastor* knows each nanny and her kid, although sometimes the kids and nannies are numbered in large flocks. This method makes it easier for the *pastor*, as kids are not exposed to predators or to being lost, nor are they exposed as much to cold or wet weather. Also, the nannies browse more efficiently without kids trying to nurse and butting their hindquarters off the ground!

If you can buy a kid (from a Spanish goat, or *española*, not from an angora goat), then you should try to cook it *al pastor*, or over the coals. The tasty result is called *cabrito asado*.

After the kid is killed and hung up by the hind legs to bleed (the Mexicans save the blood), it is skinned out (try to avoid getting its hair on the meat). The glands are removed from the legs and the rectum, and the kid is halved lengthwise and spitted on green sticks or pieces of iron re-bar (*varillas*). The carcass is salted and usually rubbed with cooking oil or lard, and then it is cooked slowly over the coals. Cook until tender inside and slightly brown and crusty on the outside, never over direct flame.

| | |
|---|---|
| How delicious! | *¡Qué sabroso!* |
| Do you have any kid goats for sale or eating? | *¿Tiene cabritos de venta? (¿Vende usted cabritos?)* |
| Where are the kids? | *¿Dónde están los cabritos?* |
| I want to kill a kid. | *Quiero matar un cabrito.* |
| I would like to buy a fat kid if the price is not too high. | *Quiero comprar un cabrito si no está muy caro.* |
| Show me what kids you have, please. | *Enséñeme los cabritos, por favor.* |
| That one will do. | *Está bien* (pointing). |
| What price do you want for him (her)? | *¿Cuánto por él (ella)?* |
| I will pay you —— pesos, no more. | *Le pago —— pesos, no más.* |
| You ask too much. | *Pide mucho. (Es muy caro.)* |
| Will you kill it and skin it for me now? | *¿Podría matarlo y desollarlo ahorita? (¿Lo prepara, por favor?)* |
| After you kill the kid, you'll have to skin it. | *Después de matar el cabrito, tendrá usted que desollarlo.* |
| Careful with the skin. | *¡Cuidado con la piel (el cuero)!* |
| I don't want any hair on the meat. | *No quiero pelo en la carne.* |
| You can keep the skin, head, blood, and kidneys if you wish to do so. | *Si le gusta, quédese con la piel, la cabeza, el sangre, y los riñones.* |
| Be sure to bleed it well. | *Desángrelo bien.* |
| Please cut the meat. | *Por favor, corte la carne.* |
| How do you prepare *cabrito*? | *¿Cómo prepara usted el cabrito?* |
| Will you cook it for me *pastor*-style? | *¿Lo prepara al pastor, por favor?* |
| Roast it over the live coals. | *Áselo sobre las brazas (las ascuas).* |
| Baste the kid with lard every half hour. | *Unte usted el cabrito con manteca cada media hora.* |
| These are excellent cuts of meat. | *Estos son excelentes trozos de carne.* |

| | |
|---|---|
| Do you like *cabrito*? | *¿Le gusta el cabrito?* |
| Yes, I like it. It is very good. | *Sí, me gusta. Está muy sabroso.* |
| Sit down and eat with us, friend. | *Siéntese a comer con nosotros, amigo.* |
| You can eat here. | *Puede comer aquí.* |
| Show me the best wood for cooking the kid. | *Enséñeme qué clase de leña sirve para asar el cabrito.* |
| Please cut me some clean spits for the kid. | *Córteme unos palitos muy limpios, por favor.* |
| Sharpen the end of the stick a little. | *Afile un poco la estaca.* |
| Where can we find firewood? | *¿Dónde hay leña?* |
| I'm going to light a fire. | *Voy a encender una lumbre.* |
| Have you any chips to start the fire? | *¿Tiene usted astillas para encender el fuego?* |
| Should I chop more wood? | *¿Corto más leña?* |
| That large log will choke the fire! | *¡Ese leño grande ahogará el fuego!* |
| A loop of the fatty intestine of a freshly killed goat or sheep, tied on a stick and broiled over coals | *Macho* (m.); *machitos* (m.); *burritos* (m.) |
| Skewered meat chunks | *Carne en alambres* (f.); *alambritos* (m.); *alambres de carne* (m.) |

## THE *COMAL*

You should acquire a *comal*. *Comales* can be made of anything from the cut out top of an oil drum, to the hood of an old car, to a clay plate. The *comal* is a basic Mexican cooking tool, and we always carry one with us for heating our *tortillas* at supper and breakfast. A sheet of steel plate about eight inches wide by twelve inches long and about one-quarter inch thick is ideal. Support it on rocks or pieces of iron re-bar over the coals and use it to warm your *tortillas* or other food. When the *tortillas* puff up, poke them down in the middle with a forefinger. *Tortillas* that have dried out can be salvaged by a sprinkle of water. Learn to catch them deftly on the *comal* with the fingertips and flip them without getting burned! You are then *un hombre de campo* (a country man). Mexican *vaqueros* (cowboys) and *candelilla* wax gatherers (*cereros*) have hands so tough they can light a smoke by picking up a live coal with their bare fingers.

It is traditional to turn *tortillas* three times. Warm one side, turn and heat until it puffs up, then a quick final turn back to the original down side and it's ready to eat. Fill the hot *tortilla* with *salsa, queso* (cheese), *chile con carne* (chile with meat), or even butter and syrup,

and roll it into a tube. Put your index finger over the top of the roll at
its middle, and support the two ends with thumb and ring or middle
finger, then push down with the index finger and the rolled *tortilla* is
formed into a bent tube, with the middle lower than each end. This
keeps the filling from running out the other end when you take a bite.
There is true artistry involved!

## STAYING HEALTHY

Fresh fruit and vegetables can be made safe to eat raw if you soak them
for thirty minutes in iodized water. Iodine (*yodo para lavar verduras*)
can be purchased in pharmacies. Two or three drops per quart of clean
water will do. Do not use tincture of iodine, as it is too weak.

Raw milk and pressed white country cheese can carry serious risks.
Adequate cooking is required of these (and all) foods to destroy patho-
gens and parasites.

| | |
|---|---|
| Where can I take a bath? | *¿Dónde puedo bañarme?* |
| Where can I wash my hands? | *¿Dónde puedo lavarme las manos?* |

You should assume that all rural water sources are polluted and pu-
rify the water in a manner proven effective. It is usually safe to drink
coffee in a Mexican village if it is hot and right from the pot. Bottled
sodas and beer are safe, but you should open them personally and in-
spect them. If they have been "cooled" in polluted water, as is frequently the case, you should at least wipe dry the cap and neck before
opening it or rinse the unopened bottle in water of known purity. Ice
cannot be relied on to be free of pollution.

Despite our own knowledge of the risks, we have eaten and drunk
items of uncertain purity many times when judgment was overruled
by hunger or thirst or in order not to offend a new friend. Still, the risk
is actual and substantial enough to warrant preventive measures.

### Avoiding More Serious Diseases and Parasites

Because you will be in the backcountry and sleeping outdoors, you are
exposed to more risk of acquiring certain diseases and parasites than is
the typical tourist who visits the cities, stays mainly in hotels, and
travels by automobile or airplane. The extra risk is not high, but can
be substantially eliminated by the following steps. We are not medical
doctors, and you are encouraged to consult competent medical spe-
cialists who have knowledge of the medical needs of international
travelers and who maintain current knowledge of the suggestions of
the Centers for Disease Control, Atlanta, Georgia 30333.

TETANUS: if you have not had a booster within the past ten years, you should have one.

POLIO: if you are an adult, a Salk (killed-vaccine) booster injection is advised. For children and young adults, a booster of live vaccine can be taken orally.

RABIES: if you are a cave explorer, or a zoologist who will be handling road-killed animals and trapped animals, you may wish to undergo rabies immunization (over a period of about two months). Rabies can be transmitted, although rarely, by inhalation of the dust or aerosols in caves frequented by certain bats, and zoologists are always looking for skeletons, no matter how smelly they may be. The risk is not great, but immunization is easily acquired before exposure.

TYPHOID: immunization takes about a month. In areas of polluted drinking water, such as much of lowland or tropical Mexico, it is worthwhile.

HEPATITIS: a single 2-ml injection of immune (gamma) globulin offers protection for a couple of months. In lowland or tropical Mexico or anywhere in Mexico where you cannot rely on clean food and drink, it is worthwhile. Take it before leaving home.

MALARIA: we went for years to Mexico, and even to Central American jungles, without worrying about antimalaria protection. However, it is one of the most serious diseases of travelers to the tropics and is spreading worldwide. Chemical protection is cheap, easy to use, and has proved to be very safe. In Mexico all of the lowland tropical areas place one at risk of infection, and the most recent surveys by the Centers for Disease Control show that even parts of lowland Chihuahua, Sonora, Durango, Jalisco, and Sinaloa are risky. These are states of mountains and canyons and offer some of the best hiking and exploring in Mexico, so you will want to go there. Risks can be considered to exist all year, and at all places below 3,000 feet (1,000 meters) elevation. In Mexico chloroquine-resistant strains of the parasite have not been found, so the basic adult dose is 300-mg base (500-mg salt) of chloroquine phosphate taken orally once a week beginning two weeks before entering Mexico and continuing for six weeks after your return. Remember, take that weekly tablet! Insect repellant, substantial clothing with long pants and shirtsleeves, and sleeping under a mosquito net all help reduce the chances of infection. Since the *Anopheles* mosquito feeds mainly between dusk and dawn, protection and avoidance in those hours is also a help. However, nothing beats good chemical protection with cloroquine.

When discussing your immunization needs with medical doctors, be sure to point out that you are not a typical tourist and that you will be on foot, in canoes or rafts, on muleback, and sleeping out of doors.

Be sure also to advise that you may be drinking water of uncertain purity and that you may be eating foods in native villages without assurance of quality. Of course, this may simply provoke the response, "Don't do it"!

## Sickness and Emergencies

| | |
|---|---|
| What is the matter with you? | *¿Qué tiene usted? (¿Qué le pasa?)* |
| Call a doctor. | *Llame usted un médico.* |
| Send for a doctor. | *Mande usted por el médico.* |
| At once. | *¡Pronto!* |
| I am very sick. | *Estoy muy enfermo(a).* |
| It hurts me here (pointing). | *Me duele aquí.* |
| Do you know a good doctor? | *¿Conoce un buen médico?* |
| Help me! | *¡Ayúdeme, por favor!* |
| Help | *Ayuda (socorro)* |
| Take me to a hospital. | *Lléveme al hospital.* |
| Take me to a doctor. | *Lléveme a un médico.* |
| Take me there. | *Lléveme allá.* |
| Come quickly! | *¡Venga pronto!* |
| Go quickly! | *¡Vaya pronto!* |
| Bring help! | *¡Traiga ayuda!* |
| Please don't move him (her)! | *¡No lo (la) mueva!* |
| Where is a hospital (doctor)? | *¿Dónde está un hospital (médico)?* |
| I've sprained my ankle. | *Me he torcido el tobillo.* |
| I've something in my eye. | *Tengo algo en el ojo.* |
| I have a terrible toothache. | *Tengo un dolor de muelas horroroso.* |
| Please don't move. Sit still. | *No se mueva, por favor. Estése quieto. (Siéntese quieto.)* |
| Point to where it hurts. | *Indíqueme dónde le duele.* |
| Show me where you hurt and try to tell me what's wrong. | *Indíqueme dónde le duele y trate de decirme lo que tiene.* |
| I want to see the doctor (clergyman) (lawyer). | *Deseo ver al médico (a un ministro o pastor) (a un abogado).* |
| I want to lie down (to go back to bed) (to get up) (to sit up) (to sit down). | *Deseo acostarme (volver a la cama) (levantarme) (sentarme en la cama) (sentarme).* |
| May I have ———? | *¿Puedo tomar ———?* |
| I cannot sleep (walk) (get up). | *No puedo dormir (caminar) (levantarme).* |
| I have a pain in my head (back) (chest) (legs). | *Tengo dolor de cabeza (de espalda) (en el pecho) (en las piernas).* |
| Am I better? Am I worse? | *¿Estoy mejor? ¿Estoy peor?* |

When is the doctor coming? | ¿Cuándo viene el doctor?
Please | Tenga la bondad de; por favor
I would like ———. | Yo quisiera ———.
Did you call? Just a minute, please. What is your problem? | ¿Usted llamó? Un momento por favor. ¿Cuál es su problema?
Good morning. How are you today? Did you sleep well? | Buenos días. ¿Cómo está usted hoy? ¿Durmió bien?
Good night. I hope you sleep well. | Buenas noches. Espero que duerma bien esta noche.

What is your religion? | ¿A qué religión pertenece usted?
Would you like to see a minister (priest)? | ¿Quiere ver a un padre o un ministro?
How do you feel? Are you all right now? | ¿Cómo se siente? ¿Está bien ahora?
Do you feel weak or strong? | ¿Se siente débil o fuerte?
Don't be afraid. It is nothing serious. | No tenga miedo. No es nada serio.
I feel fine. | Me siento bien.
I feel ill. | Me siento malo.
Did you rest well? | ¿Durmió bien?
I think I have a cold. | Pienso que estoy resfriado(a).
I will take you to the doctor. | Lo llevo a usted al doctor (médico).

Stretcher | Camilla (f.)
A short fervent prayer | Jaculatoria (f.)

# 12. Entertainment

**M**uch has been written about the ball games and footraces of the Indians of the western Sierra Madre, so no account will be given here of those events. However, you might be interested in other games and sports played by rural Mexicans, particularly by children, as there is much to be learned from their approach to entertainment.

We became interested in games and children's play after coming upon some temporary camps that had been abandoned. In each instance we found evidence that the children had been building small villages of stones, sticks, and native materials. We found pens of sticks, with "goats" of small round stones, and herders made of tied plant fibers. Some of these were so clever and artistic that we photographed them and showed them to our children when we returned home. As a result, our daughters (three between us) learned to make dolls, animals, pens, sheds, houses, and kitchen utensils from the native materials found at any spot they happened to be. Whenever we stop for a lunch break on a desert hike, or when we camp for the night, the girls usually end up making a small *rancho* or a village, populating it with dolls and animals made of whatever vegetable materials are at hand, using the native rock, dried plant remains, and grass for thatching. The skill has furnished them many hours of educational play, and they have taught it to many other children, with whom it has always been a hit. It has helped keep our children out of the "Barbie culture" and has taught them the very valuable lesson that you do not need to have a lot of material goods or toys to have fun; all you need is imagination and the will to invent your own playthings.

Although baseball and soccer are highly popular in Mexico, and probably dominate the game field in urban areas, we have not seen much evidence of either sport in the high mountains or in the deserts. We did pick up a child's hand-carved baseball bat abandoned when some timber cutters left an area, but that is about the only evidence we have found of these otherwise popular games. Volleyball (*vólibol*), however, is popular in even remote desert *ejidos*. It is playable in a small cleared area and does not have the space requirements of·soccer or baseball. Men, women, and children all play, sometimes all at the same time, sometimes in more organized teams.

Volleyball is a valuable aid to breaking the ice in a Mexican village. If you carry a net, ball, and some portable poles, you can get a game going almost anywhere. It takes no language to communicate in a sport with universally known rules. If you wish to provide something for the benefit of a rural school, a net and ball are always valued gifts. Get the weatherproof type of net, of nylon, and get a ball designed for scuffing. It is also a good idea to put some leak sealant in the ball before you leave home, as there are lots of thorns and sharp sticks around the volleyball courts of rural Mexico. Leak sealants really do the job. Be sure to provide a hand pump and a couple of needles with the ball, as they are hard to come by in Mexico's outback.

### Game Vocabulary

| | |
|---|---|
| Do you want to play volleyball? | ¿Quiere usted jugar al vólibol? |
| Do you play volleyball? | ¿Sabe usted jugar al vólibol? |
| Let's play a game! | ¡Vamos a jugar un partido! |
| What do you want to play? | ¿Qué quiere jugar? |
| It's your turn. | Le toca a usted. |
| Let's join hands. | Juntemos las manos. |
| Hold hands. | Cójanse de la mano. |
| Let's play this game. | Vamos a jugar este juego. |
| What are the rules? | ¿Cuáles son las reglas? |
| They wanted to see who could throw the farthest. | Querían ver quién podía tirar más lejos. |
| Pitch (toss) the ball to me. | Tíreme (Aviénteme) la pelota. |
| What is our score? | ¿Cómo estamos de tantos? |
| Whose turn is it to serve? | ¿A quién le toca sacar? |
| It's your serve. | Usted tiene el saque. |
| That was some throw! | ¡Ese fue un buen tiro! |
| Who threw that? | ¿Quién tiró eso? |
| Who goes first? | ¿Quién va primero? |
| I don't think we can tie the score now. | No creo que podamos empatar ahora. |
| Tough luck! | ¡Mala suerte! |
| Good luck! | ¡Buena suerte! |
| They won 20 to 12. | Ganaron por veinte tantos a doce. |
| Shall we play a game of volleyball? | ¿Nos echamos una partida de vólibol? |
| The ball fell out of bounds! | ¡La pelota cayó fuera del campo (de la cancha)! |

| Was that play fair or foul? | ¿Fué la jugada limpia o sucia? |
| Ball | Pelota (f.) |
| Ball game | Juego de pelota (m.) |
| To play ball | Jugar a la pelota |
| Playing field, court | Cancha (f.) |
| Net | Red (f.) |
| Volley (bat the ball back and forth) | Volear; volea (f.) |
| Serve the ball | Sacar la pelota |
| Points or score | Tanto (m.) |

## Singing

Discussion of entertainment would not be complete without considering singing. We always carry guitars, mandolins, and other instruments with us and sit around and play and sing in the evening. When you camp in or near a Mexican village, you will usually get some singers and players to come forth, and you can have a good jam session. There are good rural musicians all over Mexico, and singing and playing are popular forms of entertainment in the back country. Your ability to sing and play will help you break the ice and make friends more quickly. Singing Mexican folksongs in Spanish is also a good way to learn the language. A *gringo* who can sing like a Mexican is always an instant hit!

## Popcorn

Popcorn is an inexpensive treat that goes a long way. A little popcorn, cooking oil (*aceite comestible*), salt (*sal*), and a pan with a lid and you can treat all the visitors to your camp. Popcorn (*palomitas, esquite, rosetas, palomitas de maíz,* or *maíz chapolote*) was developed by the Indians who preceded many of the Spanish-speaking peoples of Mexico, Central and South America. Native popcorn is grown in many of Mexico's rural areas. Remember as you select a can of popcorn at the supermarket that long before the discovery voyages of Columbus the Indian agriculturists of Mexico and nations south of it had developed many varieties of corn (*maíz*), not to mention tomatoes, peppers, potatoes, vanilla, chocolate, squash, pumpkin, and other plants that have so greatly enriched our diets. Taking popcorn to Mexico is akin to carrying coals to Newcastle!

## Soap Bubbles

Small children love to blow soap bubbles (*ampollas* or *burbujas*). Carrying along some cheap plastic bubble blowers and plenty of mixture for the bubbles will furnish much fun for you, the children, and their parents, at little cost.

The child's blowing soap bubbles!    *¡El niño hace pompas de jabón!*

## Tape Recordings

In these days of the portable tape recorder (*grabadora de cinta*), it is easy to record singers, or children at play, and playing back their own voices usually creates a lot of interest. "Mike fright" is common, so it is easier and less distracting to use the mike that is a part of most recorders, rather than an external mike with a wire. Never poke it in their faces.

| | |
|---|---|
| To tape record | *Grabar en cinta* |
| Recording | *Grabación* (f.) |
| I'm going to make a recording. | *Voy a hacer una grabación.* |

# 13. Adaptability to the Environment

**M**uch of northern Mexico is desert country, the Chihuahuan Desert and the Sonoran Desert both being recognized as such. It is a harsh environment in which to wrest a living from the soil by any of the means commonly resorted to. Constant exposure to such an environment toughens the *gente* and makes for self-reliant individuals. Examples of this toughness and self-reliance are easy to come by, but let us give four that illustrate the point well.

PATRICIO DOMÍNGUEZ. We first met Patricio Domínguez in about 1973 in the old mining and ranching village of San Carlos (now Ejido Manuel Benavides), some thirty or forty miles southeast of Ojinaga, Chihuahua. He was an old man then, in his seventies, and no doubt has passed on, although he was vigorous and appeared healthy at that time.

When we encountered him, he was making fiber rope (*mecate*) from the fibers (*ixtle*) of the *lechuguilla* plant, a common *agave* of his area. He was twisting the fibers into rope, in a manner described in chapter 10. We stopped to watch him work and to learn his technique and soon struck up a friendship. Since we were at that point starting a ten-day ramble across Chihuahua and Coahuila on unmapped roads, and since we were gathering information about the plants, roads, mountains, and water sources of the area, we asked him if he would like to take a trip with us. He said, *"¡Si, con mucho gusto!"* went into his *jacal*, grabbed a straw *sombrero* and a fiber *morral*, and got in with us, without hesitation or goodbye to anyone, to go with us to any place we decided to go. It turned out that we could not have made a better choice. He had been born in Redford (then called Polvo), Texas, just across the river, and had lived on the border all his life, living first on one side then the other, depending on the "heat," as he had been a revolutionary in the Mexican Revolution and also an outlaw and rustler on the Texas side. He knew every road, trace, and trail, every pass and mountain range, every spring and waterhole within a vast area of country.

None of the information he gave us has ever turned out to be in error.

He had a great sense of humor. We passed a *campo santo* (graveyard), and he described it as "a very quiet *ejido*." He saw Bob Burleson's key ring, with its dozens of keys to ranch and farm gates, office, home, etc., and said he "didn't know there were that many locks in the whole world."

Finally, over a hundred miles from his home, he said it was time to get back, and we let him out, at a tiny place called Puesto del Lucio at a fork in the road, with nothing more than he started with, no food, no water, and no ride. We offered to take him to some other place, or to wait until he got a ride, but he merely laughed and said he could get home from anywhere "with a penny in my sandal" (*con un centavo en mi chancla*). No doubt he made it back without any problem at all. He confided to us with a wink that he had "family" in virtually every *jacal* and *rancho*.

MARCARIO HINOJOSA. Marcario was a very old man when we first met him in the mid-1960s at Terlingua, Texas, where he lived in an old rock house near the store that was then in operation. (We learned later of his death.) Marcario had been a miner (*minero*) in nearly all the mining areas in the Big Bend area, on both sides. He took us to some mines that he had worked in, tiny, airless shafts, barely wide enough for a slender man to pass through while stooped over. He demonstrated how they worked with *sotol* torches and kerosene lanterns for smoky light, breaking the ore out with picks and bars and hauling it to the surface in large *ixtle* fiber bags (*costales*) with a tumpline or strap from the top of the bag to the forehead of the miner, to help support the load. Under certain conditions the miners worked naked because of the heat and poor ventilation in the shafts and tunnels. Many of them became poisoned by certain types of ore (probably mercury poisoning), and it must have been one of the toughest life-styles imaginable. Mines we have visited in Mexico are even narrower and more poorly ventilated than those around Terlingua. Marcario had long outlived all his contemporaries and was hanging on as one of the few then still alive who had worked the Terlingua mines in the early days. He knew most of the people buried in the Terlingua *campo santo* and had helped bury a good many of them.

RAMÓN URESTE. Ramón is an *arriero*, a burro driver, and we once employed him and five of his burros to haul water to the tops of some dry mountains where we wished to set up a base camp and explore. We also thought how nice it would be to have the burros haul our packs up the 6,000 vertical feet to the top, but after beating them up the moun-

Marcario Hinojosa and his puppy.
Marcario was then in his nineties.
(Mickey Burleson photo)

tain we calculated that the energy savings were somewhat overesti-
mated in our advance plans, as you work harder trying to get burros up
a trackless mountain than you do climbing it with the pack on your
own back! However, that is a different story.

Ramón showed up for this hike, which was in February, cold and
foggy at the start, with a climb to an elevation of about 8,000 feet,
without a bedroll, dressed in street shoes, a flannel cap, a denim
jacket, jeans, and a thin shirt. We had *ponchos*, down jackets, wool
pants, hiking boots, and all the rest of the gear that *gringos* (*alpinistas*)
burden themselves with. Since we were to stay about five days and four
nights on top, we asked Ramón what he intended to do at night, what
he intended to eat, and what he would do if the weather turned worse.
He seemed unconcerned and answered that he would build a small fire
and sit close, he would eat what we gave him, if he could stand it, and
if not he would eat nothing, and if the weather got worse it was God's
will and he would sit closer to his fire or look for a hole to get into!

As matters turned out, we had sleet the first night out, and we
moved Ramón into a tent. He was able to eat *some* of our food (but not
the freeze-dried stew), and despite the cold he refused to put on a
sweater that was offered him as we hiked out each day from the base
camp. His shoes came apart (both heels came off on the way up), but he
never showed any sign of sore feet. As he hopped from boulder to boul-

der, whacking and cursing the burros, he appeared totally unconcerned about the unreasonably steep game trail, the drops of several
hundred feet yawning a single misstep off the trail, and never seemed
to tire.

Ramón is not exceptional. We have run into Mexicans hiking trails
in the blaze of summer's heat and the freezing winter many miles from
any village or habitation, in daylight or by moonlight, without what
we consider proper clothing, without proper shoes or boots, and usually without a sign of a water jug or canteen. They know their country
and are just flat tougher than we are. Just for kicks, sometime, try heft-
ing and carrying on your back one of the loads of wood that you see old
men or women or young boys packing up a Mexican mountain, or put
a tumpline around your forehead and try marching off through the
jungle or swamp with a *costal* of dried ears of corn. That 100-pound
old woman or 135-pound old man or boy can probably haul more of a
load than you can, and haul it a lot farther and not complain one bit in
the process.

VAQUEROS. Back in the early 1970s we made a trip to climb one of
the higher peaks in northern Coahuila, El Centinela. On the way up
we found a rather interesting "boundary marker" created by a black
bear (*oso negro*), apparently a pretty good-sized one. A pine tree about
eight inches in diameter was growing at a low spot in the ridge, a natural place for animals to cross. This tree was mutilated and "wounded"
by many long sets of claw marks, starting above our heads and coming
down to about three feet off the ground. These were all around the
tree, always vertical, and were of varying ages, some relatively fresh
and oozing sap, and others older and healed. Abundant black bear hair
stuck in the tree's bark, clearly showing what animal had made the
scratches (as if there could be any doubt). There was a good bit of bear
scat (easily identifiable by its large size and the abundance of acorn
hulls it contains) along the game trail we had been following. Presumably, this was a marker tree, marked and probably also scented with
urine as a warning to other male bears to avoid the area. In several en-
counters with bears at close range in these mountains, the unanimous
action of the bears had been a "woof" and a retreat at amazing speed,
convincing us that if a bear ever charged as fast as it retreated, we were
in trouble for sure! Since we were not hunting and were unarmed, we
wondered, as we observed the impressive depth and width of these claw
marks in live wood, what we would do if we ever met a bear that did not
"woof" and run away. Frankly, that question remains unanswered.

This, however, is not a bear story but a story about Mexican *vaqueros* and territorial markers.

Ramón Ureste of Ejido Jaboncillos, Coahuila, a fine *arriero*. He sits atop the Sierra del Carmen, Coahuila, overlooking Boquillas Canyon. (Will Thompson photo)

After leaving the bear's boundary marker (*jalón*), we finished the climb of El Centinela and, after enjoying the beautiful 360-degree view from its relatively tiny top, we decided to play *alpinistas* and leave a record of our conquest. We wrote our names, addresses, and a short history of our climb, along with the date, and placed it in an aluminum 35mm film can with screw top (the old style, not made in recent years). The can was one of those that was painted bright yellow. We left the can under a cairn of flat rocks right on the highest point of the peak, thinking that perhaps some day one of us would get back up there with his children and could show them that daddy had left his mark on the mountain just like the bear did.

In about 1981, we were some ten miles or so south of Pico El Centinela, in the area of Rancho El Club, driving our truck over rutted roads flowing with clear water like mountain streams after unusually heavy rains, when we encountered a group of *vaqueros* jerking meat. They had accidentally killed a cow while working stock (a frequent occurrence, as *vaqueros* are traditionally pretty rough with livestock and will forefoot an animal with the *lazo* where rough ground almost guarantees injury) and had butchered it on the spot. Strips of red meat, cut with the grain, were hanging out to dry into *carne seca* on *lazos* strung from tree to tree, and meat for the evening meal was cooking on the fire.

These *vaqueros* were from a nearby *ejido*, and they were not happy to see us. They were not overtly hostile, but definitely were not friendly, an uncommon reaction in our experience. After talking a while, it became clear what the problem was. They thought from our massive *doble tracción* truck, with winch and big mud tires (we call it Supertruck) that we were miners (*mineros*) or timber cutters (*leñeros*) exploring for timbers for the mines, and they had been having trouble with some of these folks cutting their fences, poaching their game, and disputing their boundaries. They thought we might be scouting for these competitors for the available natural resources.

After making friends, we visited an hour or so with them before going on to make camp for the night near a gushing spring. It turned out that they had been having trouble with soldiers (*soldados*) also, coming in and killing game (*caza*). These men were among the few we have talked with from the *ejidos* who seemed to have any idea at all of conservation, because they volunteered that it was obvious that if people killed game for food or fun whenever they felt inclined, there would soon be no game. They also said that they were not all that concerned about mountain lions (*leones*) and bear, because "there is a place for everything in this world and we all need to live together." Also, it seems that the Indians (*los indios*) from the Kickapoo village near Músquiz, 80 miles or more to the south, would periodically come to this area for communal hunts and kill much game (white-tailed deer). We were already aware of this fact from previous trips and conversation with ranchers down the mountain chain toward Músquiz.

In the course of the conversation, we asked where the boundary of their *ejido* ran, and they said "from the top of El Centinela to the Cerro Colorado," and this got us to talking about the mountain. We told them that "*en años pasados*" we had climbed El Centinela and described the arduous climb. Then they told us this story:

*Vaqueros* head for home on tired horses, followed by tired cowdogs, after a long day of gathering cattle in the Coahuilan brush. (Earl Nottingham photo)

We were in a dispute with the *mineros* and the *leñeros* about the true boundary of our *ejido*, and we were told that our boundary started at the top of the Pico el Centinela. So, we decided to climb up there and see if we could find our *jalón*, which marks the boundary. We started off early in the morning, and that was some climb! It took us all day, and we were hot and tired. But it was worth it, for when we got to the top we found the *jalón*, a little stack of rocks for a marker, and when we opened the *jalón* we found this yellow can with some papers inside. We could not read them, but because we knew that they were important to our title [*título*], we took the yellow can and the papers back to the *ejido* to keep it safely among our documents, thinking all the while that, indeed, someone else had claim to our territory.

So much for our cairn and our film can. Now when our children climb Pico El Centinela on their own, they will never believe we were there before them. Come to think of it, neither will you!

# PART II. LANGUAGE

# 14. A Brief Guide to Spanish Grammar and Pronunciation

**A**lthough Spanish is a relatively easy language to learn, its grammar is, to the beginner, a formidable undertaking. It has a familiar or friendly form and a formal or polite form. There are regular verbs and irregular verbs and of course all manner of tenses. Adjectives must agree in gender with nouns they modify. Nouns and articles have masculine and feminine forms. There are prefixes, suffixes, diminutives, augmentatives, depreciatives, and so on. Spanish is an expressive, colorful language. Our guide assumes that you have some knowledge of and grasp of conversational Spanish, or that you are willing to acquire it by self-study.

For those who may want to delve further into this wonderfully expressive language and its grammar, we recommend to you the following materials.

One of the best general, practical introductions to Spanish grammar is found in the U.S. Immigration and Naturalization Service's "A Practical Spanish Grammar for Border Patrol Officers" (1972 revision, GPO, Washington, D.C.). This book provides an intense but practical course in Spanish and although the vocabulary is meant for the Border Patrol (*la migra*) it works very well indeed for most purposes.

For those more academically inclined, there are any number of fine Spanish textbooks. Concise grammars can be found in every dictionary. Our favorite is the "Elements of Spanish Grammar" in Simon and Schuster's *International Dictionary*; this version is especially concise and to the point.

Unlike English, Spanish is completely phonetic. The simple pronunciation guide that follows will allow you to pronounce most words in this guide correctly the first time. As you listen to and talk with native speakers your accent will improve rapidly. Our guide is intended to help you communicate in Spanish through a gradual vocabulary-building and thus conversation-building process.

We invite you to jump in and enjoy conversational Spanish and thus the people and the country. This experience will only stimulate you to learn more about the language, since communication is the key to understanding the land and its people.

## PRONUNCIATION

Although you may not believe it, the pronunciation of Spanish words is actually simpler than English pronunciation. There is less variation in sounds and the rules are less complicated. The Spanish vowels are represented by the letters *a, e, i, o,* and *u,* as in English.

*a*    is always pronounced like the *a* in the English word *mama.*
    *casa   pasa   masa*

*e*    is pronounced much like the long *a* in *rate.*
    *mesa   te   peso*
    In a syllable that ends in a consonant, *e* is pronounced like the *e* in *let.*
    *es   del   este   tengo*

*i*    is pronounced like the *ee* in *feet* or *peek.*
    *si   ranchito   cabrito   mina*

*o*    is pronounced like the *o* in *so* or *go.*
    *solo   oro   río   beso*

*u*    is pronounced like the *oo* in *boot.*
    *su   tu   subir   usted*

The consonants are pronounced as follows:

*b*    *b* and *v* are pronounced so much alike that uneducated Mexicans often interchange them in spelling. *Vaca* is sometimes spelled "*baca*" and *veinte* is sometimes spelled "*beinte,*" for example. At the beginning of a word and after the letters *m* and *n,* they sound like the *b* in *book.*
    *bonito   bajo   ambos*
    At all other times the *b* and *v* are pronounced like the *v* in *level.*
    *beber   vivir   baile   libro   cabra*

*c*    sounds like *k* in English unless it is followed by an *e* or an *i,* in which case it sounds like the English *s.*
    *como   campo   casa   ciudad   cera*

*ch*    is a single letter and sounds like the *ch* in *church.*
    *chalar   mucho   chica   muchísimo   macho*

*d*    is similar to the *d* in English; however, between vowels it sounds like the *th* in *they.*
    *dar   donde   lado   vado*

*f*    sounds essentially the same as its English counterpart.
    *falcete   frente   freno   fuego*

*g*    is the same as the *g* in English, unless followed by an *e* or *i,* and then it is like an *h* in English.

*gato   pago   gente   girasol*

*h*    is always silent in Spanish. It takes some practice for the English speaker to leave it silent.

*hijo   hora   hoy   huevo   hablar*

*j*    is always like the English *h*.

*Juan   hijo   frijol   jinete*

*k*    is not found in the Spanish alphabet, although it does appear in words of foreign origin. It is pronounced like the *k* in English.

*kilo   kilómetro*

*l*    sounds much the same as in English.

*leche   lado   libra   lejos*

*ll*   is treated as a single letter in the Spanish alphabet and sounds like the *y* in *yellow*.

*lleno   llano   caballo   llevar*

*n*    is much like the *n* in English.

*nunca   noche   nada   niño*

*ñ*    is a separate letter and sounds like the *ny* in *canyon*.

*mañana   leña   cañón   año*

*p*    sounds much the same as in English.

*poder   padre   primero   poner*

*q*    is much like the *k* in English and is always followed by a silent *u*.

*quiote   queso   que   quiero*

*r*    is a difficult letter to pronounce in Spanish. It is similar to the English *r* but is slightly trilled or rolled. It is more strongly trilled at the beginning of a word than within a word.

*rancho   robar   rojo   rico   rastro   pero*

*rr*   is a separate letter. It is very strongly trilled. Say the English word *ladder* several times in rapid succession, faster and faster, and you will be saying the Spanish *rr*.

*perro   carro   correr   cigarro*

*s*    is sounded much like the English *s*. Before *d* and *m* it sounds more like a *z*.

*solo   sacar   mismo   sed*

*t*    is much like its English counterpart.

*tome   tiene   todo   tuvo*

*v*    is explained under *b*.

*w*    is not a part of the Spanish alphabet.

*x*    sounds like the English *gs* when found between vowels.

*exacto   examin*

When it is followed by a consonant it sounds more like the English *s*, although this distinction is not made by all Spanish speakers and some pronounce it the same as the English *x*.

*explicar   extensión   expreso*

*y*   is sounded like the long *e* in English,
        *ley   y   rey*
      or as a consonant like the *y* in *Yuma.*
        *yucca   yo   leyes   ayer*
*z*   sounds much like the English *s.*
        *zorro   zero   zapato*

## ACCENTUATION

In Spanish you raise your voice higher on one syllable than on another, to add inflection or emphasis (this is the accented syllable). Words that end in a vowel or *n* or *s* are pronounced with stress on the next-to-last syllable. All other words are stressed on the last syllable, unless there is a written accent mark.

| | |
|---|---|
| *ca*sa | trac*tor* |
| *va*mos | algo*dón* |
| *pa*se | pa*sar* |
| ca*ba*llo | fri*jol* |
| *ha*blan | |

# 15. Specific Vocabulary, Phrases, and Conversations

**O**ne major weakness of most phrase books is the fact that they usually give only one side of the conversation. Where practical we have attempted to work in typical responses to your questions or statements, to help you understand and communicate that much better. Not all of these conversations are complete, and not all of them make sense alone, but they should help you flesh out your communicating abilities. We have grouped them under the following topics, to help you locate the conversation you need for a given situation. We have tried to give you alternate ways of saying the same thing where good alternatives are known to us.

| | |
|---|---|
| Buying and Bargaining | Ownership and Property |
| Clothing | Parts of the Body and Health |
| Coming, Going, and Travel | Problem Solving |
| Commands | Sayings |
| Emotions and Feelings | Simple Ideas, Concepts, and Wants |
| Fault and Blame | Time and Dates |
| Hunting and Predators | Warnings and Cautions |
| Idiomatic and Slang Expressions | Weather |
| Marital and Family Relations | The World |
| Observations (general) | |

Certainly it is not possible to gather under these limited headings everything that you may need under every possible circumstance, but after you go through them we believe you will agree that it is a pretty good start. Your suggestions for improvement will be appreciated.

## BUYING AND BARGAINING

In most of the Mexican backcountry, you won't be doing much shopping, except for gasoline from drums, sodas, fruit juice in cans, or perhaps some fruit or produce. Some of the small rural *tiendas* (stores), though, have interesting items, including locally made equipment, and in Indian areas there are open-air markets and market days that are worthwhile. In the more tropical regions you find more markets, market days, and things to shop for. All we intend to do here is give you some basic shopping and bartering language and a few hints.

Outside the main cities, most prices will be the same for you as for a Mexican; the double price list is uncommon in rural areas. Still, you need to exercise good judgment in shopping anywhere, so that you don't pay too much and be thought a fool.

Most vendors in markets in Mexico expect to haggle over prices and will usually set their first price higher than they expect to sell for. Don't hesitate to bargain, shop around, and haggle over prices, as it is all part of the game and a custom of the country. In *tiendas*, the prices are less flexible.

Gasoline prices, even from a drum in a remote village, are pretty much standard and are not usually the subject of bargaining. Services such as guide fees and driver fees are subject to bargaining. It helps to stand around awhile and watch the natives doing their shopping. Watch what they do, see what they pay, and keep an eye out for the price of the objects you are interested in. It pays off.

It's hard to bargain effectively if you are unwilling to walk off and never look back if you cannot get a decent price. Steel yourself, there's always something else down the line that you will like as well, or better, and at a better price.

Bargaining is a calm, deliberate discussion, not a disagreement. Keep it that way. If your Spanish is inadequate, use gestures and facial expressions to convey your meaning, and keep trying until you get the hang of it.

Always use Mexican currency if at all possible. With the devaluation of the peso, it goes farther. Learn the exchange rate, as it is easy to calculate.

Start with a polite greeting. (*"Buenos días"*; *"¿Qué tal?"*)

Examine the wares or produce carefully, to be sure of its condition. Examine everything top and bottom.

Ask what the price is, as it is never marked. Price the same item at several places, if possible. Watch out if any price is unusually high. Watch the eyes and side glances of the seller, and watch for grins on the faces of spectators!

Make a counteroffer, say 25 percent to 50 percent below the asking price, and always less than you would be willing to pay.

Barter back and forth until you have made your final offer.

Wait around and give the other person time to think about the deal, then speak politely as if you are leaving.

You may even have to take a few steps away. If necessary, just keep going. As long as you still have your money, it has been cheap recreation. Sometimes you may want to count out the money (your offer) into your hand and then repeat your offer with the cold cash in plain view.

| Good morning. | *Buenos días.* |
| How much? | *¿Cuánto, por favor?* |
| At how much do you sell this? | *¿A cómo vende usted esto?* |
| At what price do you give it? | *¿A cómo lo da, Señora?* |
| How much does it cost? | *¿Cuánto cuesta, por favor?* |
| What is it worth? | *¿Cuánto vale, Señor?* |
| It is worth 50 pesos. | *Vale cincuenta pesos.* |
| How much is it? | *¿Cuánto es, por favor?* |
| I'll give you 20 pesos (a counteroffer less than asking price). | *Le doy veinte pesos (emphasis on veinte).* |
| Won't it go for 20 pesos? | *¿No sale (Lo deja) en veinte pesos?* |
| I'll take it for 20 pesos. | *Lo llevo por veinte pesos.* |
| Won't you give it to me for 20 pesos? | *¿No me lo da (deja) por veinte pesos?* |

It's not customary to run down the merchandise. That's not polite. Also, food items usually have a lower markup than hardware or craft items, so set your offer accordingly. Don't show a lot of money. Carry small bills and in different pockets, with plenty of change in rural areas. Also remember that in the small *tiendas* there is less tendency to bargain than in markets (prices are more rigid).

| It is worth 5 pesos. | *Vale cinco pesos.* |
| It is as I said. | *Es como yo digo.* |
| It is too expensive; I will give you 20 pesos. | *¡Está muy caro! Le doy a usted veinte pesos.* |
| I cannot reduce the price a penny more. | *No puedo rebajar el precio ni un centavo.* |
| I find that price too high. | *Está muy caro.* |
| Is there another one cheaper? | *¿No hay otro más barato?* |
| Can't you make it less? | *¿No puede rebajarlo?* |
| What is your bottom price? | *¿Cuál es el último precio?* |
| You ask me too much. | *Usted me pide demasiado.* |
| I won't pay that much. | *No puedo pagar tanto.* |
| The price is very high. | *El precio es muy caro.* |
| I do not like to haggle over prices. | *No me gusta regatear.* |
| It is (They are) very cheap. | *Está (Están) muy barato(s).* |
| It is a bargain. | *Es una ganga. (¡Qué ganga!)* |
| You'll find many bargains here. | *Usted encontrará aquí muchas gangas.* |

| | |
|---|---|
| It is a very low price. | *Es un precio muy bajo.* |
| I'll make a bargain with you. | *Haré un trato con usted.* |
| Very moderate. | *Muy módico(a).* |
| Very reasonable. | *Muy equitativo(a) (razonable;* |
| | *justo(a)).* |
| Payment in advance | *Pago adelantado* |
| Now, tell me what I owe you. | *Ahora, dígame cuánto le debo.* |
| It comes to 100 pesos. | *Le sale cien pesos.* |
| Are you mistaken? | *¿No se equivocaría usted?* |
| | *(¿Está equivocado(a)?)* |
| Give me back 10 pesos; you | *Haga el favor de devolverme diez* |
| charged me too much. | *pesos; me cobró de más.* |
| I lack ——— pesos. | *Me faltan ——— pesos.* |
| The account is right. | *La cuenta está exacta (correcta).* |
| I didn't buy it because of the high | *No lo compré por el alto precio.* |
| price. | |
| It comes out cheaper if you buy | *Le sale más barato si compra* |
| five at a time. | *cinco una vez.* |
| Both good and cheap. | *Es bueno y barato a la vez.* |
| That's a good buy. | *Es una buena compra.* |
| I don't call this cheap! | *¡No le llamo a esto barato!* |
| I will take this. | *Me llevo esto. (Llevaré esto.)* |
| I'll take this one. | *Me quedo con este(a).* |
| Show me some others (something | *Enséñeme usted otros (algo* |
| different). | *diferente).* |
| I will think it over and call again. | *Lo pensaré y regresaré.* |
| It doesn't fit (you, me). | *No (le, me) queda.* |
| This is too (large) (small) (long) | *Esto está demasiado (grande)* |
| (short) (tight). | *(chico) (largo) (corto) (ajustado).* |
| I would like to buy ———. | *Deseo (Quiero) comprar ———.* |
| Do you sell Pepsi-Cola here? | *¿Venden Pepsi aquí?* |
| | *(¿Hay Pepsi?)* |
| Give me a bottle, please. | *Por favor, déme una botella* |
| | *(cáscara).* |

(Note: There is always a deposit [*depósito, embase*] on the empty bottle [*cáscara*]. Return bottle to claim it.)

| | |
|---|---|
| Is there ———? | *¿Hay ———?* |
| There is no ———. | *No hay ———.* |

(Note: See the discussion of the use of *tener* vs. *haber* on pages 104–105.)

| | |
|---|---|
| I want to buy ———. | *Yo quiero comprar ———.* |
| Is it cheaper or more expensive? | *¿Es más barato o más caro?* |

| | |
|---|---|
| I also want ———. | También quiero ———. |
| Would you like to buy ———? | ¿Le gustaría comprar ———? |
| I'll buy it. | Lo compro. |
| It's rather expensive. | Es bastante caro. |
| Then I will take the cheapest. | Escogeré entonces el más barato. |

(Note: When buying fresh meat, specify "pedazo entero" [whole piece] or the butcher may chop it up without asking.)

| | |
|---|---|
| We bargained with him before buying. | Estuvimos regateando con él antes de comprar. |
| Don't go above 20 pesos. | No pase de veinte pesos. |
| What's the actual cost? | ¿Cuál es el costo real? |
| Be careful you are not cheated! | ¡Cuidado que no le engañen! |
| Are these eggs fresh? | ¿Están frescos estos huevos? |
| How much are eggs by the dozen? | ¿Cuánto vale la docena de huevos? |
| These eggs are 5 pesos a dozen. | Estos huevos son a cinco pesos la docena. |
| Is your offer still open? | ¿Está todavía en pie la oferta? |
| Choose one or the other. | Elija uno u otro. |
| I don't want this one but the other. | No deseo éste, sino el otro. |
| What is his range of prices? | ¿Cuál es su escala de precios? |
| This is the standard size (price). | Este es el tamaño (precio) corriente. |
| How much for it as is? | ¿Cuánto quiere usted por ello, tal como está? |
| I know a store where you can buy that. | Conozco una tienda donde puede usted comprar eso. |
| Let's make a trade. | Hagamos un cambio. |
| Let's settle accounts. | Vamos a ajustar las cuentas. |
| There seems to be an error in the bill. | Parece que hay un error en la cuenta. |
| This account is correct. | Esta cuenta está justa. |
| They gave me this for good measure. | Me dieron esto de pilón (yapa). |
| Do you want anything more? | ¿Desea algo más? |
| No, that's all. | No. Eso es todo. |
| Can't you knock down the price a couple of pesos? | ¿No podría rebajar el precio un par de pesos? |
| Knock something off the price. | Rebaje un poco el precio. |
| That's the most I can pay. | Eso es lo máximo (más) que puedo pagar. |
| This cost me more than I expected. | Esto me ha costado más de lo que esperaba. |

## CLOTHING

| | |
|---|---|
| Clothing (general term) | Ropa (f.); vestidos (m.) |
| What size? | ¿Qué tamaño? (¿Qué talla?) |
| Does it fit? | ¿Cabe? (¿Le queda?) |
| It doesn't fit. | No cabe. (No me queda.) |
| Bag, purse; pocket | Bolsa (f.); bolsillo (m.) |
| Belt | Cinturón (m.); cinto (m.) |
| Blouse | Blusa (f.) |
| Boot | Calzado (m.); bota (f.) |
| Bra | Brasiér (m.); sostén (m.) |
| Button | Botón (m.) |
| Buttonhole | Ojal (m.) |
| Cap | Cachucha (f.) |
| Coat | Chaqueta (f.); saco (m.) |
| Diaper | Pañal (m.) |
| Dress | Vestido (m.) |
| Eyeglasses | Anteojos (m.); lentes (m.) |
| Glove | Guante (m.) |
| Handkerchief | Pañuelo (m.) |
| Hat | Sombrero (m.) (means "maker of shade") |
| Heel (of shoe) | Talón (m.) |
| Jacket (heavy) | Chamarra (f.); saco (m.) |
| Overcoat | Abrigo (m.) |
| Panties | Pantaletas (f.) |
| Pants | Pantalones (m.); calzones (m.) |
| Pantyhose | Pantimedias (f.) |
| Sandals | Huaraches (m.); chanclas (f.) |
| Shirt | Camisa (f.) |
| Shoe | Zapato (m.); calzado (m.) |
| Shorts | Calzoncillos (m.) |
| Skirt | Falda (f.); enagua (f.) |
| Sleeve | Manga (f.) |
| Slip | Fondo (m.) |
| Socks | Calcetines (m.) |
| Sole (of shoes) | Suela (f.) |
| Stockings | Medias (f.) |
| Suit | Traje (m.) |
| Sweater | Suéter (m.); sudador (m.) |
| Swim suit | Traje de baño (m.); traje de natación (m.) |
| Underpants | Trusas (f.) |

| Undershirt | *Camiseta* (f.) |
| Underwear | *Ropa interior* (f.) (*calzones* [m.]) |
| Zipper | *Cierre relámpago* (m.); *riqui* (m.) |

## COMING, GOING, AND TRAVEL

| Did you have any trouble keeping up with the others? | *¿Tuvo usted dificultad en mantenerse al paso con los demás?* |
| Do you think you can last another mile (kilometer)? | *¿Cree usted que puede durar una milla (kilómetro) más? (¿Cree usted que puede aguantar [resistir] una milla más?)* |
| Are you all ready? | *¿Están listos(as)?* sing.: *¿Está listo(a)?* |
| Let me by, please. | *Por favor, déjeme pasar.* |
| The burros were carrying heavy packs. | *Los burros llevaban cargas pesadas.* |
| That is too heavy a load for the burro. | *Es una carga demasiado (muy) pesada para el burro.* |
| We have to lighten the load. | *Tenemos que aligerar la carga.* |
| Be sure to lock the gate when you leave the ranch. | *Cerciórese que haya usted cerrado la puerta con llave al salir del rancho.* |
| Do you have a lock for the gate? | *¿Tiene usted un candado para la puerta?* |
| Do you know where they are moving to? | *¿Sabe usted adónde van a cambiarse?* |
| They are always on the move. | *Siempre andan de acá para allá.* |
| The trip is off. | *Se ha suspendido el viaje.* |
| You should go in the opposite direction. | *Debe usted ir en la dirección opuesta.* |
| Where are the others? | *¿Dónde están los otros?* |
| You can't see them? | *¿No se los ve?* |
| One can see them. | *Se los ve.* |
| My staying here is out of the question. | *Es imposible que me esté aquí.* |
| It is 10 kilometers over that way. | *Está a diez kilómetros hacia allá (en esa dirección).* |
| I intend to stop there overnight. | *Pienso (Mi intención es) pasar la noche allí.* |
| Point out the place you told me about. | *Muéstreme (Indíqueme) el lugar de que me habló.* |

Can you go and be back on the same day?

*¿Puede usted ir y volver el mismo día?*

This is the best season for hiking.

*Esta es la mejor temporada para hacer excursiones a pie.*

We are taking off on our hike tomorrow morning.

*Saldremos de caminata mañana por la mañana.*

Is there a shortcut home?

*¿Hay algún atajo de aquí a casa?*

Where is the source of this river?

*¿Dónde nació este río?*

Don't go far.

*No se vaya lejos.*

Your house is farther away than mine.

*Su casa está más lejos que la mía.*

We went as far as we could.

*Fuimos lo más lejos que pudimos.*

Even at full speed it would take us an hour to get there.

*Aún cuando fuéramos a toda velocidad nos tardaríamos una hora en llegar.*

I took the trip all by myself.

*Hice el viaje completamente solo(a).*

Are they leaving today?

*¿Se van hoy?*

I think so.

*Creo que sí.*

May I come too?

*¿Puedo ir yo también?*

You can't go where I'm going.

*Adónde voy no puede ir usted.*

He hasn't arrived yet.

*No ha llegado todavía.*

Let's go outside.

*Vamos afuera.*

Don't go too far away.

*No se aleje demasiado.*

Has anybody come?

*¿Ha venido alguien?*

Let's go that way.

*Vamos hacia allá.*

We took a long hike up to the summit.

*Dimos una gran andada para llegar a la cumbre.*

I've been chasing around all day!

*¡He andado andando (caminando) todo el día!*

The mules balked halfway there.

*Las mulas se armaron a medio camino.*

This mule can't carry a heavier load.

*Esta mula no puede llevar más carga.*

Let's go up.

*Vamos para arriba.*

It is time to leave.

*Es la hora de salida. (Es hora de irnos.)*

Let's wait for the others.

*Esperemos a los demás.*

They are coming along behind.

*Vienen detrás.*

We followed the course of the river.

*Seguimos el curso del río.*

We went along a narrow road.

*Pasamos por un camino estrecho.*

Please step aside; you are blocking the way.

*Retírese de ahí, por favor; usted está impidiendo el paso.*

| | |
|---|---|
| He spent two hours going 5 kilometers. | Invirtió dos horas para recorrer cinco kilómetros. (Cubrió [Recorrió] cinco kilómetros en dos horas.) |
| When will we arrive at Las Norias Ranch? | ¿Cuándo llegaremos al Rancho las Norias? |
| We will arrive in three hours on horseback. | Yendo a caballo llegaremos en tres horas. |
| They have already left. | Ya se fueron. |
| We will meet at the usual place. | Nos encontraremos en el lugar acostumbrado. |
| He went out very early in the morning. | Salió muy de mañana. |
| When are you leaving? | ¿A qué hora se marcha (va) usted? |
| I cannot wait any longer for him. | No puedo esperarlo más. |
| He left for Chihuahua. | Salió con rumbo a Chihuahua. |
| He has not arrived yet. | Todavía no ha llegado. |
| They went through the woods. | Fueron a través del bosque (monte). |
| When do you start on your trip? | ¿Cuándo sale usted de viaje? |
| Do you want to come? | ¿Quiere usted venir? |
| Of course. | Ya lo creo. (Claro que sí.) (Por supuesto.) |
| Where shall I leave the key? | ¿Dónde dejo la llave? |
| I don't know where they hid the key. | No sé dónde escondieron la llave. |
| Is he going with you? | ¿Va él contigo? |
| Are you going to town? | ¿Va usted al pueblo? |
| When are you going to town? | ¿Cuándo va usted al pueblo? |
| I have to go to town today. | Yo tengo que ir al pueblo hoy. |
| Do I have to walk? | ¿Tengo que caminar? |
| Yes. You have to walk. | Sí. Usted tiene que caminar. |
| Do you want to come with me? | ¿Quiere venir conmigo? |
| What are we going to do? | ¿Qué vamos a hacer? |
| Where are you going? | ¿Para dónde va usted? |
| At what time did you arrive? | ¿A qué hora llegó usted? |
| It was about 2:00. | Serían como las dos. |
| Be here at 3:00 sharp! | ¡Esté aquí a las tres en punto! |
| Are you going to leave? | ¿Va a salir? (¿Va a irse?) |
| Is it necessary to go to ——? | ¿Es necesario ir a ——? |
| Bring her along. | Tráigala consigo. |
| Come along with me. | Venga usted conmigo. (Vengan ustedes conmigo.) |

| | |
|---|---|
| You may also come. | *También usted puede venir.* |
| I'll be there, although I may be late. | *Estaré allá, aunque llegue tarde.* |
| I cannot stay any longer. | *No puedo quedarme más.* |
| He ought to be there by now. | *Ya debe haber llegado allí.* |
| You forgot to bolt the gate. | *Se le olvidó echar el cerrojo a la puerta.* |
| Where are you bound for? | *¿A dónde se dirige usted?* |
| Wait for us where the road branches to the right. | *Espérenos donde el camino se bifurca a la derecha.* |
| I'll get there in an hour. | *Llegaré allí dentro de una hora.* |
| When did you get back? | *¿Cuándo regresó usted?* |
| I want to get away from the noise. | *Quiero alejarme del ruido.* |
| Let's go on toward the mountain. | *Vamos hacia la sierra.* |
| When are you going away? | *¿Cuándo se marcha usted?* |
| When do you expect to go back? | *¿Cuándo piensa volver?* |
| When did he go? | *¿Cuándo se fue?* |
| We plan to go by mule. | *Pensamos ir en mula.* |
| I wish to go to Durango. | *Deseo ir a Durango.* |
| How long do you plan to be in the mountains? | *¿Qué tiempo piensa permanecer en las sierras?* |
| Do you plan to spend many days in the mountains? | *¿Viene usted a pasarse muchos días en las sierras?* |
| I think it will be two or three weeks. | *Creo que unas dos o tres semanas.* |
| Do you plan to go by pack animal or truck? | *¿Piensa ir en troca o por bestia?* |
| I plan to go by animal. | *Pienso ir por bestia.* |
| I am leaving. | *Yo me voy. (Voy a salir.)* |
| We are leaving. | *Vamos a salir. (Salimos.)* |
| I need to leave. | *Necesito salir.* |
| We are almost finished. | *Ya estamos casi terminando.* |
| I'm coming! | *¡Ahí voy! (¡Allí voy!)* |
| I'm going right now. | *Ya voy.* |
| He is going to leave for Texas. | *El va a salir para Tejas. (Se va para Tejas.)* |
| I will open the gate. | *Yo abro la puerta.* |
| Come this way. | *Pase (usted) por aquí.* |
| Did you see anyone as you came in? | *¿Vió usted a alguien cuando entró?* |
| He went out the back door. | *Salió por la puerta de atrás.* |
| It is necessary that you come. | *Es necesario que usted venga.* |
| He has gone "over there." (said of | *Se fue "pa' allá" (para allá).* |

someone who has gone to parts
unknown; "pa' allá" is slang
and bad Spanish, but common)

| | |
|---|---|
| He left here very early in the morning. | Salió de aquí tempranito. |
| I am also going to ———. | También voy a ———. |
| Are you going to ———? | ¿Va usted a ———? |
| I'm afraid I'm going to be late. | Temo que voy a llegar tarde. |
| I was here two years ago. | Estuve aquí hace dos años. |
| He left a while ago. | Salió hace un rato. |
| I've been waiting all day. | He estado esperando todo el día. |
| I'll be at home. | Estaré en casa. |
| I'm going to go right away. | Me voy a ir en seguida. |
| Do you want me to go with you? | ¿Quiere que le acompañe? |
| Please go to the ——— now. | Por favor vaya al (a la) ——— ahora. |
| Why did you stop? | ¿Por qué paró usted? |
| He is going to leave for Boquillas. | Él va a salir para Boquillas. |
| I will take them in the truck. | Yo los llevo en la troca (camioneta). |

## COMMANDS

These phrases are mostly direct orders, as you would give to an employee or person under your command. You can add "por favor" at the end, or "podría usted" (could you) at the beginning of some and make them less imperative and more polite.

| | |
|---|---|
| Be quiet! | ¡Cállese! (¡Silencio!) |
| Bring me water. | Tráigame agua. |
| Come here. | Venga acá. |
| Come quickly. | Venga pronto. (¡Apúrese!) |
| Hurry! | ¡Apúrese usted! (¡Ándele!) |
| Return quickly. | Vuelva pronto. |
| Come in. | Entre usted. (Pase; siga.) |
| Come this way. | Pase usted por acá. (Pase usted por aquí.) |
| Enough! | ¡Basta! |
| Halt! | ¡Alto! |
| Stop! | ¡Párese! |
| Look. | Mire. |
| Stand up (get up). | Levántese. (Póngase en pie.) |
| Sit down. | Tome asiento. (Siéntese.) |

| | |
|---|---|
| Watch out. | Cuidado. (Precaución.) |
| Wait. | Espere. |
| Wait outside. | Espere fuera. |
| Wait a moment. | Espéreme un momento. |
| Wait until I come back. | Espere hasta que yo regrese. |
| Let me alone! | ¡Déjeme en paz! |
| Pay him off and get rid of him! | ¡Páguele y despídalo! |
| Let's not have any argument! | ¡No disputemos (discutamos)! |
| Please take this away. | Haga el favor de llevarse esto. |
| Don't throw anything away. | No tire nada. |
| Do this before anything else. | Haga usted esto antes que nada. |
| Let me know before you come. | Avíseme antes de que usted venga. |
| Have you left anything behind? | ¿Ha olvidado usted algo? |
| Be careful not to break it. | Tenga cuidado de no romperlo. |
| Bring it with you. | Tráigalo con usted. |
| Open the gate (gap). | Abra la puerta (el falcete). |
| Open the window. | Abra la ventana. |
| Close the (gate) (gap) (window). | Cierre (la puerta) (el falcete) (la ventana). |
| | |
| Stop, we have gone too far! | ¡Alto! ¡Nos hemos pasado! |
| No. | No. (Que no.) |
| Go away! | ¡Váyase! |
| Go quickly. | Vaya pronto. |
| Take me there. | Lléveme allá. |
| Give me a hand. | Déme una manita. (Ayúdeme, por favor.) |
| | |
| Handle this very carefully. | Maneje esto con mucho cuidado. |
| Wait for me here. | Espéreme aquí. |
| Take me to this address. | Lléveme a esta dirección. |
| I do not want to be disturbed. | No quiero que me molesten (llamen). |
| | |
| Carry this. | Lleve éste. |
| Take it to him. | Lléveselo a él. |
| Lend a hand. | Dar la mano. |
| Give it to me. | Démelo. |
| You are mistaken. | Usted se equivoca. (Está equivocado[a].) |
| | |
| Hurry, it's getting late! | ¡Apúrese, se hace tarde! |
| Get in (a vehicle). | Suba. (Súbase.) |
| Get in the car. | Súbase al carro. |
| Get out of the car. | Bájese del carro. |
| Follow me. | Sígame. |
| Stop or stand up. | Párese. |

| Show me the (road) (trail). | *Enséñeme (el camino) (la vereda; el sendero).* |
|---|---|
| If you see him, let us know. | *Díganos si lo ve.* |
| How did this come about? | *¿Cómo pasó esto?* |
| Start cooking dinner now. | *Empiece a cocinar ahorita.* |
| Leave it inside (here). | *Déjelo adentro (aquí).* |
| Bring it. | *Tráigalo.* |
| Tell me again. | *Dígame otra vez.* |
| Go over there. | *Vaya allá.* |
| Be here tomorrow. | *Esté aquí mañana. (Venga mañana.)* |
| Come here early tomorrow. | *Venga aquí temprano en la mañana.* |
| Look for it. | *Búsquelo.* |
| Give me the ———. | *Deme la (el) ———.* |
| Do it right now. | *Hágalo ahorita.* |
| Repeat, please. | *Repita, por favor.* |
| Speak louder. | *Hable más fuerte.* |
| Sit down. | *Siéntese.* |
| Turn around. | *Voltéese.* |
| Carry this pack. | *Lleve esta paca (este equipaje).* |
| Put it over there. | *Póngalo allá.* |
| Load this box. | *Cargue esta caja.* |
| Unload this equipment. | *Descargue este equipaje.* |
| Take the lead. I will follow. | *Ándele y yo seguiré.* |
| Help me carry this equipment to the pickup. | *Ayúdeme a llevar este equipaje a la camioneta.* |
| Help me unload the pickup. | *Ayúdeme a descargar la camioneta.* |
| Wake me at 6:00 A.M. | *Despiérteme a las seis de la mañana.* |
| Do not fail to ———. | *No deje usted de ———.* |
| Listen to me! | *¡Escúcheme! (¡Escuche!)* |
| Gather the burros now. | *Recoja las bestias ahora.* |
| Load up and let's go. | *¡Cargue y vámonos!* |
| Bring them here. | *Tráigalas aquí.* |
| Bring them. | *Tráigalos.* |
| Bring the sacks. | *Traiga los sacos.* |
| Don't forget. | *No se olvide.* |
| Come to work at 8 in the morning. | *Venga a trabajar a las ocho de la mañana.* |
| Put it on the table. | *Póngala(lo) en la mesa.* |
| Put them against the wall. | *Póngalas(los) aquí contra la pared.* |

| | |
|---|---|
| Take it off. | *Quítelo(la).* |
| Let's take it off. | *Vamos a quitarla(lo).* |
| I will help you. | *Yo le ayudo.* |
| Put it on the truck. | *Póngala(lo) en la troca.* |
| We are going to unload the truck. | *Vamos a descargar la troca.* |
| Move the boxes to the side. | *Mueva las cajas a un lado.* |
| Take the equipment to the truck. | *Llévese el equipaje a la troca.* |
| Leave it open. | *Déjelo abierto.* |
| Get out here. | *Bájense aquí.* |
| I will call you if I need anything. | *Le llamo si necesito algo.* |
| Do it any way you can. | *Hágalo cómo pueda.* |

**Polite Forms**

| | |
|---|---|
| Could you be quiet? | *¿Podría usted callarse?* |
| Could you bring me water? | *¿Podría usted traerme agua?* |
| Could you come here? | *¿Podría usted venir acá?* |
| Could you come quickly? | *¿Podría usted apurarse?* |
| Could you hurry? | *¿Podría usted apresurarse?* |
| Could you come in? | *¿Podría usted entrar?* |
| Could you come this way? | *¿Podría usted venir por acá?* |
| Could you get in (vehicle)? | *¿Podría usted subirse?* |
| Could you stop? | *¿Podría usted detenerse?* |
| Could you return quickly? | *¿Podría usted regresar pronto?* |
| Could you stand (get) up? | *¿Podría usted levantarse?* |
| Could you sit down? | *¿Podría usted sentarse?* |
| Could you watch out? | *¿Podría usted ser precavido?* |
| Could you wait? | *¿Podría usted esperar?* |
| Could you wait outside? | *¿Podría usted esperar fuera?* |
| Could you wait a moment? | *¿Podría usted esperarme un momento?* |
| Could you wait until after I get back? | *¿Podría usted esperar hasta que yo regresara?* |
| Could you let me alone! | *¡Podría usted dejarme solo(a)!* |
| Could you do this before anything else? | *¿Podría usted hacer esto antes que nada?* |
| Can you bring it with you? | *¿Podría usted traerlo con usted?* |
| Can you open the (gate) (window) (gap)? | *¿Podría usted abrir (la puerta) (la ventana) (el falcete)?* |
| Can you close the (gate) (gap) (window)? | *¿Podría usted cerrar (la puerta) (el falcete) (la ventana)?* |
| Can you leave? | *¿Podría usted irse?* |
| Could you go quickly? | *¿Podría usted ir pronto?* |
| Could you give me a hand? | *¿Podría usted ayudarme? (¿Podría usted darme una manito?)* |

Could you handle this very carefully?

*¿Podría usted manejar esto con mucho cuidado?*

## EMOTIONS AND FEELINGS

He lives a lonely life.
*Lleva una vida solitaria.*

Aren't you lonely without your friends (family)?
*¿No se siente usted solo(a) sin sus amigos (su familia)?*

We are not on speaking terms.
*No nos hablamos.*

He doesn't know the meaning of fear.
*No sabe lo que es miedo.*

There is no fear of anything like that taking place.
*No hay ningún peligro de que suceda eso.*

You have nothing to fear.
*No tiene usted nada que temer.*

He is having a hard time.
*Está pasando tiempos duros.*

I wish I could stay here longer.
*Me gustaría quedarme aquí más tiempo.*

I'm very glad to see you.
*Me alegro mucho de verle.*

I hope you will come again someday.
*Espero que usted regrese algún día.*

We have had a bad time.
*Hemos pasado un mal rato.*

Everything is going very badly.
*Todo va muy mal.*

He drinks to excess.
*Bebe sin medida.*

I'm dying of thirst!
*¡Estoy muerto(a) de sed!*

Why are you worried?
*¿Por qué está usted preocupado(a)?*

Because I'm afraid of the storm.
*Porque tengo miedo de la tempestad.*

Fall is my favorite season.
*El otoño es mi estación favorita.*

Why are you upset?
*¿Por qué está usted mortificado(a)? (¿Molesto?)*

Because I have problems.
*Porque tengo problemas.*

My husband has abandoned me.
*Mi esposo me ha abandonado.*

Why are you angry?
*¿Por qué está usted enojado(a)?*

Because I don't like that man.
*Porque no me gusta ese señor.*

Are you angry at him?
*¿Está usted enojado (sentido) con él?*

He's mad at me.
*Está enojado (sentido) conmigo.*

But I'm tired!
*¡Pero estoy cansada(o)!*

I'm not at all tired.
*No estoy nada cansado(a).*

Do you want something?
*¿Desea algo?*

You are among friends.
*Usted está entre amigos.*

Don't give up hope.
*No pierda usted la esperanza.*

What is the matter with you?
*¿Qué tiene usted? (¿Qué le pasa?)*

| How sad! What a pity! | *¡Qué lastima! (¡Qué triste!)* |
| I'm sorry. | *Lo siento mucho.* |
| I'm very interested. | *Me interesa mucho.* |
| How interesting! | *¡Qué interesante!* |
| I want to tell you something. | *Quiero decirle algo.* |
| What do you think? | *¡Qué le parece? (¡Qué piensa?)* |
| No way! | *¡De ninguna manera!* |

## FAULT AND BLAME

| Don't blame me! | *¡No me eches la culpa!* |
| Who, me? | *¡Quién, yo?* |
| I don't know what you are talking about! | *¡No sé de qué habla usted!* |
| It is not your fault. | *Usted no tiene la culpa.* |
| Who is to blame? | *¡Quién tiene la culpa?* |
| I think that it is your fault. | *Me parece que es culpa suya.* |
| It is my fault. | *Es mi culpa.* |
| It is not my fault. | *No es mi culpa.* |
| Whose fault is it? | *¡Quién tiene la culpa?* |
| I know. | *Yo sé.* |
| I do not know. | *Yo no sé.* |
| Forgive me. | *Dispénseme. (Disculpeme.)* |
| That was a close call! | *¡Qué poco faltó!* |
| His recklessness cost him his life. | *Su temeridad le costó su vida.* |

## HUNTING AND PREDATORS

| Do you like to hunt? | *¡Le gusta cazar?* |
| He doesn't know anything about hunting. | *No sabe nada de la caza.* |
| Are you going on the hunt? | *¡Va usted ir a la cacería?* |
| There is a lot of hunting in this mountain. | *Hay mucha caza en esta sierra.* |
| They are gone hunting deer. | *Están cazando venados.* |
| The hunters brought home the dressed game. | *Los cazadores se llevaron las piezas a sus casas.* |
| The hunter was skinning the deer. | *El cazador estaba desollando el venado.* |
| This is a mountain lion (bear) trap. | *Esta es una trampa para leones (osos).* |
| He fell into the trap (snare) they set for him. | *Cayó en la trampa (la red) que le tendieron.* |

| | |
|---|---|
| They caught the mountain lion by the foot. | *Cogieron el león de una pata.* |
| At night you can hear the howl of wolves (coyotes). | *De noche se puede oír el aullido de los lobos (coyotes).* |
| The coyote is howling over there. | *El coyote está aullando allá.* |
| They hunted him down. | *Le persiguieron hasta capturarlo.* |
| A mountain lion attacked our goats! | *¡Un león atacó nuestras cabras!* |
| Here are the tracks! | *¡Aquí están las huellas!* |
| Let's follow his tracks and see where he went. | *Sigamos sus huellas para ver adonde fue.* |
| The dog followed the hot trail. | *El perro siguió el rastro fresco.* |
| We were hot on the trail! | *¡Les seguíamos de cerca!* |
| When they reached the river the dogs lost the trail. | *Los perros perdieron el rastro al llegar al río.* |
| Something's in the wind! | *¡Algo se está tramando!* |
| The dogs got wind of the mountain lion! | *¡Los perros olfatearon el rastro del león!* |
| You're on the right trail! | *¡Va usted por la buena huella!* |
| That shot sounded very close! | *¡Ese tiro sonó muy cerca!* |
| They have caught a mountain lion! | *¡Capturaron un león!* |
| Did you hear a shot? | *¿Oyó usted un disparo?* |
| Are there any game wardens around here? | *¿Hay por aquí algunos forestales?* |

## Mexico's Wildlife

Although abuse of the soil and water resources of the nation has turned many parts of Mexico into desert, there are still areas, mainly in the major mountain ranges or in isolated mountain "islands in the sky," that have enough elevation to catch moisture, resulting in timbered peaks and well-watered valleys. Natural areas and abundant wildlife, much as all of the country must have supported before European contact, still exist in these areas, primarily those still in private hands.

The following terms will help you ask about local wildlife resources.

| | |
|---|---|
| Alligator | *Lagarto* (m.); *caimán* (m.) |
| Anteater (tropics) | *Hormiguero* (m.); *oso hormiguero* (m.) |
| Antelope (Pronghorn) | *Berrendo* (m.) (rare) |
| Armadillo | *Armadillo* (m.); *armado* (m.) |
| Badger | *Tejón* (m.); *tlalcoyote* (m.) |
| Beaver | *Castor* (m.) |

| | |
|---|---|
| Bird (generic) | *Ave* (f.); *pájaro* (m.) |
| Black bear | *Oso negro* (m.) (confined mainly to mountain regions, but common there) |
| Bobcat | *Gato de montes* (m.) |
| Buzzard | *Aura* (f.), black vulture, but is also a general term sometimes used for any large bird of prey (*aves de rapiña*), including hawks, eagles, and ravens. *Zopilote* usually refers to the red-headed turkey vulture. |
| Chachalaca (generic) | *Chachalaca* (f.) |
| Coatimundi | *Pisote* (f.); *choluga* (f.) |
| Cottontail rabbit | *Conejo* (m.) |
| Coyote | *Coyote* (m.) |
| Deer (generic) | *Venado* (m.) |
| Den (hole of small animal) | *Agujero* (m.) |
| Den (of animal) | *Caverna* (f.); *guarida* (f.); *escondrijo* (m.); *lugar de retiro* (m.); *cueva de fieras* (f.) |
| Desert bighorn sheep | *Borrego cimarrón* (m.) (rare) |
| Dove (generic) | *Paloma* (f.) |
| Ducks (generic) | *Patos* (m.) |
| Falcon | *Halcón* (m.) |
| Eagle | *Águila* (f.) |
| Fish (caught) | *Pescado* (m.) |
| Fish (in water) | *Pesca* (m.); *pez* (m.) |
| Flock of birds | *Bandada* (f.) |
| Fox | *Zorra* (f.) |
| Goose (generic) | *Ansar* (m.) |
| Grizzly bear | *Oso plateado* (m.); *oso grande* (m.) (confined to a small area of mountains in Chihuahua and nearing extinction) |
| Hawk | *Halcón* (m.); *gavilán* (m.) |
| Jackrabbit | *Liebre de cola negra* (m.); *liebre* (m.) |
| Jaguar | *Tigre* (m.) |
| Lizard (generic) | *Lagartija* (f.) |
| Monkey (tropics) | *Chango* (m.); *mono* (m.); *mico* (m.) (long-tailed) |
| Mountain lion | *León* (m.); *pantera* (f.) |

| | |
|---|---|
| Mule deer | *Bura* (m.); *venado de cola negra* (m.) |
| Opossum | *Tlacuache* (m.) |
| Owl | *Tecolote* (m.); *buho* (m.); *lechuza* (f.) |
| Peccary | *Javelina* (f.); *jabalí* (m.) |
| Quail (generic) | *Codorniz* (m.) |
| Blue quail | *Tostón* (m.) |
| Raccoon | *Mapache* (m.) |
| Rattlesnake | *Cascabel* (m.); *víbora* (f.) |
| Raven | *Cuervo* (m.) |
| Ringtail | *Cacomixtle* (m.) |
| Sandhill crane | *Grulla* (f.) |
| Shark | *Tiburón* (m.) |
| Skunk | *Zorrillo* (m.) |
| Snake (generic) | *Culebra* (f.) |
| Squirrel | *Ardilla* (f.) |
| Tapir (southern tropic lowlands only) | *Tapir* (m.); *danta* (f.) |
| Turtle (generic) | *Tortuga* (f.) |
| Vulture or buzzard | *Zopilote* (m.); *aura* (f.) |
| Weasel | *Comadreja* (f.) |
| Whitetail deer | *Venado* (m.); *venado de cola blanca* (m.) |
| Wild beast (fierce) | *Fiera* (f.) |
| Wildlife (general term) | *Animales silvestres* (m.); *vida silvestre* (f.) |
| Wild turkey | *Pavo de monte* (m.); *guajolote silvestre* (m.); *cócono* (m.) |
| Wolf | *Lobo* (m.) (nearing extinction) |

## IDIOMATIC AND SLANG EXPRESSIONS

| | |
|---|---|
| In spite of | *A pesar de* |
| I'm getting along o.k. | *Pasándola.* |
| It makes little difference. | *Importa poco.* |
| Since | *Puesto que* |
| Countless | *Sin cuenta* |
| Among themselves | *Entre sí* |
| Anglo or any foreign white person | *Gringo; bolillo* |
| By means of | *Por medio de* |
| Meanwhile | *Mientras tanto* |
| At the beginning of | *Al principio de* |

| | |
|---|---|
| He (she) uses | Se sirve de |
| It can be said that | Se puede decir que |
| Pedalpushers or short pants | Brinca charcos ("puddle jumpers") |
| Not at all. | De ninguna manera. |
| Are you ready? | ¿Están listos(as)? |
| At once. | Inmediatamente. |
| Carry on | Sigue con |
| Carry out | Llevar a cabo |
| Feel like | Tener ganas de |
| Keep on | Seguir |
| Lend a hand. | Ayúdanos. |
| Leave us (me) alone. | Déjenos (Déjame) en paz. |
| Out of order | Descompuesto(a) |
| Watch out for ———! | ¡Cuidado con ———! |
| A shallow river one can wade in with clothes on. | Río pasito |
| To cross the Río Grande (Río Bravo del Norte) | Brincar el charco (said of "wetbacks" or mojados) |
| Don't worry. | No tenga pena. |
| We need them. | Nos hacen falta. |
| Really! | ¡De veras! |
| On the way to ——— | Camino a ——— |
| Something to eat | Algo que comer |
| What is the date? | ¿Cuál es la fecha? |
| To do it in great style. | ¡Como gringo! |
| Heads or tails | Aguila o sol |
| Like two cats in a sack! | ¡Como dos gatos en un costal! |
| Look out! Watch out! | ¡Aguas! ¡Águila! |
| Since then | Desde entonces |
| To work hard | A darle duro |
| To get the show on the road | Dar un empujón |
| What's up? | ¿Quiúbole? (¿Qué húbole?) |
| With great pains | A duras penas |
| What can it be? | ¿Qué será? |
| Yes, indeed. | Ya lo creo. |
| We need water. | Nos hace falta agua. (Necesitamos agua.) |
| In time | Con el tiempo |
| Suddenly | De repente |
| Under the command of | A mando de |
| So that | De modo que |

The following are Mexican border slang expressions collected by Rex R. Kelly and George W. Kelly, Vanderpool, Texas, and are used with their permission:

*A las migas* — To go to dinner. From the Spanish word *migas*, which means "crumbs."

*Al caliche* — To go to jail (prisoners dig caliche).

*Andar escuadra* — Flat broke.

*Aplátose, por favor.* — Please sit down.

*Caer al pelo* — To come in handy or be just right: "*Esta cerveza me cayó al pelo.*"

*¡Dale prisa!* — Hurry up! Come on!

*Dar un manito (dar una mano)* — To ask for help: "Lend a hand."

*Decir a lo macho* — To say it like a man: "*Se lo dijo a lo macho.*"

*Despagar* — To cut weeds, etc. Probably derived from *despajar*, to separate wheat or grain.

*Dormírsele el gallo* — To be caught loitering or loafing. The Mexicans say, "*Se le durmió el gallo*" (He was caught loafing on the job). The correct English translation would be, "The rooster goes to sleep."

*Estar muy piocha* — To be right or just right.

*Fue gallo.* — "It was a lucky break." This is a very commonly used expression. The Mexicans on the border use *gallo* in many expressions pertaining to luck.

*Gancharse* — A slang expression meaning to get married. Corresponds to the English expression "to get hitched" (from *enganchar*, "to hook").

*Ir al remoje* — To go swimming (from *remoje*, to soak or wet).

*Ir al yugo* — To go to work (from *yugo*, a yoke used on oxen).

*Irse por el arrastradero* — To go by a cow trail or follow animal tracks (from the Spanish expression referring to a trail made by dragging a dead bull from the ring).

| | |
|---|---|
| *Irse volado* | To go in a hurry (from *ir* and *volar*, to go and to fly). |
| *No pica.* | "He will not do a thing" (from *picar*, to bite). |
| *Ojos cueveños* | Those having light eyes. Used on the lower border for people with light eyes (from a story of people with light eyes who came from the Las Cuevas Ranch). |
| *Patrón* | Used when a person is addressing a superior. *Patrón* means a landlord, but the Mexicans use it for any person of means. |
| *Puro aire* | One who talks a great deal and says nothing: *"Ud. es puro aire,"* corresponding to the English slang "You are a windbag." |
| *¡Qué parada!* | What a surprise! (How exciting!) |
| *¿Qué pasó?* | Derived from *pasar*, but has many meanings on the border, such as, "What do you want?" or "What are you doing?" or "What's going on?" |
| *Ser gallo* | To have a lucky break (from *gallo*, rooster). |

## MARITAL AND FAMILY RELATIONS

| | |
|---|---|
| He is older than I. | *Él es mayor que yo.* |
| Who lives next door? | *¿Quién vive en seguida?* |
| The family lived in poverty. | *La familia estaba en la miseria.* |
| They pay him a pittance. | *Lo que le pagan es una miseria.* |
| He took the job to keep from starving to death. | *Aceptó aquel trabajo para no morirse de hambre.* |
| They lived in thatched huts. | *Vivían en casitas (jacales) de paja.* |
| Do you have any family here? | *¿Tiene usted familia aquí?* |
| Yes, I have family here. | *Sí, tengo familia aquí.* |
| Are they your parents (brothers) (sisters) (children)? | *¿Son sus padres (hermanos) (hermanas) (hijos)?* |
| Yes, they are my parents (brothers and sisters) (children). | *Sí, son mis padres (hermanos) (hijos).* |
| How many children do you have? | *¿Cuántos hijos tiene usted?* |

| | |
|---|---|
| I have four children: one son and three daughters. | *Tengo cuatro hijos: un hijo y tres hijas.* |
| What is your father's (mother's) name? | *¿Cómo se llama su padre (madre)?* |
| My father's (mother's) name is John (Mary). | *Mi padre (madre) se llama Juan (María).* |
| What is his relationship to you? | *¿Qué parentesco tiene con usted?* |
| He is my son. | *Es mi hijo.* |
| What age is your son? | *¿Qué edad tiene su hijo?* |
| He is twelve years old. | *Tiene doce años.* |
| How is she related to you? Is she your daughter? | *¿Qué es de usted? ¿Es su hija?* |
| Yes, she is my daughter. | *Sí, es mi hija.* |
| How is she related to you? | *¿Qué parentesco tiene con usted?* |
| She is my aunt. | *Es mi tía.* |
| Is your papa (mama) at home? | *¿Está (aquí) su papá (mamá) en casa?* |
| He (She) isn't here. | *No está aquí. (No está en casa.)* |
| He is not going to be home today. | *Él no estará hoy en casa.* |
| There is nobody else here. | *No hay nadie más aquí.* |
| Where is your mother (father)? | *¿Dónde está su madre (su padre)?* |
| She (He) is outside. | *Está afuera.* |

(Note: The familiar form is used in many of the following sentences, as a Mexican mother might speak to her child.)

| | |
|---|---|
| Listen, love. | *Oye, amorcita(o).* |
| Listen, my little one. | *Oye, mi hijito(a).* |
| Look, dear. | *Mira, muchachito(a).* |
| Darling | *Nene(a)* |
| Sweetheart | *Niñito(a); nenito(a)* |
| Come on, precious. | *Ven, precioso(a).* |
| That's good! | *¡Qué bueno!* |
| Give me a hug (kiss). | *Déme un abrazo (un besito).* |
| How pretty! | *¡Qué bonito(a)!* |
| How cute! | *¡Qué mono!* |
| How darling! | *¡Qué precioso(a)!* |
| Stay nice and quiet. | *Estate tranquilito(a).* |
| Sleep well. | *Duerme tranquilito(a).* |
| I don't want to! | *¡No tengo ganas! (¡Si no quiero!)* |
| Leave me alone! | *¡Déjame!* |
| Darling, be good! | *¡Mi hijito(a), sé bueno(a)!* |
| Darling, go to sleep! | *¡Mi hijito(a), duérmete!* |
| Darling, be quiet! | *¡Mi hijito(a), cállate!* |

| | |
|---|---|
| Little one, how do you feel? | Chiquito(a), ¿cómo te sientes? |
| Sweetheart, don't talk now. | Precioso(a), no hables ahora. |
| Don't be afraid. | No tengas miedo. |
| I'm never afraid! | ¡Yo nunca tengo miedo! |
| I'm strong. | ¡Yo soy fuerte (valiente)! |
| Yes, I forgot. | Sí, se me olvidó. |
| Get up, little one. | Levántate, chica(o). |
| Did you sleep well? | ¿Dormiste bien? |
| Do you feel better now? | ¿Te sientes mejor? |
| Honey, what do you want? | Querido(a), ¿qué quieres? |
| I don't want anything. | No quiero nada. |
| Do you want your toys (storybook) (doll)? | ¿Quieres tus juguetes (tu librito de cuentos) (tu muñeca)? |
| Little one, do you want to come with me? | Chiquitín, ¿quieres ir conmigo? |
| Yes, I want to. | Sí, quiero. |
| No, I don't want to. | No, no quiero. |
| Not now. | No ahora. |
| Later. | Luego. |
| Do you want to play? | ¿Quieres jugar? |
| Do you want to have something to drink? | ¿Quieres tomar algo? |
| Let me ———. | Déjame ———. |
| I hope so! | ¡Ojalá que sí! |
| Do you like ———? | ¿Te gusta ———? |
| When is mama coming? | ¿Cuándo viene mamá? |
| We have to go. | Tenemos que ir. |
| But I don't want to go! | ¡Pero no quiero ir! |
| Have you had your dinner? | ¿Ya comió? (¿Ya comiste?) |
| It's done! | ¡Ya acabó! |
| Is there anyone to look after the children? | ¿Hay alguien que cuide a los niños? |
| Adopted | Adoptado(a); adoptivo(a) |
| Bachelor, single | Soltero(a) |
| Brother, sister | Hermano; hermana |
| Brother-, sister-in-law | Cuñado(a) |
| Cousin | Primo(a) |
| Daughter | Hija (f.) |
| Daughter-in-law | Nuera (f.) |
| Divorced | Divorciado(a) |
| Family name | Apellido (m.) |
| Father, dad | Padre; papá (m.) |

| | |
|---|---|
| Father-in-law | *Suegro* (m.) |
| Female | *Mujer* (f.); *femenina* (f.) |
| Fiancé (fiancée) | *Prometido(a)*; *entendido(a)* |
| First cousin | *Primo(a) hermano(a)* |
| First name | *Nombre de pila* (m.) |
| Foster parents | *Padres adoptivos* (m.) |
| Foster son, daughter | *Hijo(a) adoptivo(a)* |
| Girlfriend; boyfriend | *Novia; novio* |
| Grandchildren | *Nietos* (m.) |
| Grandparents | *Abuelos* (m.) |
| Grandson; granddaughter | *Nieto; nieta* |
| Grandfather, grandmother | *Abuelo; abuela* |
| Half-brothers | *Medio hermanos* (m.) |
| Husband | *Esposo* (m.); *marido* (m.) |
| Maiden name | *Apellido de soltera* (m.) |
| Male | *Varón* (m.); *masculino; macho* (m.) |
| Man | *Hombre* (m.) |
| Married | *Casado(a)* |
| Mother; mom | *Madre* (f.); *mamá* (f.) |
| Mother-in-law | *Suegra* (f.) |
| Nephew (niece) | *Sobrino(a)* |
| Nickname | *Apodo* (m.) |
| Orphan | *Huérfano(a)* |
| Parents | *Padres* (m.) |
| Separated | *Separados(as)* |
| Son | *Hijo* (m.) |
| Son-in-law | *Yerno* (m.) |
| Stepfather | *Padrastro* (m.) |
| Stepmother | *Madrastra* (f.) |
| Stepson | *Hijastro* (m.) |
| Twins | *Mellizos* (m.); *gemelos* (m.); *cuates* (m.) |
| Uncle (aunt) | *Tío(a)* |
| Widower (widow) | *Viudo(a)* |
| Wife | *Esposa* (f.); *mujer* (f.) |
| Woman | *Mujer* (f.) |
| Youth | *Joven* (m. or f.) |

## OBSERVATIONS (GENERAL)

| | |
|---|---|
| The trucks make a lot of noise. | *Los camiones hacen mucho ruido.* |
| What a man! | *¡Qué hombre!* |

What a mess! | ¡Qué lío! (¡Qué mugrero!)

He is the only one there. | Es el único que está allí.

The house is in a clearing in the woods. | La casa está en un claro (desmonte) en el bosque.

He lives in an out-of-the-way place. | Vive él en un sitio muy apartado (muy retirado).

They pipe the water here from a spring. | Traen el agua por cañería (tubería) desde el manantial (el ojo de agua).

The spring (well) never runs dry. | El manantial (La noria) nunca se seca.

Did you see that puff of smoke? | ¿Vió esa bocanada de humo?

Do you smell smoke (also)? | ¿Huele usted humo (también)?

That slope is steeper than it looks. | Esta cuesta es más empinada de lo que parece.

I stepped in a puddle. | Pisé en un charco.

The first good rainstorm will wash it away! | ¡La primera lluvia fuerte se lo llevará!

The ground is firm here. | El suelo es firme aquí.

He shouted and we heard the echo. | Gritó y oímos el eco.

They lived close to the river. | Vivían cerca del río.

There was a curtain of smoke over the area. | Había una cortina de humo sobre la zona.

I wonder where that column of smoke comes from? | ¿De dónde saldrá esa columna de humo?

The sun just went down. | Acaba de ponerse el sol.

I see them a way off. | Los veo a lo lejos.

I hear someone yelling for help. | Oigo que alguien pide auxilio a gritos.

They exhausted all the resources of the country. | Han acabado con todos los recursos del país.

He is up there waiting for you. | Está allá arriba esperándole.

Your friends are in there. | Allá dentro están sus amigos.

I must change a string on the guitar. | Tengo que cambiar una cuerda de la guitarra.

From above one could see the river. | Desde arriba se veía el río.

Although I was not born in the country, I know it well. | Aunque no nací en el país, lo conozco muy bien.

This tank has a capacity of 30 liters. | Este tanque tiene una capacidad de treinta litros.

The traffic is congested. | El tráfico está congestionado.

The descent was very dangerous. | La bajada era muy peligrosa.

The road is very dusty in this weather.

*En este tiempo se empolva mucho el camino.*

Everything is covered with dust.

*Todo está lleno (cubierto) de polvo.*

He climbed the tree.

*Se subió al árbol.*

This well is very deep.

*Este pozo (Esta noria) es muy hondo(a).*

The house caved in.

*La casa se hundió.*

The pool is full of clean water.

*La tinaja (piscina) está llena de agua limpia.*

They are ahead of us.

*Están adelante de nosotros.*

The lumber is still green.

*La madera está verde todavía.*

There will be a full moon tonight.

*Esta noche habrá luna llena.*

They were walking in the moonlight.

*Estaban paseando a la luz de la luna.*

I cannot see in this light.

*No puedo ver con esta luz.*

I cannot see.

*No puedo ver.*

Today is Monday.

*Hoy es lunes.*

The truck stopped in the middle of the road.

*La troca (El camión) se paró en medio del camino.*

He climbed to the very top of the mountain.

*Subió hasta lo más alto de la sierra.*

The forest (jungle) was so thick that one could hardly walk through it.

*El bosque (La selva) era tan espeso(a) que casi no se podía andar.*

They came to look for us.

*Vinieron a buscarnos.*

They had a hard time getting here.

*Llegaron a duras penas.*

The journey was very hard.

*La jornada fue muy dura.*

Yesterday we covered 10 kilometers.

*Ayer recorrimos diez kilómetros.*

What a strange thing!

*¡Qué cosa tan rara! (¡Qué curiosidad!)*

The afternoon's getting cooler.

*Está refrescando la tarde.*

The road was (is) very slippery.

*El camino era (es) muy resbaloso.*

He ran a big risk.

*Corrió mucho riesgo.*

The truck (stone) was rolling (is rolling) downhill.

*El camión (La piedra) rodaba (roda) cuesta abajo.*

There is not enough room for everyone.

*No hay lugar para todos.*

He sought the shade of the tree.

*Buscó la sombra del árbol.*

The trees give shade.

*Los árboles dan sombra.*

It is all gone!

*¡Se acabó!*

This is for the better.

*Más vale así.*

| | |
|---|---|
| I thought I heard a rifle shot! | *¡Me pareció oír un rifle!* |
| We could hear the sound of the gun. | *Oímos el disparo del arma.* |
| Everyone else has gone. | *Todos los demás se han ido.* |
| There is nobody else here. | *No hay nadie más aquí.* |
| I hear someone coming. | *Oigo que alguien viene.* |
| The flies around here are terrible. | *Son terribles las moscas de aquí.* |
| He climbed up so high that we could not see him. | *Subió a tal altura que no lo podíamos ver.* |
| There were trees on either side of the road. | *Había árboles a ambos lados del camino.* |
| You are mistaken. | *Se equivoca.* |
| There come the men. | *Allá vienen los hombres.* |
| He bought them. | *Las compró.* |
| I see her. | *La veo.* |
| I see him. | *Lo veo.* |
| I see the man (the woman). | *Veo al hombre (a la mujer).* |
| I see them. | *Los veo.* |
| It is not worthwhile. | *No vale la pena.* |
| I should like ———. | *Quisiera ———.* |
| I am looking for ———. | *Busco a ———.* |
| I don't see them. | *No los veo.* |
| Don't you see them? | *¿No se ve?* |

## OWNERSHIP AND PROPERTY

| | |
|---|---|
| Do you own any land? | *¿Tiene usted terreno?* |
| I own no land. | *No tengo terreno.* |
| Do you have title to this house? | *¿Tiene usted el título de propiedad de esta casa?* |
| It is not my own. | *No es mía.* |
| Are these your things? | *¿Son éstas sus cosas?* |
| Who owns this property? | *¿De quién es esta propiedad?* |
| That man owns a large tract of land. | *Ese hombre es dueño de una gran extensión de terreno.* |
| What is the size of this property? | *¿Cuál es la extensión de la propiedad (la finca)?* |
| This farm runs about a mile from the north to the south. | *La extensión de la finca de norte a sur es una milla.* |
| Is this house for rent? | *¿Se renta esta casa?* |
| Who owns this house? | *¿Quién es el dueño de esta casa?* |
| Where does he live? | *¿En dónde vive el dueño?* |
| How much is it per month? | *¿Cuánto es por mes?* |
| We have nothing to sell. | *No tenemos nada que vender.* |

## PARTS OF THE BODY AND HEALTH

It is safer to sleep under a net in this climate.
En este clima es más seguro dormir con mosquitero.

He was run down by a truck.
Lo atropelló un camión.

His death was due to an accident.
Su muerte fue ocasionada por un accidente.

This is where he died.
Aquí está en donde murió.

He was killed in an auto accident.
Se mató en un choque.

He died last year.
Se murió el año pasado.

I have to wash my hands and brush my teeth.
Tengo que lavarme las manos y cepillarme los dientes.

I'd like to take a bath before dinner.
Me gustaría bañarme antes de comer.

I'm out of breath.
Estoy echando los bofes.

Are you comfortable?
¿Está usted cómodo(a)?

What is the matter with you?
¿Qué le pasa? (¿Qué tiene usted?)

I feel really bad.
Me siento muy mal.

Why? Do you have a headache?
¿Por qué? ¿Tiene dolor de cabeza?

It's more than that. I'm very weak.
Es más que eso. Tengo mucha debilidad. (Estoy muy débil.)

Be calm!
¡Cálmese!

Your condition is serious.
Su condición está seria.

How long have you had this problem?
¿Desde cuándo tiene esta condición (este problema)?

I have had it six months.
Tengo este problema (esta condición) desde hace seis meses.

What do you feel?
¿Qué siente?

A pain here.
Un dolor (Duele) aquí.

Do you have much pain?
¿Tiene usted mucho dolor?

Yes, I have a lot.
Sí, tengo bastante dolor.

I'm exhausted!
No puedo más. (¡Ya no puedo!) (¡Ya no tengo ganas!)

What is the matter?
¿Qué tiene usted?

Do you feel better?
¿Se siente mejor?

I have to wash the wound.
Tengo que lavar la herida.

Don't be afraid.
No tenga miedo.

He has a snakebite!
¡El tiene una mordida de víbora!

Is he going to live?
¿Va a vivir?

When can I go home?
¿Cuándo puedo irme a casa?

After a bath I feel more comfortable.
Después del baño me siento más cómodo(a).

He didn't come because he got sick.
No vino porque se enfermó.

| | |
|---|---|
| Abdomen | *Abdomen* (m.) |
| Ankle | *Tobillo* (m.) |
| Arm | *Brazo* (m.) |
| Artery | *Artería* (f.) |
| Back | *Espalda* (f.) |
| Bald head | *Calva* (f.) |
| Beard | *Barba* (f.) |
| Bellybutton | *Ombligo* (m.) |
| Blood | *Sangre* (f.) |
| Body | *Cuerpo* (m.) |
| Bone | *Hueso* (m.) |
| Brain | *Cerebro* (m.) |
| Breast | *Seno* (m.); *chiche* (f.) (slang) |
| Buttocks | *Nalgas* (f.) |
| Cheek | *Mejilla* (f.); *cachete* (m.) |
| Chest | *Pecho* (m.) |
| Chin | *Barbilla* (f.); *barba* (f.) |
| Ear | *Oreja* (f.) |
| Elbow | *Codo* (m.) |
| Eye | *Ojo* (m.) |
| Eyeball | *Globo del ojo* (m.) |
| Eyebrow | *Ceja* (f.) |
| Eyelash | *Pestaña* (f.) |
| Eyelid | *Párpado* (m.) |
| Face | *Cara* (f.) |
| Finger | *Dedo* (*de la mano*) (m.) |
| Fist | *Puño* (m.) |
| Foot | *Pie* (m.); *pata* (f.) (usually an animal's) |
| Forehead | *Frente* (f.) |
| Front teeth | *Dientes* (m.) |
| Hair | *Cabello* (m.); *pelo* (m.) |
| Hand | *Mano* (f.) |
| Head | *Cabeza* (f.) |
| Heel | *Talón* (m.) |
| Heart | *Corazón* (m.) |
| Hip | *Cadera* (f.) |
| Jaw | *Quijada* (f.) |
| Knee | *Rodilla* (f.) |
| Leg | *Pierna* (f.) |
| Lip | *Labio* (m.) |
| Liver | *Hígado* (m.) |
| Lung | *Pulmón* (m.) |

| Molar | Muela (f.) |
|---|---|
| Mole | Lunar (m.) |
| Mouth | Boca (f.) |
| Muscle | Músculo (m.) |
| Mustache | Bigote (m.) |
| Nail | Uña (f.) |
| Neck | Cuello (m.); pescuezo (m.) |
| Nipple | Teta (f.) |
| Nose | Nariz (f.) |
| Palm | Palma de la mano (f.) |
| Ribs | Costillas (f.) |
| Shoulder | Hombro (m.) |
| Skull | Cráneo (m.); calavera (f.) |
| Sole of foot | Planta del pie (f.) |
| Sore | Grano (m.) |
| Spine | Columna vertebral (f.); espina (f.) |
| Stomach | Estómago (m.) |
| Thigh | Muslo (m.) |
| Thumb | Pulgar (m.) |
| Toe | Dedo (del pie) (m.) |
| Tongue | Lengua (f.) |
| Tooth | Diente (m.); muela (f.) |
| Trunk | Tronco (m.) |
| Vein | Vena (f.) |
| Waist | Cintura (f.) |
| Wound | Herida (f.) |

## PROBLEM SOLVING

| | |
|---|---|
| The pipeline is leaking at the joints. | Se sale el agua por las junturas de la cañería (tubería). |
| There is a leak in that pipe. | Hay un escape en esa cañería. |
| There is a leak in the roof. | Hay una gotera (un agujero) en el techo. |
| | |
| He lost his way in the woods. | Se perdió en el bosque. |
| I came near getting lost. | Estuve a punto de perderme. |
| That's the very most I can do. | Eso es lo más que puedo hacer. |
| What shall I do next? | ¿Qué hago después? |
| There is a hole in the roof of this house. | Hay un agujero en el techo (tejado) de esta casa. |
| The power is off. | No hay corriente. |
| Does this happen often? | ¿Pasa esto muy seguido? |
| How often? | ¿Cada cuánto tiempo? |

The cables parted under the strain.

*Los cables se rompieron bajo el peso.*

We'll burn our trash in a pit.

*Quemaremos la basura en el hoyo (pozo).*

Can you repair my pickup in a hurry?

*¿Puede usted componerme la camioneta muy pronto?*

A complete repair job will take ten days.

*Se tardarán diez días en hacer todas las reparaciones.*

Roll over!

*¡Dése la vuelta!*

It doesn't fit!

*¡No cabe!*

If I can do it, so can you.

*Si yo lo puedo hacer, también puede usted.*

Is there room for one more?

*¿Hay sitio (lugar) para uno más?*

Is there enough room in the pickup for everyone?

*¿Hay bastante sitio (lugar) en la camioneta para todos?*

Is there any space for my equipment?

*¿Hay espacio para mi equipaje?*

The spring (of an auto, or truck) seems to be broken.

*Parece que el resorte (muelle) está roto.*

The motor's stalled again, darn it!

*¡Demonio! Se ha atascado de nuevo el motor.*

Start the engine!

*¡Arráncale!*

What is the next step?

*¿Qué hacemos ahora?*

We need an expert mechanic for this job.

*Necesitamos un mecánico experto para este trabajo.*

These tires are done for.

*Estas llantas están gastadas.*

The accident damaged the pickup.

*El accidente (choque) estropeó la camioneta.*

How much damage has been done?

*¿Cuáles han sido los daños causados?*

He estimated the damages at close to 2,000 pesos.

*Estimó que el daño causado llegaba aproximadamente a dos mil pesos.*

This truck is ready to fall apart.

*Esta troca (Este camión) está a punto de desbaratarse.*

There is not a drop of water left.

*No queda ni una gota de agua.*

This hole should be stopped up.

*Hay que tapar este agujero.*

I've been in tight spots before.

*He pasado por dificultades antes de ahora.*

Can you light the way?

*¿Puede alumbar el camino?*

A truck stopped (is stopped) in the road.

*Se atravesó (Se atraviesa) un camión en el camino.*

I'm going to chock the wheels so the pickup won't roll.

*Voy a calzar las ruedas para que no se mueva la camioneta.*

| How can I help you? | ¿En qué puedo ayudarlo? |
| We make all kinds of repairs. | Hacemos toda clase de reparaciones. |
| Turn on the ignition. | Encienda el contacto. (Dale.) (Dale una vez.) |
| Have you anything to cut this string? | ¿Tiene usted algo con que cortar esta cuerda? |
| The bridge collapsed. | El puente se derrumbó. |
| There's a landslide on the road. | Hay un derrumbe en el camino. |
| I lost my bearings when I came out of the canyon. | Me desorienté al salir del cañón. |
| The axle is broken. | El eje está roto (quebrado). |
| Please turn on the light. | Haga el favor de prender la luz. |
| Who is in charge of this matter? | ¿Quién se encarga de este asunto? |
| There is very little gasoline left in the tank. | Queda muy poca gasolina en el tanque. |
| Gasoline is scarce around here. | La gasolina es rara por aquí. |
| He sank in mud to his knees. | Se hundió en el lodo hasta las rodillas. |
| Who can prevent it? | ¿Quién lo puede impedir? |
| I forgot the key to the gate. | Olvidé la llave de la puerta. |
| We are taking two spare tires. | Llevamos dos llantas extras (de repuesto). |
| What shall we do afterwards? | ¿Qué haremos luego? |
| Will you give me a light? | ¿Quiere usted darme lumbre? |
| He couldn't (can't) start the motor. | No podía (puede) poner en marcha el motor. |
| I see no means of solving this. | No veo medio de resolver esto. |
| He refuses to help me. | El niega (rehusa) ayudarme. |
| I couldn't (can't) find it anywhere. | No lo encontré (encuentro) por ningún lado. |
| They had (have) to stop halfway there. | Tuvieron (Tienen) que parar a medio camino. |
| We will have (had) to repair the damage. | Tenemos (Tuvimos) que reparar el daño. |
| The water line broke. | La cañería (tubería) se reventó. |
| A tire blew out. | Se reventó una llanta. |
| I cannot (could not) follow you. | No puedo (pude) seguirle. |
| It is impossible to do it! | ¡Es imposible hacerlo! |
| What are the rules? | ¿Cuáles son las reglas? |
| What is the matter? | ¿Qué pasó? |
| What is the matter with him? | ¿Qué le pasa? |
| What must be done? | ¿Qué hay que hacer? |
| What should I do? | ¿Qué debo hacer? |

| | |
|---|---|
| I cannot do this all alone. | *No puedo hacerlo solo.* |
| The nut's loose on this bolt. | *La tuerca del tornillo está floja (suelta).* |
| It won't come loose! | *¡No quiere!* (idiomatic or slang expression) |
| I'll have to look around for it. | *Tendré que buscarlo por aquí.* |
| Do you know who (how, why)? | *¿Sabe usted quién (cómo, por qué)?* |
| I don't know. | *Yo no sé.* |
| Yes, I know. | *Sí, lo sé.* |
| Do you have enough money? | *¿Tiene bastante dinero?* |
| Can you lend me ———? | *¿Puede prestarme ———?* |
| Now, do you have everything? | *¿Ahora, tiene todo?* |
| What else do you all want? | *¿Qué más quieren?* |
| I can't do better than this. | *No lo puedo hacer mejor que esto.* |
| Do me a favor. | *Hágame un favor.* |
| Do you need anything? | *¿Necesita algo?* |
| May I help you? | *¿Puedo servirle?* |
| What's up? | *¿Qué hubo?* (*¿Qué pasó?*) |
| What happened? | *¿Qué pasó?* |
| I ask (need) nothing. | *No me falta nada.* |
| They are of no use. | *No sirven.* |
| Don't worry. | *No se preocupe.* |
| We need them. | *Nos hacen falta.* |
| By moonlight | *A la luz de la luna* |
| Many years ago | *Hace muchos años; en años pasados* |
| | |
| All or part | *Todo o partes* |
| Do you need help? | *¿Necesita ayuda?* |
| What can it be? | *¿Qué será?* |
| Water is needed. | *Falta agua.* |
| See if you can flag a passing truck. | *Mire si haciendo señales puede parar algún camión.* |
| Can you fix me up with a place to sleep? | *¿Puede proporcionarme un sitio (lugar) donde pudiera dormir?* |
| Can you fix this? | *¿Puede usted componer esto?* |
| Where can we get this flat fixed? | *¿Dónde nos pueden arreglar esta llanta ponchada?* |
| Put it in gear. | *Póngalo en marcha.* |

## SAYINGS

| | |
|---|---|
| God willing. | *Si Dios quiere.* (*Con el favor de Dios.*) (*Dios mediante.*) |

Each man's head is a world unto itself.

*Cada cabeza es un mundo.*

It is God's will.

*Sea por Dios.*

A man may do what he wants, but everything is God's will.

*Haga uno lo que haga, todo es lo que Dios quiere.*

Man proposes, God disposes.

*El hombre propone, Dios dispone.*

What comes out of the water returns to the water (easy come, easy go).

*Lo del agua, al agua.*

Dead men tell no tales!

*¡Los muertos no hablan!*

Hunger is the best sauce!

*¡A buen hambre no hay gordas duras!*

Each man knows best about the load in his sack.

*Cada quien sabe lo que carga en su costal.*

In jail you know your friends.

*En la cárcel se conocen los amigos.*

To try to suck both teats (play both ends against the middle)

*Mamar a dos tetas*

The barking dog does not bite.

*Perro que ladra no muerde.*

There is nothing good without a drawback, nor bad without some saving grace.

*No hay bien sin pero, ni mal sin gracia.*

God will pay (reward) you (said when one cannot pay or when an offer of payment for a service is refused).

*Dios se lo pague. (Que Dios se lo pague.)*

The liver doesn't exist! (a toast among hard drinkers)

*¡El hígado no existe!*

Everyone has his own way of killing fleas.

*Cada uno tiene su modo de matar pulgas.*

50/50

*Mitad y mitad*

Which is the lesser of two evils?

*¿De los dos males, cuál es el menor?*

God bless you!

*¡Qué Dios le bendiga!*

Happiness is a matter of moderation.

*La felicidad consiste en la moderación.*

We all have our faults.

*Todos tenemos nuestras faltas.*

There's no life without hardships.

*No hay vida sin fatigas.*

The good always pay for the wicked.

*Siempre pagan justos por pecadores.*

He who sings drives away his grief.

*Quien canta, su mal espanta.*

He was caught in the act.

*Le cogieron con las manos en la masa. (Lo pescaron en la movida.)*

| | |
|---|---|
| That happens to all mortals. | *Eso le ocurre a todos los mortales.* |
| May he rest in peace. | *Que en paz descanse.* |
| Everything is catching except beauty! | *¡Todo se pega menos la belleza!* |
| The road to Hell is paved with good intentions and little else! | *El infierno está empedrado de buenos propósitos y nada más!* |
| Come Hell or high water. | *Contra viento y marea.* |
| Against the wind | *Con viento contrario* |
| It's getting hard to make both ends meet. | *Se está haciendo difícil vivir con lo que se tiene.* |
| Who knows what the end will be? | *¿Quién sabe cuál será el fin?* |
| He who is lost tries anything. | *El perdido se va a todo.* |
| The priest has testicles just like me. | *El padre tiene huevos como yo.* |
| Health and money and time to enjoy them! | *¡Salud y dinero y tiempo para gustarlos!* |
| Enough is enough! | *¡Basta y sobra!* |
| He who is guilty of nothing fears nothing. | *Él que nada debe nada teme.* |

## SIMPLE IDEAS, CONCEPTS, AND WANTS

To give the opposite of many basic expressions you can simply use *no* with them. To make it a question, show the question by voice inflection and look. A liberal use of the "please" ending (*por favor*) will show courtesy.

| | |
|---|---|
| I want ———. | *Quiero ———.* |
| I don't want ———. | *No quiero ———.* |
| I want to eat ———. | *Quiero comer ———.* |
| Please. | *Sírvase. (Por favor.)* |
| Where is ———? | *¿Dónde está ———?* |
| At what time? | *¿A qué hora?* |
| What time does ——— start? | *¿A qué hora empieza ———?* |
| What time does ——— leave? | *¿A qué hora sale ———?* |
| When does ——— leave? | *¿Cuándo sale ———?* |
| Bring help! | *¡Traiga ayuda!* |
| I am your friend. | *Soy su amigo(a).* |
| We want ———. | *Queremos ———.* |
| Bring me ———. | *Tráigame ———.* |
| I need ———. | *Necesito ———.* |
| Give me ———. | *Déme ———.* |
| Where can I get ———? | *¿Dónde puedo conseguir ———?* |

| | |
|---|---|
| I have ———. | *Tengo* ———. |
| I don't have ———. | *No tengo* ———. |
| We have ———. | *Tenemos* ———. |
| We don't have ———. | *No tenemos* ———. |
| Have you ———? | *¿Tiene usted* ———? |
| Is there ———? | *¿Hay* ———? |
| There is no ———. | *No hay* ———. |
| I want to buy it. | *Quiero comprarlo.* |
| Where can I find ———? | *¿Dónde puedo hallar* ———? |
| Where is there ———? | *¿Dónde hay* ———? |
| Where is ———? | *¿Dónde está* ———? |
| I am | *Estoy* or *soy* |
| He is | *Está* or *es* |
| Are you ———? | *¿Está usted* ———? |
| We are | *Estamos* |
| They are | *Están* or *son* |
| Is it ———? | *¿Está* ———? (generally used for location or condition) |
| It is ———. | *Está* ———. |
| This is ———.   · | *Esto está* ———. |
| That is ———. | *Aquello está* ———. |
| It is not ———. | *No está* ———. |
| It is (too, very) ———. | *Está muy* ———. |
| Is it ———? | *¿Es* ———? |
| It is ———. | *Es* ———. |
| This is ———? | *¿Esto es* ———? |
| This is ———. | *Esto es* ———. |
| That is ———. | *Aquello es* ———. |
| It is not ———. | *No es* ———. |
| Are you ———? | *¿Están ustedes* ———? |
| They are ———. | *Están* ———. |
| We are ———. | *Estamos* ———. |
| I can ———. | *Puedo* ———. |
| You can ———. | *Usted puede* ———. |
| Come. | *Venga.* |
| Come here. | *Venga acá.* |
| Go. | *Vaya.* |
| Go away. | *Váyase.* |
| What is it? | *¿Qué es?* |
| Who is it? | *¿Quién es?* |
| Take me there. | *Lléveme allá.* |
| I am hot. | *Tengo calor.* |
| I am tired. | *Estoy cansado(a).* |

| | |
|---|---|
| Where are they? | ¿Dónde están? |
| Which is ———? | ¿Cuál es ———? |
| Show me ———. | Enséñeme ———. |
| Take me to ———. | Lléveme a ———. |
| My ——— doesn't work. | No sirve mi ———. |
| Pass me ———. | Alcánzeme ———. |
| Does it fit? | ¿Cabe? |
| It doesn't fit. | No cabe; no queda. |
| We need ———. | Necesitamos ———. |
| It needs ———. | Se necesita ———. |
| We want ———. | Queremos ———. |
| Where can we ———? | ¿Dónde podemos ———? |
| Where is ——— sold? | ¿Dónde se vende ———? |
| Why is it ———? | ¿Por qué es ———? |
| Please ———. | Por favor ———. |
| I have been able to ———. | He podido ———. |
| I (You) want to ———. | Quiero (Quiere) ———. |
| I (You) have to ———. | Tengo (Tiene) que ———. |
| It's necessary to ———. | Es necesario ———. |
| I (You) should ———. | Debo (Debe) ———. |
| It's possible to ———. | Es posible ———. |
| I'm (You're) going to ———. | Voy (Va) a ———. |
| I'm (You're) not going to ———. | No voy (va) a ———. |
| This, that | Esto(a), Eso(a) |
| Here, there | Aquí, allá |
| Everywhere | A todas partes |
| It's (not) o.k. | (No) está bien. |
| I can (cannot). | (No) puedo. |
| I have (have not) just | (No) acabo de |
| Which one? What? | ¿Cuál? |
| Who? | ¿Los cuáles? |
| How? | ¿Cómo? |
| When? | ¿Cuándo? |
| Where from? | ¿De dónde? |
| Where to? | ¿Adónde? |
| How much? | ¿Cuánto? |
| How many? | ¿Cuántos? |
| Where? | ¿Dónde? |
| Why? | ¿Por qué? |
| Whom? | ¿Quién? |
| Whose? | ¿De quiénes? |
| More than | Más que |
| I am hot (cold) (hungry) (thirsty) (sleepy). | Tengo calor (frío) (hambre) (sed) (sueño). |

| | |
|---|---|
| I am ill. | *Estoy enfermo(a).* |
| I am hot (mad)! | *¡Estoy caliente (enojado[a])!* |

## Basic Questions

| | |
|---|---|
| How? | *¿Cómo?* |
| How many? | *¿Cuántos(as)?* |
| How much? | *¿Cuánto(a)?* |
| How often? | *¿Con qué frecuencia?* |
| How many times? | *¿Cuántas veces?* |
| How far? | *¿A qué distancia? (¿Qué tan lejos?)* |
| How long? (time) | *¿Cuánto tiempo?* |
| How long? (length) | *¿De qué largo?* |
| What? | *¿Qué? (¿Mande?)* |
| What for? | *¿Para qué?* |
| What else? | *¿Qué más?* |
| What about? | *¿Y de?* |
| Which? | *¿Cuál?* |
| What is ———? | *¿Qué es ———?* |
| Which ones? | *¿Cuáles?* |
| What was ———? | *¿Qué era ———?* |
| Who? | *¿Quién? (¿Quiénes?) (¿Cuáles?)* |
| What were ———? | *¿Qué eran ———?* |
| Who is ———? | *¿Quién es ———?* |
| When? | *¿Cuándo?* |
| Who are ———? | *¿Quiénes son ———?* |
| Where? | *¿Dónde?* |
| Where from? | *¿De dónde?* |
| Where about? | *¿En dónde?* |
| Where is ———? | *¿Dónde está ———?* |
| Where is the toilet? | *¿Dónde está el excusado (sanitario)?* |
| Whose? | *¿De quién?* |
| Where to? | *¿A dónde?* |
| Why? | *¿Por qué?* |
| Why not? | *¿Por qué no?* |
| When? | *¿Cuándo?* |
| How high? | *¿De qué altura?* |
| How deep? | *¿De qué hondo?* |
| How narrow? | *¿De qué ancho?* |
| What size? | *¿De qué tamaño?* |
| How heavy? | *¿Qué pesa?* |
| For when? | *¿Para cuándo?* |
| Who did it? | *¿Quién lo hizo?* |

Where did he go? — ¿Adónde se fue?
What was he like? — ¿Cómo era?
Where do you live? — ¿Dónde vive usted?
Where were you born? — ¿Dónde nació usted?
Where is the entrance (exit)? — ¿Dónde está la entrada (salida)?
Whom do I pay? — ¿A quién pago?
When can I have this? — ¿Cuándo puedo tener eso?
May I speak to ———? — ¿Puedo hablar con ———?
May I have a word with you? — ¿Me permite hablarle un momento?

What is the size? — ¿De qué tamaño es?
What do you want? — ¿Qué quiere usted? (¿Qué desea usted?)

Do you want ———? — ¿Desea usted ———?
Are you single or married? — ¿Es soltero(a) o casado(a)?
How old are you? — ¿Qué edad tiene? (¿Cuántos años tiene?)

What is your occupation? — ¿Cuál es su ocupación?
What is the name of this? — ¿Cómo se llama esto?
What do you mean? — ¿Qué quiere decir?
What is there? — ¿Qué hay?
Who knows? — ¿Quién sabe?
Who is it? — ¿Quién es? (¿Quién vive?)
It's me! — ¡Soy yo!
Where's he from? — ¿De dónde es?
From Boquillas. — De Boquillas.
Whose is it? — ¿De quién es?
It's hers. — Es de ella.

## General Conversation

Does anyone here play an instrument? — ¿Hay aquí alguien que toque algún instrumento?
Are there musicians in this village? — ¿Hay músicos en este pueblo?

Is this for me? — ¿Esto es para mí?
What do you mean by that? — ¿Qué quiere decir usted con eso?
I missed what you said. — Se me escapó lo que usted dijo.
I want you to meet my father. — Quiero que conozca a mi padre. (Quiero presentarle a mi padre.)

I want to leave a message. — Quiero dejar un recado.
Please take a message. — Tome un recado, por favor.
You must be mistaken. — Usted debe estar equivocado(a).
Who is next? — ¿A quién le toca? (¿Quién sigue?)

| | |
|---|---|
| I was next in line. | *Seguía yo.* |
| What next? | *¿Y ahora qué? (¿Y luego qué?)* |
| What's next (more)? | *¿Qué más?* |
| Did you have a nice time? | *¿Pasó un rato agradable? (¿Se divirtió usted?)* |
| This is only for you. | *Esto es únicamente para usted.* |
| Where's your mother? | *¿Dónde está su madre?* |
| She's outside. | *Está allá fuera.* |
| What's going on over there? | *¿Qué pasa allí?* |
| Let's get to the point! | *¡Vamos al grano!* |
| Really! | *¡De veras! (¡No me lo diga!)* |
| Let's stay in the shade. | *Quedémonos en la sombra.* |
| Shall I wait? | *¿Espero? (¿Debo esperar?) (¿Me espero?)* |
| So they say. | *Así dicen.* |
| Generally, he's home every evening. | *Generalmente, está en casa todas las noches.* |
| Let's get a drink of cool spring water. | *Bebamos un poco de agua fresca del ojo de agua.* |
| Step back a little, please. | *Por favor, retírese usted un poco.* |
| Will you step aside, please? | *¿Quiere hacerse a lado, por favor?* |
| Can't you get up earlier? | *¿No puede usted levantarse más temprano?* |
| Hold still a minute. | *Estése quieto(a) un momento.* |
| I have it on the tip of my tongue! | *¡Lo tengo en la punta de la lengua!* |
| Business is on the rise. | *Los negocios van para arriba.* |
| What are you doing up there? | *¿Qué está usted haciendo allí arriba?* |
| Which way did he go? | *¿Por dónde se fue él?* |
| You will have to wait a while before you can see him. | *Tendrá usted que esperar un rato antes de verle.* |
| Is this your seat? | *¿Es este su asiento?* |
| Is your papa at home? | *¿Está su papá?* |
| He isn't here. | *No está aquí. (No está en casa.)* |
| He is not going to be home today. | *Él no estará hoy en casa.* |
| What was the cause of his delay? | *¿Cuál fue la causa de su retraso?* |
| Do you know Mr. García? | *¿Conoce usted al señor García?* |
| How many will come? | *¿Cuántos vendrán?* |
| When will you come? | *¿Cuándo vendrá usted?* |
| Here I am. | *Aquí estoy.* |
| Say it in plain terms. | *Dígalo en lenguaje llano.* |
| I'll do it later. | *Luego lo haré.* |
| What are you looking at? | *¿Qué mira usted?* |

| | |
|---|---|
| He didn't even say goodbye. | No dijo ni adiós. |
| Go out and see what is happening. | Salga usted a ver que ocurre. |
| Have you forgotten something? | ¿Ha olvidado usted algo? |
| Do you remember what I told you? | ¿Recuerda usted lo que le dije? |
| Let's cool off in the shade of the trees. | Vamos a refrescarnos en la sombra de los árboles. |
| Don't laugh! | ¡No se ría usted! |
| What are you laughing at? | ¿De qué se ríe usted? |
| I cannot do it now. | Yo no puedo hacerlo ahorita. |
| How many times? | ¿Cuántas veces? |
| Have you ———? | ¿Ha usted ———? |
| I want you to meet my friend. | Quiero presentarle a mi amigo(a). |
| Glad to know you. | Mucho gusto. |
| What happened then? | ¿Qué hizo usted entonces? |
| You cannot. | No puede. |
| Please come with me to the truck. | Por favor, venga conmigo a la troca. |
| You need to write your address. | Usted necesita escribir su dirección. |
| O.K., I'm going to write my address. | Muy bien. Voy a escribir mi dirección. |
| Do I have to get up now? | ¿Tengo que levantarme ahorita? |
| Yes, you have to get up now. | Sí, usted tiene que levantarse ahorita. |
| Are you going to give it to me? | ¿Me lo va a dar? (¿Va a dármelo?) (¿Me lo da?) |
| I'm going to give it to you. | Se lo voy a dar. |
| What a scare! | ¡Qué susto! |
| I wonder who he was? | ¿Quién sería él? |
| At what time did you get up this morning? | ¿A qué hora se levantó usted esta mañana? |
| I got up at 6:00 this morning. | Me levanté a las seis esta mañana. |
| Are you wide awake? | ¿Está usted bien despierto(a)? |
| What is he like? | ¿Cómo es él? |
| What is Joe like? | ¿Cómo es José? |
| He is fat (thin). | Es gordo (flaco). |
| What are Michael and Helen like? | ¿Cómo son Miguel y Elena? |
| They are very old. | Son muy viejos. |
| They are very rich. | Son muy ricos. |
| What are your children like? | ¿Cómo son sus hijos? |
| They are ingrates (loving)! | ¡Mis hijos son ingratos (afectuosos)! |
| Where shall I put ———? | ¿Dónde pongo ———? |

| | |
|---|---|
| Please open the window (door). | *Favor de abrir la ventana (puerta).* |
| Should I ———? | *¿Debo ———?* |
| Do you have to use ———? | *¿Tiene que usar ———?* |
| Why are you ———? | *¿Por qué está usted ———?* |
| Is it necessary to call ———? | *¿Es necesario llamar a ———?* |
| What does he say? | *¿Qué dice él?* |
| He says ———. | *Dice que ———.* |
| We are going to do ———. | *Vamos a hacer ———.* |
| Take off ———, please. | *Quítese ———, por favor.* |
| What do you use? | *¿Qué usa usted?* |
| What do you buy? | *¿Qué compra usted?* |
| What do you have? | *¿Qué tiene usted?* |
| What was it? | *¿Qué fue?* |
| Who was it? | *¿Quién fue?* |
| How many are there in all? | *¿Cuántos hay en total?* |
| How do you tell the two apart? | *¿Cómo puede distinguir uno del otro?* |
| | |
| We are giving this away free. | *Estamos dando esto gratis.* |
| What is this weed (plant) called? | *¿Cómo se llama esta yerba (planta)?* |
| | |
| It is a saltbush (pigweed, careless weed). | *Es una chamiza (un quelite).* |
| I'll be right with you. | *En seguida le atiendo.* |
| What do you mean? | *¿Qué quiere decir usted?* |
| Do you remember ———? | *¿Se acuerda usted de ———?* |
| Wait and see. | *Espere y verá.* |
| Who knows? | *¿Quién sabe?* |
| That is all right. | *Eso está bien.* |
| I'll talk to you later. | *Yo le hablo más tarde.* |
| What else do we need? | *¿Qué más necesitamos?* |
| Come now! You don't say! | *¡Vaya! ¡No me diga!* |
| Come what may. | *Venga lo que venga.* |
| As soon as possible. | *Lo más pronto posible.* |
| More than ever. | *Más que nunca.* |
| Again. | *Otra vez.* |
| Let's see. | *A ver.* |
| Let's go see. (We'll see.) | *Vamos a ver.* |
| What did they say? | *¿Qué dijeron?* |
| Little by little. | *Poco a poco.* |
| Step by step. | *Paso a paso.* |
| More or less. | *Más o menos.* |
| By hook or by crook. | *Por las buenas o las malas.* |
| For the time being. (For now.) | *Por lo pronto.* |

| | |
|---|---|
| At least. | *Por lo menos.* |
| Just in case. | *Por si acaso.* |
| As an average. | *Por término medio.* |
| What is the date? | *¿Qué día del mes es hoy? (¿Cuál es la fecha?)* |
| What has become of ———? | *¿Qué se ha hecho de ———?* |
| By hand | *A mano* |
| On foot | *A pie* |
| Again | *De nuevo; otra vez* |
| Idle; free | *Libre; suelto(a)* |
| Standing | *De pie* |
| Suddenly | *De pronto; de repente* |
| Just right | *Al punto* |
| What size is it? | *¿De qué tamaño es?* |
| From time to time. | *De vez en cuando.* |
| No sooner said than done. | *Dicho y hecho.* |
| In other words | *En otras palabras (en otros términos)* |
| In broad daylight | *En pleno día* |
| Instead of | *En vez de* |
| Aloud | *En voz alta* |
| Whisper | *En voz baja* |
| That's it! | *¡Eso es!* |
| All right. | *Está bien (bueno).* |
| I am ———. | *Yo soy ———.* |
| I am not ———. | *Yo no soy ———.* |
| Then | *Entonces* |
| Along | *A lo largo de; a lado de* |
| To the (At the) other side | *Al (Del) otro lado* |
| Enough! | *¡Basta!* |
| On the road to; on the way to | *Al camino de* |
| As usual | *Como de costumbre* |
| To believe (think) not | *Creer que no* |
| To believe (think) so | *Creer que sí* |
| I think not. | *Creo que no.* |
| Regardless of cost (Cost what it may.) | *Cueste lo que cueste.* |
| Since | *Puesto que; desde que* |
| Countless | *Sin cuenta* |
| In their turn | *A su vez* |
| Instead of | *En vez de* |
| Everywhere | *A todas partes* |
| By means of | *Por medio de* |

| | |
|---|---|
| Meanwhile | *Mientras tanto* |
| On the heights | *En las alturas* |
| Let's sing. | *Cantemos. (Vamos a cantar.)* |
| Everybody join in the chorus! | *¡Todos a cantar en coro!* |
| All of you listen. | *Todos escuchen.* |
| I am ready. | *Estoy listo(a).* |
| Don't hurry. | *No se dé prisa.* |
| Share them. | *Compártelos. (Repártelos.)* |
| Read it. | *Léalo.* |
| I want you to read this, please. | *Deseo que lea esto, por favor.* |
| Print your name here. | *Deletree (Escriba) su nombre aquí, con letras de molde.* |
| At about two o'clock. | *Como a las dos.* |
| What is the date? | *¿A cuánto estamos? (¿La fecha, por favor?)* |
| Piggyback | *A cuestas* |
| Crawling | *A gatas (gatear) (a cuatro patas)* |
| Beside | *A lado de* |
| In the dark | *A obscuras* |
| At full speed | *A toda velocidad (a todo correr)* |
| To the right | *A la derecha* |
| To the left | *A la izquierda* |
| Straight ahead | *Siempre derecho; vaya derecho* |

(Note: Be careful not to confuse *derecho* [ahead] with *derecha* [right]. Watch which way your informant points, and go that way!)

## Intentions

| | |
|---|---|
| What is your reason for coming here? | *¿Qué objeto tiene su venida aquí?* |
| I shall do it. | *Lo haré.* |
| I'll be back soon. | *Regreso pronto.* |
| I'm going to return tomorrow. | *Voy a regresar mañana.* |
| State your business, please. | *Por favor, diga usted lo que quiere.* |
| I'll be back within a few hours. | *Volveré dentro de unas horas.* |
| I'm going inside. | *Voy a ir adentro.* |
| I'm going to take a bath. | *Voy a bañarme.* |
| I'm going to call my wife (husband). | *Voy a llamar a mi esposa (esposo).* |
| I'm going to measure ———. | *Voy a medir ———.* |
| How cold! I'm going to wear ———. | *¡Qué frío! Voy a ponerme ———.* |
| I want to go see him. | *Quiero ir a verlo.* |
| I will see. | *Voy a ver.* |

## TIME AND DATES

### Time

| | |
|---|---|
| Midnight | *Medianoche* (f.) |
| Morning (A.M.) | *Mañana* (f.) |
| Noon | *Mediodía* (m.) |
| 12 midnight | *Doce de la noche* (f.) |
| Predawn hours | *Madrugadas* (f.) |
| From 1:00 to 11:00 | *De la una a las once* |
| 12 noon | *Doce del día* (f.) |
| Afternoon (P.M.) | *Tarde* (f.) |
| Evening; night (P.M.) | *Noche* (f.) |
| From 1:00 to 6:00 | *De la una a las seis* |
| From 7:00 to 12:00 | *De las siete a las doce* |
| It is 1:15. | *Es la una y quince.* |
| It is 2:30. | *Son las dos y treinta (y media).* |
| At 1:00. | *A la una.* |
| At 2:00. | *A las dos.* |
| What time is it? | *¿Qué hora es?* |
| What time is it? | *¿Qué horas son?* |

### Days of the Week

| | |
|---|---|
| Sunday | *Domingo* |
| Monday | *Lunes* |
| Tuesday | *Martes* |
| Wednesday | *Miércoles* |
| Thursday | *Jueves* |
| Friday | *Viernes* |
| Saturday | *Sábado* |

### Dates (*Fechas*)

| | |
|---|---|
| On January 1, 1976 | *El primero de enero de mil novecientos setenta y seis* |
| On August 12, 1980 | *El doce de agosto de mil novecientos ochenta* |
| On November 14, 1914 | *El catorce de noviembre de mil novecientos catorce* |

### Months (*Los Meses del Año*)

| | |
|---|---|
| January | *Enero* |
| February | *Febrero* |
| March | *Marzo* |
| April | *Abril* |

| May | *Mayo* |
| June | *Junio* |
| July | *Julio* |
| August | *Agosto* |
| September | *Septiembre* |
| October | *Octubre* |
| November | *Noviembre* |
| December | *Diciembre* |

## The Seasons (*Las Estaciones del Año*)

| Spring | *Primavera* (f.) |
| Summer | *Verano* (m.) |
| Autumn, fall | *Otoño* (m.) |
| Winter | *Invierno* (m.) |

## Miscellaneous

| Year | *Año* (m.) |
| Yearly | *Anualmente* |
| Month | *Mes* (m.) |
| Monthly | *Mensualmente* |
| Week | *Semana* (f.) |
| Next week | *La semana que entra* |
| Weekly | *Semanalmente* |
| Day | *Día* (m.) |
| Daily | *Diariamente* |
| Hour | *Hora* (f.) |
| Hourly | *Cada hora* |
| Half hour | *Media hora* |
| Minutes | *Minutos* (m.) |
| Seconds | *Segundos* (m.) |
| Day after tomorrow | *Pasado mañana* |
| Tomorrow | *Mañana* |
| Today | *Hoy* |
| Tonight | *Esta noche* |
| Last night | *Anoche* |
| Night before last | *Anteanoche* |
| Yesterday | *Ayer* |
| Day before yesterday | *Anteayer* |
| Two days ago | *Hace dos días* |
| Morning | *Mañana* (f.) |
| In the morning | *Por la mañana* |
| Every morning | *Todas las mañanas* |
| All morning | *Toda la mañana* |

| | |
|---|---|
| Yesterday morning | *Ayer por la mañana* |
| Then | *Entonces* |
| Afterward | *Luego; después; desde* |
| As soon as possible | *Lo más pronto posible* |
| On time | *A tiempo* |
| Never | *Nunca* |
| Also | *También* |
| Earlier | *Más temprano* |
| In years past | *En años pasados* |
| A week from today | *De hoy en ocho días* |
| Two weeks from today | *De hoy en quince días* |
| Have you been here long? | *¿Hace mucho tiempo que usted está aquí?* |
| For three years. | *Por tres años.* |
| I arrived three days ago. | *Llegué hace tres días.* |
| I came here two days ago. | *Yo vine hace dos días.* |
| Schedule | *Horario (m.)* |
| You arrived just in time. | *Llegó usted muy a tiempo.* |
| Next week | *La semana que entra* |
| Last week | *La semana pasada* |
| Three years ago | *Hace tres años* |
| This week | *La semana corriente; esta semana* |
| Ten days from now | *De aquí en diez días* |
| Seldom | *Pocas veces* |
| Nowadays | *Hoy día; estos días* |
| Finally | *Por fin; en fin* |
| Afternoon | *Mediodía (m.); tarde (f.)* |
| Every afternoon | *Todas las tardes* |
| All afternoon | *Toda la tarde* |
| In the afternoon | *Por la tarde* |
| Evening, night | *Tarde (f.); noche (f.)* |
| In the evening; at night | *Por la noche* |
| Every evening; every night | *Todas las noches* |
| From; since | *Desde* |
| Always | *Siempre* |
| Never | *Nunca* |
| Lately | *Últimamente* |
| Now | *Ahora; ahorita* |
| Right away | *Ahora mismo; ahorita; luego* |
| Before | *Antes* |
| After | *Después; desde; luego* |
| Later | *Más tarde* |
| Next | *Próximo(a); en seguida* |

| | |
|---|---|
| Until | *Hasta* |
| As soon as | *Tan pronto como* |
| Within a short while | *Dentro de poco* |
| Since then | *Desde entonces* |
| Ago | *Hace* (plus a period of time) |
| Late in, toward the end of (week, month, year, etc.) | *A fines de* |
| About the middle of (week, month, year, etc.) | *A mediados de* |
| Often | *A menudo; frecuentemente; muchas veces* |
| Early in, about the first of (week, month, year, etc.) | *A principios de* |
| At what time? | *¿A qué hora?* |
| At times | *En ratos* |
| At the end of the month | *Al fin del mes* |
| Sometimes; at times | *A veces* |
| At sunset | *Al caer la tarde; al atardecer* |
| At sunset | *A la caída (puesta) del sol* |
| In the wee hours of the morning | *En la madrugada* |
| At dawn (daybreak) | *Al amanecer* |
| At dusk (nightfall) | *Al anochecer* |
| At the end of the year | *Al fin del año* |
| In the end | *Al fin; al cabo* |
| At first | *Al principio* |
| At the end (last) | *Al último* |
| At about | *Como a* |
| In about | *Como en* |
| From then on | *De allí en adelante* |
| From now on | *De aquí en adelante* |
| From that time on | *Desde entonces* |
| From now on | *De hoy en adelante* |
| Very early in the morning | *Muy de mañana* |
| Immediately | *En seguida; inmediatamente* |
| Years later | *Años después* |
| Years past | *En años pasados* |
| In time | *Con el tiempo* |
| On arrival | *Al llegar* |
| At the same time | *A su vez* |
| Not right now | *Ahorita no* |
| A few days | *Pocos días* |
| Take your time. | *Tome su tiempo.* |
| I'll leave at once. | *Salgo en seguida.* |

| | |
|---|---|
| Be ready to leave at a moment's notice. | *Prepárese a salir (para irse) en cuanto le avisen.* |
| We must start early so as to be on time. | *Debemos irnos temprano (pronto) para llegar a tiempo.* |
| I want to leave as soon as possible. | *Quiero salir tan pronto que se pueda.* |
| I must go, as it's late. | *Tengo que irme porque es tarde.* |
| He's late as usual. | *Está retrasado como de costumbre.* |
| I'll be back at 4:00. | *Regresaré a las cuatro.* |
| Back in 1975 | *Allá por el año de mil novecientos setenta y cinco* |
| I went to bed late. | *Me acosté tarde.* |
| They'll come before long. | *Vendrán dentro de poco.* |
| I'll meet you between 6:00 and 7:00. | *Lo encontraré entre seis y siete.* |
| I'll see you by and by. | *Lo veré más tarde.* |
| What is the cause of the delay? | *¿Cuál es la causa de la demora?* |
| I'll come by your house tonight. | *Pasaré por su casa esta noche.* |
| He'll come out soon. | *Saldrá pronto.* |
| We will return at dusk. | *Regresaremos al crepúsculo.* |
| I want to leave. | *Quiero salirme (irme).* |

## WARNINGS AND CAUTIONS

| | |
|---|---|
| Don't step in the ———. | *No pise usted en ———.* |
| Try not to lose your nerve. | *Procure no perder el valor.* |
| Watch your step! | *¡Tenga usted cuidado!* |
| Don't fall over the edge! | *¡No se caiga por el borde!* |
| Don't step on the snake in the grass! | *¡No pise sobre la culebra en el zacate!* |
| No trespassing! | *¡Prohibido el paso!* |
| Trespassing on that property is not allowed. | *Se prohibe pasar por esa propiedad.* |
| You had better remove your wet clothes. | *Es mejor que se quite la ropa mojada.* |
| Bend down, the ceiling is low. | *Agachen la cabeza porque el techo es muy bajo.* |
| Be careful going down. | *Tenga cuidado al bajar.* |
| The descent was (is) very dangerous. | *El descenso fue (es) muy peligroso.* |
| This is a dangerous thing to do. | *El manejo de esto ofrece peligro.* |
| The handling of dynamite is dangerous. | *El manejo de la dinamita es peligroso.* |

| | |
|---|---|
| Look out! It's going to fall! | ¡Ojo! ¡Que se va a caer! |
| The pass is dangerous at night. | El paso es peligroso por la noche. |
| The dog has rabies. | El perro tiene rabia. |
| You have to obey the rules. | Usted tiene que obedecer las reglas. |
| This is a very dangerous jump (waterfall). | Este salto (salto del agua) es muy peligroso. |
| You should not drink that water! | ¡No debe tomar de esa agua! |
| Why not? | ¿Por qué no? |
| It will make you sick. It is contaminated. | Le enferma. Está contaminada. |
| You should not eat that food! | ¡No debe comer esa comida! |
| Why not? | ¿Por qué no? |
| Is it spoiled? | ¿Está corrompida (perdida)? |
| It is spoiled (bad). | Está corrompida (mala). |
| Look out! | ¡Cuídese usted! |
| Do you dare go there alone? | ¿Se atreve usted a ir solo allá? |
| Be careful you are not cheated! | ¡Cuidado que no le engañen! |

## WEATHER

| | |
|---|---|
| It is cold. | Hace frío. |
| It is hot. | Hace calor. |
| It is bad weather. | Hace mal tiempo. |
| It is going to rain. | Va a llover. |
| Rain | Lluvia (f.) |
| Mist or drizzle | Llovizna (f.); nublinazo (m.) |
| Fog | Neblina (f.) |
| Drought | Sequía (f.) |
| Ice | Hielo (m.) |
| Frost | Helada (f.) |
| It is very windy. | Hace mucho viento. |
| Wind | Viento (m.) |
| Storm | Tormenta (f.); tronada (f.); tempestad (f.) |
| Stormy | Tempestuoso(a); borrascoso(a) |
| Thunder | Truenos (m.) |
| Thunderstorm | Chubasco (m.); tronada (f.); borrasca (f.) |
| Dew | Rocío (m.) |
| Snow | Nieve (f.) |
| Hail | Granizo (m.) |
| Light | Luz (f.) |
| Darkness | O(b)scuridad (f.) |

| | |
|---|---|
| Shade | *Sombra* (f.) |
| Lightning | *Rayos* (m.); *foco(s)* (m.); *relámpago* |
| Rainbow | *Arco iris* (m.) |
| Dust devil | *Remolino de polvo de arena* (m.) |
| Did it rain much yesterday? | *¿Llovío mucho ayer?* |
| I should say so! | *¡Ya lo creo!* |
| The rain is over. | *La lluvia se paró.* |
| To weather the storm | *Aguantar el chubasco* |
| How is the weather? | *¿Cómo está el clima (tiempo)?* |
| The day is cloudy. | *El día esta nublado.* |
| Don't you think it will rain? | *¿No cree usted que va a llover?* |
| What is the temperature by the thermometer? | *¿A cuántos grados está el termómetro?* |
| To pour down rain | *Llover a chorros* |
| Deluge | *Chaparrón* (m.) |
| Flood | *Diluvio* (m.) |
| Dust cloud or dust storm | *Polvareda* (m.) |
| Blizzard | *Ventisca* (f.); *norteño* (m.) |
| Hurricane | *Huracán* (m.) |
| The weather is fine. | *Hace buen tiempo.* |
| What sort of weather have we? | *¿Qué tiempo hace?* |
| I am warm. | *Tengo calor.* |
| I am cold. | *Tengo frío.* |
| Very damp | *Muy húmedo(a)* |
| It is sunny. | *Hay sol.* |
| It is cool. | *Hace (Está) fresco.* |
| It is very muddy. | *Hay mucho lodo.* |
| It is very dusty. | *Hay mucho polvo.* |
| It is dark. | *Está obscuro.* |
| It rains. | *Llueve.* |
| It is raining. | *Está lloviendo.* |
| Do you think it will be good weather? | *¿Cree usted que hará buen tiempo?* |
| It is a beautiful night. | *Es una noche hermosa.* |
| The weather is very changeable. | *El tiempo está muy variable.* |
| It is threatening to rain. | *Quiere llover.* |
| When does the rainy season start? | *¿Cuándo empieza la temporada de lluvias (las aguas)?* |
| | |
| The ground is wet with dew. | *Hay mucho rocío.* |
| There was heavy dew last night. | *Hubo bastante rocío anoche.* |
| It is very windy. | *Hace mucho viento. (Está muy vientoso.)* |

|  |  |
|---|---|
| Look at those dark clouds! | *¡Mire aquellas nubes negras!* |
| There comes the rain! | *¡Allá viene la lluvia!* |
| It is beginning to rain. | *Empieza a llover.* |
| We will wait a while. | *Esperamos poco tiempo.* |
| It is no longer raining. | *Ya no llueve.* |
| It rained an inch. | *Llovió una pulgada.* |
| We've been having awful weather! | *¡Hemos tenido un tiempo horrible!* |
| It's a bad day to go out. | *Es mal día para salir.* |
| We had better go before it rains. | *Sería mejor que nos fuéramos antes de que lloviera.* |
| The lightning blinded me for a while. | *El relámpago me cegó por un momento.* |
| The wind will blow hard tonight. | *El viento soplará fuerte esta noche.* |
| A storm may blow up this afternoon. | *Puede desencadenarse una tormenta esta tarde.* |
| Did you hear that clap of thunder? | *¿Oyó usted ese trueno?* |
| The skies are clearing now. | *El cielo se está despejando.* |
| In July the heat is intense. | *En julio el calor es intenso.* |
| The sun's awfully hot today. | *El sol está que quema hoy.* |
| The rain has not let up for two days. | *La lluvia no ha cesado por dos días.* |
| The rains started late this year. | *Este año han empezado tarde las lluvias.* |
| The rainy season set in early this year. | *La estación de lluvias comenzó temprano este año.* |
| The wind has shifted. | *El viento ha cambiado de dirección.* |
| How does the sky look today? | *¿Cómo está el cielo hoy?* |
| The sky is overcast. | *El cielo está nublado.* |
| There is a south wind. | *Sopla viento sur.* |
| Every summer this stream dries up. | *Esta corriente se seca todos los veranos.* |
| It has been a dry summer. | *Ha sido un verano seco.* |
| There is not even a drop of water. | *No hay ni una gota de agua.* |
| The air is very still. | *El aire está muy quieto. (No corre ningún viento.)* |
| We had a big storm yesterday. | *Ayer tuvimos una gran tormenta.* |
| We have had a streak of very hot weather. | *Hemos tenido una racha de tiempo muy caluroso.* |
| It is very sunny today. | *Hoy hay mucho sol.* |
| Wasn't that a terrible storm last night? | *¿Verdad que fue terrible la tormenta de anoche?* |

| | |
|---|---|
| The wall protected me from the rain. | *La pared me abrigaba de la lluvia.* |
| We are having a rainy spell. | *Ahora hace un tiempo de agua.* |
| There is a very strong wind blowing. | *Sopla un aire muy fuerte.* |
| It is very warm today. | *Hoy hace mucho calor.* |
| The water became muddy because of the rain. | *El agua se enturbió con la lluvia.* |
| A very strong north wind is blowing. | *Sopla un norte muy fuerte.* |
| A strong wind was blowing. | *Sopló mucho viento.* |
| A strong wind is blowing. | *Sopla un viento fuerte.* |
| What was the weather yesterday? | *¿Qué tiempo hizo ayer?* |
| Yesterday the weather was bad. | *Ayer hizo mal tiempo.* |
| It is very hot. | *Hace mucho calor.* |
| The water is very cold. | *El agua está muy fría.* |
| Now that the rain has stopped, we can leave. | *Ahora que ha cesado la lluvia, podemos marcharnos (podemos irnos).* |
| The cold froze the water in the pipes. | *El frío congeló el agua en las cañerías (los tubos).* |

## THE WORLD

| | |
|---|---|
| Sky, heaven | *Cielo* (m.) |
| Moon | *Luna* (f.) |
| Planets | *Planetas* (m.) |
| Rainbow | *Arco iris* (m.) |
| Fire | *Fuego* (m.) |
| Sand | *Arena* (f.) |
| Mud | *Lodo* (m.); *zoquete* (m.) |
| Ocean | *Océano* (m.) |
| Beach, dry lake | *Playa* (f.) |
| Bay | *Bahía* (f.) |
| Tide | *Marea* (f.) |
| Dam | *Presa* (f.) |
| River | *Río* (m.) |
| Waterfall | *Cascada* (f.); *salto del agua* (m.); *caída* (f.) |
| Mountain | *Sierra* (f.); *montaña* (f.) |
| Valley | *Valle* (m.) |
| Sun | *Sol* (m.) |
| Stars | *Estrellas* (f.) |

| | |
|---|---|
| Clouds | *Nubes* (f.) |
| Air | *Aire* (m.) |
| Water | *Agua* (f.) |
| Dust | *Polvo* (m.) |
| Island | *Isla* (f.) |
| Coast | *Costa* (f.) |
| Sea | *Mar* (m.) |
| Gulf | *Golfo* (m.) |
| Lake | *Lago* (m.) |
| Lagoon | *Laguna* (f.) |
| Current | *Corriente* (f.) |
| Peak | *Pico* (m.); *cumbre* (f.); *cima* (f.) |
| Ridge | *Loma* (f.); *cuesta* (f.) |
| Cliff | *Peñasco* (m.) |
| Rocks | *Rocas* (f.); *piedras* (f.) |
| Hill | *Colina* (f.); *loma* (f.) |
| Dry lake bed | *Playa* (f.); *laguna* (f.) |
| Flats near river | *Vegas* (f.) |
| High plains | *Llanos* (m.) |
| Edge of river, cliff, steep place, or body of water | *Orilla* (f.) |
| Canyon | *Cañón* (m.); *barranca* (f.) |
| Volcano | *Volcán* (m.) |
| Sinkhole | *Sumidero* (m.); *sótano* (m.) |
| Swamp | *Pantano* (m.) |
| Jungle | *Selva* (f.) |
| Forest | *Bosque* (m.) |
| Desert | *Desierto* (f.) |
| Brackish or salty water | *Agua salobre* (f.); *agua salada* (f.) |
| Salt crystals or salty, white evaporite found in desert washes or near desert seep springs | *Salitre* (m.); *salumbre* (m.) |
| Hot spring | *Ojo termal* (m.); *ojo caliente* (m.) |
| Box or blind canyon | *Cañón sin salida* (m.); *cañón ciego* (m.) |
| Sand dunes | *Médanos* (m.); *dunas de arena* (f.) |
| Canebrake | *Carrizal* (m.) |

# 16. References

## MAPS

Raisz, Erwin. *Landforms of Mexico*. Available from 130 Charles Street, Boston, MA 02114, 617/523-4520; 41" × 28", less than $2.00 + $2.50 postage for rolled/tube mailing. Great introduction to physiographic features of Mexico.

García, José. *Maps of the Chihuahuan Desert Region.* 1976. (Supplement to *Gazeteer of the Chihuahuan Desert Region*, by James Henrickson and Richard M. Straw. Los Angeles: California State University, 1976.) Available for $15.00 from Dr. James Henrickson, Department of Botany, University of Texas at Austin 78712. Includes separate gazeteer of the Chihuahuan Desert Region, which lists all locales, place names, elevations, *municipios*, etc. Provides access to hard-to-get military maps of northern Mexico. The handy size makes it very convenient. Roadways are not always accurate and, especially with the influx of *ejido* development, some of the cultural names are now outdated. A must for the desert traveler.

NOAA. *Sectional Aeronautical Chart.* Scale 1:500,000. Folded format; about $3.50 each.

a. El Paso (Chihuahua, Coahuila)

b. San Antonio (Coahuila)

c. Brownsville (Coahuila, Nuevo León, Tamaulipas)

Available at most private airports. These maps are air navigation maps but they are excellent for general orientation. In the old days, we used them extensively for getting around, despite their weakness of scale. Culture is scant but most ranches with airstrips show up and the spot elevations are useful. They are also useful for note taking, planning, and general discussion. One of the best uses, if you know where you are, is to calculate latitude and longitude. In this sense, they're very good for biologists, geologists, and others who may need to document their location.

Coordinación General Nacional del Sistema de Información (CGNSI, formerly DETENAL). Available from Agencia CGNSI Balderas, Bal-

deras no. 71, México 6, D.F., México. Excellent series of modern topographic maps equivalent to USGS 7½ minute series. Write for
free index. The showroom in Mexico City is a must for the serious
Mexicophile. By the time this book goes to press coverage will be
available for almost the entire nation. These are good maps, but
their scale makes them cumbersome for use on road trips. If you are
in major cities, such as Guadalajara, Monterrey, or Ciudad Juárez,
there are map shops that carry limited coverage in this series. When
ordering by mail, be sure to send the purchase price by international
money order in pesos.

The following references are included to give the serious student
some idea of sources available to help you understand the Mexican
countryside. All are relatively inexpensive and are readily available.
There are thousands of references on Mexican history, art, archeology,
folklore, architecture, and the like.

## NATURAL HISTORY

### Geology

Smith, C. I. Geologic Map of Northern Coahuila, Mexico. In *Lower
Cretaceous Stratigraphy, Northern Coahuila, Mexico.* Rept. No. 65.
Austin: Bureau of Economic Geology, University of Texas, 1970.

### Biotic Communities

Brown, David E., ed. Biotic Communities of the American Southwest—
United States and Mexico. In *Desert Plants.* Vol. 4, nos. 1–4, 1982.
342 pp. Available at $13.95 from Boyce Thompson Southwestern Ar-
boretum, P.O. Box AB, Superior, AZ 85273. Excellent introduction
to plant communities in the Southwest, with hundreds of color and
black-and-white photographs.

### Vegetation

Rzedowski, Jerzy. *Vegetación de México.* 1978. 432 pp. About $15.00
from Editorial LIMUSA, Arcos de Belén 75, México 1, D.F., México.
Comprehensive treatment of Mexico's vegetation in Spanish with
color and black-and-white photographs.

### Plant Identification

Little, Elbert L., Jr. *The Audubon Society Field Guide to North American Trees: Western Region.* New York: Knopf, 1980. 640 pp. Excellent guide with all color photographs. Includes most species of
northern Mexico. Available at all good bookstores.

Spellenberg, Richard. *The Audubon Society Field Guide to North American Wildflowers: Western Region*. New York: Knopf, 1979. 862 pp.

Vines, Robert A. *Trees, Shrubs, and Woody Vines of the Southwest*. Austin: University of Texas Press, 1960. 1104 pp. Valuable, standard lay reference, now available in paperback sections (Central, North, and East Texas). Illustrated with generally excellent line drawings.

Warnock, Barton H. *Wildflowers of the Big Bend Country, Texas*. Alpine, TX: Sul Ross State University, 1970.

————. *Wildflowers of the Guadalupe Mountains and the Sanddune Country, Texas*. Alpine, TX: Sul Ross State University, 1974.

————. *Wildflowers of the Davis Mountains and Marathon Basin, Texas*. Alpine, TX: Sul Ross State University, 1977. All color photographs. These three books by one of the great West Texas botanists will guide you to most common wildflowers in northern Mexico.

### Reptiles and Amphibians

Conant, Roger. *A Field Guide to Reptiles and Amphibians of Eastern and Central America*. 2d ed. Boston: Houghton Mifflin, 1975. Indispensable reference, which also covers part of South Texas.

King, F. Wayne, and John Behler. *The Audubon Society Field Guide to North American Reptiles and Amphibians*. New York: Knopf, 1979. All color photographs.

### Birds

Birkenstein, Lillian R., and Roy E. Tomlinson, comps. *Native Names of Mexican Birds*. USDI Fish and Wildlife Service Resource Publication 139. Washington, D.C., 1981. An important work.

Peterson, Roger Tory. *A Field Guide to the Birds of Texas and Adjacent States*. Boston: Houghton Mifflin, 1960. Includes many birds in the border region that are not illustrated in the Mexican reference.

————, and Edward L. Chalif. *A Field Guide to Mexican Birds*. Boston: Houghton Mifflin, 1973. Standard reference.

Wauer, Roland H. *A Field Guide to Birds of Big Bend*. Austin: Texas Monthly Press, 1985.

### Wildlife/Mammals

Davis, William B. *The Mammals of Texas*. Texas Parks and Wildlife Department Bulletin 41, rev. Available for about $3.00 from TPWD at 4200 Smith School Road, Austin, TX 78744. Generalized discussion of all mammals in the area, with some black-and-white photographs.

Leopold, A. Starker. *Wildlife of Mexico: The Game Birds and Mam-*

*mals.* Berkeley and Los Angeles: University of California Press, 1972. One of the standard and classic references on wildlife conservation in Mexico.

Schmidly, David J. *The Mammals of Trans Pecos Texas.* College Station: Texas A&M University Press, 1977. Includes information on all mammals of Trans Pecos Texas, which includes adjacent Mexico. The best reference for the area.

Whitaker, J. O., Jr. *The Audubon Society Field Guide to North American Mammals.* New York: Knopf, 1980. Excellent color photography of all mammals.

### Environment and Early Cultures

West, Robert C., ed. *Natural Environment and Early Cultures.* Vol. 1, *Handbook of Middle American Indians,* ed. Robert Wauchope. Austin: University of Texas Press, 1964.

### Natural History/Biota General

Gehlbach, Frederick R. *Mountain Islands and Desert Seas: A Natural History of the U.S. Mexican Borderlands.* College Station: Texas A&M University Press, 1981.

Wauer, Roland H. *Naturalist's Big Bend.* College Station: Texas A&M University Press, 1980. Excellent introduction to natural history of the area, including adjacent Mexico.

————, and D. H. Riskind, eds. *Transactions of the Symposium on the Biological Resources of the Chihuahuan Desert Region, U.S. and Mexico.* USDI, NPS, Transactions and Proceedings Series 3. Washington, D.C.: GPO, 1978. Available from Chihuahuan Desert Research Institute (CDRI), Box 1334, Alpine, TX 79831-1334. Standard reference overview of the biological resources of the region.

## GENERAL GUIDES

Forsyth, Adrian, and Ken Miyata. *Tropical Nature.* New York: Charles Scribner's Sons, 1984. This is the best overall guide to understanding the tropical jungles and rainforests of Mexico and Central America. It contains a good section on hiking at night in the jungle and general advice on gear and technique that is very accurate and reliable.

Franz, Carl. *The People's Guide to Mexico.* Santa Fe, NM: John Muir Publications, 1972 (Box 613, 87501).

————. *The People's Guide to Backpacking, Boating, and Camping in Mexico.* Santa Fe, NM: John Muir Publications, 1981 (Box 613, 87501). Both of the foregoing works by Carl Franz have been reviewed by us to compare them to our present work. We believe they are worth adding to your library. They are generally accurate and helpful and are always entertaining. We are inclined to discount as apocryphal some of the rather bizarre situations the author claims to have encountered and survived, but the general content of both books is reliable and they nicely complement our present work. They would be of particular value to one planning to travel in Mexico by camper or minibus with the intention of sticking pretty close to the main highways and public areas or of camping and beachcombing along the coasts.

## PERSONAL HEALTH IN THE TROPICS

Persons traveling in lowland Mexico, or even in the *sierras* in the tropic zone, will do well to consider malaria prevention and other potentially serious diseases that can be acquired anywhere in Mexico's backcountry. You can judge for yourself the extent of the risk you are willing to take, but in case you are interested in prevention, the following references will be helpful. Remember, this sort of information always needs updating, so seek the most current edition of these references in every instance.

Centers for Disease Control. "Prevention of Malaria in Travelers." *Morbidity and Mortality Weekly Report* (Suppl.) 31, no. 1S (April 16, 1982). Available from Centers for Disease Control, Center for Infectious Diseases, Parasitic Diseases Division, Atlanta, GA 30333.

Neumann, Hans H., M.D. *Foreign Travel and Immunization Guide.* Oradell, NJ: Medical Economics Books, 1982.

The foregoing two volumes will give you all the basic information needed to avoid the most serious diseases that may be encountered anywhere in Mexico and Central America.

## LANGUAGE AIDS

Castillo, Carlos, and Otto F. Bond, comps. *University of Chicago Spanish/English English/Spanish Dictionary.* New York: Washington Square Press, 1968. One of the best pocket dictionaries to pack away for trips; emphasizes New World usages.

Galván, Roberto A., and Richard U. Teschner, comps. *El Diccionario del Español de Tejas.* Silver Spring, MD: Institute of Modern Languages, 1975.

Jiménez, A. *Picardía Mexicana.* Mexico City: Editorial B. Costa-Amic, 1975.

Kelly, Rex R., and George W. Kelly. *Farm and Ranch Spanish.* Vanderpool, TX: Kelly Bros., 1960.

————. *Spanish for the Housewife.* Vanderpool, TX: Kelly Bros., 1973.

Kercheville, F. M. *Practical Spoken Spanish.* 7th ed. Albuquerque: University of New Mexico Press, 1959.

Krack. *Tabú Spanish of Mexico (Words your teacher never taught you).* 1976. Available from author at 3385 30th Street, San Diego, CA.

Miller, J. Dale. *1,000 Spanish Idioms.* Provo, UT: Brigham Young University Press, 1981.

Rosensweig, Jay B. *Caló: Gutter Spanish.* New York: E. P. Dutton, 1973. Another unusual Spanish dictionary, but not nearly as good as *Tabú* or *El Diccionario del Español de Tejas.*

Santamaría, Francisco J. *Diccionario de Mexicanismos.* Mexico City: Editorial Porrúa, 1959.

Simon and Schuster's International Dictionary: *English/Spanish Spanish/English.* New York: Simon & Schuster, 1973. In our experience this is the best desk dictionary for Spanish terms and vernacular as spoken in Mexico.

Technical Information Dept., Engineering Office, Chrysler Corp. *Glossary of Automotive Terminology: Spanish-English; English-Spanish.* 1978. Available from Society of Automotive Engineers, Inc., 400 Commonwealth Drive, Warrendale, PA 15096.

U.S. Department of Justice, Immigration and Naturalization Service. *A Practical Spanish Grammar for Border Patrol Officers.* Washington, D.C.: GPO, 1972.

## Spanish Language Courses on Cassette Tapes

One of the fastest and easiest ways to improve your Spanish is to listen to it while driving. Even short drives, such as to and from work, will give you a surprising amount of time to study your Spanish without taking valuable time away from family, recreation, and friends. On long trips, particularly for those who travel often by automobile, many hours of Spanish study can be gained out of otherwise wasted time on the road.

The trick is to use your car's cassette player (or a portable cassette player plugged into the cigarette lighter socket for a power source) to play Spanish language music, study courses, and conversations. The following courses are the best we have seen for this use because you can benefit from them without having a written manual open before you. The tapes contain the entire course (although there is a manual and vocabulary guide), and the English translation is given immediately following the Spanish. With these courses you can use all the wasted time that you're behind the wheel, including long trips or the time you're stuck in a traffic jam on the freeway. Make a point of listening to the course, over and over, every day and you will have a much better command of Spanish in less than a month without cracking a book! It is really painless.

Write to Advance Memory Research, Inc. (AMR), 800 Roosevelt Road, Building A, Glen Ellyn, IL 60137, 312/858-1900 or 1-800-323-2500. Four courses are offered at present: Spanish I, Spanish II, Spanish for Police and Firemen, and Spanish for Medical Personnel. You should acquire all of them, even the course for the police and firemen, as each has a slightly different approach and vocabulary. Using them in rotation cuts down on boredom.

# 17. Glossaries

The following glossaries contain most of the vocabulary found in Part I. For more detail, however, you should consult the appropriate section of Part I dealing with culture and lifeways.

## SPANISH TO ENGLISH

| | |
|---|---|
| *A causa de; por* | Because of |
| *A lo largo de; a lado de* | Along; alongside |
| *A llegar* | Arrive |
| *A media cabeza* | By the half-head, said of a loop of rope that catches the cow only by one horn and the face |
| *A menudo* | Often |
| *A pie* | Afoot |
| *A quien* | Whom |
| *A través de* | Across |
| *A; en* | At |
| *A; hasta* | To |
| *Abajo; bajo* | Down |
| *Abanico* (m.); *ventilador* (m.) | Fan |
| *Abarrotes* (m.); *comestibles* (m.); *comida* (f.) | Groceries; food |
| *Abdomen* (m.) | Abdomen |
| *Abeja* (f.) | Bee |
| *Abertura* (f.) | Hole (as in a wall) |
| *Abierto(a)* | Opened |
| *Abrazadera* (f.) | Hose clamp |
| *Abrazo* (m.) | Hug, embrace |
| *Abrelatas* (m.) | Can opener |
| *Abrigo* (m.) | Overcoat |
| *Abrir* (m.) | Open |
| *Abuelo* (m.); *abuela* (f.) | Grandfather; grandmother |

| | |
|---|---|
| *Abuelos* | Grandparents |
| *Acabar; terminar* | End |
| *Acampar* | Camp |
| *Aceite* (m.) | Oil |
| *Acequia* (f.); *zanja* (f.); *ditche* (m.) | Irrigation ditch |
| *Acostarse* | Lie down |
| *Acumulador* (m.) | Battery |
| *Adelante; delante* | Forward |
| *Adiós* | Goodby (or casual "hello") |
| *Adobes* (m.) | Adobe bricks |
| *Adoptado(a); adoptivo(a)* | Adopted |
| *Aduana* (f.) | Customs |
| *Afinación* (f.) | Tune up of instruments |
| *Afinar* | Tune (a car) |
| *Aflojar; soltar* | Loosen, relax |
| *Afuera; fuera* | Outside |
| *Agarrar* | Grasp |
| *Agarrar; coger; pescar* (fish) | Catch |
| *Agua* (f.) | Water |
| *Aguada* (f.); *laguna* (f.) | Small lake or big puddle; intermittent lake bed in desert |
| *Agua potable* (f.) | Drinking water |
| *Águila* (f.) | Eagle (slang: Watch out!) |
| *Agujero* (m.) | Den (hole of small animal) |
| *Agujero* (m.) | Hole (as in small hole, leak, or mouse or rat hole) |
| *Ahora; ahorita* | Now |
| *Aire* (m.) | Air |
| *Alacranes* (m.) | Scorpions |
| *Alambre* (m.) | Wire; fence |
| *Alambre de pico* (m.); *alambre de púas* (m.) | Barbed wire |
| *Alambre de tela* (m.) | Net wire |
| *Alambre liso* (m.) | Wire (slick) |
| *Álamo* (m.) | Cottonwood tree |
| *Alfiler* (m.); *alfiler de seguridad* | Pin; safety pin |
| *Alforjas* (f.) | Saddlebags |
| *Algo; alguna cosa* | Something |
| *Algodón* (m.) | Cotton |
| *Alguien* | Anybody |
| *Alguien; alguna persona* | Somebody |
| *Alguna cosa; algo* | Anything |
| *Alguno(a)* | Any |

| | |
|---|---|
| *Alguno(a); unos(as)* | Some |
| *Algunos(as)* | Several |
| *Alicates* (m.) | Needlenose pliers |
| *Alimento* (m.); *comida* (f.) | Food |
| *Allá* | Yonder |
| *Allá; allí; ahí* | There |
| *Almohada* (f.) | Pillow |
| *Alpinista* (m. or f.) | Mountaineer |
| *Alrededor* | Around |
| *Alternador* (m.) | Alternator |
| *Alto(a)* | High; tall |
| *Alto; hacer alto; parar* | Halt |
| *Altura* (f.); *estatura* (f.) | Height |
| *Ama de la casa* | Lady of the house |
| *Amanecer* (m.); *madrugada* (f.) | Dawn |
| *Amarre* (m.) | Tie |
| *Ambos(as); los dos* | Both |
| *Amigo(a)* | Friend |
| *Amortiguador* (m.) | Shock absorber |
| *Amparo* (m.) | Protection (aid, favor) |
| *Amparo* (m.); *denuncio de una mina* | Mining rights (claim) |
| *Ancho(a)* | Broad, wide |
| *Andar* | Walk |
| *¡Ándele!* | Go on, Shoo! Scat! |
| *Angosto(a); estrecho(a)* | Narrow (passage) |
| *Anillo* (m.) | Ring |
| *Animales silveres* (m.); *vida silvestre* (f.); *fauna* (f.) | Wildlife (general term) |
| *Anoche* | Last night |
| *Anochecer* (m.) | Evening; to grow dark |
| *Ansar* (m.) | Goose (generic) |
| *Anteanoche* | Night before last |
| *Anteayer* | Day before yesterday |
| *Anteojos* (m.); *lentes* (m.) | Eyeglasses |
| *Anterior* | Preceding |
| *Antes de* | Before (time) |
| *Añadir* | Add |
| *Año* (m.) | Year |
| *Aparejo* (m.); *fuste* (m.) | Packsaddle |
| *Apellido* (m.) | Family name |
| *Apellido de soltera* (m.) | Maiden name |
| *Apodo* (m.) | Nickname |

| | |
|---|---|
| *Apretado(a)* | Tight (squeezed) |
| *Apretar* | Tighten |
| *Apuntar* | Point, show |
| *Aquel; ese* | That (demonstrative) |
| *Aquí; acá* | Here |
| *Arado* (m.) | Plow |
| *Arandelas* (f.) | Washers |
| *Arañas* (f.); *sartenes* (f.) | Spiders |
| *Araño* (m.); *rasguño* (m.) | Scratch |
| *Árbol* (m.) | Tree |
| *Arco iris* (m.) | Rainbow |
| *Ardilla* (f.) | Squirrel |
| *Arena* (f.) | Sand |
| *Árido(a)* | Barren, dry |
| *Arma* (f.) | Gun |
| *Armadillo* (m.); *armado* (m.) | Armadillo |
| *Arqueólogo* (m.) | Archeologist |
| *Arranque* (m.) | Starter |
| *Arrastrarse; gatear* | Crawl |
| *Arrastrarse; jalar* | Drag |
| *Arreglar; reparar; componer* | Fix |
| *Arriba* | Up, upstairs |
| *Arriero* (m.) | Mule or burro driver |
| *Arroyo* (m.); *cañada* (f.) | Gully, ravine |
| *Arroz* (m.) | Rice |
| *Artefacto* (m.) | Artifact |
| *Así; de este modo* | Thus |
| *Así; tan* | So |
| *Asiento* (m.) | Seat |
| *Áspero(a)* | Rough |
| *Atajo* (m.) | Shortcut |
| *Atascadero* (m.) | Mudhole |
| *Atascado(a); Atascar* (v.) | Stuck; to get stuck |
| *Atrás* | Back |
| *Atrás; detrás* | Behind |
| *Atrasado(a); hacia atrás* | Backward |
| *Ataúd* (m.) | Coffin |
| *Automático(a)* | Automatic |
| *Avance* (m.) | Advance |
| *Ave* (f.); *pájaro* (m.) | Bird (generic) |
| *Aventón* (m.) | Ride |
| *Aves de corral* (f.) | Domestic fowl, fowl |
| *Avión fumigador* (m.); *aeroplano* (m.) | Crop duster (airplane) |

| | |
|---|---|
| *Avisador* (m.) | Warner (one who warns), seer |
| *Avisar* | Warn |
| *Aviso* (m.) | Warning, notice |
| *Avispa* (f.) | Wasp |
| *Avispero* (m.) | Wasps' nest |
| *Ayer* | Yesterday |
| *Ayudar; ayuda* (f.); *asistir; socorro* | Help |
| *Ayuste* (m.) | Splice (wood or rope) |
| *Azadón* (m.) | Hoe |
| *Azotea* (f.) | Roof (flat) |
| *Azúcar* (m.); *piloncillo* (m.) | Sugar; brown sugar |
| *Azucarera* (f.) | Sugar bowl |
| | |
| *Bahía* (f.) | Bay |
| *Bajada* (f.) | Dip, downward slope or path |
| *Bajarse de* | Get down (out of or off a vehicle) |
| *Bajo llave* | Under lock and key |
| *Bajo(a); abajo* | Low |
| *Bajo; abajo; debajo* | Under |
| *Bajo* (m.); *bajío* (m.); *banco de arena* (m.) | Shoal |
| *Bala* (f.); *balazo* (m.); *disparo* (m.) | Shot |
| *Balde* (m.); *bote* (m.); *tina* (f.) | Bucket |
| *Baleros* (m.) | Ball bearings |
| *Balsa* (f.) | Raft |
| *Banca* (f.) | Bench; riverbank |
| *Bandada* (f.) | Flock of birds |
| *Banda de ventilador* (f.) | Fan belt |
| *Bañera* (f.); *batea* (f.) | Tub |
| *Barba* (f.) | Beard |
| *Barbilla* (f.); *barba* (f.) | Chin |
| *Barra* (f.) | Crowbar |
| *Barranca* (f.); *banco* (m.); *orilla* (f.) | Bank |
| *Barrer* | Sweep |
| *Barril* (m.) | Barrel |
| *Barril de agua* (m.) | Water barrel |
| *Barro* (m.) | Clay |
| *Bastante* (m.); *suficiente* | Enough |
| *Bastidor* (m.) | Frame |
| *Bastón* (m.) | Stick |
| *Basura* (f.); *desperdicio* (m.) | Letter; trash (garbage), waste |
| *Bataría* (f.); *luz* (f.) | Flashlight |

*Batea* (f.)

Pan (shallow bowl of wood for collecting gold dust)

*Batea* (wood) (f.); *cuenco* (m.); *trazón* (m.)

Bowl

*Batea* (f.); *bandeja* (f.)

Mixing bowl

*Batear*

To pan for gold

*Batería* (f.); *pila* (f.); *acumulador* (m.)

Battery

*Baúl* (m.)

Trunk

*Bayoneta* (f.)

Dipstick

*Beber*; *tomar*; *trago* (m.)

Drink

*Becerros* (m.); *terneras* (f.)

Calves

*Berrendo* (m.)

Antelope (pronghorn)

*Bestias* (f.)

Pack animals

*Bicho* (m.)

Conenose bug (kissing bug)

*Bigote* (m.)

Mustache

*Blanquillos* (m.)

Eggs

*Bloques* (m.)

Blocks (chain)

*Blusa* (f.)

Blouse

*Bobina* (f.)

Coil (of a car)

*Boca* (f.)

Mouth

*Boca abajo*

Face down

*Boca arriba*

Face up

*Bocina* (f.)

Horn

*Bodega* (f.)

Warehouse, storeroom

*Bolsa* (f.)

Pocket (of ore)

*Bolsa* (f.); *bolsillo* (m.)

Bag, purse; pocket

*Bomba* (f.)

Pump

*Bonanza* (f.)

Strike (rich ore)

*Bondadosa(o)*

Kind (agreeable)

*Bonito(a)*; *lindo(a)*; *hermoso(a)*; *chula(o)*

Pretty

*Boñiga* (f.)

Cow dung

*Boñiga* (f.); *estiércol* (m.)

Dung (manure)

*Boquilla* (f.)

Mouth; gap; opening; entrance to canyon

*Borde* (m.); *saliente* (m.)

Shoulder (of road)

*Bordo* (m.)

All-weather road, built up road with deep bar ditches on both sides

*Bordo* (m.); *orilla* (f.)

Edge

*Borrada* (cicatriz de viruelas)

Pockmarked

*Borrascoso(a)*; *áspero(a)*

Rough

| | |
|---|---|
| *Borrego cimarrón* (m.) | Desert bighorn sheep (rarely seen now) |
| *Borrego* (m.); *oveja carnero* (f.) | Sheep |
| *Bosque* (m.) | Forest |
| *Bosque* (m.); *monte* (m.); *selva* (f.) | Woods |
| *Botella* (f.) | Bottle |
| *Botón* (m.) | Button |
| *Brasier* (m.); *sostén* (m.) | Bra |
| *Brazo* (m.) | Arm |
| *Brida* (f.); *frena de caballo* (f.); *cabestro* (m.) | Bridle |
| *Brincar*; *saltar* | Jump |
| *Brizna de sacate* (f.) | Blade of grass |
| *Bronco*(*a*) | Wild |
| *Broqueta* (f.); *alambre* (m.); *palito* (m.) | Skewer |
| *Bueno*; *lo mejor* | Good (relative term); the best |
| *Buey* (m.) | Big steer, ox |
| *Búho* (m.); *lechuza* (f.) | Owl |
| *Bujía* (f.) | Spark plug |
| *Bura* (f.); *venado de cola negra* (m.) | Mule deer |
| *Buscar* | Hunt for, look for, seek, search for |
| | |
| *Caballada* (f.); *remuda* (f.) | Horse herd |
| *Caballo* (m.) | Horse (male) |
| *Caballo de loma hundido* (m.) | Sway-backed horse |
| *Cabello* (m.); *pelo* (m.) | Hair |
| *Caber* | Contain; be contained in; to fit |
| *Cabestro* (m.) | Halter |
| *Cabeza* (f.) | Head |
| *Cable* (m.) | Cable |
| *Cables* (*para cargador de batería*) (m.) | Jumper cables |
| *Cabra* (f.); *chivo* (m.) | Goat |
| *Cabrito* (m.); *chivito* (m.) | Kid goat |
| *Cacerola* (f.) | Saucepan |
| *Cacomixtle* (m.) | Ringtail |
| *Cachucha* (f.) | Cap |
| *Cada*; *todo*(*a*) | Each |
| *Cada*; *todos*(*as*) | Every |
| *Cadena* (f.) | Chain |
| *Cadera* (f.) | Hip |

| | |
|---|---|
| *Caer* | Fall |
| *Café* (m.) | Coffee |
| *Cafetera* (f.) | Coffeepot |
| *Cagajón* (m.) | Horse dung (slang: horseshit) |
| *Cagarruta* (slang) (f.) | Rat dung |
| *Caja de herramientas* (f.) | Tool box |
| *Caja* (f.); *cajón* (m.) | Box |
| *Caja* (f.) | Coffin |
| *Calabaza* (f.) | Squash |
| *Calcetines* (m.) | Socks |
| *Caldera* (f.) | Boiler |
| *Calibrador* (m.) | Gauge |
| *Caliente, caluroso*(*a*) | Hot |
| *Calor* (m.) | Heat |
| *Calva* (f.) | Bald head |
| *Calzado* (m.); *bota* (f.) | Boot |
| *Calzoncillos* (m.) | Shorts |
| *Cama* (f.) | Bed |
| *Camilla* (f.) | Stretcher |
| *Caminata* (f.); *andada* (f.) | Long walk or hike |
| *Camino* (m.) | Road |
| *Camión* (m.); *troca* (m.); *troque* (m.) | Truck |
| *Camisa* (f.) | Shirt |
| *Camiseta* (f.) | Undershirt |
| *Campo* (m.); *campamiento* (m.) | Camp |
| *Campo santo* (m.) | Graveyard |
| *Canal* (m.) | Outspout, to keep water from roof away from the base of an *adobe* wall; channel |
| *Canasta* (f.) | Basket |
| *Canción* (f.); *canto* (m.); *corito* (m.) | Song |
| *Cancha* (f.) | Playing field or court |
| *Candado* (m.); *cerrar con llave* (v.); *cerradura* (f.) | Lock (usually with chain) |
| *Candela* (f.); *vela* (f.) | Candle |
| *Canina* (f.) | Dog dung |
| *Canoa* (f.) | Canoe; feed trough (usually long and of wood) |
| *Cansado*(*a*) | Tired |
| *Cansar* | Tire (v.) |
| *Cantar* | Sing |
| *Cantimplora* (f.) | Canteen |

| | |
|---|---|
| *Cañada* (f); *quebrada* (f.) | Gulch |
| *Cañón* (m.); *barranca* (f.) | Canyon |
| *Cañón sin salida* (m.) | Box or blind canyon |
| *Caporal* (m.) | Ranch foreman |
| *Caporal* (m.); *jefe* (m.); *rallador* (m.); *mayordomo* (m.) | Foreman |
| *Cara* (f.) | Face |
| *Carbón* (m.) | Charcoal, coal |
| *Carburador* (m.) | Carburetor |
| *Cárcel* (f.) (*"en el bote"*) | Jail |
| *Carga* (f.) | Load, burden |
| *Cargador* (m.); *portero* (m.) | Porter |
| *Cargadores* (m.) | Loaders; cartridge clips |
| *Carne seca* (f.) | Dried meat; jerky |
| *Carozo* (m.) | Corn cob |
| *Carpa* (f.) | Tent |
| *Carpintero* (m.) | Carpenter; woodpecker |
| *Carreta* (f.) | Ox cart |
| *Carretera* (f.) | Highway, improved road |
| *Carretilla* (f.) | Wheelbarrow |
| *Carrizal* (m.) | Canebrake |
| *Carrizo* (m.); *caña* (f.) | River cane used for roof decking |
| *Carro* (m.) | Car |
| *Casa con armazón de madera* (f.) | Wood frame house |
| *Casa de estaña* (*lata*) (f.) | Tin house |
| *Casado*(*a*) | Married |
| *Cascabel* (m.); *víbora* (f.) | Rattlesnake |
| *Cascada* (f.); *salto del agua* (m.); *caída* (f.) | Waterfall |
| *Cascajo* (m.); *grava* (f.) | Gravel |
| *Cáscara* (f.) | Shell, husk, rind; empty pop bottle |
| *Casco* (m.); *mano* (front foot) (f.) | Hoof (of horse, mule, etc.) |
| *Casi* | Almost |
| *Castor* (m.) | Beaver |
| *Castrado* (m.); *capado* (m.) | Mutton goat; castrated male |
| *Causa* (f.); *causar* (v.) | Cause |
| *Cavar*; *excavar* | Dig |
| *Caverna* (f.); *guarida* (f.); *escondrijo* (m.) | Den (of animal) |
| *Cayuco* (m.) | Dugout canoe |
| *Cazador* (m.) | Hunter |
| *Cazar* | Hunt (v.) |
| *Cazuela* (f.) | Pan |

| | |
|---|---|
| *Cebo* (m.) | Bait |
| *Cebollas* (f.) | Onions |
| *Cedazo* (m.) | Sifter |
| *Cegeta* (f.); *sierra de cortar metales* (f.) | Hacksaw |
| *Ceja* (f.) | Eyebrow |
| *Cementerio* (m.) | Cemetery |
| *Cencerro* (m.) | Cowbell (also bell for goats, cattle, and ranch animals in general) |
| *Ceniza* (f.) | Ashes |
| *Cenote* (m.) | Sinkhole |
| *Cera* (f.) | Wax |
| *Cerca* (f.); *alambre* (m.) | Fence |
| *Cerca* | By (near) |
| *Cerca de* | Close to |
| *Cerebro* (m.) | Brain |
| *Cerillo* (m.); *fósforo* (m.) | Match |
| *Cerrado*(*a*) | Closed |
| *Cerrar* | Close, shut |
| *Cerrojo* (m.) | Latch bolt, bolt |
| *Cesta* (f.) | Basket (large) |
| *Chachalaca* (f.) | Chachalaca (generic: wild fowl) |
| *Chamarra* (f.); *saco* (m.) | Jacket (heavy) |
| *Chango* (m.); *mono* (m.); *mico* (long-tailed) (m.) | Monkey (tropics) |
| *Chaparro* (m.); *monte* (m.) | Brush |
| *Chaqueta* (f.); *saco* (m.) | Coat |
| *Charco* | Mudhole |
| *Chaveta* (f.) | Cotter key |
| *Chinches* (f.) | Bedbugs |
| *Chipichil* (m.); *tipichil* (m.) | Lime concrete (pea gravel aggregate) used to top off a dirt roof in old but well-built buildings |
| *Chiquero* (m.); *chivetero* (m.) | Small shelter for kid goats, made by leaning two flat rocks against each other |
| *Chispa* (f.) | Spark |
| *Chivarras* (f.); *chaparreras* (f.) | Chaps (leg protectors) |
| *Chivero* (m.); *pastor* (m.); *borreguero* (m.); *cabrero* (m.) | Goatherd |
| *Chocolate* (m.) | Chocolate |
| *Chofer* (m.) | Driver |
| *Choque* (m.) | Traffic accident, wreck |

| | |
|---|---|
| *Chorros* (m.) | Rapids |
| *Choza* (f.); *jacal* (m.); *hogar* (m.) | Hut |
| *Cielo* (m.) | Ceiling, sky, heaven |
| *Ciénaga* (f.) | Seepy area, bog, marsh |
| *Cierre relámpago* (m.); *riqui* (m.) | Zipper |
| *Ciertamente; ¿Cómo no?* | Certainly; why not |
| *Cierto(a); seguro(a)* | Certain; certainly |
| *Cilindro* (m.) | Cylinder |
| *Cima* (f.); *cumbre* (f.) | Top of hill or peak |
| *Cincel* (m.) | Cold chisel |
| *Cinta métrica* (f.) | Tape measure (metric) |
| *Cinta plástica* (f.) | Tape |
| *Cintura* (f.) | Waist |
| *Cinturón* (m.); *cinto* (m.) | Belt |
| *Claramente* | Clearly |
| *Claro(a)* | Clear, absolutely |
| *Clase* (f.) | Class |
| *Clase* (f.); *tipo* (m.) | Kind (type) |
| *Clavo* (m.) | Nail |
| *Cobertizo* (m.); *redil* (m.); *tejadillo* (m.); *tinglado* (m.) | Shed for goats or sheep |
| *Cobija* (f.); *frazada* (f.); *manta* (f.) | Blanket |
| *Cobrar* | Collect |
| *Cocina* (f.) | Kitchen |
| *Cocinera(o)* | Cook |
| *Cócono* (m.); *guajolote* (m.); *pavo* (m.) | Turkey |
| *Codo* (m.) | Elbow |
| *Codorniz* (m.) | Quail (generic); blue quail = *tostón* (m.) |
| *Cojarín* (m.) | Throw-out bearing |
| *Cojo(a)* | Crippled, lame |
| *Colador* (m.) | Strainer |
| *Colcha* (f.); *cobija* (f.) | Quilt |
| *Colchón* (m.) | Mattress |
| *Colina* (f.); *loma* (f.) | Hill |
| *Colmena* (f.); *abejera* (f.) | Beehive |
| *Colocar, poner* | Place (put on) |
| *Colonia* (f.) | Small jungle village |
| *Columna vertebral* (f.); *espina* (f.) | Spine |
| *Comal* (m.); *plancha* (f.); *tartera* (f.) | Griddle |
| *Comer* | Dine, eat |

| | |
|---|---|
| *Comestibles* (m.); *abarrotes* (m.) | Groceries |
| *Comida* (f.) | Meal |
| *Comida* (f.); *alimento* (m.) | Food |
| *¿Cómo?* | How? |
| *Como*; *lo mismo que* | Like, as, how |
| *Cómoda* (f.) | Chest of drawers |
| *Compañero*(*a*) | Companion |
| *Completar*; *acabar*; *terminar*; *completo*(*a*) (adj.) | Complete |
| *Compra* (f.) | Purchase |
| *Comprar* | Buy, purchase |
| *Comprender* | Understand |
| *Con*; *en compañía de* | With |
| *Concreto armado* (m.) | Reinforced concrete |
| *Condensador* (m.) | Condenser |
| *Conejo* (m.) | Cottontail rabbit |
| *Conocer* | Know (be acquainted with) |
| *Construir* | Build, construct |
| *Contar* | Count |
| *Contento*(*a*) | Contented, happy |
| *Contrabandista* (m.) | Smuggler |
| *Corazón* (m.) | Heart |
| *Cordón* (m.); *cuerda* (f.) | String |
| *Corona* (f.) | Saddle blanket |
| *Cortada* (f.) | Scar (cut) |
| *Cortada* (f.); *cortar* (v.) | Cut |
| *Cortapluma* (f.); *navaja* (f.) | Pocketknife |
| *Corto*(*a*); *baja*(*o*) | Short |
| *Corral* (m.) | Pen (for animals) |
| *Correa* (f.) | Strap |
| *Correcto*(*a*); *corregir* (v.) | Correct |
| *Correr* | Run |
| *Corriente* (f.) | Current |
| *Corrientes* (m.) | Skinny Mexican longhorn cattle |
| *Cosa* (f.) | Thing |
| *Cosecha* (f.) | Crop (harvest) |
| *Cosechador* (m.) | Harvester |
| *Costa* (f.) | Coast; cost |
| *Costal* (m.) | *Ixtle* fiber bag for large loads |
| *Costar* | Cost |
| *Costillas* (f.) | Ribs |
| *Coyote* (m.) | Coyote |
| *Cráneo* (m.); *calavera* (f.) | Skull |

| | |
|---|---|
| *Crecida* (f.); *creciente* (f.); *inundación* (f.) | Flood |
| *Creer* | Believe |
| *Crepúsculo* (m.) | Dusk |
| *Criar* | Raise (children or animals) |
| *Cruceta y yugo* (f.); *cardán* (f.) | Universal joint |
| *Crudo(a)* | Raw |
| *Cruzar; cruz* (f.) | Cross |
| *Cuadrado(a)* | Square |
| *Cuadros* (m.); *fotos* (f.); *retratos* (m.) | Pictures |
| *Cualquier(a)*; *lo que* | Whatever |
| *¿Cuánto(a)?* | How much? |
| *¿Cuántos(as)?* | How many? |
| *Cuarto* (m.) | Room |
| *Cubrir* | Cover |
| *Cucaracha* (f.) | Cockroach |
| *Cuchara* (f.) | Spoon |
| *Cucharón* (m.); *cazo* (m.) | Ladle |
| *Cuchillo* | Knife |
| *Cuello* (m.); *pescuezo* (m.) | Neck |
| *Cuerno* (m.); *cuerna* (f.) | Horn |
| *Cuero* (m.) | Leather |
| *Cuero crudo* (m.) | Rawhide |
| *Cuerpo* (m.) | Body |
| *Cuervo* (m.) | Raven |
| *Cuesta abajo* | Downhill |
| *Cuesta arriba* | Uphill |
| *Cueva* (f.) | Cave |
| *Cuidado* (m.) | Care |
| *Cuidadoso(a)* | Careful |
| *Cuidar* | Care (for) |
| *Cuida vaca* (f.) | Cattle guard |
| *Culebra* (f.) | Snake (generic) |
| *Culpa* (f.) | Fault |
| *Cultivador* (m.) | Cultivator |
| *Culto* (m.) | Worship |
| *Cuña* (f.) | Wedge, chock |
| *Cuñado(a)* | Brother-in-law (sister-in-law) |
| *Cuota* (f.) | Toll |
| *Curandero* | Folk medicine practitioner |
| *Cuyo* | Whose (not question) |

| | |
|---|---|
| *Dañar* (v.); *daño* (m.) | Harm, damage |
| *Dar* | Give |
| *Dar una vuelta* | Give it a turn (rope) |
| *De; desde* | From |
| *De lado* | Sideways |
| *Debajo; bajo* | Beneath |
| *Debajo de; abajo; bajo* | Below |
| *Débil* | Weak |
| *Decidir* | Decide |
| *Decir* | Say |
| *Dedo* (*de la mano*) (m.) | Finger |
| *Dedo* (*del pie*) (m.) | Toe |
| *Dejar; permitir* | Let |
| *Delante de; enfrente* | In front of |
| *Delgado*(*a*); *fino*(*a*); *flaco*(*a*) | Thin, slim |
| *Demasiado* | Too many; too much |
| *Dentro* | Inside |
| *Dentro de* | Within |
| *Denunciar* (*una mina*) | Claim (a mine) |
| *Denuncio de una mina* (m.); *amparo* (m.) | Claim (mining claim) |
| *Depósito* (m.); *embase* (m.) | Deposit |
| *Derecha* | Right (direction) |
| *Derecho; recto; directo* | Straight |
| *De repente* | Suddenly |
| *Derrubio* (m.); *fracaso* (m.) | Washout |
| *Derrumbe* (m.) | Landslide or rockfall |
| *Desarmador* (m.) | Screwdriver |
| *Desarmador de cruz* (m.) | Phillips screwdriver |
| *Descargar* | Unload |
| *Descompuesto*(*a*) | Broken |
| *Describir* | Describe |
| *Desde* | Since |
| *Desear* (v.); *deseo* (m.) | Desire |
| *Desierto* (m.) | Desert |
| *Desinflada* (f.) | Flat (tire) |
| *Desmonte* (m.) | Cleared area, abandoned field, denuded terrain |
| *Desnudo*(*a*); *en pelota* | Naked |
| *Desollar; pelar* | Skin (an animal) |
| *Despacio; lento* | Slowly |
| *Despertar* | Awaken |
| *Después* | Afterward |
| *Después* (*de*) (*que*) | After |

| | |
|---|---|
| *Destapón* (m.); *llave* (f.) | Bottle opener |
| *Destellador* (m.) | Turn signal flasher |
| *Destinación* (f.) | Destination |
| *Desviación* (f.) | Detour |
| *Detergente* (m.) | Detergent |
| *Detrás de* | After; back of |
| *Día* (m.) | Day |
| *Día de descanso* (m.) | Day of rest |
| *Diario*(*a*) | Daily |
| *Diario* (m.); *periódico* (m.) | Newspaper |
| *Dibujos* (m.) | Drawings |
| *Dicho* (m.) | Saying |
| *Diente* (m.); *muela* (f.) | Tooth |
| *Diferencial* (m.) | Differential |
| *Diferente* | Different |
| *Difícil* | Difficult |
| *Dígame.* | Tell me. (At your service.) |
| *Diluvio* (m.); *inundación* (f.) | Flood |
| *Dinero* (m.) | Money |
| *Dios* (m.) | God |
| *Dirección* (f.) | Address; direction |
| *Direccionales* (m.) | Turn signals |
| *Disco* (m.) | Disc plow |
| *Dispénseme.* | Excuse me. (Forgive me.) |
| *Distancia* (f.) | Distance |
| *Distribuidor* (m.) | Distributor |
| *Divisar* | See (to barely make out) |
| *Divorciado*(*a*) | Divorced |
| *Doblado*(*a*) | Bent |
| *Doblar* | Bend; double; turn |
| *Doblar; dar vuelta* | Turn (v.) |
| *Doble* | Double; turn |
| *Doble tracción* (f.) | 4-wheel drive |
| *Dólar* (m.) | Dollar |
| *Dolor* (m.); *doler* (v.) | Pain |
| *Dónde; adónde* (to where) | Where (in question); to where |
| *Dormir* (v.); *sueño* (m.) | Sleep |
| *Dudar* (v.); *duda* (f.) | Doubt |
| *Dueño; patrón* (m.) | Owner |
| *Dumpe* (m.); *basurero* (m.) | Dump |
| *Dunas de arena* (f.); *médanos* (m.) | Dunes (sand) |
| *Durante* | During |
| *Duro*(*a*) | Hard |

| | |
|---|---|
| *Eje* (m.) | Axle |
| *Ejidatario(a)* | Member of an *ejido* |
| *Ejido* (m.) | Communal settlement |
| *Él* | He |
| *El* (m.); *la* (f.); *los* (m. pl.); *las* (f. pl.) | The |
| *Electricidad* (f.) | Electricity |
| *Ellos* (m.); *ellas* (f.) | They; them (obj. of prep.) |
| *Elote* (m.) | Corn on the cob |
| *Embrague* (m.) | Clutch (of a car) |
| *Embudo* (m.) | Funnel |
| *Empacadora* (f.) | Baler (hay) |
| *Empacar* | Pack (v.) |
| *Empalizada* (f.) | Wooden fence |
| *Empaque* (m.) | Gasket |
| *Empezar; comenzar; principiar; ponerse en marcha* | Begin, start |
| *Empleado(a)* | Employed; employee |
| *Emplear; dar empleo; ocupar* | Employ |
| *Empleo* (m.) | Employment |
| *Empujar* | Push |
| *Empujón* (m.) | Push or shove |
| *En* | In |
| *En; sobre; encima de* | On |
| *En seguida* | Immediately, at once |
| *Encontrar* | Meet |
| *Encontrar; hallar; encuentrar* (idiomatic) | Find |
| *Engranaje* (m.) | Gear |
| *Enseñar* | Teach |
| *Enseñar; mostrar* | Show |
| *Entero(a)* | Entire |
| *Entero; todo* | Whole |
| *Enterrar; inhumar; sepultar* | Bury |
| *Entiendo.* | I understand. |
| *Entierro* (m.) | Burial |
| *Entonces; luego; después* | Then |
| *Entrada* (f.); *garita* (f.) | Entrance, entry, gateway |
| *Entrada* (f.); *puerta* (f.); *vano* (m.) | Doorway (or opening) |
| *Entrar* | Enter |
| *Entre* | Between, among |
| *Entregar* | Deliver |
| *Equipaje* (m.) | Baggage, gear, duffle |
| *Escalar; forzar la entrada en* | Break into |

| | |
|---|---|
| *Escalera* (f.) | Ladder |
| *Escaleras* (f.) | Stairs, steps |
| *Escalones* (m.) | Steps |
| *Escoba* (f.) | Broom |
| *Escobetilla* | Small whiskbroom for cleaning the *comal* |
| *Escoger* | Pick (choose) |
| *Escondido*(*a*) | Hidden |
| *Escuadra de carpintero* (f.) | Carpenter's square |
| *Escuela* (f.) | School |
| *Esos* (m.); *esas* (f.) | Those |
| *Espalda* (f.) | Back (anat.) |
| *Espantapájaros* (m.) | Scarecrow |
| *Española* (f.) | Spanish goat (for eating) |
| *Espátula* (f.) | Spatula |
| *Espejo* (m.) | Mirror |
| *Esperar; aguardar* | Wait |
| *Esposa* (f.); *mujer* (f.) | Wife |
| *Esposo* (m.); *marido* (m.) | Husband |
| *Espuelas* (f.) | Spurs |
| *Esquina* (f.) | Corner (outside) |
| *Establo* (m.); *bodega* (f.); *troje* (m.); *granero* (m.) | Barn or stable |
| *Estaca* (f.) | Stake; upright picket |
| *Estación* (f.) | Season (of the year) |
| *Estacionarse* | Park (a vehicle) |
| *Estancamientos* (m.) | Logjams or obstructions to the flow of the river |
| *Estante* (m.); *anaquel* (m.) | Shelf |
| *Estaño* (m.); *lata* (f.) | Tin |
| *Este* (m.); *esta* (f.) | This |
| *Este* (m.); *oriente* (m.) | East |
| *Estirar; tirar; arrancar; jalar* | Pull |
| *Estómago* (m.) | Stomach |
| *Estos* (m.); *estas* (f.) | These |
| *Estrecho* (m.) | Narrow passage |
| *Estrellas* (f.) | Stars |
| *Estribo* (m.) | Saddle stirrup |
| *Estudiar* (v.); *estudio* (m.) | Study |
| *Estufa* (m.) | Stove |
| *Excusado* (m.); *común* (m.); *sanitario* (m.); *alcantarillado* (m.); *letrina* (f.); *retrete* (m.) | Outhouse or latrine |

| | |
|---|---|
| *Exequias* (f.) | Funeral |
| *Extra* | Extra |
| *Extractor de engranes* (m.) | Gear puller |
| | |
| *Fácil* | Easy |
| *Falcete* (m.) | Wire gap |
| *Falda* (f.); *enagua* (f.) | Skirt |
| *Falta* (f.); *error* (m.) | Mistake |
| *Faltar* (v.); *falta* (f.) | Lack |
| *Fanga(o)* (f. or m.) | Jungle mud hole |
| *Faro* (m.); *foco* (m.) | Lantern; headlight |
| *Fechar* (v.); *fecha* (f.); *compromiso* (m.); *cita* (f.) | Date |
| *Feo(a)* | Ugly |
| *Fideo* (m.) | Spaghetti |
| *Fiera* (f.) | Wild beast (fierce) |
| *Fierro* (m.) | Brand (on an animal) |
| *Filoso(a)* | Sharp |
| *Filtro* (m.) | Filter |
| *Firma* (f.) | Signature, sign |
| *Firme; tieso(a)* | Tight (firm) |
| *Flaco(a)* | Thin; skinny; lean |
| *Flecha* (f.); *flecha cardán* (f.) | Shaft; drive shaft |
| *Flecha* (f.); *eje* (m.) | Shaft (axle or machine part) |
| *Flojo(a)* | Loose |
| *Flor* (f.) | Flower |
| *Florita* (f.) | Fluorite |
| *Foco trasero* (m.) | Taillight |
| *Focos* (m.) | Headlights, lights |
| *Fondo* (m.) | Slip (woman's clothing) |
| *Forestales* (m.) | Game wardens |
| *Fracaso* (m.) | Washout |
| *Frecuentemente; a menudo* | Frequently, often |
| *Fregadero* (m.) | Sink (kitchen) |
| *Freno* (f.); *brida* (f.) | Bridle |
| *Frenos* (m.) | Brakes |
| *Frente* (f.) | Forehead |
| *Frente* (f.); *delantero* (m.) | Front |
| *Fresco(a)* | Fresh; cool |
| *Fresno* (m.) | Ash tree |
| *Frijoles* (m.) (slang: *nacionales* [m.]) | Beans |
| *Frontera* (f.) | Border |

| | |
|---|---|
| *Fuego* (m.); *lumbre* (f.) | Fire |
| *Fuente* (f.) | Spring; fountain |
| *Fuente* (f.); *trinchero* (m.) | Plate (large platter) |
| *Fuera*; *afuera* | Outside |
| *Fuerte* | Strong |
| *Fumar* (v.); *humo* (m.) | Smoke |
| *Fundación* (f.) | Foundation (occasionally of concrete, usually of stone, and only under walls of brick or *adobe*) |
| *Funeral* (m.); *exequias* (f.) | Funeral |
| *Fusible* (m.) | Fuse |
| *Fusil* (m.); *escopeta* (f.); *carabina* (f.); *pistola* (f.); *rifle* (m.) | Gun; shotgun; carbine; pistol; rifle |
| *Gabinete* (m.) | Cabinet |
| *Gallina* (f.); *gallina ponedora* (f.) | Hen; setting hen |
| *Gallo* (m.) | Rooster; cocky fellow (slang) |
| *Gambusino* (m.) | Prospector |
| *Gancho* (m.); *anzuelo* (m.) | Hook; hay hook; chain hook |
| *Garita* (f.) | Entrance gate or way |
| *Garrafón* (m.); *tinaja* (f.) | Water jug (large) |
| *Garrapatas* (f.) | Ticks |
| *Gasolina* (f.) | Gasoline |
| *Gasolinera* (f.) | Gas station |
| *Gastos* (m.); *coste* (m.) | Expense |
| *Gato*(*a*) | Cat |
| *Gato* (m.) | Jack (for car) |
| *Gato de montes* (m.) | Bobcat |
| *Gemelos* (m.); *miralejos* (m.) | Binoculars |
| *Generador* (m.) | Generator |
| *Gente* (f.) | People |
| *Globo del ojo* (m.) | Eyeball |
| *Gobierno* (m.) | Government |
| *Golfo* (m.) | Gulf |
| *Golpear*; *pegar* | Hit |
| *Gordo*(*a*); *grueso*(*a*) | Fat |
| *Gorgojos* (m.) | Weevils |
| *Gota* (f.) | Drop |
| *Gotera* (f.) | Leak |
| *Grabar* | Record (a tape) |
| *Gracias* (f.) | Thanks |
| *Grampas, grapas* (f.) | Staples |
| *Grande* | Big, large |

|  |  |
|---|---|
| *Granero* (m.); *troje* (m.) | Barn |
| *Granja* (f.) | Farm |
| *Granjero* (m.); *ranchero* (m.) | Farmer |
| *Grano* (m.) | Sore (wound) |
| *Grasa* (m.) | Grease |
| *Grava* (f.) | Gravel |
| *Gringo*(*a*) | Term applied to Anglo-looking foreigners |
| *Gritar*; *grito* (m.) | Yell, shout |
| *Grúa* (f.); *remolque* (m.) | Tow truck, wrecker |
| *Grueso*(*a*); *denso*(*a*); *espeso*(*a*) | Thick |
| *Grulla* (f.) | Sandhill crane |
| *Guadaña* (f.); *alfanje* (m.) | Scythe |
| *Guante* (m.) | Glove |
| *Guarda vaca* (f.); *cuida vaca* (f.) | Cattle guard |
| *Guardar* | Keep; guard |
| *Guardar*; *cuidar* | Watch |
| *Guardia* (f. or m.) | Guard |
| *Guía* (f. or m.) | Guide |
| *Guisado* (m.) | Meat stew (generic) |
| *Gusanos* (m.) | Worms |
| *Gustar* | Like |
| *Habitante* (m.) | Inhabitant |
| *Hablar* | Talk |
| *Hacendado* (m.); *agricultor* (m.); *ranchero* (m.) | Farmer |
| *Hacer* | Do; make |
| *Hacer arreglos* | Take steps to |
| *Hacha* (f.) | Hatchet, axe |
| *Hacia* | Toward |
| *Halcón* (m.) | Falcon |
| *Halcón* (m.); *gavilán* (m.) | Hawk |
| *Harina de maíz* (f.) | Cornmeal |
| *Hasta*; *hasta que* | Until |
| *Hembra* (f.) | Female animal (usually domestic) |
| *Hembras* (f.) | Heifers |
| *Herida* (f.) | Wound |
| *Hermano*(*a*) | Brother (sister) |
| *Hermoso*(*a*); *lindo*(*a*); *bello*(*a*); *bonito*(*a*) | Beautiful |
| *Herramientas* (f.) | Tools (generic) |
| *Herrero* (m.) | Blacksmith; farrier |

| | |
|---|---|
| *Hiedra* (f.) | Poison ivy |
| *Hielera* (f.) | Icebox |
| *Hielo* (m.) | Ice |
| *Hierba* (f.); *mota* (f.) | Grass; marijuana |
| *Hígado* (m.) | Liver |
| *Hija* (f.) | Daughter |
| *Hijastro* (m.) | Stepson |
| *Hijo* (m.) | Son |
| *Hijo(a) adoptivo(a)* | Foster son (daughter) |
| *¡Híjole!* | Gosh! Dern it! |
| *Hilo* (m.) | Veinlet (ore), thread |
| *Hoguerra* (f.); *fogota* (f.) | Bonfire |
| *Hoja* (f.) | Blade (knife); leaf |
| *¡Hola!* | Hello! |
| *Hombre* (m.) | Man |
| *Hombro* (m.) | Shoulder |
| *Hondo(a); profundo(a)* | Deep |
| *Hora* (f.) | Hour |
| *Horario* (m.) | Schedule |
| *Hormigas* (f.) | Ants |
| *Hormiguero* (m.); *oso hormiguero* (m.) | Anteater (tropics) |
| *Horno* (m.) | Earth or stone beehive-shaped oven |
| *Horqueta* (f.) | Forked corner or center post |
| *Hoy* | Today |
| *Hoya* (f.) | River basin |
| *Hoyo* (m.); *agujero* (m.) | Hole (as in a fence) |
| *Hoz* (f.) | Sickle |
| *Huaraches* (m.); *chanclas* (f.) | Sandals |
| *Huella* (f.); *rastro* (m.) | Track (of person, vehicle, or animal) |
| *Huérfano(a)* | Orphan |
| *Hueso* (m.) | Bone |
| *Huevos* (m.); *blanquillos* (m.); *yemas* (f.) | Eggs |
| *Huracán* (m.) | Hurricane |
| *Iglesia* (f.) | Church |
| *Igriega* (f.) | Letter *y*; Y in the road |
| *Impermeable* (m.) | Raincoat |
| *Importante* | Important |
| *Imposible* | Impossible |
| *Improvisado(a); provisional* | Makeshift |

| | |
|---|---|
| *Inmediatamente* | Immediately |
| *Inseguro(a)* | Insecure; unsteady; unsafe |
| *Inyector de grasa* (m.) | Grease gun |
| *Ir* | Go |
| *Irse* | Go away |
| *Isla* (f.) | Island |
| *Ixtlero* (m.) | Fiber gatherer |
| *Izquierda* (f.) | Left |
| | |
| *Jabón* (m.) | Soap |
| *Jacal* (m.) | *Adobe* hut |
| *Jalón* (m.); *mojón* (m.) | Boundary marker |
| *Jamás* | Never |
| *Jardín* (m.) | Garden, yard |
| *Jarra* (f.); *garrafón* (m.) | Water jug |
| *Jarra de café* (f.); *cafetera* (f.) | Coffee pot |
| *Javelina* (f.); *jabalí* (m.) | Peccary |
| *Jefe* (m.) | Chief, boss |
| *Jejenes* (m.); *moscos* (m.) | Gnats |
| *Jinete* (m.) | Horse breaker, horseman |
| *Jineteada* (f.) | Horsebreaking |
| *Jira* (f.); *merienda de campo* (f.) | Picnic |
| *Jornada* (f.) | Day's walk |
| *Joven* (m. or f.) | Youth, young person |
| *Junta* | Council |
| *Juntar; unir* | Join |
| | |
| *Klaxon* (m.); *bocina* (f.) | Horn |
| | |
| *Labio* (m.) | Lip |
| *Labrador* (m.); *cultivador* (m.); *sembrador* (m.) | Farm laborer |
| *Lado* (m.) | Side |
| *Ladrillero* (m.) | Brickmaker |
| *Ladrillo* (m.) | Brick |
| *Ladrillos* (m.) | Fired bricks |
| *Ladrón* (m.) | Thief, outlaw |
| *Lagartija* (m.) | Lizard (generic) |
| *Lagarto* (m.); *caimán* (m.) | Alligator |
| *Lago* (m.) | Lake |
| *Laguna* (f.); *playa* (f.) | Lagoon; dry lake holding water after rain |
| *Lamentar* | Mourn |

| | |
|---|---|
| *Lámina* (f.) | Corrugated sheet iron |
| *Lámpara* (f.) | Lamp |
| *Lancha* (f.); *kajak* (m.) | Kayak |
| *Lápida* (f.) | Gravestone |
| *Lápiz* (m.) | Pencil |
| *Largo*(*a*) | Long |
| *Largo* (m.) | Length |
| *Lata* (f.); *bote* (m.) | Tin can |
| *Latillas* (f.); *savinos* (m.); *latas* (f.); *tablas* (f.) | Roof cross-decking |
| *Lavabo* (m.) | Wash basin |
| *Lazada* (f.) | Loop of rope |
| *Lazo* (m.); *reata* (f.) | Lasso |
| *Leche* (f.) | Milk |
| *Leer* | Read |
| *Legua* (f.) | League (distance) |
| *Lejano*(*a*) | Remote |
| *Lejos* | Far (away) |
| *Lejos de* | Far from |
| *Lengua* (f.) | Tongue |
| *Leña* (f.) | Firewood |
| *Leñador* (m.); *hachero* (m.) | Woodcutter |
| *León* (m.); *pantera* (f.) | Mountain lion |
| *Levantar*; *alzar* | Lift |
| *Levantar*; *coger* | Pick (up) |
| *Levantarse* | Get up |
| *Ley* (f.) | Law |
| *Libre*; *gratis* | Free (cost) |
| *Liebre de cola negra* (f.); *liebre* (f.) | Jackrabbit |
| *Ligero*(*a*) | Light (weight) |
| *Lima* (f.) | File (tool) |
| *Limpia parabrisas* (f.) | Windshield wiper |
| *Limpiar* (v.); *limpio*(*a*) | Clean |
| *Línea* (f.); *raya* (f.) | Line |
| *Liso*(*a*) | Slick, smooth |
| *Listo*(*a*) | Ready |
| *Liviano*(*a*) | Wild, unbroken animal |
| *Lobo* (m.) | Wolf |
| *Lodo* (m.); *zoquete* (m.) | Mud |
| *Lodoso*(*a*); *zoquetoso*(*a*) | Muddy |
| *Loma* (f.); *cuesta* (f.) | Ridge |
| *Lomo* (m.) | Back (animal) |
| *Lona* (f.); *tarpa* (f.) | Tarpaulin |

| | |
|---|---|
| *Los* (m.); *las* (f.) | Them (direct object) |
| *Luego* | Later, then |
| *Lugar* (m.); *sitio* (m.) | Place (location) |
| *Lumbre* (f.); *fuego* (m.) | Fire |
| *Luna* (f.) | Moon |
| *Lunar* (m.) | Mole |
| *Luto* (m.) | Mourning |
| *Luz* (f.); *luminar* (v.) | Light |
| | |
| *Llamar* | Call |
| *Llamar con señas* | Beckon |
| *Llamarse* | Be named |
| *Llanos* (m.) | Plains |
| *Llanta* (f.); *neumático* (m.) | Tire (for wheel) |
| *Llave* (f.) | Wrench (generic); key |
| *Llave astria* (f.) | Box-end wrench |
| *Llave de alan* (f.) | Allen wrench |
| *Llave de bujía* (f.) | Spark plug wrench |
| *Llave de cruz* (f.) | Lug wrench |
| *Llave de dado* (f.) | Socket wrench |
| *Llave de switch* (f.) | Ignition key |
| *Llave de gringo* (f.) | Crescent wrench |
| *Llave española* (f.) | Open-end wrench |
| *Llave Stillson* (f.) | Pipe wrench |
| *Llegar* | Arrive |
| *Llenar* | Fill |
| *Lleno*(*a*) | Full |
| *Llevar* | Carry |
| *Llevar*; *tener puesto* | Wear |
| *Llover* (v.); *lluvia* (f.) | Rain |
| | |
| *Macho* (m.) | Male animal; brave |
| *Madera* (m.) | Wood; timber |
| *Madrastra* (f.) | Stepmother |
| *Madre* (f.); *mamá* (f.) | Mother, mom |
| *Madrina* (f.) | Lead mare (bell mare) |
| *Madrugadas* (f.) | Predawn hours |
| *Maduro*(*a*); *sazonado*(*a*) | Ripe |
| *Maestro*(*a*) | Teacher |
| *Maíz* (m.) | Corn |
| *Majada* (f.) | Large flock of goats |
| *Malacate* (m.); *molinete* (m.) | Winch |
| *Malo*(*a*); *muy feo*(*a*); *muy malo*(*a*) | Bad |

| | |
|---|---|
| Malsano(a) | Unsanitary; unhealthy |
| Manada (f.) | Mares under a stallion |
| Mancornador (m.) | Yoke |
| Mandar; enviar; expedir | Send |
| Manejar; guiar | Drive |
| Manga (f.) | Sleeve |
| Mango (m.); tirador (m.); manubrio (m.) | Handle |
| Manguera (f.) | Hose |
| Manguera de gasolina (f.) | Fuel line |
| Manivela (f.); manubrio (m.) | Crank |
| Mano (f.) | Hand; grinding handstone; forefoot of animal |
| Manojo (m.) | Handful |
| Manso(a) | Tame |
| Manteca (f.) | Lard; grease; fat |
| Mantequilla (f.) | Butter |
| Mañana (f.) | Morning; tomorrow |
| Mapache (m.) | Raccoon |
| Máquina (f.) | Machine |
| Máquina de coser (f.) | Sewing machine |
| Mar (m.) | Sea |
| Marca (f.) | Brand (of product or animal) |
| Marcha (f.) | Starter |
| Marea (f.) | Tide |
| Mariposa (f.) | Butterfly |
| Martillo (m.) | Hammer |
| Marrano (m.); puerco (m.); cerdo (m.); cochi (m.) | Pig (hog) |
| Más | More |
| Más bajo; más abajo | Lower |
| Más grande | Larger |
| Más grande (m. or f.) | Largest |
| Más lejos | Farther |
| Más o menos | More or less |
| Más que | More than |
| Más tiempo | Longer (time) |
| Mata (f.) | Plant, bush, or shrub |
| Mata cabras (f.) | Norther, severe winter storm |
| Matamosca (f.) | Flyswatter |
| Matar | Kill |
| Matas (f.) | Stalks |
| Materia prima (f.) | Raw material |

| | |
|---|---|
| *Maza* (f.); *marro* (m.); *pisón* (m.) | Hammer (sledge; maul) |
| *Mazorca* (f.) | Dried corn on the cob |
| *Mecate* (m.); *cuerda* (f.) | String; cord |
| *Mecha* (f.) | Wick |
| *Médanos* (m.); *dunas de arena* (f.) | Sand dunes |
| *Medianoche* (f.) | Midnight |
| *Medias* (f.) | Stockings |
| *Médico* (m.); *doctor* (m.) | Doctor |
| *Medio hermanos* (m.) | Half-brothers |
| *Medio* (m.); *mitad* (f.) | Half |
| *Mediodía* (m.) | Noon |
| *Mejilla* (f.); *cachete* (m.) | Cheek |
| *Mejor; mucho mejor; lo mejor* | Better; much better; the best |
| *Mellizos* (m.); *gemelos* (m.); *cuates* (m.) | Twins |
| *Menos* | Less |
| *Menos de* | Fewer than |
| *Mensajero* (m.); *avisador* (m.) | Messenger; advisor (brings warnings) |
| *Mercado* (m.) | Market |
| *Merienda* (f.) | Afternoon snack |
| *Mes* (m.) | Month |
| *Mesa* (f.) | Table |
| *Mesquital* (m.) | Mesquite woodland |
| *Metate* (m.); *molcajete* (m.) | Grinding slab |
| *Mezcla* (f.); *mortero* (m.); *cemento* (m.) | Mortar |
| *Mientras* | While |
| *Mientras tanto* | Meanwhile |
| *Migas* (f.) | Crumbs (slang: supper); also a dish made from eggs and left-over *tortillas* |
| *Milpa* (f.) | Cornfield |
| *Milpa* (f.); *labor* (m.); *sembrado* (m.) | Field |
| *Mina* (f.) | Mine |
| *Mineral* (m.) | Ore |
| *Minero* (m.) | Mill (general) |
| *Minutos* (m.) | Minutes |
| *Miralejos* (m.) | Binoculars |
| *Mire; vea* | Look at (command) |
| *Mismo; igual* | Same |
| *Mochila* (f.); *tendido* (m.) | Backpack; bedroll |

| | |
|---|---|
| *Mochilero(a)* | Backpacker |
| *Moer* (m.) | Mohair (goat hair) |
| *Mofle* (m.) | Muffler |
| *Mojar* (v.); *mojado(a)*; *húmedo(a)* | Wet |
| *Mojón* (m.); *jalón* (m.); *monumento* (m.) | Marker (stone pile) |
| *Molde de madera* (m.) | Mold for brick making (also concrete form) made of wood |
| *Molida* (f.) | Feed (ground) |
| *Molino* (m.) | Mill |
| *Montar en pelo* | Ride bareback |
| *Monte* (m.); *chaparral* (m.); *matorral* (m.) | Thicket |
| *Monumento* (m.) | Gravestone |
| *Mordida* (f.) | Bite; bribe (slang) |
| *Morillo* (m.); *viga* (f.) | Roof beam or rafter |
| *Morir* | Die |
| *Moscas* (f.) | Flies |
| *Mosquitero* (m.) | Mosquito net |
| *Mota* (f.) | Marijuana |
| *Motor* (m.) | Motor |
| *Motosierra* (f.) | Chain saw |
| *Mucho(a)* | Much |
| *Muebles* (m.) | Furniture |
| *Muela* (f.) | Molar |
| *Muerte* (f.) | Death |
| *Muerto(a)* | Dead |
| *Mujer* (f.) | Woman |
| *Mula* (f.); *acémila* (f.); *bestia* (f.) | Mule |
| *Múltiple* (m.) | Manifold (exhaust) |
| *Municipio* (m.) | Local governmental unit |
| *Murciélagos* (m.) | Bats |
| *Muro* (m.); *muralla* (f.); *pared* (f.) | Wall |
| *Músculo* (m.) | Muscle |
| *Músico* (m.) | Musician |
| *Muslo* (m.) | Thigh |
| | |
| *Nacer* | Be born |
| *Nada* | Nothing |
| *Nadie* | Nobody |
| *Nalgas* (f.) | Buttocks |
| *Nariz* (f.) | Nose |
| *Naufragio* (m.) | Shipwreck |

| | |
|---|---|
| *Navaja* (f.); *cuchillo* (m.) | Knife |
| *Neblina* (f.) | Fog |
| *Necesario(a)* | Necessary |
| *Necesitar; faltar* | Need |
| *Necesitar; querer; desear* | Want |
| *Nevar* (v.); *nieve* (f.) | Snow |
| *Ni; tampoco* | Neither |
| *Nieto(a)* | Grandson (granddaughter) |
| *Nietos* (m.) | Grandchildren |
| *Niguas* (f.); *chigoes* (m.) | Chiggers |
| *Ninguno(a)* | None |
| *Niña* (f.); *muchacha* (f.) | Girl |
| *Niño* (m.); *muchacho* (m.) | Boy |
| *Nivel* (m.) | Level |
| *No* | Not; no |
| *Noche* (f.) | Night |
| *Nombre* (m.) | Name |
| *Nombre de pila* (m.) | First name |
| *Noria* (f.); *pozo* (m.) | Well |
| *Norte* (m.) | North |
| *Nos* | Us (obj.) |
| *Nosotros(as)* | We; us (obj. of prep.) |
| *Novia(o)* | Girlfriend (boyfriend) |
| *Novillos* (m.) | Steers |
| *Nubes* (f.) | Clouds |
| *Nublado(a)* | Overcast |
| *Nudo ciego* (m.) | Knot (hard knot) |
| *Nuera* (f.) | Daughter-in-law |
| *Nuevo(a)* | New |
| *Nunca; jamás* | Never |
| | |
| *O* | Or |
| *O* (conj.); *tampoco* (adv.) | Either |
| *Obscuridad* (f.) | Darkness |
| *Obscuro(a)*; *moreno(a)*; *prieto(a)*; *trigueño(a)* | Dark |
| *Obstáculo* (m.); *barrera* (f.) | Barrier |
| *Océano* (m.) | Ocean |
| *Ocupado(a)* | Busy |
| *Ocupar; dar empleo* | Hire |
| *Oeste* (m.) | West |
| *¡Oiga!* | Listen! |
| *Oír; oír decir* | Hear |

| | |
|---|---|
| Ojal (m.) | Buttonhole |
| Ojo (m.) | Eye |
| Ojo de agua (m.); manantial (m.); ojo (m.) | Spring of water |
| Ojo termal (m.); ojo caliente (m.) | Hot spring |
| Olla (f.) | Pot |
| Olla (f.); olla de barro (m.) | Water jug (glazed clay pot holding one liter of water) |
| Ollera (f.) | Pottery maker |
| Ombligo (m.) | Bellybutton |
| Oreja (f.); oído (m.) | Ear |
| Orilla (f.) | Bank (of ditch or stream); edge of river, cliff, steep place, or body of water |
| Orilla (f.); banca (f.); ribera (f.) | Bank (river) |
| Orilla (f.); playa (f.) | Shore |
| Oro (m.) | Gold |
| Oso negro (m.) | Black bear (confined mainly to mountain regions, but common there) |
| Oso plateado (m.); oso grande (m.) | Grizzly bear (confined to a small area of mountains in Chihuahua and nearing extinction) |
| Otra vez; de nuevo | Again |
| Otro(a) | Another, other |
| Otro lado (m.) | Other side |
| Paca (f.) | Bale |
| Padrastro (m.) | Stepfather |
| Padre (m.); papá (m.) | Father, dad |
| Padres (m.) | Parents |
| Padres adoptivos (m.) | Foster parents |
| Página (f.) | Page |
| Paisano (m.) | Roadrunner; native, countryman |
| Paja (f.) | Straw |
| Pala (f.) | Shovel |
| Pala (f.); remo de canoa (m.) | Paddle |
| Pala de recoger la basura (el polvo) (f.); recojedor (m.) | Dustpan |
| Palanca (f.); maneral (m.) | Lever or handle |
| Palapa choza (f.) | Palm leaf hut |
| Palisado (m.); palizada (f.) | Wall of upright posts, pickets, or quiotes |

| | |
|---|---|
| *Palitos* (m.); *estacas* (f.) | Upright pickets used in house walls |
| *Palma de la mano* (f.) | Palm of hand |
| *Palma* (f.); *yucca* (f.) | Giant *yucca* (dagger) plant |
| *Palo* (m.) | Pole; stick |
| *Paloma* (f.) | Dove (generic) |
| *Palomitas* (f.) | Popcorn |
| *Panal* (m.) | Honeycomb |
| *Panocha* (f.) | Raw sugar |
| *Pantaletas* (f.) | Panties |
| *Pantalones* (m.); *calzones* (m.) | Pants |
| *Pantano* (m.) | Swamp |
| *Panteón* (m.) | Cemetery |
| *Pantimedias* (f.) | Pantyhose |
| *Pañal* (m.) | Diaper |
| *Pañuelo* (m.) | Handkerchief |
| *Papalote* (m.) | Windmill |
| *Papas* (f.) | Potatoes |
| *Papel* (m.) | Paper |
| *Papel de lija* (m.) | Sandpaper |
| *Paquete* (m.); *bulto* (m.) | Bundle |
| *Paquete cama* (m.) | Sleeping bag |
| *Par* (m.) | Even (number) |
| *Para; por* | For |
| *Parabrisas* (f.) | Windshield |
| *Paradero* (m.) | Whereabouts; stopping place |
| *Parar; tapar* | Stop up |
| *Parche* (m.) | Patch |
| *Parecer* | Seem |
| *Pared* (f.); *muralla* (f.); *muro* (m.) | Wall |
| *Parilla* (f.) | Grill; grate |
| *Párpado* (m.) | Eyelid |
| *Parque* (m.) | Park |
| *Parte* (f.); *partir* (v.) | Part |
| *Partir; salir* | Depart |
| *Pasable* | Passable |
| *Pasado(a); último(a)* | Past |
| *Pasaje* (m.) | Passage |
| *Pasajero* (m.) | Passenger |
| *Pasar* | Spend (time); pass |
| *Pasar de contrabando* | Smuggle |
| *Paso* (m.) | Step; pass |
| *Pastero* (m.) | Fence (boundary) rider (It is the |

custom of the *pastero* to cut a green, leafy branch from time to time and hang it over the fence, to prove how recently he has passed.)

| | |
|---|---|
| *Pasto* (m.) | Pasture |
| *Pasto* (m.); *zacate* (m.) | Grass |
| *Pastor* (m.) | Shepherd |
| *Pastura* (f.) | Hay; pasture |
| *Patio* (m.); *yarda* (f.); *jardín* (m.) | Yard (house) |
| *Pato* (m.) | Duck |
| *Patria* (f.) | Country |
| *Patrón* (m.); *mayordomo* (m.); *jefe* (m.); *cabo* (m.) | Boss |
| *Patrón* (m.); *mayordomo* (m.) | Employer |
| *Pavimentado*(a) | Paved |
| *Pavimento* (m.) | Pavement |
| *Pavo de monte* (m.); *guajolote silvestre* (m.); *cócono* (m.) | Wild turkey |
| *Pecho* (m.) | Chest (anat.) |
| *Pedazo* (m.); *pieza* (f.) | Piece |
| *Pedernales* (m.) | Flints (arrow points) |
| *Peligro* (m.) | Danger |
| *Peligroso*(a) | Dangerous |
| *Pelota* (f.) | Ball |
| *Pensar*; *creer* | Think |
| *Peña* (f.); *roca* (f.) | Boulder |
| *Peñasco* (m.) | Cliff |
| *Peor* | Worse |
| *Pequeño*(a); *chico*(a); *chiquito*(a) | Small; little (size) |
| *Perder* | Lose |
| *Perdido*(a) | Lost |
| *Perico* (m.); *cresciente* (m.) | Crescent wrench |
| *Permiso* (m.); *permisión* (f.) | Permission; permit |
| *Permitir*; *dejar* | Allow; permit |
| *Perno* (m.) | Pin |
| *Pero*; *sino*; *más* | But |
| *Perro* (m.) | Dog |
| *Perros de caza* (m.); *sabuesos* (m.) | Dogs (hunting) |
| *Perros juanes* (m.) | Dogs (hound) |
| *Pesado*(a); *grueso*(a) | Heavy |
| *Pesca* (f.); *pez* (m.) | Fish (in water) |
| *Pescado* (m.) | Fish (caught) |

| | |
|---|---|
| *Pestaña* (f.) | Eyelash |
| *Petate* (m.) | Mat |
| *Picante* | Hot (spicy) |
| *Pico* (m.) | Chisel plow; pick |
| *Pico* (m.); *cumbre* (f.); *cima* (f.) | Peak |
| *Pie* (m.); *pata* (animal) (f.) | Foot |
| *Piedra* (f.) | Stone |
| *Piedra* (f.); *roca* (f.) | Rock |
| *Piel* (f.); *cuero* (m.) | Hide, skin of animal |
| *Piel* (f.); *cutis* (f.) | Skin |
| *Pierna* (f.) | Leg |
| *Pila* (f.) | Water trough (circular); battery; fountain |
| *Pilón* (m.) | Boot (something extra in trade) |
| *Pimienta* (f.) | Pepper |
| *Pinturas* (f.) | Art; paintings |
| *Pinzas* (f.); *tenazas* (f.) | Pliers |
| *Pinzas de extensión* (f.) | Water pump pliers |
| *Pinzas de presión* (f.) | Vise grips |
| *Piojos* (m.) | Lice |
| *Pipa* (f.); *tubo* (m.) | Pipe |
| *Piquete* (m.) | Bite (or small wound) |
| *Piscar; coger* | Gather |
| *Piso* (m.); *suelo* (m.) | Floor |
| *Pisote* (m.); *choluga* (f.) | Coatimundi |
| *Pistola* (f.) | Pistol |
| *Pizarra* (f.) | Blackboard |
| *Planetas* (f.) | Planets |
| *Plano* (m.); *nivel* (m.) | Flat area; level |
| *Planta del pie* (f.) | Sole of foot |
| *Plata* (f.) | Silver |
| *Platinos* (m.) | Points (of a car ignition) |
| *Plato* (m.) | Plate |
| *Plato de presión* (m.) | Pressure plate (clutch) |
| *Playa* (f.) | Beach |
| *Playa* (f.); *laguna* (f.) | Dry lake bed; temporary lake |
| *Plomo* (m.) | Lead |
| *Pluma* (f.) | Wiper blade; pen |
| *Pobre* | Poor |
| *Poco(a)* | Little (quantity) |
| *Pocos* | Few |
| *Poder* | Can (to be able); may |
| *Polillas* (f.) | Moths |

| | |
|---|---|
| *Polín* (m.); *viga* (f.) | Roof beam |
| *Polines* (m.); *vigas* (f.) | Floor beams or joists |
| *Pollo* (m.) | Chicken; chicken meat |
| *Polvear; envenenar* | Dust crops |
| *Polvo* (m.) | Dirt; dust |
| *Polvoriento*(*a*); *polvoroso*(*a*) | Dusty |
| *Poner; colocar* | Set; put |
| *Popa* (f.) | Stern (of canoe or raft) |
| *Poquito* (m.) | Little bit |
| *Por* | By; through |
| *Por favor* | Please |
| *Por medio de* | By means of |
| *Porque; pues* | Because |
| *Por todas partes* | Everywhere |
| *Porvenir* (m.) | Future |
| *Posible* | Possible |
| *Poste* (m.); *palo* (m.) | Post |
| *Pote* (m.); *olla* (f.); *marmita* (f.) | Pot |
| *Potrero* (m.); *trampa* (f.) | Trap; small holding pasture or meadow |
| *Potro* (m.) | Colt |
| *Pozo* (m.); *hueco* (m.) | Hole (in the ground) |
| *Pozo* (m.); *noria* (f.) | Water well |
| *Pozo de mina* (f.); *tiro de mina* (m.) | Mine shaft |
| *Precio* (m.) | Price |
| *Precipicio* (m.) | Steep place; cliff |
| *Precipitoso*(*a*); *muy alto*(*a*) | Steep |
| *Preferencia* (f.) | Preference, i.e., right of way (traffic sign) |
| *Pregunta* (f.); *questión* (f.) | Question |
| *Preguntar* | Ask (question) |
| *Prensa* (f.) | Tortilla press |
| *Presa* (f.) | Dam |
| *Presentar* | Present (v.) |
| *Presente* (m.) | Present |
| *Primer gallo* (m.) | First rooster to crow in the A.M. |
| *Primo*(*a*) | Cousin |
| *Primo hermano* (m.) | First cousin |
| *Proa* (f.) | Bow (of canoe or raft) |
| *Problema* (m.) | Problem |
| *Prometido*(*a*); *entendido*(*a*) | Fiancé(e) |
| *Pronto* | Quickly; soon |

| | |
|---|---|
| *Pronto(a); rápido(a)* | Quick |
| *Propiedad* (f.); *finca* (f.) | Property, land |
| *Próxima(o); que viene; siguiente* | Next |
| *Pueblo* (m.); *aldea* (f.); *villa* (f.) | Village |
| *Puente* (m. or f.) | Bridge |
| *Puerta* (f.) | Gate; door |
| *Puerta* (f.); *entrada* (f.) | Gate |
| *Puerta de tablones* (f.) | Door made of roughsawn planks |
| *Pues; bien* | Well |
| *Puesto* (m.) | Small outpost |
| *Pulga* (f.) | Flea |
| *Pulgada* (f.) | Inch |
| *Pulgar* (m.) | Thumb |
| *Pulmón* (m.) | Lung |
| *Punto* (m.); *punta* (f.) | Point |
| *Punzón* (m.); *sacabocados* (m.) | Punch (or awl) |
| *Puño* (m.) | Fist |
| *Puro(a)* | Pure |
| | |
| *Que* | That (relative pron.) |
| *Quebrar; romper* | Break |
| *¿Qué húbole?; ¡Oíga!; ¡Hola!* | Hello! |
| *Quelite* (m.) | Careless weed |
| *Querer; desear* | Wish |
| *Querer decir* | Mean |
| *Queso* (m.) | Cheese |
| *¿Quién?* | Who? |
| *Quijada* (f.) | Jaw |
| *Quiotes* (m.); *piquetes* (m.) | Horizontal latticework between upright posts, usually made of *sotol* or *agave* flower stalks |
| *Quiotes* (m.); *piquetes* (m.); *palisados* (m.) | Upright pickets made of *agave* or *sotol* flower stalks |
| *Quitar* | Take away |
| *Quitarse* | Take off |
| | |
| *Radiador* (m.) | Radiator |
| *Radio* (f.) | Radio |
| *Raíces* (f.) | Roots |
| *Rama* (f.) | Branch |
| *Ramada* (f.) | Unwalled arbor for shade |
| *Ranchero(a)* | Rancher |
| *Rancho* (m.); *granja* (f.) | Farm |

| | |
|---|---|
| *Rancho* (m.) | Ranch |
| *Rastreador* (m.); *rastrear* (v.) | Scout (searcher); search for |
| *Rastrillo* (m.) | Harrow |
| *Ratas* (f.) | Rats |
| *Ratones* (m.) | Mice |
| *Rayo* (m.); *foco* (m.); *relám-pago* (m.) | Lightning |
| *Raza* (f.) | Race (of people) |
| *Reata* (f.); *lazo* (m.); *mecate* (m.); *cuerda* (f.); *soga* (f.) | Rope |
| *Rebaño* (m.); *hato* (m.) | Herd or flock |
| *Recio; aprisa; rápido* | Fast |
| *Red* (f.); *malla* (f.) | Net |
| *Redondo(a)* | Round |
| *Refaccionaria* (f.) | Auto parts store |
| *Refacciones* (f.) | Repair parts |
| *Refrescos* (m.) | Refreshments |
| *Refrigerador* (m.) | Refrigerator (very rare) |
| *Refugiarse* | Take shelter |
| *Regalo* (m.) | Present (gift) |
| *Regar* | Irrigate |
| *Regresar* (v.); *volver* (v.); *regreso* (m.); *vuelta* (f.) | Return |
| *Regulador de voltaje* (m.) | Voltage regulator |
| *Relé* (m.) | Relay |
| *Remiendo* (m.) | Patch |
| *Remo* (m.) | Oar |
| *Remolcar* | Tow |
| *Remolinos* (m.); *olas* (f.) | Eddies, waves, and whirls |
| *Rentar* | Rent |
| *Reparar; componer* | Repair |
| *Reparo* (m.) | Repair |
| *Repetir* | Repeat |
| *Resbaloso(a)* | Slippery |
| *Resorte* (coil) (m.); *muelle* (leaf) (m.) | Spring |
| *Respeto* (m.) | Respect |
| *Retén* (m.) | Seal |
| *Retirado(a)* | Remote |
| *Retrato* (m.) | Photograph |
| *Rico(a)* | Rich |
| *Riego* (m.) | Irrigation |
| *Riendas* (f.) | Reins |

| | |
|---|---|
| *Riesgo* (m.); *peligro* (m.) | Danger, risk |
| *Rincón* (m.) | Corner (inside) |
| *Río* (m.) | River |
| *Río abajo* | Downstream |
| *Río arriba* | Upstream |
| *Rocas* (f.); *piedras* (f.) | Rocks |
| *Rocío* (m.) | Dew |
| *Rocoso*(a); *roqueño*(a) | Rocky |
| *Rodada* (f.) | Rut |
| *Rodilla* (f.) | Knee |
| *Ropa* (f.); *vestidos* (m.) | Clothing (general term) |
| *Ropa de cama* (f.) | Bedding |
| *Ropa interior* (f.); *calzones* (m.) | Underwear |
| *Ropero* (m.) | Closet (almost never seen) |
| *Roto*(a); *quebrado*(a) | Broken |
| *Rotor* (m.) | Rotor |
| *Rótula* (f.) | Ball joint |
| *Rueda* (f.) | Wheel |
| *Rueda de repuesto* (f.) | Spare wheel and tire |
| *Ruido* | Noise |
| *Ruinas* (f.) | Ruins |
| *Rumbo* (m.); *ruta* (f.) | Route; direction |
| | |
| *Sábana* (f.) | Sheet (bed) |
| *Saber* | Know (a fact) |
| *Sabio*(a); *docto*(a); *erudito*(a) | Wise |
| *Sacar* | Take out |
| *Saco* (m.); *costal* (m.) | Sack |
| *Sal* (f.) | Salt |
| *Salera* (f.) | Salt box (for livestock) |
| *Salero* (m.) | Salt shaker |
| *Saliente* (m.); *borde* (m.) | Shoulder (of road) |
| *Salir; dejar; partir* | Leave |
| *Salitre* (m.); *salumbre* (m.) | Salt crystals or salty, white evaporite found in desert |
| *Salobre; agua salada* (f.) | Brackish; brackish or salty water |
| *Salsa de tomate* (f.) | Tomato sauce |
| *Salto* (m.); *salto de agua* (m.); *caída* (f.); *catarata* (f.); *cascada* (f.) | Waterfall |
| *Salvavidas* (m.) | Life jacket |
| *Salvo*(a); *seguro*(a) | Safe |
| *Sangre* (f.) | Blood |

| | |
|---|---|
| *San José* | Patron saint of miners |
| *Sartén* (f.) | Frying pan |
| *Se acabó* | All gone; finished |
| *Secar* (v.); *seco*(*a*); *árido*(*a*) | Dry |
| *Seguir la pista; seguir el rastro* | Track (to trail) |
| *Segundo* (m.) | Second-in-command |
| *Seguro*(*a*); *cierto*(*a*) | Sure |
| *Selva* (f.) | Jungle |
| *Selva* (f.); *bosque* (m.) | Forest |
| *Semáforo* (m.) | Traffic light |
| *Semana* (f.) | Week |
| *Sembrador* (m.); *labrador* (m.) | Farm worker |
| *Sembradora* (m. or f.) | Planter |
| *Sembranda* (f.) | Planting |
| *Semejante* | Like |
| *Semilla* (f.); *pepa* (fruit) | Seed |
| *Senda* (*de pie*) (f.); *sendero* (m.); *vereda* (f.); *rastro* (m.) | Footpath; trail |
| *Seno* (m.) | Breast |
| *Sentado*(*a*) | Seated |
| *Sentarse* | Sit down |
| *Señal* (m.) | Traffic sign |
| *Separados*(*as*) | Separated |
| *Sepultura* (f.) | Grave; burial |
| *Ser; estar* | Be |
| *Serrucho* (m.); *sierra* (f.); *segueta* (f.) | Saw |
| *Servilletas* (f.) | Napkins |
| *Sesteadero* (m.) | Shaded spot where livestock rest during heat of the day |
| *Si* | Whether; if |
| *Sí* | Yes |
| *Siempre* | Always |
| *Sierra* (f.); *loma* (f.); *cerro* (m.); *colina* (f.) | Hill |
| *Sierra* (f.); *montaña* (f.) | Mountain |
| *Silla* (f.) | Chair |
| *Silla de montar* (f.); *montura* (f.) | Saddle |
| *Sin embargo* | However; nevertheless |
| *Sin riesgo; sin peligro* | Without danger |
| *Sitio* (m.); *lugar* (m.) | Spot (place) |
| *Sobre; encima de* | Over; upon |
| *Sobre; encima; arriba* | Above |

| | |
|---|---|
| *Sobrino(a)* | Nephew (niece) |
| *Sol* (m.) | Sun |
| *Soldar* | Weld |
| *Solenoide* (m.) | Solenoid |
| *Solo(a)* | Alone |
| *Soltero(a)* | Bachelor, single person |
| *Sombra* (f.) | Shade |
| *Sombrero* (m.) | Hat |
| *Su; sus* | Its; your; their |
| *Suave; liso(a); llano(a)* | Smooth |
| *Subir* | Climb |
| *Subirse a* | Get (into vehicle) |
| *Suegra* (f.) | Mother-in-law |
| *Suegro* (m.) | Father-in-law |
| *Suela* (f.) | Sole (of shoes) |
| *Sueldo* (m.); *salario* (m.) | Wages, salary |
| *Suelo* (m.); *piso* (m.) | Floor |
| *Suelo* (m.); *tierra* (f.) | Ground |
| *Suelto(a); flojo(a)* | Loose |
| *Suelto(a); no atado(a)* | Free (unattached) |
| *Suelto(a)* | Loose (slang: not doing much) |
| *Suerte* (f.) | Luck |
| *Suéter* (m.); *sudador* (m.); *chamarra* (f.) | Sweater |
| *Sumidero* (m.); *sótano* (m.) | Sinkhole |
| *Sur* (m.) | South |
| *Surco* (m.); *raya* (f.) | Row |
| *Suyo(a)* | Theirs |
| | |
| *Tabla* (f.) | Board |
| *Tabla* (f.); *puente de pie* (m.) | Footbridge |
| *Tablón* (m.) | Plank |
| *Taburete* (m.) | Stool |
| *Tahona* (f.); *arrastra* (f.) | Ore mill (hand or burro powered) |
| *Tajar; cortar; picar* | Chop |
| *Taladro* (m.) *y pizcas* (f.) | Drill and bits |
| *Talón* (m.) | Heel (of shoe) |
| *Tal vez; quizás* | Maybe; perhaps |
| *Taller* (m.) | Shop |
| *También* | Also |
| *También; además* | Too |
| *Tanque* (m.); *estanque* (m.) | Stock tank |
| *Tanto(a)* | So much |

| | |
|---|---|
| *Tantos(as)* | So many |
| *Tapa* (f.) | Cap, lid |
| *Tapadero* (m.) | Saddle toe fender |
| *Tapia* (f.) | *Adobe* wall (usually a ruin) |
| *Tapir* (m.); *danta* (f.) | Tapir (southern tropical lowlands only) |
| *Tapón* (m.) | Plug; lid (cap); tap |
| *Tarántula* (f.) | Tarantula |
| *Tarde* (f.) | Afternoon; late |
| *Taza* (f.) | Cup |
| *Tecolote* (m.) | Owl |
| *Techo* (m.); *tejado* (m.) | Roof |
| *Tejas* (f.) | Tiles (usually hooked over or nailed to *tablas*) |
| *Tejedora* (f.) | Weaver |
| *Tejón* (m.); *tlalcoyote* (m.) | Badger |
| *Tela metálica* (f.) | Screen (windows and doors) |
| *Telaraña* (f.) | Spider web |
| *Temer* (v.); *tener miedo* (v.); *temor* (m.) | Fear |
| *Tempestuoso(a)* | Gusty |
| *Tendedero* (m.); *lazo* (m.) | Clothesline |
| *Tendido* (m.) | Bedroll |
| *Tenedor* (m.) | Fork |
| *Terrón* (m.) | Clod (of earth) |
| *Teta* (f.) | Nipple |
| *Tetera* (f.) | Teapot |
| *Tiburón* (m.) | Shark |
| *Tiempo* (m.) | Weather; time |
| *Tienda* (f.); *taller* (m.) | Shop |
| *Tienda de abarrotes* (f.) | Grocery store |
| *Tienda de campaña* (f.) | Tent |
| *Tierra* (f.); *suelo* (m.) | Soil |
| *Tierra* (f.); *terreno* (m.) | Land |
| *Tigre* (m.) | Jaguar |
| *Tijeras* (f.) | Scissors |
| *Tinaja* (f.) | Tank (natural rock water hole) |
| *Tío; tía* | Uncle; aunt |
| *Tirar; disparar; fusilar* | Shoot |
| *Tiro* (m.); *disparo* (m.); *balazo* (m.) | Gunshot |
| *Tiza* (f.) | Chalk |
| *Tlacuache* (m.) | Opossum |
| *Toalla* (f.) | Towel |

| | |
|---|---|
| *Tobillo* (m.) | Ankle |
| *Tocador* (m.) | Dresser |
| *Tocante*(*a*); *respecto*(*a*); *acerca de*; *encuanto*(*a*) | Concerning |
| *Tocino* (m.) | Salt pork; bacon |
| *Todavía*; *ya*; *aún* | Yet; still |
| *Todo* | All |
| *Todo*; *todo lo que* | Everything |
| *Todo el mundo* | Everybody |
| *Toma de agua* (f.); *termostato* (m.) | Thermostat |
| *Tomar*; *llevar*; *aceptar* | Take |
| *Tomate* (m.) | Tomato |
| *Tope* (m.) | Speed bump across road |
| *Tormenta* (f.); *tronada* (f.); *tempestad* (f.) | Storm |
| *Tornillo* (m.) | Vise |
| *Tornillo* (m.); *cerrojo* (m.) | Bolt |
| *Torno* (m.); *chilillo* (m.) | Screw |
| *Toro* (m.) | Bull |
| *Toro orejano* (m.) | Maverick bull (no ear marks) |
| *Torrente* (m.) | Torrent |
| *Tortón* (m.) | Big truck |
| *Tortuga* (f.) | Turtle (generic) |
| *Trabajador* (m.); *jornalero* (m.) | Worker |
| *Trabajar* (v.); *obrar* (v.); *trabajo* (m.); *empleo* (m.); *obra* (f.) | Work |
| *Trabas* (f.) | Hobbles (for burros) |
| *Tractor* (m.) | Tractor |
| *Traer* | Bring |
| *Traje* (m.) | Suit |
| *Traje de baño* (m.); *traje de natación* (m.) | Swimsuit |
| *Tranquilo*(*a*) | Quiet, still |
| *Transbordador* (m.); *barca de pasaje* (f.); *chalán* (f.) | Ferryboat |
| *Tránsito* (m.) | Traffic; traffic policeman |
| *Transmisión* (f.); *caja* (f.) | Transmission |
| *Trapeador* (m.) | Mop |
| *Trapo* (m.); *garra* (f.) | Rag |
| *Trasquilador* (m.) | Shearer of sheep or goats |
| *Tratar de*; *procurar* | Try |
| *Triste* | Sad |
| *Tronco* (m.) | Tree trunk; trunk |

| | |
|---|---|
| *Troneras* (f.) | Holes for muskets or rifles to fire through, found in very old stone buildings |
| *Tropilla* (f.) | Horse herd led by a bell mare |
| *Troquero* (m.) | Trucker |
| *Truenos* (m.) | Thunder |
| *Trusas* (f.) | Underpants |
| *Tubería* (f.) | Pipeline |
| *Tubo corto* (m.) | Short pipe |
| *Tubo de escape* (m.) | Exhaust pipe |
| *Tuerca* (f.) | Nut |
| *Tumba* (f.) | Grave |
| *Túnel* (m.) | Tunnel (mine) |
| | |
| *Último(a)* | Last |
| *Una vez* | Once |
| *Único(a); solo(a); solamente* | Only |
| *Unido(a)* | Joined; together |
| *Uno y otro(a)* | Either |
| *Uña* (f.) | Fingernail; claw |
| | |
| *Vacas* (f.); *ganado* (m.); *res* (m.) | Cattle |
| *Vacío(a)* | Empty |
| *Vaciero* (m.) | Sheepboss |
| *Vadear; andar a pie por el agua* | Wade |
| *Vado* (m.) | Ford; dip in road |
| *Vagoneta* (f.) | Station wagon |
| *Vajillas* (f.); *trastes* (m.) | Dishes |
| *Valer* (f.) | Be worth |
| *Válvulas* (f.) | Valves |
| *Valle* (m.) | Valley |
| *Vaquero* (m.) | Cowboy |
| *Vara* (f.) | Stick |
| *Varilla de dirección* (f.) | Tie rod |
| *Varón* (m.); *masculino; macho* | Male |
| *Vaso* (m.) | Glass |
| *Vegas* (f.) | Flats near river |
| *Vela* (f.) | Candle |
| *Velar* | Hold a wake |
| *Velocidad* (f.) | Speed |
| *Velorio* (m.); *velatorio* | Wake (funeral) |
| *Vena* (f.) | Vein |
| *Venado* (m.) | Deer (generic) |

| | |
|---|---|
| *Vender* | Sell |
| *Veneno* (m.); *envenenar* (v.) | Poison |
| *Venir* | Come |
| *Ventana* (f.); *ventanilla* (f.); *vidrio* (m.) | Window |
| *Ventilador* (m.); *abanico* (m.) | Fan |
| *Ver* | See |
| *Verdad* (f.) | Truth |
| *Verdadero(a)* | True; truthful |
| *Vereda* (f.) | Trail |
| *Vestido* (m.) | Dress |
| *Veta* (f.) | Vein (ore) |
| *Viajar; caminar* | Travel |
| *Viaje* (m.) | Trip |
| *Viajero(a); pasajero(a)* | Traveler |
| *Víbora* (f.); *cascabel* (m.) | Rattlesnake |
| *Vida* (f.) | Life |
| *Viejo(a)* | Old |
| *Viento* (m.); *aire* (m.); *brisa* (f.) | Wind |
| *Vientre* (m.); *panza* (f.) | Belly |
| *Viga* (f.) | Joist |
| *Vigor* (m.); *fuerza* (f.) | Strength |
| *Vista* (f.) | Sight |
| *Viuda* (f.) | Widow |
| *Viudo* (m.) | Widower |
| *Volante* (m.) | Steering wheel |
| *Volcán* (m.) | Volcano |
| *Volear* | Volley |
| *Vólibol* (m.) | Volleyball |
| *Vulcanizador* (m.) | Tire repair shop |
| | |
| *Ya* | Already |
| *Yegua* (f.) | Mare |
| *Yerba* (f.) | Weed; plant; herb |
| *Yerno* (m.) | Son-in-law |
| *Yugo* (m.); *mancornador* (m.) | Yoke (for oxen) |
| | |
| *Zacatal* (m.) | Grassland |
| *Zacate* (m.); *pasto* (m.) | Grass |
| *Zanja* (f.) | Ditch |
| *Zancudos* (m.); *moyotes* (m.) | Mosquitoes |
| *Zapato* (m.); *calzado* (m.) | Shoe |
| *Zona escolar* (f.) | School zone |

| | |
|---|---|
| *Zona fronteriza* (f.) | Border zone |
| *Zopilote* (m.); *aura* (f.) | Vulture or buzzard (*Aura*, used for black vultures, is also a general term sometimes used for any large bird of prey [*aves de repiña*], including hawks, eagles, and ravens. *Zopilote* usually refers to the red-headed turkey vulture.) |
| *Zorra(o)* | Fox |
| *Zorrillo* (m.) | Skunk |

## ENGLISH TO SPANISH

| | |
|---|---|
| Above | *Sobre; encima; arriba* |
| Accident (auto) | *Choque* (m.) |
| Across | *A través de* |
| Add | *Añadir* |
| Afoot | *A pie* |
| After (time) | *Despúes* (*de*) (*que*) |
| After (location) | *Detrás de* |
| Afterwards | *Después* |
| Again | *Otra vez; de nuevo* |
| All | *Todo(a)* |
| All gone | *Se acabó* |
| Allow | *Permitir; dejar* |
| Almost | *Casi* |
| Alone | *Solo(a)* |
| Along | *A lo largo de* |
| Alongside | *A lado de* |
| Already | *Ya* |
| Also | *También* |
| Always | *Siempre* |
| Among | *Entre* |
| Another | *Otro(a)* |
| Any | *Alguno(a)* |
| Anybody | *Alguien* |
| Anything | *Alguna cosa* (f.); *algo* |
| Around | *Alrededor* |
| Arrive | *Llegar* |
| As | *Como* |
| Ask (question) | *Preguntar* |
| Ask (for) | *Pedir* |

| | |
|---|---|
| At | *A, en* |
| At once | *En seguida; ahorita* |
| Automatic | *Automático* |
| Awaken | *Despertar* |
| | |
| Back (location) | *Atrás* |
| Back of (location) | *Detrás de* |
| Back (animal) | *Lomo* (m.) |
| Back (human) | *Espalda* (f.) |
| Backward | *Atrasado(a); hacia atrás* |
| Baggage | *Equipaje* (m.) |
| Bait | *Cebo* (m.) |
| Bank | *Barranca* (f.); *banco* (m.); *orilla* (f.) |
| Barbed wire | *Alambre de pico* (m.); *alambre de púas* (m.) |
| Barn | *Granero* (m.); *troje* (m.) |
| Barrel | *Barril* (m.) |
| Barren (arid) | *Árido(a)* |
| Barrier | *Obstáculo* (m.); *barrera* (f.) |
| Basket (large) | *Cesta* (f.) |
| Basket | *Canasta* (f.) |
| Battery | *Batería* (f.); *pila* (f.); *acumulador* (m.) |
| | |
| Be | *Ser; estar* |
| Be able | *Poder* |
| Be acquainted with | *Conocer* |
| Beans | *Frijoles* (m.) (slang: *nacionales*) |
| Beautiful | *Hermoso(a); lindo(a); bello(a); bonito(a)* |
| | |
| Be born | *Nacer* |
| Because | *Porque; pues* |
| Because of | *A causa de; por* |
| Beckon | *Llamar con señas* |
| Bed | *Cama* (f.) |
| Bedding | *Ropa de cama* (f.) |
| Bedroll | *Mochila* (f.); *tendido* (m.) |
| Bee | *Abeja* (f.) |
| Beehive | *Colmena* (f.); *abejera* (f.) |
| Before (time) | *Antes de* |
| Before (location) | *Delante de; enfrente* |
| Begin | *Empezar; comenzar; principiar* |
| Behind (location) | *Atrás; detrás* |
| Believe | *Creer* |

| | |
|---|---|
| Belly | *Vientre* (f.); *panza* (f.) |
| Below | *Debajo de; abajo; bajo* |
| Be named | *Llamar* |
| Bend (fold) | *Doblar* |
| Beneath | *Debajo; bajo* |
| Bent | *Doblado(a)* |
| Best | *El mejor* |
| Better | *Mejor* |
| Between | *Entre* |
| Be worth | *Valer* |
| Big | *Grande* |
| Binoculars | *Miralejos* (m.); *gemelos* (m.) |
| Bite (or small wound) | *Piquete* (m.) |
| Blackboard | *Pizarra* (f.) |
| Blade (grass) | *Brinza de zacate* (f.) |
| Blade (knife) | *Hoja* (f.) |
| Blade (paddle) | *Pala* (f.) |
| Blanket | *Cobija* (m.); *manta* (f.) |
| Bolt | *Cerrojo* (m.) |
| Bonfire | *Hoguerra* (f.); *fogata* (f.) |
| Boot (something extra in trade) | *Pilón* (m.) |
| Boot (footwear) | *Bota* (f.) |
| Border | *Frontera* (f.) |
| Boss | *Patrón* (m.); *mayordomo* (m.); *jefe* (m.); *cabo* (m.) |
| Both | *Ambos; los dos* |
| Bottle | *Botella* (f.) |
| Bottle opener | *Destapador* (m.); *llave* (f.) |
| Boundary marker | *Jalón* (m.); *mojón* (m.) |
| Box | *Caja* (f.); *cajón* (m.) |
| Boy | *Niño* (m.); *muchacho* (m.) |
| Brakes | *Frenos* (m.) |
| Branch | *Rama* (f.) |
| Break | *Quebrar; romper* |
| Break into | *Escalar; forzar la entrada en* |
| Brick | *Ladrillo* (m.) |
| Bridge | *Puente* (m. or f.) |
| Bridle | *Freno* (m.); *brida* (f.) |
| Bring | *Traer* |
| Broad | *Ancho(a)* |
| Broken | *Roto(a); quebrado(a)* |
| Bucket | *Balde* (m.); *bote* (m.); *tina* (f.) |
| Build | *Construir* |

| | |
|---|---|
| Bundle | *Paquete* (m.); *bulto* (m.) |
| Burden | *Carga* (f.) |
| Busy | *Ocupado(a)* |
| But | *Pero; sino; más* |
| Butterfly | *Mariposa* (f.) |
| Buy | *Comprar* |
| By (agent) | *Por* |
| By (near) | *Cerca* |
| By means of | *Por medio de* |
| | |
| Call | *Llamar* |
| Camp | *Campo* (m.); *campamento* (m.) |
| Can (tin) | *Lata* (f.); *bote* (m.) |
| Can (to be able) | *Poder* |
| Candle | *Vela* (f.) |
| Can opener | *Abrelatas* (m.) |
| Cap (bottle) | *Tapón* (m.) |
| Care (to take) | *Cuidar* |
| Care | *Cuidado* (m.) |
| Carefully | *Cuidadoso* |
| Carry | *Llevar* |
| Cat | *Gato* (m.) |
| Catch | *Agarrar; coger; pescar* |
| Cattle guard | *Guarda vaca* (f.); *cuida vaca* (f.) |
| Cause | *Causa* (f.); *causar* (v.) |
| Ceiling, sky | *Cielo* (m.) |
| Certain | *Cierto(a); seguro(a)* |
| Certainly | *Cierto; seguro* |
| Certainly | *Ciertamente; ¡Cómo no?; Seguro que sí* |
| | |
| Chain | *Cadena* (f.) |
| Chain hook | *Gancho* (m.) |
| Chain saw | *Motosierra* (f.) |
| Chalk | *Tiza* (f.) |
| Chop | *Tajar; cortar; picar* |
| Church | *Iglesia* (f.) |
| Claim (mining claim) | *Denuncio de una mina* (m.); *amparo* (m.) |
| | |
| Claim (a mine) | *Denunciar* |
| Class | *Clase* (f.) |
| Clean | *Limpiar* (v.); *limpio(a)* |
| Clear | *Claro(a)* |
| Clearly | *Claramente* |

| | |
|---|---|
| Climb | *Subir* |
| Clod (of earth) | *Terrón* (m.) |
| Close | *Cerrar* (v.) |
| Closed | *Cerrado(a)* |
| Close to | *Cerca de* |
| Clothesline | *Tendedero* (m.); *lazo* (m.) |
| Collect | *Cobrar* |
| Collide | *Chocar* |
| Collision | *Choque* (m.) |
| Come | *Venir* |
| Companion | *Compañero(a)* |
| Complete | *Completar* (v.); *acabar* (v.); *termi-*<br>*nar* (v.); *completo(a)* |
| Concerning | *Tocante(a)*; *respecto(a)*; *acerca de*;<br>*en cuanto(a)* |
| Construct | *Construir* |
| Contain | *Contener* |
| Contain (be contained in) | *Caber* |
| Contented | *Contento(a)* |
| Corn | *Maíz* (m.) |
| Corner (inside) | *Rincón* (m.) |
| Corner (outside) | *Esquina* (f.) |
| Cornfield | *Milpa* (f.) |
| Cornmeal | *Harina de maíz* (f.) |
| Correct | *Correcto(a)*; *corregir* (v.) |
| Cost | *Costar* |
| Cotton | *Algodón* (m.) |
| Count | *Contar* |
| Cover | *Cubrir* |
| Crawl | *Arrastrarse*; *gatear* |
| Crippled | *Cojo(a)* |
| Cross | *Cruzar* (v.); *cruz* (f.) |
| Cut | *Cortada* (f.); *cortar* |
| | |
| Daily | *Diario* |
| Dam | *Presa* (f.) |
| Danger | *Peligro* (m.) |
| Dark | *Obscuro(a)*; *moreno(a)*; *prieto(a)*;<br>*trigueño(a)* |
| Date | *Fechar* (v.); *fecha* (f.); *compromiso*<br>(m.); *cita* (f.) |
| Dawn | *Amanecer* (m.); *madrugada* (f.) |
| Day | *Día* (m.) |

| | |
|---|---|
| Day of rest | *Día de descanso* (m.) |
| Dead | *Muerto(a)* |
| Death | *Muerte* (f.) |
| Decide | *Decidir* |
| Deep | *Hondo(a); profundo(a)* |
| Deliver | *Entregar* |
| Depart | *Partir; salir* |
| Describe | *Describir* |
| Desert | *Desierto* (m.) |
| Desire | *Desear* (v.); *deseo* (m.) |
| Destination | *Destinación* (f.) |
| Dew | *Rocío* (m.) |
| Die | *Morir* |
| Different | *Diferente* |
| Difficult | *Difícil* |
| Dig | *Cavar; excavar* |
| Dine | *Comer* |
| Dirt | *Polvo* (m.); *tierra* (f.) |
| Distance | *Distancia* (f.) |
| Do | *Hacer* |
| Dollar | *Dólar* (m.) |
| Door | *Puerta* (f.) |
| Double | *Doble; doblar* (v.) |
| Doubt | *Dudar* (v.); *duda* (f.) |
| Down | *Abajo; bajo* |
| Down (get) | *Bajarse de* |
| Down (face down) | *Boca abajo* |
| Downhill | *Cuesta abajo* |
| Drag | *Arrastrarse; jalar* |
| Drink | *Beber* (v.); *tomar* (v.); *trago* (m.) |
| Drive | *Manejar; guiar* |
| Drop (of liquid) | *Gota* (f.) |
| Dry | *Secar* (v.); *seco(a); árido(a)* |
| Dump | *Dumpe* (m.); *basurero* (m.) |
| During | *Durante* |
| Dusk | *Crepúsculo* (m.) |
| Dust | *Polvo* (m.) |
| | |
| Each | *Cada; todo(a)* |
| Easy | *Fácil* |
| Eat | *Comer* |
| Edge | *Bordo* (m.); *orilla* (f.) |
| Either | *O* (conj.); *tampoco* (adv.) |

| | |
|---|---|
| Either | *Uno y otro* |
| Electricity | *Electricidad* (f.) |
| Employ | *Emplear; dar empleo; ocupar* |
| Employed | *Empleado(a)* |
| Employee | *Empleado* (m.) |
| Employer | *Patrón* (m.); *mayordomo* (m.) |
| Employment | *Empleo* (m.) |
| Empty | *Vacío(a)* |
| End | *Acabar; terminar* |
| Enough | *Bastante; suficiente* |
| Enter | *Entrar* |
| Entire | *Entero(a)* |
| Entrance | *Entrada* (f.) |
| Entrance gate | *Garita* (f.) |
| Entry | *Entrada* (f.) |
| Even (number) | *Par* |
| Ever | *Jamás; alguna vez; siempre* |
| Every | *Cada; todos* |
| Everybody | *Todo el mundo* |
| Everything | *Todo; todo lo que* |
| Everywhere | *Por todas partes* |
| Expense | *Gastos* (m.); *coste* (m.) |
| Extra | *Extra* |
| | |
| Fall | *Caer* |
| Far (away) | *Lejos* |
| Far from | *Lejos de* |
| Farm | *Rancho* (m.); *granja* (f.) |
| Farmer | *Hacendado* (m.); *agricultor* (m.); *ranchero* (m.) |
| Farm laborer | *Labrador* (m.); *cultivador* (m.); *sembrador* (m.) |
| Farther | *Más lejos* |
| Fast | *Recio(a); aprisa; rápido(a)* |
| Fat | *Gordo(a); grueso(a)* |
| Fear | *Temer* (v.); *tener miedo* (v.); *temor* (m.) |
| Fence | *Cerca* (f.) |
| Ferryboat | *Transbordador* (m.); *barca de pasaje* (f.); *chalán* (f.) |
| Few | *Pocos(as)* |
| Fewer than | *Menos de* |
| Fill | *Llenar* |

| | |
|---|---|
| Find | *Encontrar; hallar* |
| Fire | *Fuego* (m.); *lumbre* (m.) |
| Fix | *Arreglar; reparar; componer* |
| Flashlight | *Batería* (f.) |
| Flea | *Pulga* (f.) |
| Flood | *Diluvio* (m.); *inundación* (f.) |
| Floor | *Suelo* (m.); *piso* (m.) |
| Flower | *Flor* (f.) |
| Footbridge | *Tabla* (f.); *puente de pie* (m.) |
| Footpath | *Senda* (*de pie*) (f.); *sendero* (m.); *vereda* (f.) |
| For | *Para; por* |
| Forest | *Selva* (f.); *bosque* (m.) |
| Forward | *Adelante; delante* |
| Free | *Suelto*(*a*); *no atado*(*a*); *libre; gratis* |
| Frequently | *Frecuentemente; a menudo* |
| Fresh | *Fresco*(*a*) |
| From | *De; desde* |
| Front | *Frente; delantero*(*a*) |
| Front of | *Delante de* |
| Full | *Lleno*(*a*) |
| Future (the) | *Porvenir* (m.) |
| Gap | *Boquilla* (f.); *falcete* (wire gap) (m.) |
| Gate | *Puerta* (f.); *entrada* (f.) |
| Gate (entrance) | *Garita* (f.) |
| Gather | *Piscar; coger* |
| Get (into vehicle) | *Subirse a* |
| Get (out of or off a vehicle) | *Bajarse de* |
| Get up | *Levantarse* |
| Girl | *Niña* (f.); *muchacha* (f.) |
| Give | *Dar* |
| Go | *Ir* |
| Goatherd | *Chivero* (m.); *pastór* (m.); *borreguero* (m.); *cabrero* (m.) |
| Go away | *Irse* |
| God | *Dios* (m.) |
| Government | *Gobierno* (m.) |
| Grasp | *Agarrar* |
| Grass | *Pasto* (m.); *zacate* (m.) |
| Gravel | *Cascajo* (m.); *grava* (f.) |
| Groceries | *Abarrotes* (m.); *comestibles* (m.); *comida* (f.) |

| | |
|---|---|
| Ground | *Suelo* (m.); *tierra* (f.) |
| Grow dark | *Anochecer* |
| Guard | *Guardar* (v.); *guardia* (f. or m.) |
| Gulch | *Cañada* (f.); *quebrada* (f.) |
| Gun | *Fusil* (m.); *escopeta* (shotgun) (f.); *carabina* (f.); *pistola* (f.) |
| Gunshot | *Tiro* (m.); *disparo* (m.); *balazo* (m.) |
| Gusty | *Tempestuoso*(a) |
| | |
| Half | *Medio; mitad* (f.) |
| Halt | *Alto; hacer alto* (v.); *parar* (v.) |
| Handful | *Manojo* (m.) |
| Handle | *Mango* (m.); *tirador* (m.); *manubrio* (m.) |
| Hard | *Duro*(a) |
| Hard (difficult) | *Difícil* |
| Harm | *Dañar* (v.); *daño* (m.) |
| He | *Él* |
| Hear | *Oír; oír decir* |
| Heat | *Calor* (m.) |
| Heavy | *Pesado*(a); *grueso*(a) |
| Height | *Altura* (f.); *estatura* (f.) |
| Hello | *¡Qué húbole!; ¡Oíga!; ¡Hola!* |
| Help | *Ayudar* (v.); *ayuda* (f.); *asistir* (v.); *socorro* (m.) |
| Herd | *Rebaño; hato* (m.); *manada* (f.) |
| Here | *Aquí; acá* |
| Hidden | *Escondido*(a) |
| Hide (skin of animal) | *Piel* (f.); *cuero* (m.) |
| Hide (from sight) | *Ocultar; esconder* |
| High | *Alto*(a) |
| Hill | *Sierra* (f.); *loma* (f.); *cerro* (m.); *colina* (f.) |
| Hire | *Ocupar; dar empleo* |
| Hit | *Golpear; pegar* |
| Hole (as in wall) | *Abertura* (f.) |
| Hole (as in fence) | *Hoyo* (m.) |
| Hole (as in roof) | *Agujero* (m.) |
| Hole (as in ground) | *Pozo* (m.); *hoyo* (m.); *hueco* (m.) |
| Hole (as in small hole or mouse or rat hole) | *Agujero* (m.) |
| Hoof (of horse, mule, etc.) | *Casco* (m.); *mano* (front hoof) (m.) |
| Hook | *Gancho* (m.); *anzuelo* (m.) |

| | |
|---|---|
| Hot | *Caliente; caluroso(a)* |
| Hot (spicy) | *Picante* |
| How? | *¿Cómo?* |
| However | *Sin embargo* |
| How many? | *¿Cuántos(as)?* |
| How much? | *¿Cuánto(a)?* |
| Hunt | *Cazar* |
| Hunt for something | *Buscar* |
| Hunter | *Cazador* (m.) |
| Hut | *Choza* (f.); *jacal* (m.) |

| | |
|---|---|
| If | *Si* |
| Immediately | *Inmediatamente; en seguida* |
| Important | *Importante* |
| Impossible | *Imposible* |
| In | *En* |
| Inch | *Pulgada* (f.) |
| In front of | *Delante de* |
| Inhabitant | *Habitante* (m.) |
| Insecure | *Inseguro(a)* |
| Inside | *Dentro* |
| Its | *Su* |

| | |
|---|---|
| Jail | *Cárcel* (f.) (slang: *en el bote*) |
| Jerk (sudden) | *Tirón* (m.); *cimbrón* (m.) |
| Join | *Juntar* (v.); *unir* (v.); *unida* (f.) |
| Jump | *Brincar; saltar* |

| | |
|---|---|
| Keep | *Guardar* |
| Key | *Llave* (f.) |
| Kill | *Matar* |
| Kind (type) | *Clase* (f.); *tipo* (m.) |
| Kind (agreeable) | *Bondadoso(a)* |
| Knife | *Navaja* (f.); *cuchillo* (m.) |
| Know (a fact) | *Saber* |
| Know (be acquainted with) | *Conocer* |

| | |
|---|---|
| Lack | *Faltar* (v.); *falta* (f.) |
| Ladder | *Escalera* (f.) |
| Land | *Tierra* (f.); *terreno* (m.) |
| Large | *Grande* |
| Larger | *Más grande* |
| Largest | *El* or *la más grande* |

| | |
|---|---|
| Lasso | *Lazo* (m.) |
| Last | *Último*(*a*) |
| Latch bolt | *Cerrojo* (m.) |
| Lean (thin) | *Flaco*(*a*) |
| Leave | *Salir; dejar; partir* |
| Length | *Largo* (m.) |
| Less | *Menos* |
| Let | *Dejar; permitir* |
| Level | *Plano*(*a*); *llano*(*a*); *nivel* (m.) |
| Lid (cap) | *Tapón* (m.) |
| Lie down | *Acostarse; tenderse* (lay out the dead) |
| Life | *Vida* (f.) |
| Lift | *Levantar; alzar* |
| Light (weight) | *Ligero*(*a*) |
| Light | *Luz* (f.); *iluminar* (v.) |
| Like (similar) | *Semejante* |
| Like (as) | *Como; lo mismo que* |
| Like (v.) | *Gustar* |
| Line | *Línea* (f.); *raya* (f.) |
| Listen! | *¡Oiga!* |
| Litter | *Basura* (f.); *desperdicio* (m.) |
| Little (size) | *Pequeño*(*a*); *chico*(*a*); *chiquito*(*a*) |
| Little (quantity) | *Poco*(*a*) |
| Load | *Carga* (f.); *cargar* (v.) |
| Loaders; cartridge clips | *Cargadores* (m.) |
| Lock | *Candado* (m.); *cerrar con llave* (v.); *cerradura* (f.) |
| Long | *Largo*(*a*) |
| Longer (time) | *Más tiempo* |
| Look at (command) | *Mire; vea* |
| Look for | *Buscar* |
| Loose | *Suelto*(*a*) (slang: not doing much) |
| Loosen | *Aflojar; soltar* |
| Lose | *Perder* |
| Low | *Bajo*(*a*); *abajo* |
| Lower | *Más bajo*(*a*); *más abajo* |
| Lumberjack | *Leñador* (m.); *hachero* (m.) |
| Make | *Hacer* |
| Makeshift | *Improvisado* (*a*); *provisional* |
| Man | *Hombre* (m.) |
| Marker (stone pile) | *Mojón* (m.); *jalón* (m.); *monumento* (m.) |

| | |
|---|---|
| May (to be able) | *Poder* |
| Maybe | *Tal vez; quizás* |
| Meal | *Comida* (f.) |
| Mean (intend) | *Querer decir* |
| Meanwhile | *Mientras tanto* |
| Meet (encounter) | *Encontrar* |
| Meet (become acquainted) | *Conocer* |
| Messenger | *Mensajero* (m.); *avisador* (brings warnings) (m.) |
| Mining rights (claim) | *Amparo* (m.); *denuncio de una mina* (m.) |
| Mistake | *Falta* (f.); *error* (m.) |
| Mohair (goat hair) | *Moer* (m.) |
| Money | *Dinero* (m.) |
| More | *Más* |
| More or less | *Más o menos* |
| More than | *Más que* |
| Much | *Mucho(a)* |
| Mud | *Lodo* (m.); *zoquete* (m.) |
| | |
| Naked | *Desnudo(a); en pelota* |
| Narrow | *Angosto(a); estrecho(a)* (passage) |
| Necessary | *Necesario(a)* |
| Need | *Necesitar; faltar* |
| Neither | *Ni; tampoco* |
| Net | *Red* (f.); *malla* (f.) |
| Net wire | *Alambre de tela* (m.) |
| Never | *Nunca; jamás* |
| New | *Nuevo(a)* |
| Newspaper | *Diario* (m.); *periódico* (m.) |
| Next | *Próximo(a); que viene; siguiente* |
| Nickname | *Apodo* (m.) |
| Nobody | *Nadie* |
| Noise | *Ruido* (m.) |
| None | *Ninguno(a)* |
| Not | *No* |
| Nothing | *Nada* |
| Notice | *Aviso* (m.) |
| Now | *Ahora; ahorita* |
| | |
| Often | *A menudo* |
| Old | *Viejo(a)* |
| On | *En; sobre; encima de* |

| | |
|---|---|
| Once | *Una vez* |
| Only | *Único(a); solo(a); solamente* |
| Open | *Abrir* |
| Opened | *Abierto(a)* |
| Or | *O* |
| Other | *Otro(a)* |
| Out | *Fuera; afuera* |
| Outside | *Afuera; fuera* |
| Over (on top of) | *Sobre; encima de* |
| Over yonder | *Allá* |
| | |
| Pack | *Empacar* |
| Page | *Página* (f.) |
| Pain | *Dolor* (m.); *doler* (v.) |
| Paper | *Papel* (m.) |
| Park | *Parque* (m.) |
| Park (a car) | *Estacionarse* |
| Part | *Parte* (f.); *partir* (v.) |
| Pass | *Pasar* (v.); *paso* (m.) |
| Passage | *Pasaje* (m.) |
| Passenger | *Pasajero* (m.) |
| Past | *Pasado(a); último(a)* |
| Pasture | *Pastura* (f.); *pasto* (m.) |
| Path | *Sendero* (m.); *vereda* (f.) |
| Paved | *Pavimentado(a)* |
| Pencil | *Lápiz* (m.) |
| People | *Gente* (f.) |
| Permission | *Permiso* (m.); *permisión* (f.) |
| Permit | *Permitir* (v.); *permiso* (m.) |
| Pick (choose) | *Escoger* |
| Pick (up) | *Levantar; coger* |
| Picnic | *Jira* (f.); *merienda de campo* (f.) (afternoon snack = *merienda*) |
| Piece | *Pedazo* (m.); *pieza* (f.) |
| Pin | *Alfiler* (m.); *alfiler de seguridad* (safety pin) |
| Pistol | *Pistola* (f.) |
| Place (location) | *Lugar* (m.); *sitio* (m.) |
| Place (put on) | *Colocar; poner* |
| Plug | *Tapón* (m.) |
| Pockmarked | *Borrada* (f.); *cicatriz de viruelas* (f.) |
| Point | *Punto* (m.); *punta* (f.) |
| Poison | *Veneno* (m.); *envenenar* (v.) |

| | |
|---|---|
| Poison ivy | *Hiedra* (f.) |
| Pole | *Palo* (m.) |
| Poor | *Pobre* |
| Porter | *Cargador* (m.); *portero* (m.) |
| Possible | *Posible* |
| Post | *Poste* (m.); *palo* (m.) |
| Pot | *Pote* (m.); *olla* (f.); *marmita* (f.) |
| Preceding | *Anterior* |
| Present | *Presente* |
| Present (gift) | *Regalo* (m.); *pilón* ("boot" or something extra) (m.) |
| Present (v.) | *Presentar* |
| Pretty | *Bonito(a)*; *lindo(a)*; *hermoso(a)*; *chula(o)* |
| Price | *Precio* (m.) |
| Property | *Propiedad* (f.); *finca* (land) (f.) |
| Protection (aid, favor) | *Amparo* (m.) |
| Pull | *Estirar*; *tirar*; *arrancar*; *jalar* |
| Pump | *Bomba* (f.) |
| Purchase | *Comprar* (v.); *compra* (f.) |
| Pure | *Puro(a)* |
| Push | *Empujar* |
| Put | *Poner*; *colocar* |
| | |
| Question | *Pregunta* (f.); *cuestión* (f.) |
| Quick | *Pronto(a)*; *rápido(a)* |
| Quickly | *Pronto* |
| | |
| Radio | *Radio* (f.) |
| Rag | *Trapo* (m.); *garra* (f.) |
| Rain | *Llover* (v.); *lluvia* (f.) |
| Raincoat | *Impermeable* (m.) |
| Raise (animals or children) | *Criar* |
| Ranch | *Rancho* (m.) |
| Rancher | *Ranchero* (m.); *ranchera* (f.) |
| Ranch foreman | *Caporal* (m.) |
| Rattlesnake | *Víbora* (f.); *cascabel* (m.) |
| Ravine | *Arroyo* (m.); *cañada* (f.) |
| Raw | *Crudo(a)* |
| Raw material | *Materia prima* (f.) |
| Read | *Leer* |
| Ready | *Listo(a)* |
| Relax | *Aflojar*; *soltar* |

| | |
|---|---|
| Rent | *Rentar* |
| Repair | *Reparar* (v.); *componer* (v.); *reparo* (m.); *arreglar* (v.) |
| Repeat | *Repetir* |
| Return | *Regresar* (v.); *volver* (v.); *regreso* (m.); *vuelta* (f.) |
| Rich | *Rico*(*a*) |
| Ripe | *Maduro*(*a*); *sazonado*(*a*) |
| River | *Río* (m.) |
| Road | *Camino* (m.) |
| Rock | *Piedra* (m.); *roca* (f.) |
| Roof | *Techo* (m.) |
| Room | *Cuarto* (m.) |
| Rope | *Reata* (f.); *lazo* (m.); *mecate* (m.); *cuerda* (f.); *soga* (f.) |
| Rough | *Áspero*(*a*) |
| Round | *Redondo*(*a*) |
| Route | *Rumbo* (m.); *ruta* (f.) |
| Run | *Correr* |
| | |
| Sack | *Saco* (m.); *costal* (m.); *bolsa* (f.) |
| Sad | *Triste* |
| Safe | *Salvo*(*a*); *seguro*(*a*) |
| Salary | *Sueldo* (m.); *salario* (m.) |
| Salt | *Sal* (f.) |
| Same | *Mismo*(*a*); *igual* |
| Sand | *Arena* (f.) |
| Saw | *Serrucho* (m.); *sierra* (f.) |
| Say | *Decir* |
| Scar (cut) | *Cortada* (f.) |
| School | *Escuela* (f.) |
| Scout | *Rastreador* (m.); *rastrear* (v.) |
| Scratch | *Araño* (m.); *rasguño* (m.) |
| Search for | *Buscar* |
| Seat | *Asiento* (m.) |
| Seated | *Sentado*(*a*) |
| See | *Ver* |
| See (to barely make out) | *Divisar* |
| Seed | *Semilla* (f.); *pepa* (fruit seed) (f.) |
| Seek | *Buscar* |
| Seem | *Parecer* |
| Sell | *Vender* |
| Send | *Mandar; enviar; expedir* |

| | |
|---|---|
| Set | *Poner; colocar* |
| Several | *Algunos(as)* |
| Shaft (axle or machine part) | *Flecha* (f.); *eje* (m.) |
| Shaft (mine) | *Pozo de mina* (m.); *tiro de mina* (m.) |
| Shelter (to take) | *Refugiarse* |
| Shoe | *Zapato* (m.) |
| Shoot | *Tirar; disparar; fusilar* |
| Shop | *Tienda* (f.); *taller* (m.) |
| Shore | *Orilla* (f.) |
| Short | *Corto(a); bajo(o)* |
| Shot | *Bala* (f.); *balazo* (m.); *disparo* (m.) |
| Show | *Enseñar; mostrar* |
| Shut | *Cerrar* |
| Side | *Lado* (m.) |
| Sideways | *De lado* |
| Sifter | *Cedazo* (m.) |
| Sight | *Vista* (f.) |
| Signature | *Firma* (f.) |
| Since | *Desde* |
| Sing | *Cantar* |
| Sit down | *Sentarse* |
| Skin | *Piel* (f.); *cutis* (f.) |
| Skin (an animal) | *Desollar; pelar* |
| Skinny | *Flaco(a); delgado(a)* |
| Sky | *Cielo* (m.) |
| Sleep | *Dormir* (v.); *sueño* (m.) |
| Slick | *Liso(a)* |
| Slim | *Delgado(a); flaco(a)* |
| Slowly | *Despacio; lento* |
| Small | *Pequeño(a); chico(a)* |
| Smear | *Untar; embarrar* |
| Smoke | *Fumar* (v.); *humo* (m.) |
| Smooth | *Suave; liso(a); llano(a)* |
| Smuggle | *Pasar de contrabando* |
| Smuggler | *Contrabandista* (m.) |
| Snow | *Nevar* (v.); *nieve* (f.) |
| So | *Así; tan* |
| Soap | *Jabón* (m.) |
| Soil | *Tierra* (f.); *suelo* (m.) |
| Some | *Alguno(a); algunos(as)* |
| Somebody | *Alguien; alguna persona* |
| Something | *Algo; alguna cosa* |

| | |
|---|---|
| So much | *Tanto(a)* |
| So many | *Tantos(as)* |
| Song | *Canción* (f.); *canto* (m.); *corito* (m.) |
| Soon | *Pronto* |
| Spark | *Chispa* (f.) |
| Speed | *Velocidad* (f.) |
| Spend (time) | *Pasar* |
| Splice (wood or rope) | *Ayuste* (m.) |
| Spot (place) | *Sitio* (m.); *lugar* (m.) |
| Spring of water | *Ojo de agua* (m.); *manantial* (m.); *ojo* (m.) |
| Spurs | *Espuelas* (f.) |
| Square | *Cuadrado(a)*; *cuadrar* (v.) |
| Stairs | *Escaleras* (f.) |
| Stake | *Estaca* (f.) |
| Stake a claim (mine) | *Denunciar una mina* |
| Start | *Empezar; comenzar; principiar; ponerse en marcha* |
| Steep | *Precipitoso(a)* |
| Steep place | *Precipicio* (m.) |
| Step | *Paso* (m.) |
| Steps (stairs) | *Escaleras* (f.) |
| Stick | *Palo* (m.); *bastón* (m.) |
| Stick (in mud) | *Atascarse* |
| Still | *Todavía; tranquilo(a)* (quiet) |
| Stone | *Piedra* (f.) |
| Stop | *Alto* |
| Stop up | *Parar; tapar* |
| Storeroom | *Bodega* (f.) |
| Stove | *Estufa* (m.) |
| Straight | *Derecho; recto; directo* |
| Strainer | *Colador* (m.) |
| Strength | *Vigor* (m.); *fuerza* (f.) |
| String | *Cordón* (m.); *cuerda* (f.) |
| Strong | *Fuerte* |
| Stuck | *Atascado(a)* |
| Study | *Estudiar* (v.); *estudio* (m.) |
| Suddenly | *De repente* |
| Sure | *Seguro(a)*; *cierto(a)* |
| Take | *Tomar; llevar; aceptar* |
| Take away | *Quitar* |

| | |
|---|---|
| Take off | *Quitarse* |
| Take out | *Sacar* |
| Take steps to | *Hacer arreglos* |
| Talk | *Hablar* |
| Tall | *Alto(a)* |
| Tank (natural rock water hole) | *Tinaja* (f.) |
| Tank (dirt or metal) | *Tanque* (m.); *estanque* (m.) |
| Tap | *Tapón* (m.) |
| Tarpaulin; canvas | *Lona* (f.); *tarpa* (f.) |
| Teach | *Enseñar* |
| Teacher | *Maestro(a)* |
| Tent | *Carpa* (f.) |
| That (rel. pron.) | *Que* |
| That (demonstrative) | *Aquél; ése* |
| The | *El* (m.); *la* (f.); *los* (m. pl.); *las* (f. pl.) |
| Their | *Su; sus* |
| Theirs | *El suyo; la suya; los suyos; las suyas* |
| Them (dir. obj.) | *Los; las* |
| Them (obj. of prep.) | *Ellos; ellas* |
| Then | *Entonces; luego; después* |
| There | *Allá; allí; ahí* |
| These | *Estos* (m.); *estas* (f.) |
| They | *Ellos* (m.); *ellas* (f.) |
| Thick | *Grueso(a); denso(a); espeso(a)* |
| Thief | *Ladrón* (m.) |
| Thin | *Delgado(a); fino(a); flaco(a)* |
| Thing | *Cosa* (f.) |
| Think | *Pensar; creer* |
| This | *Este* (m.); *esta* (f.) |
| Those | *Esos* (m.); *esas* (f.) |
| Through (pass) | *Por; a través de* |
| Through (finished) | *Acabado(a)* |
| Thus | *Así; de este modo* |
| Tight (squeezed) | *Apretado(a)* |
| Tight (firm) | *Firme; tieso(a)* |
| Time (period) | *Tiempo* (m.) |
| Tin | *Estaño* (m.); *lata* (f.) |
| Tire (for wheel) | *Llanta* (f.); *neumático* (m.) |
| Tire (v.) | *Cansar* |
| Tired | *Cansado(a)* |
| To | *A; hasta* (until) |

| | |
|---|---|
| Today | *Hoy* |
| Toll | *Cuota* (f.) |
| Too | *También; además* |
| Tools | *Herramientas* (f.) |
| Too many | *Demasiado(a)* |
| Top of hill or peak | *Cima* (f.); *cumbre* (f.) |
| Tow | *Remolcar* |
| Toward | *Hacia* |
| Towtruck | *Grúa* (f.); *remolque* (m.) |
| Track (of man, vehicle, or animal) | *Huella* (f.); *rastro* (m.) |
| Track (v.) | *Seguir la pista; seguir el rastro; perseguir* |
| Trail | *Sendero* (m.); *vereda* (f.) |
| Trap | *Potrero* (m.); *trampa* (f.) |
| Trash (garbage) | *Basura* (f.); *desperdicio* (m.) |
| Travel | *Viajar; caminar* |
| Traveler | *Viajero(a); pasajero(a)* |
| Tree | *Árbol* (m.) |
| Tree trunk | *Tronco* (m.) |
| Truck | *Camión* (m.); *troca* (m.); *troque* (m.) |
| Trucker | *Troquero* (m.); *chofer* (m.) |
| True | *Verdad* (f.) |
| Truthful | *Verdadero(a)* |
| Try | *Tratar de; procurar* |
| Turn | *Doblar; dar vuelta a* |
| | |
| Ugly | *Feo(a)* |
| Under | *Bajo; abajo; debajo* |
| Under lock and key | *Bajo llave* |
| Unhealthy | *Malsano(a)* |
| Unload | *Descargar* |
| Unsafe | *Inseguro(a)* |
| Unsanitary | *Malsano(a)* |
| Unsteady | *Inseguro(a)* |
| Until | *Hasta; hasta que* |
| Up | *Arriba* |
| Up (face up) | *Boca arriba* |
| Up (get) | *Levantarse* |
| Uphill | *Cuesta arriba* |
| Upon | *Sobre; encima de* |
| Upstairs | *Arriba* |
| Us (obj. of prep.) | *Nosotros(as)* |

| | |
|---|---|
| Us (obj.) | *Nos* |
| Use (v.) | *Usar* |
| Village | *Pueblo* (m.); *aldea* (f.); *villa* (f.) |
| Wade | *Vadear; andar a pie por el agua* |
| Wages | *Sueldo* (m.) |
| Wait | *Esperar; aguardar* |
| Walk | *Andar* |
| Wall | *Pared* (f.); *muralla* (f.); *muro* (m.) |
| Want | *Necesitar; querer; desear* |
| Warehouse | *Bodega* (f.) |
| Warm | *Caliente; caluroso(a); calentar* (v.) |
| Warn | *Avisar* |
| Warner (one who warns) | *Avisador* (m.) |
| Warning | *Aviso* (m.) |
| Wasp | *Avispa* (f.) |
| Wasp's nest | *Avispero* (m.) |
| Watch (over) | *Guardar; cuidar* |
| Water hammer (in piping) | *Choque de agua* (m.) |
| Water jug | *Garrafón* (m.); *tinaja* (f.) |
| We | *Nosotros(as)* |
| Weak | *Débil* |
| Wear | *Llevar; tener puesto* |
| Weather | *Tiempo* (m.) |
| Well (water) | *Pozo* (m.); *noria* (f.) |
| Well (interj.) | *Pues bien; pues* |
| Well (very, properly) | *Bien* |
| Wet | *Mojar* (v.); *mojado(a); húmedo(a)* |
| Whatever | *Cualquier(a); lo que* |
| Wheel | *Rueda* (f.) |
| Where (in a question) | *Dónde; adónde* (to where) |
| Whereabouts | *Paradero* (m.) |
| Whether | *Si* |
| While | *Mientras* |
| Who (in a question) | *Quién* |
| Whole | *Entero(a); todo(a)* |
| Whom | *A quién* |
| Whose (not question) | *Cuyo* |
| Wide | *Ancho(a)* |
| Wind | *Viento* (m.); *aire* (m.); *brisa* (f.) |
| Windmill | *Papalote* (m.) |
| Window | *Ventana* (f.); *ventanilla* (f.); *vidrio* (m.) |

| | |
|---|---|
| Wire | *Alambre* (m.) |
| Wire (slick) | *Alambre liso* (m.) |
| Wise | *Sabio(a); erudito(a)* |
| Wish | *Querer; desear* |
| With | *Con; en compañía de* |
| Within | *Dentro de* |
| Without (outside) | *Fuera; afuera* |
| Without | *Sin* |
| Without a doubt | *Sin embargo; sin duda* |
| Woman | *Mujer* (f.) |
| Wood | *Madera* (m.) |
| Wood (for a fire) | *Leña* (f.) |
| Woods | *Bosque* (m.); *monte* (m.); *selva* (f.) |
| Wool | *Lana* (f.) |
| Work | *Trabajar* (v.); *obrar* (v.); *trabajo* (m.); *empleo* (m.); *obra* (f.) |
| Worker | *Trabajador* (m.); *jornalero* (m.) |
| Worse | *Peor* |
| Worship | *Culto* (m.) |
| | |
| Yard (of a house) | *Patio* (m.); *yarda* (f.); *jardín* (m.) |
| Yell | *Gritar* (v.); *grito* (m.) |
| Yes | *Sí* |
| Yet | *Todavía; ya; aún* |
| Yonder | *Allá* |
| Youth | *Joven* (m. or f.) |